Soviet Central Asia

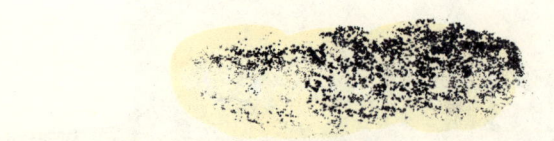

Soviet Central Asia

The Failed Transformation

EDITED BY
William Fierman

WITH A FOREWORD BY
Teresa Rakowska-Harmstone

Westview Press
BOULDER • SAN FRANCISCO • OXFORD

This Westview softcover edition is printed on acid-free paper and bound in library-quality, coated covers that carry the highest rating of the National Association of State Textbook Administrators, in consultation with the Association of American Publishers and the Book Manufacturers' Institute.

All rights reserved. No part of this publication may be reproduced or transmitted in any form or by any means, electronic or mechanical, including photocopy, recording, or any information storage and retrieval system, without permission in writing from the publisher.

Copyright © 1991 by Westview Press, Inc.

Published in 1991 in the United States of America by Westview Press, Inc., 5500 Central Avenue, Boulder, Colorado 80301, and in the United Kingdom by Westview Press, 36 Lonsdale Road, Summertown, Oxford OX2 7EW

Library of Congress Cataloging-in-Publication Data
Soviet Central Asia : the failed transformation / edited by William Fierman : with a foreword by Teresa Rakowska-Harmstone.
  p. cm.
Includes bibliographical references and index.
ISBN 0-8133-7907-5
  1. Soviet Central Asia—Politics and government.
2. Russification—Soviet Central Asia. 3. Soviet Central Asia—Social conditions—1917– . I. Fierman, William.
DK859.S68 1991
958'.408—dc20
                                              91-13398
                                                  CIP

Printed and bound in the United States of America

∞ The paper used in this publication meets the requirements of the American National Standard for Permanence of Paper for Printed Library Materials Z39.48-1984.

10   9   8   7   6   5   4   3   2   1

To Deanna

Contents

Foreword, Teresa Rakowska-Harmstone — ix
Acknowledgments — xvii
Note on Spelling and Transliteration — xix

Introduction, *William Fierman* — 1

PART ONE: The Setting

1. The Soviet "Transformation" of Central Asia, *William Fierman* — 11
2. Implications of Ethnic and Demographic Trends, *Nancy Lubin* — 36
3. Central Asia's Cotton Economy and Its Costs, *Boris Z. Rumer* — 62

PART TWO: Politics

4. Power and Politics in Soviet Uzbekistan: From Stalin to Gorbachev, *Donald S. Carlisle* — 93
5. Prelude to "Independence": How the Uzbek Party Apparatus Broke Moscow's Grip on Elite Recruitment, *James Critchlow* — 131

PART THREE: Identity and Religion

6. Ethnic Attitudes and Relations in Modern Uzbek Cities, *Ronald Wixman* — 159
7. Islam and Atheism: Dynamic Tension in Soviet Central Asia, *Azade-Ayse Rorlich* — 186

| 8 | Forging a Soviet People: Ethnolinguistics in Central Asia, *Isabelle Kreindler* | 219 |

PART FOUR: Socioeconomic Issues

9	Women and Society in Central Asia, *Martha Brill Olcott*	235
10	Central Asian Youth and Migration, *William Fierman*	255
	Conclusion, *William Fierman*	290

Glossary   309
About the Editor and Contributors   311
Index   313

Foreword

Stripped of political rhetoric of the "achievements of socialism" and "benefits of fraternal assistance," the fate of Soviet Central Asia represents perhaps the most tragic and least reversible example of the failure of the Soviet experiment that, in the name of an ideological goal, led to near destruction of a region, its peoples, and its culture.

Prior to the Gorbachev era even most skeptical observers accepted the claim that the modernization under Soviet rule brought significant benefits to the region, notwithstanding the costs of transforming a feudal imperial backwater into a showcase of Soviet "socialism." The Soviet-style modernization was comparable in many respects to that introduced by Western imperial powers in their colonies, but it was more sweeping and was characterized by ideological and political constraints. A mass-based education system, operating both in local languages and in Russian, stimulated the emergence of modernized elites. Development of indigenous cultures was promoted, modern communications systems were developed, and a network of state-run social and health services was set up. Last but not least, the region underwent an accelerated economic change and development as the Soviet Union's primary cotton producer. However inadequate the results were by Western standards (or even in comparison with the Soviet West), and however staggering the price, this change meant progress in a society whose growth had been arrested in the Middle Ages, and it compared favorably with neighboring countries.

Among the costs were the break-up of the region's natural unity and the destruction of the traditional society, which led to the suppression of Islam and violation of its cultural norms. It also meant the obliteration of successive generations of indigenous leaders who dared to defend local interests and the deaths of millions during the collectivization campaign. It also brought total subordination of local interests to Moscow.

In the light of glasnost, the benefits of Soviet-type progress in the Central Asian republics appear to have been, at best, a mixed blessing. Educational and cultural policies, determined by the center and ideologically slanted, were applied in total disregard of local needs and requirements, and carried a strong Russifying impact. The conflicting socialization by both traditional and modern agents opened the way for the emergence of culturally ambivalent elites. Caught between new Soviet (*de facto* Russian) values and their traditional Islamic roots, and between their dependence on Moscow and their need for support based in old kinship and regional ties, the elites acted as a go-between but did not fully identify either with the old or with the new community. The bearers of Moscow's messages and executors of Moscow's policies, they were distrusted locally. Yet they could not integrate into the new society because they were not accepted as equal by the Russians, who remained firmly convinced of the superiority of their culture and of their "civilizing mission" in the imperial periphery.

The indigenous communists were formally in charge of their republics. But "parachuted" functionaries of the central party and state *apparat* were placed in politically strategic positions throughout the region, while immigrants effectively manned the regional administrative and managerial infrastructure and dominated urban and industrial centers. Central Asia was flooded by Russians, other Slavs, members of other groups in pursuit of a warmer climate and better wages, and by successive waves of involuntary settlers. "Enemies of the people," individuals as well as entire social and national groups such as the *kulak*s and Soviet Germans and Crimean Tatars, were deported to the region. The Muslim masses, on the other hand, continued to dominate the countryside of cotton-growing kolkhozes and sovkhozes and persisted in their traditional life, refusing a change that would mean an acceptance of foreign ways.

The masses' social resistance can be measured by their lack of progress in learning Russian, the effective language of universal communication in the Soviet Union and the indispensable tool for progress up the social, political, and economic ladder. The results of the last two Soviet population censuses (1979 and 1989) indicated that fully one-half to three-fourths of the native populations of Central Asia and Kazakhstan could not understand or speak Russian and that non-speakers of the language were more numerous among the young people than they were among the older generation. The resulting alienation between rural/traditional/indigenous and urban/modernized/immigrant communities created an ideal breeding ground for ethnic conflict that became visible with the post-Stalin thaw, when central control and repression mechanisms were reduced and undermined.

After 1953, Muslim political elites were gradually able to gain greater political power in the management of local affairs, but the attitudes did not change on either side, and the conflict intensified. A return to traditional values and a revival of Islamic culture and religion in the Muslim community were accompanied by the growing assertion of local interests and demands in cultural, political, and economic life and an emergence of ethnic nationalism. While Islamic revival was region-wide, new nationalism aggregated on the basis of existing political-administrative structures and was articulated by the republics' indigenous political elites and supported by a wider and more broadly based Muslim cultural and professional intelligentsia. Understandably, local politicians sought the political power that had been denied them under Soviet rule and in so doing turned for approval and support to their national communities. Long-standing social, cultural, political, and economic grievances have all been placed in the context of new nationalism and national self-assertion.

Ethnic conflict has been further stimulated by perceptions of relative deprivation on the part of both the immigrant and the Muslim communities. On the one hand, the Muslims resent past persecutions, the imposition of outside controls and policies, the destruction of their traditional culture and society, the damage to their environment, and their continued low and, in fact, deteriorating living standards. The resentment is heightened by the expectations awakened by propaganda promises and comparisons made with the amenities most immigrants are believed to enjoy. The immigrants, on the other hand, complain of preferential treatment openly extended to the natives by Muslim bureaucrats ever since the bureaucrats acquired the power to do so. Immigrant settlers also have been fearful of a growing hostility toward them among the indigenous population.

Seeds of disaster are present in the deteriorating social and economic conditions. The return to traditional Islam, combined with better health and living standards in the 1950s and 1960s, led to a Muslim population explosion that largely nullified past social and economic gains. It created an enormous and growing pool in Central Asia's rural areas of unintegrated, unskilled, and basically unemployable youth, who are both unwilling and unable to relocate into the urban and industrial centers of their republics, let alone emigrate outside their home territory. The resulting poverty and unemployment breeds social discontent and intensifies hostility toward non-indigenous minorities.

The imposition on the region of a cotton monoculture to the exclusion of other crops has had negative economic, ecological, and social long-range effects. The center's insistence on ever larger yields placed a premium on quantity rather than quality of the cotton produced and stimulated intensive irrigation as well as excessive use of chemical fertilizers. For lack of adequate safeguards, both led to ecological catastrophe. The diversion of the waters of the region's two major rivers, Syrdarya and Amudarya, both emptying into the Aral Sea, caused substantial shrinking of the sea's surface. At the same time, the fertilizer overload combined with faulty irrigation ditches allowed for seepage of poisonous effluents into the subsoils affecting the region's water supply.

The emphasis on cotton left primary industries chronically underfunded, despite a long-standing verbal commitment to their development. Centrally determined planning and fiscal controls did not allow for investments into new processing and service industries, as advocated by local economists, which would have trained and absorbed the surpluses of rural manpower. There was no funding also for the most basic housing, sewage, and water supply systems to accommodate the rapid growth of the Muslim population.

The imperative to meet Moscow's planned targets at any cost and under the penalty of political oblivion or worse, has led to endemic falsification of records, corruption, and the diversion of resources for private gain by Muslim political elites, not infrequently with active cooperation of the watchdogs sent by Moscow to short-circuit any such practices. Gorbachev's anti-corruption campaign has chosen the Muslims as its primary target, but the practices are by no means unique to Central Asia and have been flourishing throughout the Soviet Union. The anti-corruption campaign in Uzbekistan and other republics resulted in a massive purge of Muslim leaders on a scale not seen since the great purges of the 1930s, albeit with less drastic consequences for the culprits. The Muslims see themselves selected as the scapegoats for sins that are common everywhere, and there is bitter resentment among them of this particular Gorbachev initiative, which has been added to their list of other grievances.

As the eighties were coming to a close, political, economic, and social frustrations erupted into sporadic violence with strong ethnic overtones throughout the region. The conditions are such that violence may accelerate instantly as sparks fly from multiple incidents of hostile confrontations, directed not only against Russians and other Europeans but also against Muslim minorities non-indigenous to the region, who may be better off than the local people. The Meskhetians, a Muslim people deported by Stalin from Georgia to Uzbekistan's Fergana Valley, are a case in point. Attacked by the Uzbeks for allegedly taking over Uzbek jobs, the Meskhetians had to be airlifted from the region in June 1989. In 1989–1990, regular Soviet troops and units of security police were repeatedly called to intervene to stop ethnic violence throughout Central Asia and Kazakhstan because local authorities were not only reluctant to protect immigrant minorities but were implicated in promoting the violence. The growth of ethnic tensions has resulted in a net outflow from the region of non-indigenous settlers noted in the last population census, which is a reversal of the trend of previous decades.

Thus as the Soviet Union disintegrates, Central Asia faces economic bankruptcy, ecological disaster, and social and political chaos. Notwithstanding the region-wide cultural unity provided by Islam, the Central

Asian republics have yet to develop regional political collaboration of a kind that has been a hallmark of Baltic nationalism. Paradoxically, as the imperial power withdraws and access to political power has finally opened up for the Muslims, the conditions for its exercise are unfavorable in the extreme.

Economically the region is in ruin, with no visible prospects for improvement, development, or diversification. Local leaders are not sure what should or can be done, and, as the center goes bankrupt and withdraws, there are no other obvious sources of assistance or investments. The ecological damage to air, water, and soil resources may well be irreversible, as in the case of the Aral Sea. At best it will take years and massive investments to overcome the deterioration of the environment and its consequences. Meanwhile it has exacted a heavy toll of disease, the incidence of which is increasing, and of growing mortality rates, especially among infants and the young.

Following the example of other Soviet republics, and riding the new wave of ethnic nationalism, all the republics in the region passed a declaration of "sovereignty" by the end of 1990. In contemporary Soviet usage the term implies the primacy of local over all-Union (federal) laws and control over the republics' resources and domestic and foreign policies, but does not exclude a continuation of ties with the center in the form of some kind of confederal rather than federal arrangement. Thus, it stops short of a demand for outright independence. At the same time, it goes much further in the assertion of the republic's power over its own affairs than the provisions for autonomy allowed under the draft "Union of Sovereign Soviet Republics" proposed by President Gorbachev in December 1990.

In contrast to the national leaders of the western Soviet republics and the republics of Transcaucasus, the Central Asian Muslim leaders have yet to articulate a blueprint for their sovereign future. They have never been allowed a real share in the Soviet model, yet find themselves connected to it by a network of dependency ties they seem unable and unwilling to break, the more so because the region has been politically fragmented. In the discussion of center-periphery relationship in the new centrally elected assemblies (the Congress of People's Deputies of the USSR and the USSR Supreme Soviet), Central Asian deputies have opposed the efforts of others, notably the Baltic republics, to become fully independent, even as they have asserted their own demands for greater autonomy.

One unresolved question is whether the new sovereignty should be expressed region-wide, on the basis of common Islamic culture and religion, or through the republics into which the region was divided in 1924. Most signs seem to point in the direction of the latter, with the republics hot in pursuit of their particular interests. As Moscow's presence withdraws, there has been a revival of intra-regional conflicts, some dating to the pre-Soviet period.

Another unresolved question is the nature of future relations with the center. Here, as noted earlier, Muslim republics are the one cluster of republics most ready to remain within a restructured union, providing their autonomy is preserved. But this attitude may change rapidly if their most basic political and economic needs are not met (which seems rather likely), especially if their new and carefully cultivated contacts with the outside Muslim world bear fruit in external support and assistance. Overall, the potential for political destabilization of the region is high.

The collection of essays that follows highlights and analyzes some of the main problems in the politics, social relations, culture, and economy of Central Asia in the period immediately preceding the crisis of 1988–1990. It brings together the consideration of the main elements that contributed to the crisis and helps to understand its nature, causes, and dimensions.

The main theme that runs through the book is the failure of the Soviet leadership, over the period of seventy years, to integrate the peoples of Central Asia into a common Soviet whole, despite claims to the contrary made by successive Soviet leaders. The failure is not unique to Soviet Central Asia but is also evident in other Soviet republics. Its cause is simple: The new "internationalist" Soviet identity, that when first introduced was meant to represent a class principle and to be supranational, ended up being an emasculated version of the old Russian imperial identity. It offered Russian cultural content, altered by the removal of the religious element and its replacement by Marxist-Leninist ideological content. Thus, the "internationalist" identity was not acceptable, in the long run, either to the Russians or to the non-Russians, and eventually had to give way to particular nationalisms in a dialectical sequence directly opposite to that predicted by Marx and Lenin. It was nation rather than class that turned out to be the ascending element in the dialectical progression of Soviet national relations.

The failure of integration was particularly glaring in the case of the Muslims of Central Asia because of the strength of their traditional culture and their lack of preparedness for the acceptance of modernity. It was the failure, primarily, of the attempt to integrate diverse perceptions and attitudes. This failure rendered meaningless the superficial integration achieved through political, administrative, and managerial linkages that run along the vertical axes of Party and state hierarchies between the republics and Moscow, and the economic "division of labor." The chapters in this book explain why the Muslims failed to develop into a new species of "Soviet man," while at the same time showing how deep are the scars left on the people and on the region by Moscow's efforts to impose this metamorphosis.

Teresa Rakowska-Harmstone

Acknowledgments

This book would never have materialized without the cooperation of all of the contributors, each of whom, certainly, also has a list of people to thank for help. As editor, however, I have the privilege of naming a few whose contributions were especially important.

My understanding of Central Asian society has benefited enormously from the opportunities I have had to work and conduct research in the region, especially in Uzbekistan. I would therefore like to thank the International Research and Exchanges Board and the University of Tennessee for making several stays in Central Asia possible over the past few years.

Among the individuals who have helped me on this project, I owe an enormous debt to James Critchlow, without whose support, encouragement, and suggestions I would have abandoned this volume long ago. I would also like to thank Teresa Rakowska-Harmstone, Azade-Ayse Rorlich, Donald Carlisle, and Muriel Atkin for reading some of my contributions to this book and offering comments that helped me clarify and revise them. I am fortunate to have worked with Rebecca Ritke, a meticulous, demanding, yet patient editor at Westview Press. Her comments and those of an anonymous outside reader have also been extremely useful.

I owe the greatest debt to my wife, Harriet, and my daughter, Deanna, who have tolerated beyond reasonable expectations the demands that this book, and my scholarly work more generally, have placed on my time. My wife also proofread all of the book's chapters.

Of course I take sole responsibility for all mistakes of fact or judgment in my own chapters. I have attempted to edit the other contributions in this volume without distorting my fellow authors' ideas. If I have made technical mistakes in editing or inadvertently injected my own views into the contributions of others, I ask for my collaborators' understanding.

William Fierman
Washington, D.C.

Note on Spelling and Transliteration

The problems of transliteration and spelling for this book were extremely complex. In large part, this was due to the region's ethnic composition and its history, but it was further complicated by the languages of the sources used by this volume's individual contributors.

Russian words and names throughout the book are generally rendered according to the Library of Congress transliteration system. However, the spelling here omits diacritical marks and ligatures as well as the soft sign (*miagkii znak*) at the end of proper names. In those instances where a common English spelling of Russian proper names exists (e.g., Tchaikovsky or Gorky), this form is used.

Common terms that refer to Islam and Islamic society are spelled in accordance with *Webster's Third New International Dictionary of the English Language* (Springfield, MA: Merriam Webster, Inc., 1986). The *Encyclopedia of Islam* was used as a guide for spellings of Islamic terms that are not in *Webster's*.

Most geographical names are spelled in accordance with *The Times Atlas of the World* (Seventh comprehensive edition) (London: John Bartholomew & Son, 1985). The most important exceptions are Tajikistan (not Tadzhikistan), Azerbaijan (not Azerbaidzhan), and Kirgizia (not Kirghizia).

The spelling of modern Central Asian personal names and place names not listed in *The Times Atlas of the World* reflects the sources used by individual contributors to this volume. Many of the authors used primarily or exclusively Russian-language Soviet materials, and the transliteration of Turkic and Tajik names in their chapters therefore reflects the Russian spelling.

As editor, I am responsible for these decisions, the last of which I took very reluctantly. However, I have no way to reconstruct many of the original Turkic- or Tajik-language names; yet only through these forms would it have been possible to transliterate Central Asian names directly (and hence more accurately) into English. I have also decided to transliterate a few other terms that refer to Central Asian society in analogous fashion. Consequently, the word for "elder" (literally "white beard") is rendered *aksakal*.

Perhaps some Central Asians, who are the focus of this volume, will feel that these decisions reflect a "colonial Russian" mentality; I hope, however, that the contents of the chapters that follow will dispel suspicions that the editor and contributors are insensitive to the concerns of the indigenous peoples of Central Asia.

W. F.

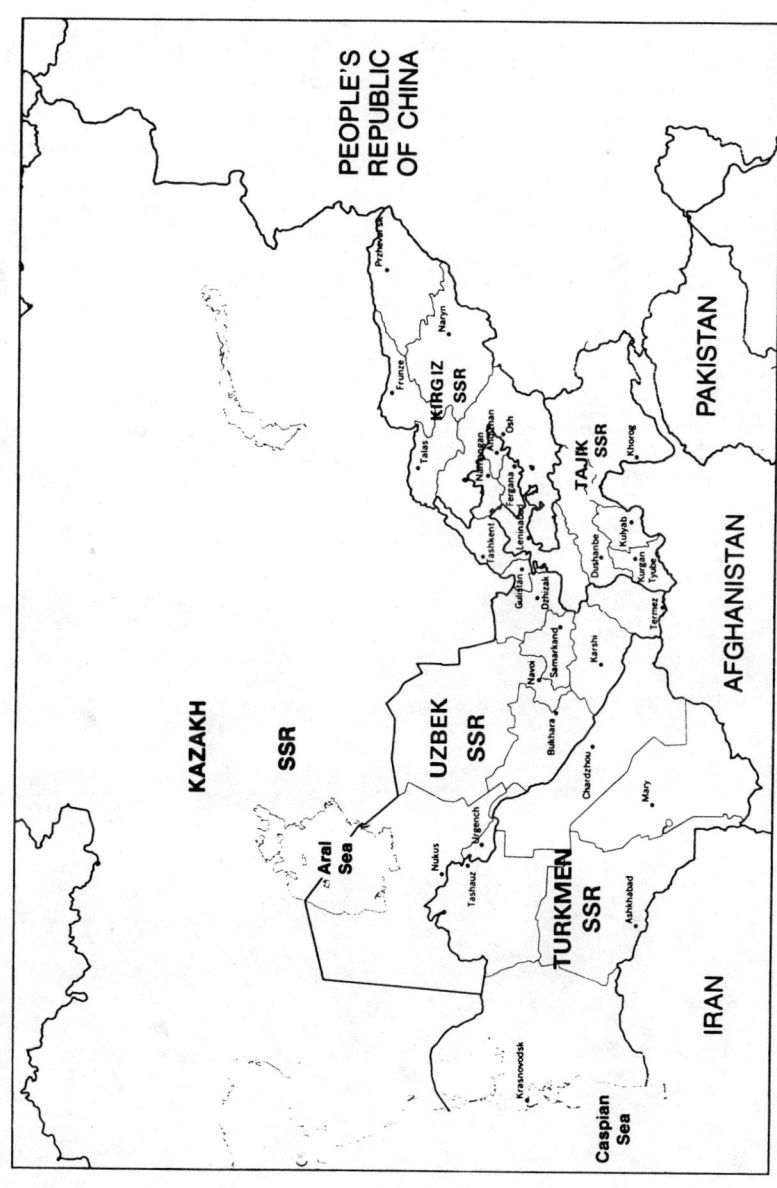

Soviet Central Asia. *Source:* Central Intelligence Agency.

Introduction

William Fierman

One of the hallmarks of the Gorbachev era has been the reassertion of national grievances among virtually every ethnic group living in the USSR. These have ranged from the spectacular to the prosaic: The world watched in awe as the Lithuanian Popular Front, Sajudis, led the small Baltic republic to reclaim its independence. Armenians and Azerbaijanis have been in a virtual state of war which Moscow seems unable to control. Less noticed, but also important, have been such processes as the cultural movement agitating in Moldavia for restoration of the Latin alphabet suppressed under Stalin. Ethnic stirrings have significantly deflected the leadership's attention away from the pressing agenda of political and economic reforms and given to conservative forces within it a bugaboo with which to resist change. Whatever the form of the various manifestations of ethnic unrest, they have pointed to a single truth: the utopian expectation nurtured for decades by the official ideology—that the disparate elements of society would coalesce into a single "Soviet nationality"—is farther than ever from fulfillment.

This projected merger of Soviet nationalities was part of a broader social and cultural transformation which the "omniscient" Communist Party claimed to be leading. Although many non-Russians living in the USSR saw this only as an excuse for political control and a new form of Russification, until Gorbachev the threat of punishment kept most of them from openly expressing their disagreement with Moscow's policies. This, perhaps, was a major reason for the belief prevalent in the 1960s and 1970s among Western journalists and even Sovietologists that the ranks of the "new" Soviet citizen—transformed and largely denationalized—were ever growing.

In the 1980s, much of the first accessible and dramatically convincing evidence which contradicted the misperception of "denationalization" came from such numerically small nationalities as the Yakuts and Crimean

Tatars, whose populations total only hundreds of thousands. Even the entire populations of the restive Baltic and Transcaucasus republics number only about some eight and sixteen million respectively. At first, there were few open signs of broadly held nationalist feelings among the most populous non-Russian nationality groups of the USSR, the Central Asians and the non-Russian Slavs.

Indeed, during the Gorbachev years prior to 1989, only one political or social problem which could be called "Central Asian" achieved headline status in the world press. This was the December 1986 disturbance in Alma-Ata (capital of Kazakhstan) following the replacement of republic Party First Secretary Dinmukhammed Kunaev (a Kazakh) by the Russian Gennadii Kolbin. Since, for reasons discussed below, Kazakhstan as a republic stands apart from Central Asia proper, it might be said that even after this event "Central Asia's" problems *still* went virtually unnoticed by most of the world. But this was soon to change. The tension in Uzbekistan's Fergana Valley exploded into violent rampages in the spring of 1989. Other major conflicts and disturbances in every Central Asian republic became major world news stories in the succeeding months.

The significance of these developments in Central Asia extends far beyond the region itself. Among the reasons are Central Asia's strategic geographic location and its large population. Far more people live in Central Asia than in the next largest non-Slavic region in the USSR. The population of Uzbekistan (Central Asia's most populous republic) alone is greater than that of all three Transcaucasus republics together, and there are more Uzbeks in the USSR than the country's combined populations of Azerbaijanis, Armenians, and Georgians.

Beyond this, however, developments in Central Asia are important because (despite the large Ukrainian and Belorussian populations in the Soviet Union) the most critical "nationality divide" in the USSR is between the Slavs (or Europeans) and traditionally Muslim groups, and the majority of Soviet Muslims—over 60 percent—are Central Asians. Indeed, among the 30 percent non-Slavic part of the Soviet population, 4 in 10 are Uzbeks, Tajiks, Turkmens, Kirgiz, or Kazakhs.

The importance of the Slavic/Muslim demographic divide in the USSR is heightened by the fundamental nature of the cultural differences. This is why Central Asia has remained the greatest stumbling-block on the path to the "merging" of Soviet nationalities. As for the Great Russians and other Europeans who live in Central Asia, they constitute an influential minority. But their physical appearance, not to mention cultural and linguistic characteristics, usually make them easily distinguishable from the indigenous peoples.

Introduction

With an important exception to be noted below, the "Central Asia" of this book refers to that part of the region of "Turkestan" which is now carved into the Soviet republics of Uzbekistan, Tajikistan, Kirgizia, and Turkmenistan (Turkmenia). For the most part, this includes the lands of *Russian* Turkestan, which at the end of the nineteenth century included territories under the Russian Governor General and the Bukharan and Khivan Khanates. However, unlike the "Central Asia" of this book, Russian Turkestan also included the southern part of today's Kazakhstan.

In turn, the larger region of "Turkestan" also included (and includes) Eastern Turkestan, which today is part of the Xinjiang Uygur Autonomous Region of the People's Republic of China, and Afghan Turkestan, an area in the north of Afghanistan. Despite current political borders, many of the bonds among Central Asians described below link all Turkestanis.

In a cultural sense, the term "Central Asians" includes Kazakhs, along with Uzbeks, Tajiks, Turkmens, Kirgiz, and some other indigenous groups whose populations in "Central Asia" are less numerous. However, as a republic, Kazakhstan in many ways is best not considered part of "Central Asia." The major reason is demographic. Kazakhs *and other Muslim nationalities combined* account for not much more than 40 percent of Kazakhstan's population. By contrast, even in Kirgizia, where the Kirgiz account for only slightly over half the inhabitants, the total for "Muslim" nationalities is about two-thirds. And the proportions in Uzbekistan, Tajikistan, and Turkmenistan are all significantly higher than in Kirgizia.

In addition to demographic characteristics which set it apart, the geography, natural resources, and economic structure of Kazakhstan also distinguish it from the four "Central Asian republics." Moreover, Kazakhstan has had a much longer history of more intensive contacts with Russia than the rest of region.

Thus, as a whole, this book is immediately concerned with developments in the four republics of Central Asia proper. One of the chapters, however—devoted to Islam—logically takes a cultural approach to the region. Consequently, it includes developments among the Kazakhs, and thus in Kazakhstan. Even though the other chapters do not explicitly treat Kazakhstan, it should be kept in mind that much of the analysis of social and political problems in "Central Asia" also applies to Kazakhstan.

It is worth pausing, if only for a moment, to consider some of the historical, linguistic, and cultural factors which link the Central Asians with one another and also isolate them from most of the rest of the USSR's inhabitants, especially the Slavic peoples. Islam, the dominant religion in Central Asia, was introduced into the region by the Arabs in the seventh century, and was eventually also adopted by the invading nomadic groups who arrived later. Although the Arabs did not establish a lasting political presence, the Islamic faith which they brought has been a fundamental force shaping Central Asian society for over a millennium. It has been woven into everyday life through social and economic structures, and has also had a major impact on the musical, literary, and other cultural traditions of the region.

The shared culture of the region is reflected also in its indigenous languages. With the exception of Tajik, all of them are Turkic; they share a large common pool of vocabulary and grammar. Because of the great historical Persian influence in the region, Tajik, too (though it is Indo-European), shares many lexical items and even grammatical structures with the most widely spoken Turkic language in the region, Uzbek. Moreover, a significant proportion of the populations of Uzbekistan and Tajikistan are fluent in both Uzbek and Tajik.

Although the Central Asian bonds are very important, "Central Asians" have what might be best understood as a layered identity. The importance of a particular element or layer of that identity depends very much on context. At one level, most Soviet Central Asians identify themselves as "Soviets." But they also have a Turkestani identity, a nationality identity (based on national republic), and local or clan identities. An Uzbek serving in the Soviet Army in Germany is undoubtedly often reminded that he is "Soviet." But in other circumstances the bonds he shares with Uygurs in China are more important than those that he shares with Russians from Leningrad. In still other circumstances, nationality (e.g., Uzbek, Tajik, etc.) or local identities manifest themselves. Regardless of their artificiality at the time of "national delimitation" in Central Asia, these categories are important markers today, and they are reinforced by print and electronic media outputs in standardized languages. At the same time, however, the more local identities are clearly salient when higher educational students of the same "nationality" form groups which clash with each other in the capital cities of their republics.

All of these "identities" and the indigenous culture of the region are crucial parts of the context in which Moscow has attempted to control and transform the region. Their importance is signalled by the difficulties which Moscow's policy of promoting mixed marriages encountered and by continuing resistance to family planning and migration. A sense of identity with one's native land was an important factor in the way in which Central Asian elites challenged Soviet hegemony in the Brezhnev era. The now notorious "cotton affair" undoubtedly lined the pockets of many Central Asian officials who falsified crop reports and engaged in other kinds of illegal and extra-legal activities, but it was also a form of passive national resistance. By short-circuiting Kremlin pressures for still more reckless expansion of cotton acreage, the "corrupt" officials helped to defend their land from further environmental degradation. The fact that some of the proceeds of their manipulations were used for public purposes, even to build mosques, also indicates that the "cotton affair" was not entirely venal in motivation.

The backdrop for today's national agitation and resistance in Central Asia is an environmental disaster of enormous proportions, seen most dramatically in the rapid drying of the Aral Sea, once the world's fourth largest inland water body. Coupled with this is economic privation, severe even by Soviet standards, that is compounded by exhaustion of resources; this becomes increasingly acute as the population grows by leaps and bounds. (In Uzbekistan, official planners anticipate an annual growth rate of more than 2.5 percent through the end of the century; at this rate the population increases by approximately one-third every eleven years.)

From one perspective, the past seventy years represent an era of enormous change in Central Asia. But this same period can also be viewed as a "totalitarian" regime's ultimately frustrated attempt to realize a very particular form of political, social, economic, and cultural transformation. This is not the place to delve into a detailed analysis of what Lenin might have envisioned as the long-term future for Central Asia. But it is plausible to assume that he believed that, under Bolshevik guidance, the region would eventually achieve economic equality and prosperity, and that nationality, religious, and linguistic differences would not serve as the bases for inter-ethnic conflict. It is also clear that Lenin recognized the need for a strong centralized political force to guide the peoples of the former Russian empire toward the communist utopia. Today, dreams of peace based on economic well-being and ethnic homogeneity seem further than ever from realization. Moreover, the political system established by Lenin appears on the verge of collapse.

This book is about the last stage of the failure of the Communist Party to achieve its transformation in Central Asia and what is likely to be viewed as "the beginning of the end" of Soviet power. A number of the contributions highlight the tremendously powerful tools which the Party wielded as it attempted to influence the course of Central Asian history. Among the most important were control of key political appointments, economic plans, the media and educational networks, and religious and social institutions. Through these instruments Moscow did, indeed, revolutionize society. But, seen against Lenin's (or even Stalin's) likely goals, it is a revolution which can be said to have miscarried. Besides destroying the natural environment, it created a host of serious social, economic, and health problems which the Party is now powerless to control. In addition to all of the above, there is a seething resentment among Central Asians toward the Russians' "civilizing" mission to transform them, an attempt which the indigenous peoples see as a tragic chapter in their history.

Until glasnost, it was not possible for Soviet Central Asians to speak openly of the most critical problems related to this failed transformation. Thus, the airing of these issues under Gorbachev is itself an amazing shift. But the Gorbachev era has involved much more than "openness." It has also brought innovative approaches designed to redress some of Central Asia's most critical problems in new ways.

Although these steps might be seen as a more enlightened approach, from another perspective they also represent a step back from Russia's earlier efforts to transform Central Asia and "civilize" it. This loosening of control may quickly be leading to genuine autonomy or political independence.

The three chapters which constitute Part One of this volume provide the historic, demographic, and economic setting against which to view the political and social processes which have been unfolding in recent years in Central Asia. Chapter 1, by William Fierman, summarizes the history of the Russian conquest and presents an outline of the most important events of Soviet rule. In Chapter 2, Nancy Lubin discusses the major demographic trends in the area and raises questions about their significance for future economic development. In the last chapter of this part, Boris Rumer examines the region's central economic problem— the cotton monoculture.

In Part Two, Donald Carlisle and James Critchlow analyze political problems. Their basis for analysis is the largest Central Asian republic, Uzbekistan; however, the general patterns they describe bear many similarities with the region's other republics. In Chapter 4, Carlisle analyzes the way in which elite political processes set in motion decades ago are still being played out today. Carlisle stresses the long-enduring power of the center to manipulate politics in the republic but suggests that these attempts at control are now bringing some unexpected and (from Moscow's perspective) very undesirable consequences. In his contribution, James Critchlow looks at elite recruitment from another perspective, highlighting some of the problems which make it difficult for Moscow to select cadres who will carry out the center's policy yet be instruments of policy acceptable to the local population.

Part Three of this volume examines identity and religion. All three chapters in this part demonstrate the failure of CPSU policies to transform Central Asians into denationalized, atheist, "Soviet" men and women. Chapter 6, by Ronald Wixman, is based on interviews conducted in Uzbekistan in three of Uzbekistan's largest cities in the summer of 1985. It clearly outlines the gulf between Slavic and Muslim cultures in Central Asian society. In Chapter 7, Azade-Ayse Rorlich analyzes CPSU policy vis-à-vis Islam and the nature of the dilemma which Islam has posed for the regime. She traces some of the changes in policy and the reasons for the regime's failure to promote atheism. Chapter 8, by Isabelle Kreindler, analyzes the attempts of the Soviet regime to use Russian language lessons as an instrument to create a new type of identity.

Part Four is devoted to socioeconomic issues. In Chapter 9, Martha Olcott considers the problems of Central Asian women. She demonstrates that more than seven decades of Soviet rule have not emancipated most of the region's female population; in fact, in some ways the life of women has become even more difficult. Chapter 10 is devoted to Central Asian youth and migration. In this chapter William Fierman examines the attempt by Moscow to encourage Central Asians to migrate outside their republics and the reasons for this effort's meager success.

The conclusion to the volume considers the phenomena described in the other contributions in a political development framework. Here Fierman reconsiders the relations among the demographic, economic, and cultural problems discussed in the earlier chapters and their implications for Moscow's political control. He suggests that the CPSU has lost much of its legitimacy in Central Asia, and that without terror to back it up, the Party is in serious danger of losing the vestiges of political control which still remain.

PART ONE

The Setting

1

The Soviet "Transformation" of Central Asia

William Fierman

Pre-Soviet History and Revolution

Western visitors to Soviet Central Asia frequently hear complaints from the indigenous Muslim population about local Russians' ignorance of Central Asian culture and lack of respect toward it. These are signs of Central Asians' resentment toward Russians who think the conquest of Turkestan and the arrival of Europeans brought Central Asia its first "civilized" culture.

Revealing their own insensitivity, many Russians exhibit a sense of frustration with the "inscrutable" indigenous peoples who still retain many of their "archaic" or "feudal" traditions. These Russians feel that Central Asians' reluctance to give up their old ways has stood in the way of their modernization. Indeed, the history of Soviet power in Central Asia can be viewed as a series of Russian attempts to transform the region. Although superficially many of these efforts were successful, the problems which plague Central Asia today bear witness to the fact that the transformation was not taking place along the lines which Moscow desired.

One of the reasons for this failure was the unattractiveness of the Russian Soviet model which the Soviet regime so strongly promoted. Although for many years they dared not make the comparison, to many Central Asians the accomplishments of Soviet society paled before the exploits of their own ancient civilizations. Almost a millennium before the Russian conquest of the region, the Central Asian cultural centers of Bukhara and Khorezm produced such important scholars and philosophers as Ibn Sina (Avicenna) (980-1037) and Abu al-Raihan Biruni (973-1048). The achievements evident today in the ruins of Afrasiyab in Samarkand and the Mausoleum of the Samanids in Bukhara attest to the great civilizations built by the ancient inhabitants of Central Asia. Although the Mongol invasion laid ruin to these centers, two of Genghis Khan's successors in the fourteenth and fifteenth centuries, the rulers Tamerlane and Ulughbek, oversaw the development of a prosperous economy and a high level of culture in these same places. Following the fifteenth century, however, the importance of the silk routes crossing Central Asia declined, and Central Asia, along with its traditional centers of high civilization, entered a period of cultural and economic stagnation. Nevertheless, as Central Asians today often proudly point out, they are heirs to a rich cultural tradition.

Because of Russia's other territorial ambitions, and because of the great distances and dangers, as late as the eighteenth century Russia had established only very limited contacts with Central Asia. True, even in the sixteenth and seventeenth centuries there was substantial trade between Russia and Central Asia. But only in the early 1800s did the tsars begin to extend their administration over the populations of the Kazakh steppe. When Kazakh resistance movements arose in the 1820s, 1830s, and 1840s, they were crushed by superior Russian might. The penetration of the steppe was important for the future of Central Asia because it broke down the barrier between Russia and the Central Asian khanates of Kokand, Bukhara, and Khiva (Khorezm).

Russia's eventual conquest of Central Asia was facilitated by internecine disputes among local leaders and frequently shifting alliances. Kokand was the first of the three states to lose territory to Russia. Adding to some other parts of the khanate conquered at the beginning of the 1860s, tsarist forces took Chimkent in 1864 and Tashkent in 1865. In 1867 the General-Governorship of Turkestan was established with Tashkent as its center. It was through this General-Governorship that Russia ruled much of today's Soviet Central Asia until after the Bolshevik Revolution. (A number of changes in administrative divisions were made, some of them to incorporate subsequent conquests.) Russia's Governor General had jurisdiction over all of the territory of the former Kokand Khanate, and parts of Bukhara and Khiva. Nevertheless, the latter two survived in truncated form as distinct states dependent on Russia until after the Bolshevik Revolution. Parts of present-day Turkmenistan were the last area of Central Asia to be brought under Russia's control. Here the tsarist forces encountered some of the fiercest opposition. In fact, in 1879 they were defeated by Teke Turkmen tribes at Gök Tepe. Two years later, however, the tsarist forces overcame fierce resistance by the Turkmens in the famous Battle of Gök Tepe. (Aside from its importance for the expansion of Russian power in Central Asia, this battle deserves mention because of the massacre by General Skobelev's forces of the local Turkmen tribes.) The rest of what was once called Transcaspia (in present day Turkmenistan) submitted without force to the Russians in 1884. Following expansion into this zone, most of the border between Russia's territories and British-dominated Afghanistan was drawn in 1887.

Contact with Russia brought major changes to the economy of Central Asia. The greatest change was the expansion in cotton cultivation and its export to Russia. Russia became interested in the cotton-producing potential of the region as the U.S. civil war cut off supplies of the valuable raw material from America. The very limited beginnings of industrial growth in Central Asia also revolved around cotton. At the same time, Turkestan became a market for raw and manufactured products (including cotton textiles) from metropolitan Russia. The tsarist regime invested in transportation in the region, constructing the Trans-Caspian and Orenburg-Tashkent railroads. Although less extensively than in Kazakhstan, the tsarist regime gave expropriated lands in Turkestan to newly arriving Russian settlers.

Despite these important economic and political changes of the late nineteenth and early twentieth centuries, in contrast to their Bolshevik successors, the tsarist colonial administration of Turkestan did not attempt to alter the traditional social structure or assimilate the local nationalities. The tsarist regime sought to weaken Islam in the region, but during most of this period, especially under the direction of Turkestan Governor General von Kaufman (1867–82), it attempted to do this by ignoring rather than attacking the religion.

The tsarist administration's cautious approach was also apparent in its educational policy in Turkestan. Russia did not disturb the traditional Islamic schools (*maktabs*), which were attended by the overwhelming majority of children of the indigenous nationalities who attended school. The tsarist administration supported the opening of only a small number of schools in which most of the tuition was in Russian for the native population; these were intended to introduce some of the elite to the Russian language and Russian culture. The only other significant educational innovation during tsarist colonial rule were the new method (*usul-i jadid*) schools; the reform-minded Muslims who organized these sought to prepare the next generation of Muslims to operate in a much more modern world. Although the colonial administration tolerated some of these schools, it did not support them. The colonial regime's suspicion of these schools was shared by the *ulema* (the traditional Islamic religious leaders), who saw these institutions as a threat to the religious and social status quo.

The *jadid* movement was an extraordinarily important source of literati and reform-minded political leadership in Central Asia both in the last years of tsarist rule and the first years following the Bolshevik Revolution.

Many *jadid*ist ideas came to Central Asia either directly or indirectly from the Tatars of Crimea and the Middle Volga. Indeed, many of the movement's leaders in Central Asia were Tatars.

After the revolution, Central Asians with *jadid* roots served in top republic leadership positions in the region until as late as 1938. *Jadid*s, though most were observant Muslims and all were loyal to their Islamic culture and heritage, felt that social reform was needed in order for Muslim society to progress.

Trade, industry, railroads, and farming all brought new Russian settlers to Turkestan. But the Russians and members of the indigenous nationalities did not mix, and typically in the towns where Russians settled, the local nationalities inhabited a separate quarter. The Russians looked upon themselves as bearers of a superior civilization, unattainable by Central Asians save possibly through assimilation. For their part, the indigenous population looked upon the Russians as infidels and intruders.

Muslims and most other non-Slavic peoples in tsarist Russia were classified as *inorodtsy* (aliens) and thus were not considered full citizens of the Russian Empire. As such, they did not enjoy the same privileges as Russians, nor did they face the same obligations; for example, they were not subject to military service.

Clumsy acts by the tsarist administration heightened Central Asians' dissatisfaction with the colonial regime and occasionally provoked violent disturbances. One such incident took place in Tashkent in 1892, when Russians ignored local custom in the measures they used to control a cholera epidemic. A series of uprisings, all led by religious leaders, occurred in the Fergana Valley in 1885, 1891, 1892, and 1898. The last, known as the Andizhan rebellion, was led by a Nakshbandi *sufi* (mystic) under the banner of "holy war." The Russians were very alarmed by this uprising, seeing it as an attempt to seize control of the entire Fergana oblast.[1] The most serious challenge to tsarist rule took place in the summer of 1916. Although the immediate cause of the uprising was a government order drafting Muslims for non-combatant military service, the roots were much deeper: the economic situation for the Central Asians had been deteriorating, most markedly since the second half of 1915. The 1916 uprising was very violent, with a thousand Central Asians reported killed in fighting around the town of Dzhizak alone. Venting their discontent, Muslims murdered large numbers of Russian peasants; a series of bloody reprisals followed. Because they reflect indigenous Central Asians' dissatisfaction with their fate as part of the Russian Empire, these disturbances, and particularly the 1916 revolt, have remained extremely sensitive topics in Soviet historiography.[2]

The revolutionary events of 1917 in Turkestan were heavily concentrated in Tashkent, the seat of colonial power, and the most active participants in the events were mainly local Slavs. The Turkestan Committee of the Provisional Government (established in April 1917) had five Russian members out of a total of nine; even the four Muslim members included non-Central Asians.[3] In its policies the Provisional Government showed little inclination to share power with the indigenous population; nor did the Tashkent Soviet, which even before the October Revolution enjoyed more authority in Tashkent than the Turkestan Committee. According to Richard Pipes, oppressive actions by members of the soviet with a "chauvinistic, colonial" mentality were in large part responsible for the growth of autonomist tendencies among the native population in the fall of 1917. However, contrary to their hopes, the situation for the indigenous nationalities did not improve immediately after the Bolshevik revolution. In November 1917, the chairman of the new Turkestan Council of People's Commissars rejected a proposal by the Turkestan Muslim Central Council to give Turkestan territorial autonomy. A resolution by the Bolshevik faction at the Turkestan Congress of Soviets refused even to consider the participation of Muslims in the new government in Central Asia, justifying this in part because "the attitude of the local population toward the Soviet of Soldiers', Workers', and Peasants' Deputies [was] quite uncertain."[4]

The Russian Bolsheviks' distrust of Central Asians, and their attempt to "import" political, economic, and social revolutions, are major themes of the history of Soviet power in the region. Below, we will follow these attempts in several areas.

The resolution by the Bolshevik faction at the Turkestan Congress and other similar actions destroyed the hopes of many Muslims that Bolshevik power would benefit Turkestan's indigenous population; in response, the Turkestan Muslim Central Council soon held an extraordinary congress in the Fergana Valley city of Kokand and proclaimed the autonomy of southern Central Asia. The autonomous government, however, was quickly crushed in February 1918 by a superior force of Bolshevik troops sent from Tashkent. Thousands of Muslims died in the massacre. The indigenous population was further alienated by the armed Soviet forces who came to the villages in search of food and booty.

Despite its ephemeral existence, the Kokand government was important as the first organized indigenous opposition to the Soviet regime and as the embodiment of the local intelligentsia's wish for self-government. Its harsh suppression and other expressions of the Russian "colonial attitude" fueled the armed guerilla struggle of the so-called *basmachi*, which began in 1918. Although *basmachi* forces were a serious challenge to the Bolsheviks in much of Central Asia until 1924, subsequently (with the exception of the period of collectivization), these guerilla bands were more an annoyance than a threat to Bolshevik power in the region.

The Bolsheviks' brutality in suppressing the government in Kokand was symbolic of the lack of sensitivity which Russians displayed toward the indigenous population over the next couple of years. The greatest excesses were committed on the initiative of local authorities rather than on instructions from Moscow. Thus, local Russian authorities were immediately responsible for the soviets' exclusion of Muslims from power and the severity of reprisals against Muslims following the defeat of Kokand. Because of the civil war, Moscow did not regain a significant degree of control over Turkestan until the end of 1919. In the fall of that year the Bolsheviks dispatched a special Commission for Turkestan Affairs (*Turkkomissiia*) to put an end to the excesses of the local Russian "revolutionaries"; some of those with the worst "colonial mentality" were sent back to Russia.

The more conciliatory policy toward the indigenous nationalities promoted by the *Turkkomissiia* was designed to win support from the local population (and especially the numerically small intelligentsia) by assuring greater participation in government by members of the Muslim nationalities. Indeed, such policies did win support from some of the Muslim nationalist reformers (in Turkestan, Khiva, and Bukhara), many of whom even joined these republics' communist parties. But many of these new "communists," while sympathetic to the goals of the Bolshevik Party, were reluctant to place power over their peoples in the hands of a Russian-dominated Party. They sought autonomy or independence, and many were sympathetic to ideas such as those expressed by the Tatar Sultan Galiev, who by 1920 had become the most important Muslim in the Commissariat of Nationalities. Several years later he became disillusioned with what the Bolshevik Revolution had brought to Russia's Muslims and began to advocate the creation of a Soviet Muslim or Turkic republic and the revival of the Muslim Communist Party.[5] Following Galiev's denunciation and arrest in 1923, however, it became ever clearer to Muslim "communists" and Muslim intellectuals sympathetic to the regime that Moscow was unwilling to permit the realization of these goals.

National Delimitation

Administratively, following April 1918, the territory which had constituted the General-Governorship became the Turkestan Autonomous Soviet Socialist Republic (TASSR), under the jurisdiction of the RSFSR (Russian Soviet Federated Socialist Republic). The revolutionary changes in the TASSR quickly spilled over into Bukhara and Khiva. With the intervention of Red Army troops, the regimes in both of these states fell in 1920; they were soon transformed into the Bukharan Soviet

People's Republic and the Khorezm Soviet People's Republic respectively. Over the next few years these units were politically and economically incorporated into the Turkestan ASSR and, thus, the rest of Russia. In 1924, the Bukharan Soviet People's Republic, the Khorezm Soviet People's Republic, and the Turkestan ASSR were all dissolved; entirely new political units were established. These units eventually were to become the Uzbek Soviet Socialist Republic, the Tajik Soviet Socialist Republic, the Turkmen Soviet Socialist Republic, and the Kirgiz Soviet Socialist Republic.

However, initially, in 1924, only two union republics were created for Central Asian nationalities, the Uzbek SSR and Turkmen SSR. Tajikistan, which was made a union republic in 1929, for five years had the status of autonomous republic under the Uzbek SSR. The Kirgiz SSR was not created until 1936; between 1924 and 1936 it existed as the Karakirgiz Autonomous Oblast under the RSFSR. The lion's share of territory divided up in the national delimitation (carved out of the 419,000 square miles of land in Turkestan, Bukhara, and Khorezm) was given to Uzbekistan and Turkmenistan; they received 154,000 and 162,000 square miles respectively. The Karakirgiz Autonomous Oblast was given only 70,000 square miles, and the Tajik ASSR only 33,000. Uzbekistan, though slightly smaller than Turkmenistan, received more than half of the region's total planted area, while the Tajik ASSR received about a quarter of it, and the other two republics inherited smaller shares. More than 60 percent of Central Asia's approximately 4 million inhabitants lived in Uzbekistan, with the remainder fairly evenly distributed throughout the other three republics.[6]

The "national delimitation," which took place in 1924–25, was part of the Bolsheviks' solution to the potential threat of pan-Turkism and pan-Islamism. While the establishment of national republics is usually viewed in terms of a Moscow policy of *divide et impera*, it should not be forgotten that even the small body of Muslim intellectuals held contradictory visions of the Muslim or Turkic community which they hoped to build. Some Central Asian intellectuals favored creation of a pan-Turkic political unit, while others were suspicious of schemes which they thought would place too much power over Central Asians in the hands of Tatar leaders. Significantly, the Bolsheviks decided not to divide Central Asia in such a way as to leave a Bukharan or a Khorezmian unit. Moreover, the units which were created were not ethnically or linguistically homogeneous. (For example, many of the inhabitants of Uzbekistan's first capital, Samarkand, were Tajik speakers.) As for the failure to create Bukharan and Khorezmian units, perhaps the Bolsheviks feared that such states would command genuine political loyalty. In any case, it should be emphasized that although Moscow exploited the many differences which divided the indigenous Central Asian intelligentsia, it did not invent them. Over the long run, such differences gave the center great leverage over local political leaders.

These republics served as the bases for newly created independent literary languages, political and economic structures, and even histories. Despite their arbitrariness and artificiality, the republic divisions acquired a greater reality as the decades passed. Individuals within distinct political units generally had more contact with other individuals from their own republic than with individuals from other ones. In turn, these more intensive intra-republic interactions engendered shared problems, perspectives, and networks of personal communication.

Economy

In terms of economic potential, Central Asia was most important to the Bolsheviks, as it had been to the tsarist regime, as a supplier of cotton. The destruction of the irrigation system and the shift of some lands from cotton to food crops in the first years after the revolution caused the production of cotton in Central Asia to fall dramatically by 1921. Almost immediately after this, the new regime began to rebuild the irrigation system. By 1927, the area devoted to cotton culture was larger than that in 1914, but the acreage of land sown with grain was still less than two-thirds of that on the eve of World War I.[7]

Ten years after the Bolshevik Revolution, the First Five-Year Plan started an economic transformation in Central Asia. The greatest changes were the collectivization of agriculture and the sedentarization of nomadic herdsmen.[8] Opposition to these policies from the indigenous Central Asian population was fierce, and the economic consequences were disastrous. Many livestock raisers slaughtered their animals or drove them across borders to China. The suffering caused by the dislocation during this period gave new life to the *basmachi*, and in some areas of Turkmenistan and Tajikistan their activities reached the proportions of renewed civil war. Despite the opposition, however, collectivization proceeded apace; the percentage of collectivized land grew in Uzbekistan from 1.2 percent in 1928–29 to 68 percent in 1932, and 95 percent in 1937.[9] Although the organization of agriculture changed, the major crop did not. Cotton remained the mainstay of the local economy.

The regime devoted far less attention to industrial development in the region than to agriculture. Between 1922 and 1928, industry in Central Asia barely recovered to the very low pre-1917 level. In the following fifteen years, especially during the first two five-year plans (1928–1937), there was a great increase in the industrial output of Central Asia. This particularly affected the power output and the development of industry related to cotton (e.g., textile mills and fertilizer plants).[10] Although it remained very small in absolute terms, the share of heavy industry grew rapidly. In 1913, it had accounted for only 2 percent of Uzbekistan's industry, but by 1940 its share had grown to over 13 percent. Meanwhile, the share of cotton ginning and oil-extracting dropped from 87 percent to 38 percent.[11]

World War II, though the front was far from the region, nevertheless had a great impact on Central Asia. As elsewhere in the USSR, thousands of men went off to battle, while women, children, and the elderly were mobilized to fill many of their positions in the work force. At the same time, some 2 million refugees were evacuated to Central Asia from the Slavic republics. Some of the new arrivals, however, such as the Koreans and Crimean Tatars, did not come voluntarily, and they were not Slavs.

The strains of the war affected every aspect of the economy. Central Asia, which had previously received grain from other areas of the USSR, was required to feed itself. Perhaps even more dramatic were the changes in industrial development. Over 300 industrial enterprises were evacuated to Kazakhstan and Central Asia,[12] with more than 100 of them being relocated in Uzbekistan alone.[13] In addition to relocated enterprises, some new ones were established. In Uzbekistan they included five large hydroelectric power stations. Coal and ferrous metal industries were also introduced into the republic, and development of a number of other industries (electrotechnical, non-ferrous metal, oil-extracting, and certain light and food industries) was speeded up.[14] Altogether, between 1940 and 1950, the output of Uzbekistan's machine building increased from 11,000 to 119,000 tons, and coal production grew five-hundred-fold, from 3,000 to 1,500,000 tons.[15]

The accelerated industrialization of Central Asia begun in World War II continued into the 1950s. Among the most important projects was the Bekabad steel plant (which produced its first rolled metal in 1946). Another surge of industrial capacity came in the 1960s, encouraged by Khrushchev's *sovnarkhoz* experiment, in which individual territorial units were given much greater control over development of their own economies. During this period, such branches of industry as chemicals, construction materials, and machine building received new attention in Central Asia. But the impact of the *sovnarkhoz* experiment on industrial growth did not extend beyond the middle of the 1970s.[16]

As before, during the Brezhnev era much of Central Asia's industry continued to revolve around agriculture, with the cotton ginning industry occupying a dominant place. Production of fertilizers and equipment needed for the planting and harvesting of cotton also grew. In addition, extractive industries became more important. Gas reserves, concentrated in Turkmenistan and Uzbekistan, were increasingly tapped. By 1982,

Turkmenistan accounted for 14 percent of all Soviet gas production, which was two-thirds of the gas produced in the region.[17] Oil extraction, especially in Turkmenistan, also remained important, though it did not grow as rapidly as gas.[18] The production of hydroelectric energy grew very rapidly in Kirgizia: whereas the republic's hydroelectric stations produced only 285.3 million kilowatts in 1960, the analogous figures for 1980 and 1985 were already 4,845.7 million and 6,063.5 million, respectively.[19] Altogether, the Central Asian electricity production in 1985 had jumped to a level eight times the figure in 1960.[20]

Because of Soviet reluctance to release relevant statistics, it is much more difficult to judge the growth of the mining industry, particularly in the case of such commodities as gold and uranium. However, it is clear that Central Asia made a significant contribution in this area. Among other things, Kirgizia is the USSR's leading producer of mercury and antimony, and one of the major producers of uranium. Gold is mined in the region's Kyzylkum Desert which is shared by Uzbekistan, Turkmenistan, and Kazakhstan.

The difficulties which plagued the growth of Central Asian industry in the Brezhnev era can be illustrated through the example of the region's largest industrial system, the South Tajikistan Territorial Production Complex. Although its major components did not begin operation until much later, it was planned in the middle of the 1960s. Constructed in a region of Tajikistan rich in hydroelectric potential and natural minerals, it includes the Nurek Hydroelectric Station, the Tajik Aluminum Plant, and the Iavan Electrochemical Plant. Like projects elsewhere in Tajikistan and in all of the other Central Asian (and other Soviet) republics, long construction delays prevented the project from beginning operation according to plan. Similarly, the quality of construction caused serious environmental damage.[21]

Still another problem of industrial development in Central Asia has been the shortage of skilled workers. This is especially remarkable in the context of a regional labor surplus, and reflects above all the small number of members of indigenous nationalities working in these areas. Among the reasons for this are the concentration of industry in urban areas, and Central Asians' lack of training in industrial skills.

Despite the growth of industry, agriculture (especially cotton) continued to dominate the region's economy after World War II. One of the major factors which permitted further expansion in this area was the opening of new lands through the extension of the irrigation system. In 1940, 923,500 acres were under cotton cultivation in Uzbekistan; despite the interruption of the war, acreage grew to 1,098,100 by 1950 and 1,549,900 by 1965.[22] Reported production also dramatically increased. In Turkmenistan, the gross harvest increased 50 percent between 1960 and

1965, and then jumped by over 90 percent in the next decade.[23] In Uzbekistan the gross cotton harvest grew more than 30 percent between 1960 and 1965, and more than another 30 percent during the following ten years. But it is obvious that the growth in production was due first of all to the mobilization of additional resources rather than to more efficient use of existing ones.[24] In Turkmenistan alone the number of acres under cotton cultivation grew from 636,000 in 1965 to 1,204,600 a decade later.[25] Though proportionally a smaller expansion, the number of acres which came under cotton cultivation in Uzbekistan was about equal.[26] However, by the time Gorbachev took over the Soviet leadership, the careless exploitation of resources had already begun to take its toll. The USSR's 1985 cotton production was 12 percent less than in 1980.[27]

The disposition of fuels, ores, and agricultural products all illustrate Moscow's treatment of Central Asia as a source for raw materials, and its refusal to do much of the processing of those materials locally. Even the area's natural gas is largely sent to other fuel-deficient areas of the country.[28] In the case of iron, the region has only one steel plant, at Bekabad, with a full metallurgical production cycle.[29] The non-ferrous metallurgy of Central Asia (though it involves some very large plants), is largely restricted to extraction and enrichment of metals. The production of finished products from these metals is completed mostly outside of the region.[30] Perhaps the clearest case of exploitation of Central Asia as a raw materials base concerns its primary agricultural crop, cotton. The vast majority of Central Asia's cotton is taken out of the region to be turned into textiles in mills located in European areas of the USSR.

Dilemmas of Nativization

As in the economic sphere, from the very early years Moscow attempted to maintain control of the political and social processes in Central Asia, transform them, and ensure dependence on the center. The national delimitation described above can be seen in this context. Especially in the early decades, the new units which the delimitation created relied on Moscow for their very existence. In a similar way, the republic Party and government officials were also dependent on the center.

But there have often been contradictions among Moscow's political, social, and economic goals. Among the most difficult problems for the regime was the contradiction between the social revolution and the goals of political control and economic efficiency. The Marxist world view of the Bolsheviks naturally inclined them to ally themselves with the poorer classes of society. But because the country's new leaders also needed literate and politically active allies in the first years of power, they were obliged to rely on some of the few members of the indigenous intelligentsia who had been educated before the revolution; most such individuals were not from poor class backgrounds. Many of this first generation of allies were themselves educated in *jadid* schools or had other ties with the "bourgeois" *jadid* movement. This heightened the new Bolshevik leaders' suspicion toward these temporary allies.

The situation was further complicated by the regime's program of *korenizatsiia* (nativization, or more literally, rooting). This policy was, among other things, an attempt by the country's new rulers to eliminate the legacy of colonialism which characterized relations between Russians and Central Asians at the time of the Bolshevik Revolution. Although *korenizatsiia* is traceable to the Turkestan Republic period, it reached its height in Central Asia (as in other non-Russian republics) after the national delimitation.

Korenizatsiia involved recruitment and training of members of the indigenous nationalities and their promotion to positions of responsibility in the Party, state, and economic bureaucracies. In nativizing, however, it was usually necessary for Bolsheviks to choose between criteria of competence and political reliability. There were few Central Asians who were both politically reliable and competent, since competence was usually accompanied by independent thinking and links to the classes that the Bolsheviks mistrusted. Political reliability was greatest among the poorest elements of society, few of whom had the benefit of much formal education.

The contradiction between reliability and competence became increasingly evident during the First Five-Year Plan. Despite the pressing need for qualified cadres, competence was increasingly sacrificed to political reliability during the early 1930s.[31] It is true that the critical shortage of Central Asians qualified to staff Party, soviet, educational, and other institutions permitted some less politically reliable individuals to continue serving in prominent posts until the middle and late 1930s. But these individuals worked under increasingly strict supervision and in an atmosphere of growing terror.

In the context of the First Five-Year Plan, *korenizatsiia* aggravated a number of already serious economic and social problems and sometimes encouraged counterproductive "solutions." Individuals were promoted into administrative posts because they possessed appropriate class and nationality credentials, even when they lacked sufficient training and experience. Because cadres of European nationalities often resisted pressures for *korenizatsiia*, the "promoted" Central Asians often occupied prominent positions, but held much less power than their titles indicated.

The early 1930s brought an end to the policy of *korenizatsiia*. With the reemergence of Russian nationalism, the regime dropped its attempt to promote individuals based on their membership in formerly "exploited" nationalities. This was apparent at the Seventeenth Congress of the Soviet Communist Party (1934), when official Soviet doctrine ceased to label "great power chauvinism" the major danger on the nationality question. In the environment of the purges of the mid-1930s, Central Asians were no longer given preferential consideration for promotion. Rapid upward mobility (with all its advantages and dangers) was reserved largely for better educated Europeans and those Central Asians who could operate in a Russian environment.

The tightening of "political reliability" criteria and its implications for competence become obvious if one examines the educational and class backgrounds of political leaders in this period. Throughout the 1920s and until the purges of the late 1930s, a number of well-educated Central Asians occupied prominent positions in their republics. Some of them came from classes which the Bolsheviks mistrusted. For example, Fayzulla Khojayev (Faizulla Khodzhaev) the first chairman of the Uzbek Council of People's Commissars after the creation of Uzbekistan, was the son of a wealthy Bukharan merchant. Khojayev had been educated in a Bukharan *madrasah* (higher religious school) and in a private school in Moscow. The first Uzbek to head the Uzbek Communist Party, Akmal Ikramov, was the son of a teacher and himself completed a teachers' course in Tashkent and briefly taught in a Soviet school. The first chairman of the Kirgiz Council of People's Commissars, Yusup Abdurakhmanov, was also well educated.

While these men held office, some others were apparently selected because of their nationality, class backgrounds, and willingness to comply with orders. This was true in the case of some chairmen of republic (or oblast) executive committees. Y. Akhunbabayev (Iu. Akhunbabaev), the chairman of Uzbekistan's Central Executive Committee, was barely literate; the same was true of A. Urazbekov, the first chairman of the Karakirgiz oblast Executive Committee. A recent historical sketch about these men alleges that besides their *batrak* (hired farm labor) origins, their poor education and unquestioning attitude toward authority were the qualities which made them attractive to authorities in Moscow.[32]

Eventually, during the purges of 1937–38, such men as Khojayev, Ikramov, and Abdurakhmanov were arrested for their "nationalist" activities; in many cases they were accused of plotting the secession of their republics from the USSR and executed. Despite their innocence, these men's names were unmentionable except in negative contexts until the late 1950s.

The fate of the members of the indigenous cultural intelligentsia who had ties with the *jadid* movement followed a similar pattern. Many of them served the Bolshevik regime during the late 1920s and the early and middle 1930s. But they, too, were vulnerable, and their members shared the tragic fate of the Party and state officials.

"Emancipation" of Women

Before considering Moscow's political control after the purges, it should be noted that the dilemmas concerning nationality, competence, and reliability were made even more acute by still other factors. Most important among these was the Bolsheviks' commitment to abolishing the exploitation of women, which Moscow viewed as characteristic of "feudal" Central Asian society. Due to this exploitation, according to one Soviet author writing in the 1920s, there was "no human being" anywhere in Russia "more ignorant, more downtrodden and enslaved" than "the Eastern woman."[33]

The Bolsheviks seem to have assumed that the social inferiority of women in Central Asia (like that of poorer classes) would ensure that they would be grateful to the Communist Party for offering them new opportunities and rights; thus, in a sense, women represented to the Bolsheviks what Gregory Massell has termed a "surrogate proletariat."[34]

As Moscow diminished its reliance on "unreliable" cadres, women became an important reserve which the regime attempted to tap. In order to mobilize women, a head-on attack (*khudzhum*) was declared on a variety of customs and taboos affecting women. Much of the assault was directed against the veil worn by Muslim women; massive public unveilings were held in 1926–28. The campaign, however, brought a backlash which united both poor and rich traditional Central Asian males in opposition.[35]

Although it quickly became evident that Central Asian Muslim women were not the easily tapped and politically reliable reserve which the regime had expected, the Bolsheviks continued to attempt to promote female cadres. However, instead of resolving the problem of *korenizatsiia*, the pressure to promote women often just added one more criterion which some proportion of promoted cadres was supposed to meet. At least throughout the years of *korenizatsiia*, it aggravated the already impossible task of finding competent and reliable individuals.

Post–World War II Political Control

The indigenous cadres who were promoted following the purges were powerful vis-à-vis other local potential leaders, but even the most prominent ones were dependent on Moscow or Moscow-appointed officials for their jobs. With the end of World War II, however, there were signs of a new indigenous political elite at higher levels of the Party and state apparatus. As Teresa Rakowska-Harmstone has noted,

> Beginning in 1944–45 a new pattern emerged in the placement of Muslim and European cadres in Central Asian republics. Muslims appeared in top "representative" positions (such as first secretaries of republican and province party organizations, ministers and chairmen of the Council of Ministers), but with Russians or other representatives of the central apparat in all of the number two "control" positions immediately below the Muslim incumbents, and occupying also most of the intermediate managerial and administrative posts in the hierarchy, as well as top positions (usually the only exceptions to the pattern) in the internal security and secret police organizations.[36]

This was accompanied by an increase in the representation of the indigenous nationalities in republic Party organizations. Between 1949 and 1959 the share of the primary indigenous nationality membership in the republic Party organization grew from 43 percent to 49 percent in Uzbekistan and 44 percent to 50 percent in Turkmenistan. The trends continued throughout the late Khrushchev and Brezhnev eras. By 1978, Uzbeks accounted for 59 percent of their republic's Party membership, and by 1983, Turkmens accounted for 62 percent in their republic.[37]

These processes began to weaken Moscow's control in the region. This became especially evident in the late Brezhnev era, when the aging leader failed to set in motion the processes—in particular, a political shakeup—which would have been necessary (though not necessarily sufficient) to reassert control. At the same time, the Central Asian political elites withheld information from the center and avoided meeting many of its demands. As their power at the republic level increased, they packed republic political, economic, and cultural institutions with their relatives, friends, political allies, and other colleagues from their home regions. Their collective "conspiracies" also contributed to maintaining silence on the increasingly serious economic problems.

Moscow's attempt to re-establish authority in Central Asia began even before Gorbachev's ascension to the post of general secretary and his policy of glasnost. In retrospect, the first sign of this may have been the sudden death in October 1983 of Sharaf Rashidov, first secretary of the Uzbek Communist Party and candidate member of the Politburo of the CPSU Central Committee. Rashidov is rumored to have realized that he was about to be disgraced by the public revelation of his "mafia's" widespread corruption, and so committed suicide. Whether true or not, a scathing report on corruption in Uzbekistan under Rashidov was delivered at a republic Party central committee plenum only months after Rashidov's death; revelations over the next two years implicated the former first secretary as a central figure in the corrupt network, who had passively if not actively opened the way to misdeeds. The revelations were accompanied by a massive purge of the republic Party apparatus. Many of the ministers and oblast Party committee secretaries who were removed were charged with criminal offenses, and some were condemned to death. Although the Party first secretaries in the other three Central Asian republics did not die in office (let alone under such mysterious circumstances as Rashidov), they were all removed within three months of each other at the end of 1985; charges of corruption and mismanagement ensued, followed by purges of their republic Party apparatuses.

Cultural Policies

Moscow's policies in the areas of culture over the past seventy years reflect its varying approaches to maintaining political dominance in the region. They also reveal the regime's persistent attempt to transform Central Asian society into something more closely resembling Soviet Russia. Thus, the Party's struggle against Islam, aside from its goal of reducing the power of the traditional leadership over Central Asian society was also an integral part of its bold attempt to replace religious and ethnic identification with an atheist, "international" one. Likewise, by maintaining tight control over the definitions of "socialist" culture and "progressive" linguistic development, the regime in Moscow sought to Russify Central Asian forms of creative expression and languages.

Islam

Moscow's division of Central Asia into individual republics reduced the threat of a "pan-Islamic" or "pan-Turkic" movement; however, Islam remained the "great divide" which distinguished Central Asians from most of the rest of the Soviet population.

In a bid to win greater support, or at least to dampen resistance, for several years following the arrival of the Commission for Turkestan Affairs, the Bolsheviks conducted a conciliatory policy toward Islam. In 1921, Friday was declared the official day of rest in Muslim areas, and the following year the *waqf* (religious endowment) lands which had previously been confiscated were returned to the mosques. Muslim schools reopened and some of the income from *waqf* lands was used to support them. *Sharia* (Islamic written law) and *adat* (customary law) courts were allowed to reassume jurisdiction, first in civil and then in criminal cases. But this policy began to be reversed already by 1924;

by 1928 polygamy, *kalym* (bride price), and other traditional family practices were prohibited, and religious courts and schools were closed. The campaign against Islam greatly intensified during the First Five-Year Plan, when crude propaganda and violence were widely used to fight religious belief and practice, and to "emancipate" women from veils and their traditional family roles. A high level of anti-Islamic propaganda was maintained throughout the rest of the period leading up to World War II.

During the war, as Moscow sought to draw on new sources of public support, its policy toward Islam (and religion more generally) became more moderate. Four Islamic spiritual directorates were established, one of them specifically to serve Central Asia and Kazakhstan. New mosques opened, and open religious observance among the population of all ages increased. The policy toward Islam remained relatively moderate until the middle of the 1950s. In fact, the Mir-i Arab Madrasah in Bukhara was reactivated in 1948 and it appears that the number of mosques in the USSR continued to grow, albeit slowly, until Stalin's death.[38] The late 1950s and early 1960s, however, witnessed an assault on Islam, with many mosques being closed amid a vigorous atheist propaganda campaign. This anti-religious activity was part of Khrushchev's attempt to eliminate religion throughout the USSR and was not directed only at Muslims.

Despite the continuation of anti-religious propaganda under Brezhnev, the regime also tolerated widespread observance of many practices popularly associated with Islam. As was revealed in the post-Brezhnev era, local Party and state officials regularly participated in religious ceremonies, and even diverted public funds to construct local mosques and "teahouses" which served religious purposes. In part, this "tolerance" may have been due to a lack of accurate information in Moscow about the widespread observance of these practices. Whatever the reasons, many of the cultural phenomena which the CPSU allowed to be "rehabilitated" during Brezhnev's tenure as part of the *national* heritage were inextricably bound to Islam.

Cultural Expression

Russification of the arts and language was especially harsh in the middle and late 1930s, when those aspects of national cultures and languages which differentiated them from the ways of the Russian "elder brother" were proclaimed archaic, dying, and even counterrevolutionary. During World War II, however, the regime sought to draw Central Asians and other non-Russians into the struggle for a Soviet homeland. Therefore, the Party was forced to reject the heavy-handed Russification which had been pursued during the late 1930s. As Stalin realized, most Central Asians were unwilling to risk their lives to defend Russia, toward which many felt indifference or even hostility. Consequently, the Party stressed the multiethnic nature of the Soviet population, and propaganda called on non-Russians to defend the USSR because it also meant defending their national homeland and traditions. No longer was the "international" character of culture judged by its "Russian-ness"; "patriotic" behavior came to mean any support for the fight with the USSR's mortal enemy. Along with an end to anti-Islamic propaganda, the denigration of national customs and heroes also ceased.

Following the war, Stalin returned to a policy of Russification. In most of the first post-war decade Moscow withheld the concessions to non-Russians' national pride that it had granted during the war. One manifestation of this in Central Asia was the campaign against the Turkic national epics in 1951–52.

Although, as described above, in the late 1950s and 1960s the Party conducted a sustained attack on Islam, in many ways nationality policy toward Central Asia in this period began to be more flexible. As part of Khrushchev's de-Stalinization campaign the leadership allowed (and perhaps encouraged) the rehabilitation of individual members of the Central Asian political leadership and cultural intelligentsia who had been purged and even shot for "nationalist" sins in the late 1930s. Selected works of some of the former "nationalist" writers, such as the Uzbek Abdulla Qadiriy (Abdulla Kadyri), were republished. Since these "nationalists" had propagated a traditional culture permeated with Islam, this eventually encouraged a changed policy toward Islam itself. But this issue was not directly confronted at this time. Rather, literary histories emphasized any evidence which—often out of context—could be understood to imply that rehabilitated writers had indeed been atheists. Sometimes their published works were edited in such a way as to omit all positive references to religion.

The more flexible policy toward culture which evolved in the 1970s reflected the beginning of the leadership's recognition that ethnic differences were not disappearing in the Soviet Union, and in particular that Central Asian Muslims were not becoming more like their Russian "elder brothers." Consequently, the definition of Soviet patriotism which evolved during the Brezhnev era increasingly rested on the assumption that all peoples of the USSR were developing stronger bonds with one another, but that for the foreseeable future they would maintain distinct national identities. In fact, the national cultures were said to be in a prolonged period of flourishing.

Thus, while official formulas describing nationality processes purported to show an increasing "coming together" (*sblizhenie*), in fact Moscow was quite tolerant of the expression of national pride in Central Asia. Local authors produced a large number of historical novels; at the same time, forgotten musical forms began to be studied openly, and the restoration of historical and architectural monuments was undertaken on a much larger scale. When criticized for displays of "nationalist" attitudes, the Central Asian intelligentsia pointed out that analogous processes were occurring throughout the USSR.

Language

Perhaps better than any other area, the Soviet policy toward language in Central Asia demonstrates how cultural policy was shaped by policy toward Islam and the complex interplay of political and economic factors. The national delimitation, of course, was itself inextricably linked to the creation of distinct literary languages for each nationality. Beyond this, however (since only a small minority of indigenous Central Asians knew much Russian), the regime's commitment to *korenizatsiia* meant that it had to attempt to provide education, services, and work environments in the local languages. Since Europeans continued to work in many administrative posts, the regime attempted to encourage them to learn the language of the majority of their republic's nationality. Indeed, at least on paper, knowledge of the local language was often made a condition for employment or promotion.

However, this effort met with opposition, derision, and avoidance from the majority of the European population, and produced few positive results. With the waning of *korenizatsiia*, the pressure was removed for government, Party, and economic personnel to conduct business in the indigenous languages; rather, they were permitted to use Russian. This killed the incentive for Slavs to learn Uzbek, Turkmen, Kirgiz, or Tajik. It also meant that those Central Asians who remained in the republic apparatus had to operate in a Russian environment. Because few Central Asians were fluent in Russian, this greatly complicated their participation. Those with no Russian skills were excluded from many activities on linguistic grounds alone.

During the next fifty years, the Party promoted Russian language instruction for Central Asians and other non-Russian nationalities. One of the first steps in this direction was the plan in 1938 to introduce universal Russian language classes for all non-Russian Soviet children. Measured by the resources which were devoted to it, the period which saw the greatest emphasis on Russian language lessons did not occur until the late Brezhnev era. Especially following 1979, the regime invested heavily in school buildings, language laboratories, teacher training, etc. as part of an effort to raise the level of Russian language skills among the local population.

This emphasis on Russian did not mean a shift in *language of instruction* for most Central Asian children. Among all the major nationalities, the vast majority of Central Asians continued to attend most of their lessons in their native tongue throughout the Brezhnev era. The need to rely on continued education in the local languages was probably most keenly felt in the period immediately following World War II, when the departure of many Slavs who had been evacuated to Central Asia required rapid training of replacements from indigenous nationalities. This was made all the more urgent by the disruption of education caused by the war.

A small proportion of indigenous nationality parents (especially in the republic capitals and certain other cities) sent their children to Russian-language schools. In many cases this was motivated by the (generally correct) view that Russian-language schools provided a better quality of education and by the knowledge that much of higher and specialized secondary education was available only in Russian.

Though Islam was not an important factor shaping the Party's policy toward language *status* (i.e., the functions assigned to each language), it was very apparent in policy toward language *corpus* (i.e., the development of the body of the local languages themselves). As a result of the All-Union Turcological Congress held in 1926, all Central Asian languages shifted to the Latin alphabet. (The Arabic script, which had been used to write Central Asian forms of Turkic as well as Tajik, was considered holy by many believers; moreover, it was a symbolic bond linking all believers with the language of the Koran.) In parallel fashion, many Arabic words were eliminated from Central Asian languages in the 1920s and 1930s and replaced with "international" (i.e., Russian) ones. Indeed, basing themselves on the linguistic theories of Nikolai Marr, Soviet scholars began to claim that national languages (along with other nationality divisions) in the USSR would soon disappear; they predicted that before long the many different nationalities would merge into a single people. This goal of Soviet cultural policy was further manifested by the shift to writing the Central Asian languages in Cyrillic at the end of the 1930s.

Although even under the more relaxed cultural policy of the Brezhnev era the Central Asian languages never returned to the Arabic (or Latin) script, the less strident anti-Islamic policy did have an important effect on vocabulary. Some of the previously discarded "archaic" Arabic vocabulary began to reappear in Central Asian publications.

Educational Achievement and Problems

The Bolshevik leaders hoped that the educational system would play an important role in raising the future citizens of a transformed and modern Central Asia. Naturally, educational and language policies were closely linked. There is evidence that (aside from the break with the Islamic world) one of the reasons the Bolsheviks promoted the Latin alphabet was that they thought learning to read was easier with Latin letters than with Arabic ones. Until the late 1980s, standard Soviet accounts claimed that at the time of the Bolshevik Revolution the literacy rate in Central Asia was no more than 2 or 3 percent.[39] Whatever the real rate at the time of the revolution, it is obvious that, despite its promises to provide the local population with native-language education, the Turkestan ASSR achieved only a modest improvement in literacy rates. A tremendous literacy campaign coincided with the shift to the Latin alphabet (and the First Five-Year Plan), but it is extremely difficult to tell how many people learned to read with the "new" letters. The literacy data from the late 1930s are also problematic. Until recently, Soviet histories insisted that literacy levels of 80 percent or even 90 percent were achieved in this period. Although these figures are certainly inflated, there is no doubt that the regime was successful in teaching basic literacy skills to a large segment of the population in a short period. At the same time, however, the shift to the Cyrillic alphabet made millions of people "illiterate" overnight. (Until recently, this fact was never mentioned in Soviet accounts of this second shift.)

As everywhere else in the USSR, World War II disrupted the educational system in Central Asia. Moreover, because of the relatively small number of births during the war, the number of children in schools was depressed even after the war: in 1940–41, grades one through eight of Central Asian primary schools had over 2 million pupils; in 1945–46, it was not much more 1.5 million. By 1950–51, the 1940–41 levels had been reached, but over the next few years there was no further growth. Only in the second half of the 1950s did the steady increase resume.[40]

One important measure to improve the standard of education in Central Asia in the first post-war decade concerned the training of teachers. This is evident in the fact that whereas in Uzbekistan in 1946–47 only 3,219 of the republic's 38,884 general educational school teachers had a higher education, a decade later, the figure had grown to 16,016 out of 69,758.[41]

The higher qualifications of teachers reflected the overall rise in the number of students attending higher educational institutions. In the four republics of Central Asia, the number of students in higher educational institutions (*vysshie uchebnye zavedeniia* or *VUZy*) in 1950–51 had already reached 64,500; this represented more than a 100 percent increase over the 1940–41 figure of 27,500. The sharp rise continued over the next two decades: by 1960–61 the number of students in Central Asian *VUZy* had again more than doubled to 151,800; it more than doubled once more by 1970 when it reached 354,900 students.[42] To judge by Uzbekistan and Kirgizia, the growth was much slower in the 1970s and early 1980s; in both of these republics the number of *VUZ* students in 1985 had grown only 20 to 25 percent over the 1970-71 figures.[43]

The 1960s also witnessed an increase in the number of students studying in Central Asia's specialized secondary educational institutions, but the most rapid growth in these schools did not take place until the next decade. Thus, the number of students in the four republics in specialized secondary educational institutions increased only from 69,400 to 94,000 between 1950-51 and 1960-61; however, by 1970-71 it had reached 269,000.[44] At least in the largest republic, Uzbekistan, the growth in the number of students receiving a specialized secondary education continued longer than growth in higher education. In Uzbekistan the number of students in specialized secondary education in 1985-86 was almost three-fourths again as large as the number in 1970-71. However, in Kirgizia the increase over the same period was less than 25 percent.[45]

The increased enrollments in *VUZ* and secondary specialized education translated into higher proportions of Central Asians with higher levels of educational achievement in the Khrushchev and Brezhnev eras. Among all of the four eponymous Central Asian nationalities the proportion of individuals with a higher education at least doubled, and in most cases almost tripled between 1959 and 1970.[46] The indicators for full general secondary education were equally dramatic. Although the proportion of females achieving these levels of education was uniformly below the level for males, the proportional increases for females were greater.

Despite the seeming progress depicted by these figures, Central Asia's educational system was growing out of touch with the needs of the economy in the Brezhnev era. Most importantly, children in Central Asia—and especially those of indigenous nationalities—did not study or learn the technical specialties most needed by their republics' economies. This is one of the primary explanations of a growing labor surplus and vacant jobs. Very few Central Asians began to work in industrial jobs. Moreover, the quality of education in Central Asia was generally poorer than in other areas of the USSR. Among the most important reasons were the poor physical plant, frequent mobilization of children for agricultural labor, and the inadequate training of teachers. Inasmuch as the Soviet leadership's hopes to transform Central Asian society required a younger generation with the skills and attitudes to revolutionize their society, the educational system did not fulfill its goals.

By the early and mid-1980s serious economic, social, and political problems had accumulated in Soviet Central Asia. True, their scale would not become evident to Western observers until the broadening of glasnost in the last years of the decade; however, the conditions which would lead to violent outbursts in such places as the Fergana Valley (summer of 1989), and later in Dushanbe, Andizhan, and Osh, were already ripening.

In retrospect, two major characteristics of Soviet policy in Central Asia in the 1980s were the Moscow leadership's insensitivity to the problems of the region and its adherence to old, familiar, and ineffective solutions. The failure of the "stale" approaches in a number of major areas is documented in the chapters which follow. Besides analyzing the reasons for these failures, the chapters also consider some of Moscow's belated major modifications of policies and its recognition of the constraints on its ability to direct a transformation of Central Asian society.

At least two sorts of constraints—economic and demographic—became acute in the 1980s. The demographic constraint—at least in the form of surplus population—did not hamper the center's ability to achieve its goals in other parts of the country: although Central Asia's population was growing rapidly, the population almost everywhere else in the USSR was barely reproducing itself. In the case of the economy, however, parallels to Central Asia's problems were abundant in every republic: While Central Asia's economy was more agricultural and the region as a whole served as a crucial raw materials base for the rest of the country, the inefficiencies and mismanagement of Central Asia—as other regions of the USSR—were also rapidly leading toward a crisis.

Because of the importance of the demographic and economic factors, the first section of this book will provide an overview of recent demographic developments and analyze more closely some of the reasons for Central Asia's present economic crisis. Following this, we will proceed to look at the failure of the political, social, and cultural transformation of Central Asian society.

Notes

1. Geoffrey Wheeler, *The Modern History of Soviet Central Asia* (New York: Praeger, 1964), p. 89.

2. On the Andizhan uprising see E. Iu. Iusupov and B. V. Lunin, "Andizhanskoe vosstanie 1898 goda v Sovetskoi istoricheskoi literature," *Obshchestvennye nauki v Uzbekistane*, no. 1 (Jan.), 1987, pp. 18–31. One of the standard works on the 1916 uprising is Kh. T. Tursunov, *Vosstanie 1916 goda v Srednei Azii i Kazakhstane* (Tashkent: Gosizdat, 1966). An Uzbek-language work by the same author and with the same title was published in 1987 as *Orta Osiya va Qazaghistanda 1916 yil khalq qozghalani* (Tashkent: Fan).

3. Hélène Carrère d'Encausse, "The Fall of the Czarist Empire," in *Central Asia: A Century of Russian Rule*, ed. Edward Allworth (New York: Columbia University Press, 1967), pp. 215–16.

4. *Nasha gazeta*, Nov. 23, 1917, cited in Richard Pipes, *The Formation of the Soviet Union* (New York: Atheneum, 1968), p. 91.
5. Pipes, *The Formation*, p. 262.
6. Alexander G. Park, *Bolshevism in Turkestan, 1917–27* (New York: Columbia University Press, 1957), p. 99.
7. Ian M. Matley, "Agricultural Development," in *Central Asia*, ed. Allworth, p. 287.
8. Ibid., p. 288.
9. Michael Rywkin, *Russia in Central Asia* (New York: Collier Books, 1963), p. 64.
10. Ian Matley, "Industrialization," in *Central Asia*, ed. Allworth, pp. 331–32.
11. S. K. Ziiadullaev, *Industriia Sovetskogo Uzbekistana* (Tashkent: Uzbekistan, 1984), p. 39.
12. S. K. Kerimbaev, *Sovetskii Kirgizstan v velikoi otechestvennoi voine 1941–1945* (Frunze: Ilim, 1980), p. 52.
13. Rywkin, *Russia in Central Asia*, p. 69.
14. *Uzbekskaia Sovetskaia Sotsialisticheskaia Respublika* (Tashkent, 1981), p. 178. This is a one-volume reference book issued as an "encyclopedia" about Uzbekistan; henceforth it will be referred to as *Uzbek Encyclopedia*.
15. Boris Rumer, *Soviet Central Asia: "A Tragic Experiment"* (Boston: Unwin Hyman, 1989), p. 54.
16. Ibid., pp. 53–59.
17. *Turkmenskaia Sovetskaia Sotsialisticheskaia Respublika* (Ashkhabad, 1984), p. 200. For reasons analogous to those cited in note 14, this will be referred to below as *Turkmen Encyclopedia*.
18. Rumer, *Soviet Central Asia*, p. 46.
19. *Narodnoe khoziaistvo Kirgizskoi SSR za gody Sovetskoi vlasti* (Frunze: Kyrgyzstan, 1987), p. 66.
20. Rumer, *Soviet Central Asia*, p. 47.
21. Bess Brown, "Economic Requests of the Central Asian Republics and Kazakhstan Presented at USSR Supreme Soviet Session," *Radio Liberty Research*, 437/80, Nov. 19, 1980, and Rumer *Soviet Central Asia*, pp. 50–52.
22. *Uzbek Encyclopedia*, p. 202.
23. *Turkmen Encyclopedia*, p. 214.
24. For a description of this process in Uzbekistan, see Alastair McAuley, "Economic Development and Political Nationalism in Uzbekistan," *Central Asian Survey*, 5, nos. 3/4 (1986), pp. 161–82.
25. *Turkmen Encyclopedia*, p. 214.
26. *Uzbek Encyclopedia*, p. 202.
27. Rumer, *Soviet Central Asia*, p. 64.
28. Ibid., p. 46.
29. Ibid., p. 49.
30. Ibid., p. 59.
31. Teresa Rakowska-Harmstone, *Russia and Nationalism in Central Asia: The Case of Tadzhikistan* (Baltimore: The Johns Hopkins Press, 1970), p. 42 and

William Fierman, "Nationalism, Language Planning and Development in Soviet Uzbekistan (1917–1941)," unpublished Ph.D. dissertation, Harvard, 1979, pp. 185–221.

32. *Komsomolets Kirgizii,* Nov. 29, 1989.

33. A. Nukhrat, *Oktiabr' i zhenshchina Vostoka* (Moscow, 1927), p. 8, cited by Gregory J. Massell, *The Surrogate Proletariat* (Princeton: Princeton University Press, 1974), p. 96.

34. Ibid., pp. 178–79.

35. Ibid., chs. VI, VII, and VIII, *passim.*

36. Teresa Rakowska-Harmstone, "Islam and Nationalism: Central Asia and Kazakhstan Under Soviet Rule," *Central Asian Survey,* 2, no. 2 (1983), p. 34.

37. *Uzbek Encyclopedia,* p. 142 and *Turkmen Encyclopedia,* p. 165.

38. Alexandre Bennigsen and S. Enders Wimbush, *Muslims of the Soviet Empire* (London: C. Hurst & Company, 1985), p. 17. In *The Modern History,* Wheeler says that Mir-i Arab Madrasah was opened in 1952. Whether opened in 1948 or 1952, it still reflects the conciliatory treatment of "official" Islam (p. 191).

39. There is considerable disagreement about the actual level of literacy in Central Asia in the first decades of the twentieth century. Some recent estimates place the rate in the range of 20 percent. See, for example, *Ozbekistan adabiyati va san"ati,* Oct. 20, 1989.

40. *Narodnoe obrazovanie, nauka, i kul'tura v SSSR: Statisticheskii sbornik* (Moscow: Statistika, 1977), pp. 72–78.

41. I. K. Kadyrov, *Ocherki razvitiia obshcheobrazovatel'noi shkoly Sovetskogo Uzbekistana* (Tashkent: Oqituvchi, 1974), p. 109.

42. *Narodnoe obrazovanie,* p. 217.

43. *Narodnoe khoziaistvo Uzbekistana v 1987 godu* (Tashkent: Uzbekistan, 1988), p. 278; *Narodnoe khoziaistvo Kirgizskoi SSR v 1971 godu* (Frunze, 1973), p. 281; and *Narodnoe khoziaistvo Kirgizskoi SSR v 1987 godu* (Frunze: Kyrgyzstan, 1988), p. 211.

44. *Narodnoe obrazovanie,* p. 156.

45. *Narodnoe khoziaistvo Uzbekistana v 1987 godu,* p. 278; *Narodnoe khoziaistvo Kirgizskoi SSR v 1971 godu,* p. 280; and *Narodnoe khoziaistvo Kirgizskoi SSR v 1987 godu,* p. 210.

46. The proportion of Uzbeks increased from 9 per 1,000 to 24 per 1,000 between 1950 and 1970. The analogous figures for Tajiks were 8 per 1,000 in 1959 and 21 per 1,000 in 1979; for Kirgiz, 9 per 1,000 and 26 per 1,000; and for Turkmens, 11 per 1,000 and 25 per 1,000 (*Itogi Vsesoiuznoi perepisi naseleniia 1970 goda* [Moscow: Statistika, 1973], vol. 4, pp. 395–403).

2

Implications of Ethnic and Demographic Trends

Nancy Lubin

Much has been written about the implications that ethnic and demographic trends in Soviet Central Asia might hold for the USSR. Throughout the 1970s and 1980s, the Central Asian population of the Soviet Union has been growing more than three to four times as fast as the USSR's ethnic Russian population. This means that at least well into the next century—should the Central Asian republics remain part of the Soviet empire—an increasing proportion of the Soviet population as a whole will be concentrated in the Central Asian republics of Tajikistan, Turkmenistan, Uzbekistan and Kirgizia with an economic infrastructure ill prepared to absorb them; and it means that a growing proportion of the Soviet population will be comprised of the ethnically Muslim Central Asian nationalities with a language, history, culture, and contemporary concerns vastly different from those of the Russians.[1]

At a time of enormous, and rising, economic, social, and nationalist pressures throughout the USSR, these demographic trends raise serious questions concerning the future both of Soviet Central Asia and of the USSR as a whole. In the context of great economic, social and nationality pressures in all of the Central Asian republics, what kinds of strains might demographic pressures suggest for the Central Asian areas themselves? In a period of tremendous uncertainty and upheaval in the USSR, what might be the impact of a rapidly expanding Central Asian population on the country as a whole? Will greater numbers of Soviet Central

---

Some of the material in this chapter first appeared in Nancy Lubin, *Labour and Nationality in Soviet Central Asia* (Princeton, NJ: Princeton University Press, 1984) and in Nancy Lubin, *Labour and Nationality in Soviet Central Asia* (London: Macmillan, 1984). Reprinted with permission.

Asians necessarily imply greater Central Asian or Muslim influence or growing political and nationalist unrest?

This chapter examines ethnic and demographic trends as a backdrop for addressing some of these larger issues. After an analysis of Central Asian demographic background, it briefly discusses some of the key issues these trends suggest, and raises questions concerning their implications for the future.

Demographic Background and Trends

Beginning in the 1960s, demographic trends in the Soviet Central Asian republics have been marked by two fundamental changes in population size and composition: the total republican populations began to grow rapidly, and the local nationalities began to comprise an increasing proportion of these total populations. These changes were due to a high rate of natural growth and low mobility among the indigenous populations, and to a lower fertility level and declining mobility among the Slavs. Although there have been some fluctuations over the past three decades, these basic trends have continued to this day.

The first of these changes, more rapid growth of the total population, was in sharp contrast to other parts of the USSR, where both the effects of past "demographic catastrophes" (two world wars, collectivization, the purges, etc.) and declining fertility levels led to a decline in the rate of population growth. In Uzbekistan, Tajikistan and Turkmenistan, for example, throughout the 1960s and 1970s, the total populations grew at least three times faster than they had during the previous two decades: while Uzbekistan's population had risen by 28 percent over the twenty-year period 1939–59 (from 6.3 to 8.1 million people) it rose by almost 90 percent over the next twenty-year period, from 8.1 million people in 1959, to 15.4 million people in 1979. Likewise, while the population of Turkmenistan grew by 16 percent between 1940–59, it grew by more than five times that rate, or by 82 percent between 1959–79. And similar patterns of overall population growth were illustrated in Tajikistan and, to a slightly lesser degree, in Kirgizia. By contrast, the population of the RSFSR grew by 8 percent and 17 percent during the same time periods. Between 1979–89, population increase remained roughly what it was during the preceding ten-year period. Thus, between 1959–70, 1970–79, and 1979–89, levels of population growth in the Central Asian republics were generally between three and four times the average for the USSR as a whole, and two to three times more rapid than they had been during the previous two decades (see Table 2.1).

The second change—i.e., the growth in Central Asia's indigenous populations—was perhaps more pronounced, for it marked a direct

TABLE 2.1
Population Size and Percentage Growth:
Central Asian Republics, RSFSR, and the USSR, 1940-89

	Total Population (in thousands)					Percent Growth		
	1940	1959	1970	1979	1989	1940-59	1959-79	1979-89
Uzbekistan	6551	8119	11,799	15,389	19,810	23.9	89.6	28.7
Tajikistan	1525	1981	2900	3806	5093	29.9	91.9	33.8
Turkmenistan	1302	1516	2159	2765	3523	16.4	82.0	27.4
Kirgizia	1528	2066	2934	3523	4258	35.2	70.8	20.9
RSFSR	110,098	117,534	130,079	137,410	147,022	6.8	17.0	7.0
USSR	194,077	208,827	241,720	262,085	285,762	7.6	25.7	9.0

Source: Narodnoe khoziaistvo SSSR v. 1983 godu, Tsentral'nyi statisticheskii upravleniie (TsSU) (Moscow: Finansy i Statistika, 1984), p. 8; 1979 and 1989 figures: Data from the State Committee for Statistics (Goskomstat) (Moscow, May 1990). See also "Nas 285, 761, 976 chelovek, i vse my zhivem v odnoi strane: Rasselenie narodov SSSR po soiuznym respublikam po perepisi 1989 g." *Soiuz*, no. 32, August 1990. Estimates from annual statistical handbooks suggest the following percent growth, 1979-89: 28.7, 34.0, 27.7, 20.7, 6.9, and 8.9.

TABLE 2.2
Population Size and Growth of the Major Central Asian Nationalities Russians and Total Population of the USSR, 1970-89

	Number of Persons of Given Nationality (in thousands)			Percentage Increase or Decrease	
	1970	1979	1989	1970-79	1979-89
Uzbeks	9195	12,456	16,698	35.5	34.1
Tajiks	2136	2898	4215	35.7	45.4
Turkmen	1525	2028	2729	33.0	34.6
Kirgiz	1452	1906	2529	31.3	32.7
Karakalpaks	236	303	424	28.5	39.9
Russians	129,015	137,397	145,155	6.5	5.6
USSR	241,720	262,085	285,761	8.4	9.0

Source: 1970 and 1979 data from Ann Sheehy, "Ethnic Muslims Account for Half of Soviet Population Increase" Radio Liberty, *Report on the USSR*, January 19, 1990, pp. 16-17. 1989 data from "Nas 285, 761, 976 chelovek, i vse my zhivem v odnoi strane: Rasselenie narodov SSSR po soiuznym respublikam po perepisi 1989 g." *Soiuz*, no. 32, August 1990.

TABLE 2.3
Nationality Composition of the Four Central Asian Republics, 1979-89

Uzbekistan

Nationality	Population (1000s) 1979	Population (1000s) 1989	1989 as % of 1979	Percent of Total 1979	Percent of Total 1989
Total Population of Which:	15389	19810	128.7	100	100
Uzbeks	10569	14142	133.8	68.7	71.4
Russians	1666	1653	99.3	10.8	8.3
Tajiks	595	934	157.0	3.9	4.7
Kazakhs	620	808	130.3	4.0	4.1
Karakalpaks	298	412	138.3	1.9	2.1
Tatars	531	468	88.1	3.5	2.4
Crimean Tatars	118	189	160.6	0.8	1.0
Kirgiz	142	175	123.0	0.9	0.9
Koreans	163	183	112.3	1.1	0.9
Ukrainians	114	153	134.6	0.7	0.8
Turkmen	92	122	131.7	0.6	0.6
Turks	49	106	--	0.3	0.5
Jews	74	65	88.6	0.5	0.3
Armenians	42	51	119.3	0.3	0.3
Uygurs	29	36	122.9	0.2	0.2
Germans	40	40	100.7	0.3	0.2
Azerbaijanis	60	44	74.3	0.4	0.2
Bashkir	26	35	134.6	0.2	0.2
Other	161	194	120.5	1.1	1.0

Tajikistan

Nationality	Population (1000s) 1979	Population (1000s) 1989	1989 as % of 1979	Percent of Total 1979	Percent of Total 1989
Total Population of Which:	3806	5093	133.8	100	100
Tajiks	2237	3172	141.8	58.8	62.3
Russians	395	388	98.3	10.4	7.6
Uzbeks	373	1198	137.2	22.9	23.5
Kirgiz	48	64	131.9	1.3	1.3
Tatars	78	72	92.4	2.0	1.4
Crimean Tatars	1.4	7.2	--	0.04	0.1
Ukrainians	36	41	115.5	0.9	0.8
Germans	39	33	84.1	1.0	0.6
Turkmen	14	20	146.4	0.4	0.4
Kazakhs	9.6	11	118.4	0.3	0.2
Koreans	11	13	120.1	0.3	0.3
Jews	13	9.7	72.4	0.35	0.19
Ossetians	7.7	7.9	101.8	0.2	0.2
Armenians	4.9	5.7	116.3	0.1	0.1
Bashkir	6.1	6.8	112.1	0.2	0.1
Belorussians	5.1	7.2	140.9	0.1	0.1
Mordvinians	6.5	5.5	85.0	0.2	0.1
Other	21	31	147.6	0.6	0.6

(continues)

TABLE 2.3 (continued)

Turkmenistan

Nationality	Population (1000s) 1979	Population (1000s) 1989	1989 as % of 1979	Percent of Total 1979	Percent of Total 1989
Total Population of Which:	2765	3523	127.4	100	100
Turkmen	1892	2537	134.1	68.4	72.0
Russians	349	334	95.6	12.6	9.5
Uzbeks	234	317	135.8	8.5	9.0
Kazakhs	80	88	110.4	2.9	2.5
Tatars	40	39	97.3	1.5	1.1
Armenians	27	32	119.6	1.0	0.9
Azerbaijanis	24	33	141.7	0.9	0.9
Baluchis	19	28	152.2	0.7	0.8
Belorussians	5.3	9.2	174.3	0.2	0.3
Persians	4.8	7.6	158.2	0.2	0.2
Kurds	3.5	4.4	124.6	0.1	0.1
Germans	4.6	4.4	97.2	0.2	0.1
Bashkir	3.9	4.7	119.5	0.1	0.1
Other	40.6	49	120.7	1.5	1.4

Kirgizia

Nationality	Population (1000s) 1979	Population (1000s) 1989	1989 as % of 1979	Percent of Total 1979	Percent of Total 1989
Total Population of Which:	3523	4258	120.9	100	100
Kirgiz	1687	2230	132.2	47.9	52.4
Russians	912	917	100.5	25.9	21.5
Uzbeks	426	550	129.1	12.1	12.9
Ukrainians	109	108	98.8	3.1	2.5
Germans	101	101	100.2	2.9	2.4
Tatars	72	70	97.7	2.0	1.6
Kazakhs	27	37	136.0	0.8	0.9
Uygurs	30	37	123.3	0.8	0.9
Tajiks	23	34	144.4	0.7	0.8
Koreans	14	18	126.8	0.4	0.4
Azerbaijanis	17	16	91.7	0.5	0.4
Kurds	9.5	14	149.4	0.3	0.3
Belorussians	7.7	9.2	119.7	0.2	0.2
Jews	6.3	5.6	88.8	0.2	0.1
Other	81	111	137.0	2.3	2.6

Source: Data from the State Committee for Statistics (Goskomstat), Moscow, May 1990.

reversal of relatively constant trends throughout the previous four decades. While Slavs—and in particular, Russians—had comprised a consistently growing share of the Central Asian population from the early 1920s until the 1959 census (rising from less than 2 percent of Uzbekistan's population, for example, in 1917, to 13.5 percent in 1959), from the 1960s on their proportion began to decline. Table 2.2 shows the difference in population increase between the Central Asian nationalities and the Russians for the USSR as a whole, 1970–89. Between 1979–89, the Central Asian nationalities grew by somewhere between 32.7 and 45.4 percent, whereas the Russians in the USSR grew by only 5.6 percent. The same trends were reflected within the Central Asian republics. Table 2.3 shows the change in nationality composition within the Central Asian republics for the intercensal period 1979–89. A steady decline in the proportion of the non-indigenous nationalities, particularly of the Russians, was illustrated in all of the Central Asian republics in this time frame. Indeed, not only the rate of growth, but the actual number of Russians declined in all of the Central Asian republics except for Kirgizia, where it grew by 0.5 percent. This contrasts markedly with a growth of between roughly 30 to 57 percent for the titular Central Asian nationalities in these republics. By 1989, the proportion of Russians in the Central Asian republics had fallen to between 7.6 and 9.5 percent of the republics' populations, with the exception of Kirgizia where the Russian population fell from a higher starting point (roughly one-fourth) to about one-fifth (21.5 percent) of the republic's population (see Table 2.3).

These figures are more dramatic when viewed over the thirty-year period, 1959–89. Table 2.4 shows the change in nationality composition for the largest of the Central Asian republics, Uzbekistan, over the past three intercensal periods: 1959–70, 1970–79, and 1979–89. Whereas the number of Uzbeks grew by almost 10 million people, 1959–89, and their proportion of Uzbekistan's total population grew from 62.1 percent to 71.4 percent, the number of Russians in Uzbekistan grew by only one-tenth that amount (by roughly 500,000 people), with their proportion of Uzbekistan's population declining from 13.5 percent in 1959 to 8.3 percent in 1989.

Natural Growth

Of the two main catalysts for population change—natural growth and migration—natural growth has been the main reason for both of these changes. While deathrates in the Central Asian republics—as elsewhere in the USSR—declined rapidly in the decades following the advent of Soviet power, birthrates in the Central Asian republics—*unlike* other

TABLE 2.4
Nationality Composition of Uzbekistan, 1959, 1970, 1979, and 1989

	Number of Given Nationality (thousands)				Nationality as Percentage of Total				1970 as Percentage of 1959	1979 as Percentage of 1970	1989 as Percentage of 1979
	1959	1970	1979	1989	1959	1970	1979	1989			
Uzbeks	5038	7725	10569	14142	62.1	65.5	68.7	71.4	153	137	133.8
Karakalpaks	168	230	298	412	2.1	2.0	1.9	2.1	137	130	138.3
Russians	1092	1473	1666	1653	13.5	12.5	10.8	8.3	135	113	99.3
Tatars	445	574	649	657[1]	5.5	4.9	4.2	3.4	129	113	101.2
Kazakhs	343	476	620	808	4.2	4.0	4.0	4.1	139	130	130.3
Tajiks	331	449	595	934	3.8	3.8	3.9	4.7	144	133	157.0
Koreans	138	148	163	183	1.7	1.3	1.1	0.9	107	110	112.3
Ukrainians	88	112	114	153	1.1	0.9	0.7	0.8	127	102	134.6
Kirgiz	93	111	142	175	1.1	0.9	0.9	0.9	119	128	123.0
Jews	94	103	100[2]	65	0.2	0.9	0.6	0.3	104	97	88.6
Turkmen	55	71	92	122	0.7	0.6	0.6	0.6	129	130	131.7
Other[3]	254	328	381	--	3.0	2.7	2.6	--	129	116	--

1. Of which 189,000 were Crimean Tatars in 1989, up from 118,000 in 1979.
2. The Goskomstat figure for number of Jews, 1979, is 74,000 rather than 100,000.
3. Other nationalities include Belorussians, Azerbaijanis, Armenians, Georgians, Bashkir, Uygurs, Moldavians, Chuvash, Germans, Turks, Ossetians, peoples of Dagestan, and Gypsies.

Source: columns 1, 2, 5, 6 TsSU, *Narodnoe khoziaistvo Uzbekskoi SSR za 60 let Sovetskoi vlasti* (Tashkent: Uzbekistan, 1977). columns 3, 7, "Vsesoiuznaia perepis' naseleniia, 1979," *Vestnik Statistiki*, no. 9, 1980, p. 61. 1979 and 1989 figures (columns 4 and 10) from data provided by the State Committee for Statistics (Goskomstat), May 1990.

areas of the USSR—were slow to follow suit. From 1940 to 1988, the birthrate in the RSFSR declined by more than half, and in the USSR as a whole, by more than one third. By contrast, despite some fluctuation throughout this almost fifty-year period, birthrates in the Central Asian republics in 1979 and 1988 were about the same level they had been in 1940 and 1959. Natural growth in the Central Asian republics, while reaching a peak during the 1960s, was about the same level in 1988 as it had been in 1970—and in some cases, such as in Tajikistan, it was higher (see Table 2.5).

Against a background of generally high fertility, vast disparities in patterns of natural growth among the nationalities accounted largely for the ethnic shifts among the populations. In 1989, one Uzbek demographer underscores, "the birthrate among the indigenous population of the UzSSR is twice as high as among the Europeans living in this republic."[2] This is certainly supported by data for Uzbekistan for the intercensal period 1959–70: while the birthrate for Uzbekistan as a whole in 1970 was quite high—at 33.5, close to twice the USSR average—it was more than twice as high among the Uzbeks (39.2 per thousand) as it was among the Russians (19.3 per thousand) in Uzbekistan, and was significantly higher among the Asian populations than among the Slavs as a whole (see Table 2.6).

Similarly, the *decline* in fertility that occurred in Uzbekistan in the 1960s and 1970s occurred largely among the European nationalities living there—i.e., among those nationality groups with the lowest birthrates in the first place. As illustrated in Table 2.6, for example, between 1959–70, birthrates among the Russians living in Uzbekistan declined by 19 percent, falling from 24 to 19 per thousand in the eleven-year period; during the same time period, birthrates among the Central Asians in Uzbekistan declined by one-third to one-half as much, and from a much higher rate. The Uzbek birthrate declined by 6 percent, from 41 to 39 per thousand; the Tajik, from 38 to 34 per thousand; and the birthrates among the Kazakhs, Kirgiz and Turkmen populations living in Uzbekistan, already high in 1959, actually rose, by as much as 8 percent, over the same eleven-year period. Thus, between 1959 and 1970, Uzbekistan's European population exhibited large declines in population reproduction from an already comparatively low level, while the Asian populations were characterized by more moderate declines, relatively stable rates, or even by slight rises.

More fragmentary data suggest that differentials in birthrate declines by nationality remained high well into the 1970s and 1980s. Another set of nationality data, for example—again for Uzbekistan—illustrates the vast differentials between the Slavic and Central Asian nationalities between 1970–78. According to these data, the annual crude birth rates

TABLE 2.5
Vital Statistics for Central Asia, the RSFSR, and the USSR, 1940-1988 (per 1000 population)

Republic	1940 BR	1940 DR	1940 NG	1960 BR	1960 DR	1960 NG	1970 BR	1970 DR	1970 NG	1980 BR	1980 DR	1980 NG	1988 BR	1988 DR	1988 NG
Uzbekistan	33.8	13.2	20.6	39.8	6.0	33.8	33.6	5.5	28.1	33.8	7.4	26.4	35.1	6.8	28.3
Tajikistan	30.6	14.1	16.5	33.5	5.1	28.4	34.8	6.4	28.4	37.0	8.0	29.0	40.0	7.0	33.0
Turkmenistan	36.9	19.5	17.4	42.4	6.5	35.9	35.2	6.6	28.6	34.3	8.3	26.0	36.0	7.8	28.2
Kirgizia	33.0	16.3	16.7	36.9	6.1	30.8	30.5	7.4	23.1	29.6	8.4	21.2	31.2	7.4	23.8
USSR	31.2	18.0	13.2	24.9	7.1	17.8	17.4	8.2	9.2	18.3	10.3	8.0	18.8	10.1	8.7
RSFSR	33.0	20.6	12.4	23.2	7.4	15.8	14.6	8.7	5.9	15.9	11.0	4.9	16.0	10.7	5.3

Source: TsSU, *Narodnoe khoziaistvo SSSR v 1983 godu* (Moscow: Finansy i statistika, 1984), pp. 32-33. Goskomstat SSSR, *Narodnoe khoziaistvo SSSR v 1988 godu* (Moscow: Finansy i statistika, 1989), p. 26.

TABLE 2.6
Changes in the Crude Birth Rate by Nationality. Uzbekistan, 1959-70

Nationality	Birthrate 1959	Birthrate 1970	1970 as Percentage of 1959	Percentage Increase/Decline 1959-70
Russians	23.7	19.3	81.0	-19.0
Ukrainians	26.0	23.0	88.4	-11.6
Belorussians	34.4	25.1	73.0	-27.0
Kazakhs	34.3	36.9	107.6	+7.6
Uzbeks	41.7	39.2	94.0	-6.0
Tajiks	38.2	34.3	89.8	-10.2
Kirgiz	29.4	31.6	107.5	+7.5
Turkmen	32.1	32.8	102.2	+2.2
Karakalpaks	39.1	33.5	85.7	-14.3
Other	36.0	22.8	63.3	-36.7
Total	37.0	33.5	90.5	-9.5

Source: Computed from I. R. Mulliadzhanov, *Naselenie Uzbekskoi SSSR* (Tashkent: Uzbekistan, 1973), p. 117.

among the indigenous Central Asians averaged between 40 and 45 births per thousand in the 1960s, and except for the Kirgiz, where the drop was more dramatic, fell to between 38 and 42 births per thousand. Among the Russians in Uzbekistan, on the other hand, the corresponding drop was from 19.0 to 16.5 per thousand, levels similar to those among the Slavic nationalities as a whole.[3] According to these statistics, therefore, the Central Asian birthrate was almost two and one-half times higher than that of the Russians, and had declined more slowly than the Russian birthrate by comparison with the preceding decade. As illustrated, even by the late 1980s, Central Asian birthrates in the USSR remained very high, and wide disparities between Slavic and Asian birthrates had not significantly diminished.

Other indicators, such as family size and fertility rates, are also important in analyzing overall population growth trends, and they, too, suggest continued high population reproduction in the Central Asian republics, particularly among the indigenous nationalities. Sociological surveys conducted in the late 1980s suggest that today, the expected number of children per married Russian female in Uzbekistan is 2.5, whereas the expected number of children per married Uzbek female is 5.6.[4] In 1979, average family size in Uzbekistan was 5.5 people, a rise from 4.6 people in 1959. Among Uzbeks, however, the average family size was 6.2 people, and more than 43 percent of all Uzbek families were comprised of seven or more members.[5] Among Russians in Uz-

TABLE 2.7
Average Family Size by Nationality, Central Asia and the RSFSR, 1979

Republic and Nationality		Average Family Size	Families with seven or more children as percent of total families of given nationality
Turkmenistan	Total	5.5	32.4
	Turkmen	6.3	44.7
	Russian	3.2	1.2
Uzbekistan	Total	5.5	32.2
	Uzbek	6.2	43.2
	Russian	3.3	1.7
Tajikistan	Total	5.7	35.5
	Tajik	6.6	48.8
	Russian	3.2	1.2
Kirgizia	Total	4.6	20.3
	Kirgiz	5.7	35.4
	Russian	3.3	1.5
RSFSR	Total	3.3	1.9
	Russian	3.2	1.0

Source: Computed from TsSU, *Chislennost' i sostav naseleniia SSSR po dannym Vsesoiuznoi perepisi naseleniia 1979 goda* (Moscow: Finansy i statistika, 1984), pp. 288-89, 298-99, 312-15, 318-19.

bekistan, on the other hand, average family size was about half that of the Uzbeks, and only 1 percent of all Russian families contained seven or more members. As illustrated in Table 2.7, similar disparities were exhibited in Tajikistan and Turkmenistan, and to a lesser extent in Kirgizia.

Likewise, total fertility rates in the Central Asian republics and among the Central Asian nationalities—while declining—are likely to remain high well into the next century.[6] Fertility rates in the Central Asian republics in 1979-80 were at about the same level they had been at in 1958-59. While these rates declined in the late 1970s and early 1980s, in many instances this decline was slight and not evident in some of the most productive age groups, such as among those in their early twenties.[7] Further decline is projected for the next seventy years. But current data suggest that the rate and magnitude of fertility declines has so far been relatively slight; they have occurred only after a rise in the mid-1970s and from a very high base; and they will certainly not be enough to offset a generally high rate of population reproduction in the near future. As a noted Uzbek demographer, Ata-Mirzaev, stated in 1989: "The high population growth of the population of Central Asia, on the order of 3.2 percent [per year], will be maintained well into the foreseeable future."[8] By the end of the 1980s, the exceedingly high birthrates and population structures of the four Central Asian republics suggested that overall population growth from natural increase, particularly among the Central Asian nationalities, would remain high for many years to come.[9]

Migration

Migratory movements over the last three decades have tended to perpetuate rather than offset these trends. While indigenous population reproduction was high during the years following the Revolution, the growth of the European population in Central Asia initially kept pace largely as a result of in-migration. In the 1920s and 1930s, for example, large numbers of Europeans were sent or migrated to Central Asia to quell resistance to the new Soviet rule, to build and staff new schools and new cultural and political institutions, or to begin industrialization and collectivization for better exploitation of the republic's natural and agricultural resources. The evacuation of factories and personnel from other parts of the USSR to Central Asia during World War II gave this growth new impetus. The first four decades of Soviet rule, therefore, saw an influx of Slavs to Central Asia coming in response to political necessity or, often, offers of lucrative jobs which the unskilled indigenous population could not or would not fill. At the same time, there was little out-migration on the part of any of the local nationalities.

Beginning in the 1950s and 1960s, however, the importance of migration in Central Asian population dynamics began to diminish. The local populations remained relatively immobile, retaining, if not increasing, their high rates of natural growth but still exhibiting practically no out-migration from their republic. The level of in-migration to Central Asia from Slavic areas for the most part remained steady or declined, in either case lagging behind rates of natural growth. Thus, for example, whereas migration had accounted for more than 42 percent of Uzbekistan's total population growth from 1939–59, from 1959–70 it accounted for only about 10 percent, and from 1971–76, only about 4 percent.[10] By 1979, 99 percent of each of the Central Asian titular nationalities were residing in Central Asia; fewer than 1 percent—or slightly over 100,000 people—were residing in the RSFSR. Indeed, the late 1970s to early 1980s saw for the first time a net migration of Europeans *out* of Soviet Central Asia rather than into it, resulting in continued high population reproduction and a growth in the indigenous nationalities as a proportion of the total republican populations.

Ethnic and Demographic Trends 49

Efforts throughout the early 1980s to encourage increase in inter-republican migration among the indigenous nationalities had little effect. The Soviet press continued to praise the continually increasing level of out-migration from the Central Asian republics to other areas of the USSR, for example, to work on the non-black earth zone (Nechernozem) or on the Baikal Amur Mainline (BAM). But Soviet articles also continued to highlight how the overall level of out-migration from the Central Asian republics to other parts of the USSR remained exceedingly low, and how the out-migrants continued to be comprised primarily of non-indigenous nationalities.[11] Most of the indigenous Central Asians who did migrate to these projects in other parts of the USSR, moreover, reportedly also returned within a relatively short amount of time. According to one report, the proportion of migrants from Central Asia working on the BAM during the early 1980s was about half the proportion of Central Asia in the population of the USSR as a whole, and representatives of the *indigenous* nationalities of Central Asia working on BAM comprised about one-twelfth of their representation in the total population, or less than one percent of the total number of workers on that project.[12]

The 1989 census data have shown an increasing net out-migration from Central Asia to other republics. Between 1979 and 1989, for example, more than 500,000 people migrated out of Uzbekistan to other republics, or roughly 11.2 percent of the population increase; in Kirgizia, this figure was roughly 20 percent of the natural increase, and in Tajikistan and Turkmenistan, between 8 and 11 percent of the increase (see Table 2.8). The out-migrants, however, continued to be overwhelmingly of the non-indigenous nationalities. Indeed, in addition to citing social, economic and political factors as accounting for low migration among the local populations, most Soviet demographers underscore that inter-republican migration among the indigenous Central Asian nationalities can hardly be expected to increase before intra-republican mobility—especially migration from rural to urban areas—increases, and this, too, remains on an exceedingly low level.[13] Thus today, while migration still accounts for a relatively small part of population change in Central Asia, the result has been to leave behind a more rapidly growing and ethnically homogeneous population than these republics have seen for some decades.

Projections for the Future

Today, while reproduction remains high, total fertility rates seem to be declining slowly, as is desired family size. But the existing demographic structure in the Central Asian republics—such as low levels of urbanization, high reproduction in the countryside, and the age and sex

TABLE 2.8
Natural Increase and Net Migration in Population Increase: Central Asian Republics, RSFSR, and the USSR, 1979-89

	Total Population Increase (in 1000s) 1979-89	Natural Increase		Net Migration	
		Absolute	% of Total	Absolute	% of Total
Uzbekistan	4515	5022	111.2	-507	-11.2
Tajikistan	1311	1413	107.8	-102	-7.8
Turkmenistan	775	859	110.8	-84	-10.8
Kirgizia	762	918	120.3	-156	-20.5
RSFSR	9835	8067	82.0	+1768	+18.0
USSR	24,281	24,450	100.7	-169	-0.7

Source: Ann Sheehy "1989 Census Data on Internal Migration in the USSR," Radio Liberty, *Report on the USSR*, November 10, 1989, p. 8.

structure of the population—suggest that these changes cannot be expected to be enough to significantly offset population trends until well into the next century.

As elsewhere in the world, urbanization in Central Asia can be expected to curtail high population reproduction. The urban population of the Central Asian republics has grown over the past several decades, rising in two of the Central Asian republics, for example—in Uzbekistan and Turkmenistan—from only 25 and 35 percent in 1940 to 42 and 47 percent of the 1986 populations respectively. But with high natural growth and low mobility particularly among the indigenous populations, this process has slowed and in some cases has reversed itself. In Tajikistan and Turkmenistan, for example, the proportion of the population that was urban either remained the same or declined between 1970–86. In Tajikistan, the decline was from 37 percent to 33 percent over the sixteen-year period.[14]

There are two complicating factors, however, to interpreting these statistics. First is the question of what is urban. Many Central Asian cities differ little from rural areas; in part this is because "urbanization" has occurred largely as a result of natural increase and reclassification rather than urban to rural migration,[15] and the growth of new cities is occurring slowly. This suggests that even as they become more urban, the local inhabitants are not necessarily transforming their way of life as much as one might expect from the demographic data; and it suggests that even urbanized Central Asians may often live in the same traditional homes and conduct their lives in the same manner as in the countryside. Often, therefore, the effect on native fertility may be more gradual than statistics alone might suggest.

Second, regardless of the rate at which urbanization has occurred, the indigenous nationalities have not been altogether included in that urbanization process and have remained largely in rural areas. In 1959, for example, only 21.8 percent of all Uzbeks in Uzbekistan lived in urban areas; in 1970, that proportion had risen only three percentage points, to 24.9 percent.[16] In 1989, according to Dr. Ata-Mirzaev, Chairman of the Economic Geography Department at Tashkent University, that proportion was back down to only 20 percent of the republic's indigenous nationalities.[17]

Urbanization, moreover, is not occurring to the exclusion of the growth of Central Asia's rural populations; their population reproduction is far more rapid, and thus rural population growth has been much higher. While an average of 37.0 births per thousand population were recorded for Uzbekistan in 1987, for example, that figure was 28.5 in urban areas and 43.2 in rural areas. And while natural growth for the republic as a whole was 30.1 in 1987, that figure was 21.9 in urban areas and 36.0

in rural areas. These figures were similar for all of the Central Asian republics. Indeed, because of high rates of population reproduction, in 1987 alone, between 60 and 75 percent of the natural growth in the four Central Asian republics occurred in the countryside—versus 24 percent in the RSFSR (see Table 2.9).

Thus, while during the 1960s–1980s the rural populations of the Slavic republics generally declined (by 27 percent, for example, in the RSFSR, and 26 percent in Belorussia), in Uzbekistan, Turkmenistan and Tajikistan, they have grown tremendously, by 75 percent, 83 percent and 97 percent respectively.[18] As Ata-Mirzaev, then Chief of the Population Laboratory at Tashkent University, noted in 1978,

> Even if one assumes that the entire urban population of Central Asia will enter into a regime of a middle or low birth rate, half of the population (the rural population) will continue to be oriented toward having many children. We must remember that in the year 2000, a population greater than the entire population of Central Asia today will be residing in rural areas alone.[19]

In addition to the potential effects of urbanization on population change, the age, sex, and nationality structures of the Central Asian republics also suggest that high population growth will be perpetuated for some time to come. Central Asia's population has been growing younger over the past two decades, so that a larger proportion falls into the lower age groups today than even ten or twenty years ago. This year (1990), the proportion of women of childbearing age is expected to be almost double the 1970 figure, and by the year 2000, 269 percent that level. Thus, even should fertility rates continue to decline, a drop in the number of births per thousand women of childbearing age would be partly offset by the "demographic momentum" set in motion or by the greater number of women of childbearing age relative to the population as a whole. This will be exacerbated by the fact that a greater proportion of the younger populations will be comprised of the indigenous nationalities, which are more oriented toward having large families than their European counterparts. And it will also be encouraged by the favorable sex ratio in the Central Asian republics as opposed to that in the republics to the north. In other words, a decline in fertility among the indigenous nationalities would still be slow in making itself felt in the republican birthrate and in population growth as a whole.

Finally, surveys and personal experience suggest that attitudinal factors also may not have changed dramatically in the 1980s. A recent survey conducted in Uzbekistan suggests that attitudes toward large families are changing in certain respects in Soviet Central Asia, especially among

TABLE 2.9
Vital Statistics by Urban and Rural Areas:
Central Asian Republics, RSFSR, and the USSR, 1987 (per thousand population)

	Birthrate			Deathrate			Natural Growth			% Natural Growth		
	Total	Urban	Rural	Total	Urban	Rural	Total	Urban	Rural	Total	Urban	Rural
Uzbekistan	37.0	28.5	43.2	6.9	6.6	7.2	30.1	21.9	36.0	100	30.7	69.3
Tajikistan	41.8	32.5	46.5	6.9	6.6	7.0	34.9	25.9	39.5	100	24.7	75.3
Turkmenistan	37.2	31.9	42.1	7.9	7.4	8.3	29.3	24.5	33.8	100	39.7	60.3
Kirgizia	32.6	25.0	37.6	7.3	6.6	7.8	25.3	18.4	29.8	100	29.0	71.0
RSFSR	17.1	16.4	19.1	10.5	9.6	13.0	6.6	6.8	6.1	100	75.9	24.1
USSR	19.8	17.6	24.0	9.9	9.0	11.7	9.9	8.6	12.3	100	58.2	41.8

Source: Goskomstat SSSR, *Naselenie SSSR 1987* (Moscow: Finansy i statistika, 1988), pp. 128, 129, 132, 139, 140, 142. Columns 10-12 calculated from pp. 110-126.

the younger generation. For example, average desired number of children among women respondents was five to six—a slight qualitative difference from the previous predominant answer of "whatever Allah brings."[20] Again, however, the question is one of *rate* of attitudinal change. Even a decline in desired family size to 5–6 children will not substantially alleviate population pressures in coming decades. Interviews throughout Central Asia over the past ten years still seem to confirm words expressed earlier, that "high birthrate indicators are connected with national traditions of having many children. . . . One must not forget that the nationality level of the birthrate is formed in the family, mainly under the influence of traditional views on number of children in the family."[21]

Taking many of these factors into account, projections for the Central Asian republics suggest that population growth will remain high to the end of the century, and differences in growth rates among the nationalities will remain wide. Taking both projected rates of natural growth and migration into account, the populations of the four Central Asian republics together are projected to comprise anywhere from 40 to 50 million people in the year 2000—or about double their 1979 size. The population of Uzbekistan alone, according to Ata-Mirzaev, will continue to grow by 500,000–600,000 people per year through the decade 2000–2010. In the year 2005, he states, 30 million people will be living in Uzbekistan— more than the population of the entire Central Asian region today— and in the year 2010, Uzbekistan's population alone will reach 33 million people.

This means that the Central Asian populations will comprise anywhere from 13 to 16 percent of the total population of the USSR within today's borders, as opposed to 9.7 percent in 1979.[22] In addition, they will be younger and more ethnically homogeneous than currently. Barring any mass deportations or major upheavals in Soviet population policies, it appears that migration cannot be expected to offset the high rates of population growth or the increasing indigenization of the republics' populations, but will remain largely a non-Asian phenomenon for some time to come.

Implications

All of these factors and trends will present serious challenges for the USSR as a whole in coming decades, regardless of any potential changes in the relationship between the Central Asian republics and Moscow. In an economy already beset by severe upheaval, for example, the fact that almost all, if not all of the growth in the Soviet working-age population in the last part of this century will be located in the south will only complicate efforts at economic change.[23] The fact that, by some estimates, already about one-third of Soviet draftees are from the Soviet southern tier—with a weak command of the Russian language, minimal technical training, often poor health, and questionable loyalty compared with their Russian counterparts—will play a significant role in new military thinking.

But the implications of demographic change in Central Asia are far more dramatic on a local scale, as these demographic trends raise more immediate and critical questions within the Central Asian republics themselves. In all four of the Central Asian republics, for example, unemployment has been growing dramatically, at the same time that a rapidly growing population is placing increasing strains on local economies to meet both consumer and producer demands. In some areas unemployment has reached a level as high as one-third of the working age populations. According to one estimate, about 1 million people are unemployed today in Uzbekistan alone, among whom a growing proportion are young. Others believe the figure is a good deal higher, perhaps 1.5 to 2 million.[24] According to yet another estimate, one in ten able-bodied citizens in Uzbekistan is now jobless, with 240,000 people entering the labor market every year.[25] And every year in Uzbekistan, reportedly more than 100,000 young people—mostly high school graduates—are joining the ranks of those employed in household and private subsidiary work.[26] Indeed, many observers in Central Asia believe that high levels of unemployment have become "critical" levels. Rising, according to one estimate, at a rate of 22,500 people per year in the Fergana Valley alone, high unemployment is considered to be one of the key reasons for the violent demonstrations that broke out in Fergana in June 1989.[27]

Likewise, there are ample indications that economic growth has already been constrained by rapid population growth.[28] In the 1970s and early 1980s, despite officially reported high percentage rises in most economic indicators, economic development in most per capita terms in Central Asia slowed; according to local interviews, this decline accelerated during the first five years of perestroika. In addition, the tremendous and growing pressure on resources and the worsening water supply in Central Asia are expected to place greater strains on producers and consumers alike. Pictures in the Central Asian press of children literally starving to death now dramatize the depth of the problem.

Another indication of economic strain is the decreasing amount of land both per capita and per agricultural worker. This problem is already contributing to growing unemployment and to the declining ability of the economy to meet the needs of a rapidly growing population. Uzbekistan, for example, currently holds only 0.2 hectares of irrigated land per capita—1.5–2 hectares per agricultural worker. In the words of one Uzbek scholar,

> a great economic burden and labor tension is being created on irrigated land. . . . In connection with the high population growth of the republic that will continue well into the foreseeable future, a severe shortage of water resources, and ecological limits for further expansion of irrigated land—and also because of the growth of industrial and housing construction—even this miserly indicator will have a tendency to contract.[29]

This scholar projects that, toward the year 2010, the population density of Uzbekistan alone will double, reaching 74 people per square kilometer and placing a further "tremendous ecological burden" on the republic's irrigated lands.

These kinds of pressures are likewise exacerbating the already serious environmental and health problems of the local populations. "As a result of a long deformation of the development of the regional economy," the same Uzbek scholar reports, "a severe ecological situation has gotten worse. . . . The high rate of population growth in Central Asia, closely connected with the low level of socioeconomic development of the region, is raising a series of complicated ecological problems."

The high use of pesticides, which was intended to keep land productive, has further aggravated environmental and health problems in the Central Asian republics. For the region as a whole, 20–25 kilograms of poisonous chemicals are used for every hectare; this compares with only 3 kilograms per hectare for the USSR as a whole. On a per capita basis, the Central Asians reportedly use 7–8 kilograms of poisons. "With such high population density in rural areas," Ata-Mirzaev writes, "the problem of applying various poisonous chemicals and fertilizers in the republics' agro-industrial complexes becomes very acute."[30]

The cumulative effect of this and other environmental catastrophes—the drying up of the Aral Sea, wind and soil erosion, contaminated drinking water, and the like—is taking its toll on the health of the Central Asian populations. While infant mortality, for example, had declined significantly since the beginning of Soviet power, the past two decades have seen a dramatic upswing in infant mortality rates in the Central Asian republics. These are seen as a direct result of environmental problems: "High mother and infant mortality [is] a result of the worsening health of the population in connection with the severe ecological situation in the republic."[31] In Uzbekistan, infant mortality rose by roughly 50 percent between 1970–89, to roughly 46 per thousand children born; in Turkmenistan, that rise was by roughly 25 percent, from 46 to 58 per thousand (see Table 2.10). Today, in some regions of the Central

TABLE 2.10
Infant Mortality in the Central Asian Republics
(number of children dying before the age of one, per thousand children born), 1970-1989

	1970	1980	1985	1986	1987	1988	1989
Uzbekistan	31.0	47.0	45.3	46.2	45.9	43.3	46
Tajikistan	45.9	58.1	46.8	46.7	48.9	48.9	46
Turkmenistan	46.1	53.6	52.4	58.2	56.4	53.3	58
Kirgizia	45.4	43.3	41.9	38.2	37.8	36.8	38
RSFSR	23.0	22.1	20.7	19.3	19.4	18.9	19
USSR	24.7	27.3	26.0	25.4	25.4	24.7	--

Source: Goskomstat SSSR, *Narodnoe khoziaistvo SSSR v 1988 godu*, p. 29; 1989 figures from Ata-Mirzaev, O.B. "Prognoz rosta chislennosti naseleniia Uzbekistana i ekologicheskaia situatsiia" (Tashkent: unpublished paper, 1989), p. 3.

Asian republics, infant mortality rates are among the highest in the world. In some areas, such as the Kungrad and Bozatau raions of the Karakalpak ASSR, more than one out of ten children die before reaching their first birthdays.

While Soviet planners are increasingly recognizing the severity of these problems, policy action remains complex and controversial, not only in Moscow, but locally. In terms of family planning, for example, Soviet policymakers have increased their efforts to encourage smaller families in Soviet Central Asia. The 1980s saw the introduction of sex education in Asian schools, including educational pamphlets both in Russian and in the native languages. Contraception is more available today than before, as small propaganda campaigns continue to aim at reducing family size in the Central Asian republics and at persuading women to have fewer children. In January 1987, a governmental campaign was reportedly launched in Tajikistan to encourage women to have fewer children, reflecting efforts started earlier in Uzbekistan to encourage families to adopt an "ideal" family size of six people.[32] Local officials and scholars have emphasized that these efforts are not meant to limit family size as much as they are meant to encourage healthier families by having greater spacing between births (two to three years). Some recent books have set out to eradicate the "backward" and "inflexible sexual ethic" in Uzbekistan, to "change and rebuild inter-relationships between man and woman" and to "create a new and healthy domestic life" among the indigenous populations.

Campaigns alone, however, have minimal effect, and many in Central Asia are debating the wisdom of such measures in addressing the growing social and economic ills of their republics. First, it is unclear how great an impact these efforts might have on future population dynamics. Contraceptives in the USSR remain of poor quality, and they are more poorly distributed and more rarely used in the Central Asian republics than elsewhere in the USSR. Sex education is still conducted on a rudimentary level, with, judging by the interviews of this author, little perceptible influence on young Central Asians in their family aspirations. And out-migration among Central Asia's indigenous nationalities is still exceedingly low.

Perhaps more importantly, local policymakers are increasingly emphasizing the importance of addressing these problems in a "complex" manner, focusing on economic, social and political measures as well as demographic policy. In one heated debate in a local Tashkent newspaper, Mukhammad Salikh, a poet and one of the founders of Uzbekistan's new "Erk" Democratic Party, argued strongly that the answer to Central Asia's problems is the development of a more rational and more vibrant economy. If Japan, "with a territory half the size of our republic . . .

and without natural resources," can have higher living standards with even higher population density than Uzbekistan, he argues, there is no reason why Central Asia cannot raise its living standard. R. Ubaidullaeva, Deputy Director of the Institute of Economics in the Uzbek Academy of Sciences, has argued vehemently on the other side in favor of strong family planning measures. The fact that Mr. Salikh and Ms. Ubaidullaeva are both Uzbeks only underscores the complexities of these problems, and how they go well beyond narrow ethnic or national interests.[33]

Clearly, population pressures are placing enormous strains on the Central Asian societies. Relieving these population pressures will demand major and fundamental changes in planning and policy in Central Asia to allow a rapidly growing population to be not only clothed and fed but also productive. This is an enormous and complex task. But unless the whole range of problems triggered by and contributing to population trends in Central Asia is addressed, then rapid population growth may present the central Soviet leadership with its most explosive catalyst for future political unrest.

Notes

1. Whereas in 1940, roughly 10 percent of all children born in the USSR were born in Central Asia and Kazakhstan, by 1985, that proportion had risen to 28 percent; whereas in 1950, about 10 percent of the USSR's population lived in Central Asia and Kazakhstan, by 1986, that had risen to 17 percent "and this proportion is continuing to rise." See A. Vishnevskii, *Kommunist*, no. 17, (Nov.), 1986, pp. 69–80.

2. M.G. Davletshin, "Mezhnatsional'nyi aspekt demograficheskoi situatsii v regione," in *Aktual'nye problemy razvitiia natsional'nykh otnoshenii v SSSR* (Tashkent: UzSSR Ministry of People's Education and Tashkent University, 1989), Material from a republican scientific-theoretical conference, Nov. 23–25, 1989, Part I, pp. 97–98.

3. See M. Feshbach, "Trends in the Soviet Muslim Population—Demographic Aspects," in *The Soviet Economy in the 1980s: Problems and Prospects Part 2*, (U.S. Congress, Joint Economic Committee, Dec. 31, 1982), p. 304.

4. M. G. Davletshin, "Mezhnatsional'nyi aspekt," p. 97.

5. Tsentral'noe statisticheskoe upravlenie, *Itogi vsesoiuznoi perepisi naseleniia 1959 goda* (Moscow: Gosstatizdat, 1962) and Tsentral'noe statisticheskoe upravlenie, *Chislennost' i sostav naseleniia SSSR po dannym Vsesoiuznoi perepisi naseleniia 1979 goda*, (Moscow: Finansy i statistika, 1984), pp. 219–358.

6. See Ward Kinkade, *Estimates and Projections of the Population, by Major Nationality, 1979–2050* (U.S. Bureau of the Census, Center for International Research, Washington, D.C., May, 1988)

7. See Ward Kinkade, unpublished tables prepared for the Center for International Research, U.S. Bureau of the Census, Washington, D.C., 1985 and N. M. Aliakberov, "Analiz sovremennykh tendentsii v rozhdaemosti v Srednei Azii,"

in *Regional'nye Demograficheskie Issledovaniia* (Tashkent: Ministry of Higher and Secondary Education, 1978), p. 21; and *Vestnik Statistiki,* Moscow: Finansy i statistika, no. 11, 1984.

8. O. B. Ata-Mirzaev, "Prognoz rosta chislennosti naseleniia Uzbekistana i ekologicheskaia situatsiia," unpublished paper, 1989, p. 1.

9. See, for example, Khodzhamakhmad Umarov, in *Voprosy ekonomiki,* no. 9 (Sep.) 1986, pp. 99–108.

10. R. A. Ubaidullaeva, "Regional'nye problemy razmeshcheniia i effektivnost' ispol'zovaniia trudovykh resursov v Uzbekskoi SSR," unpublished doctoral dissertation, Tashkent, 1974, p. 30, and data acquired by the author in Tashkent, Uzbekistan, 1979.

11. See, for example, A. Vishnevskii, in *Kommunist,* no. 17, (Nov. 1986), pp. 69–80; L. Maksakova, *Migratsiia naseleniia Uzbekistana,* (Tashkent: Uzbekistan, 1986); A. Abduganiev, "Regional'nye problemy zaniatosti," *Ekonomicheskaia gazeta,* no. 25 (June), 1985, p. 17; and L. L. Rybakovskii and N.V. Tarasova, "Vzaimodeistvie migratsionnykh i etnicheskikh protsessov," *Sotsialisticheskie issledovaniia,* no. 4, 1982, pp. 29–32.

12. Rybakovskii and Tarasova, "Vzaimodeistvie," pp. 31–32, and S. N. Zhelezko, *Sotsial'no-demograficheskiie problemy v zone BAMa* (Moscow: Statistika, 1980), p. 107.

13. See, for example, L. Maksakova, *Migratsiia naseleniia,* p. 42, and V. I. Perevedentsev, "Migratsiia naseleniia i razvitie sel'skokhoziaistvennogo proizvodstva," *Sotsiologicheskie issledovaniia,* no. 1, 1983, pp. 54–61.

14. Calculated from Tsentral'noe statisticheskoe upravlenie, *Narodnoe khoziaistvo SSSR v 1985 g.,* pp. 8–9.

15. Ibid.

16. A. S. Chamkin, "Motivy k trudu v sfere obshchestvennogo proizvodstva," unpublished doctoral dissertation, Tashkent, 1976.

17. See O. B. Ata-Mirzaev, "Demograficheskaia situatsiia i natsional'naia politika," in *Aktual'nye problemy,* p. 78.

18. See, for example, Perevedentsev, "Migratsiia naseleniia," p. 56.

19. O. B. Ata-Mirzaev, "Aktual'nye zadachi kompleksnogo issledovaniia regional'nykh problem narodonaseleniia Srednei Azii," in *Regional'nye demograficheskiie issledovaniia* (Tashkent: Ministry of Higher Education, 1978), p. 5.

20. Interview with O. B. Ata-Mirzaev at Tashkent University, Nov. 1989.

21. O. B. Ata-Mirzaev and B. Gol'dfarb, "Naselenie Uzbekistana," (v pomoshch' lektoru) Tashkent, 1978, p. 11.

22. Soviet projections suggest that by the year 2000, the number of Uzbeks alone may be almost two and one-half times the number of Belorussians in the USSR. See review by M. Atadzhanova, N. Amanmuradova, D. Karly, and Sh. Kadyrov of the book by V. I. Kozlov, *Natsional'nosti SSSR: Etnodemograficheskii obzor,* second edition, (Moscow: Finansy i statistika, 1982), printed in *Izvestiia Akademii nauk Turkmenskoi SSR. Seriia Obshchestvennykh nauk,* Apr. 7, 1984, pp. 89–91; translated in JPRS, USSR Report: Political and Social Affairs, Oct. 8, 1984, p. 54.

23. See, for example, A. Vishnevskii, in *Kommunist,* no. 17, Nov. 1986, pp. 69–80, and V. I. Perevedentsev, as cited in Murray Feshbach, "The Age Structure

of the Soviet Population: Preliminary Analysis of Unpublished Data," *Soviet Economy*, no. 2, 1985, p. 188.

24. See A. Usmanov, "Mardiker—znachit bezrabotnyi," *Uchitel'skaia gazeta*, July 15, 1989.

25. See *Pravda Vostoka*, March 24, 1990, as cited in James Critchlow, "Uzbekistan: The Next Nationality Crisis?" Radio Liberty *Report on the USSR*, May 18, 1990, p. 7.

26. A. M. Orlov, "Nekotorye problemy zaniatosti v Uzbekskoi SSR," in *Aktual'nye problemy*, p. 109.

27. See, for example, A. Usmanov, "Mardiker" and A. Kaipbergenov, "Sovietologists' Opinion on Events in Fergana oblast," *Pravda*, July 2, 1989, p. 3 translated in FBIS, Sov-89-144, July 28, 1989, p. 70. See also K. Nomerovannyi, "The Dzhizak Steppe Awaits its Conquerors," *Pravda Vostoka*, Jan. 18, 1985, p. 3 (translated in JPRS, USSR Report: Political and Sociological Affairs, March 15, 1985, p.130) and G. Toniiants, "Demograficheskoe razvitie Uzbekistana i problemy zaniatosti," *Kommunist Uzbekistana*, no. 3, (March), 1985, pp. 45–48.

28. For a discussion, see N. Lubin, *Labour and Nationality in Soviet Central Asia*, (Princeton, NJ: Princeton U. Press, 1984), pp. 49–51.

29. O. B. Ata-Mirzaev, "Demograficheskaia situatsiia," p. 79.

30. Ata-Mirzaev, "Prognoz," p. 3

31. Ibid.

32. See *Kommunist Tadzhikistana*, Jan. 20, 1987, and Ann Sheehy, "Antinatal Policy for Tajikistan," *Radio Liberty Research*, 56/87, Feb. 2, 1987.

33. See Mukhammad Salikh, "Zhenshchinam zdorov'e!" and R. Ubaidullaeva, "Da, zabota! No ne emotsii," both in *Pravda Vostoka*, March 12, 1988, p. 1.

3

Central Asia's Cotton Economy and Its Costs

Boris Z. Rumer

Introduction

Central Asia's economy is among the most specialized in the Soviet Union. In this region cotton development has always been given highest priority. It may be justifiably said that here "cotton is king." In Uzbekistan the sector of the economy directly engaged in the cultivation and processing of cotton produces more than 65 percent of the republic's gross output, consumes 60 percent of all resources, and employs approximately 40 percent of the labor force. Altogether, the republic accounts for about two-thirds of all the cotton produced in the USSR.[1] The same picture is seen in the rest of Central Asia. Thus, cotton constitutes two-thirds of the region's total output and employs more than one million people. In the main cotton-growing areas[2] the share of the land sown with cotton exceeds 70 percent.[3]

This specialization developed as a result of the region's climatic conditions and its land and water resources, which favor cotton cultivation. The Turan Lowland, which is distinguished by its warmth and abundant sunlight, makes up approximately 70 percent of the region. It has 180 to 250 frost-free days a year; the average daily temperature exceeds 20 degrees Celsius on 120 to 150 days. But rainfall in the Lowland amounts to no more than 70 to 200 mm annually, of which only 20 to 50 mm accrues during June, July, and August (the growing season for cotton).[4] Under these conditions cotton cultivation requires artificial irrigation.

This chapter is based on material excerpted from Boris Z. Rumer, *Soviet Central Asia: "A Tragic Experiment"* (Boston: Unwin Hyman, 1989), pp. 27–42 and 62–75. © 1989 by Unwin Hyman, Inc. Reprinted by permission. The present version was adapted by William Fierman.

But no more than 6 or 7 percent of the region's arable land is irrigated.[5] If the unused land were brought under irrigation, cotton production and related crops could be greatly expanded. The result has been to create a specialized infrastructure to serve the cotton industry: irrigation networks, branches of machine-building (to manufacture equipment such as cotton sowers, cultivators, harvesters, and tractors), the chemical industry (to produce mineral fertilizers and pesticides for cotton growing), cotton-processing plants (to clean the cotton and produce cottonseed oil), textile mills, and some garment factories. Central Asia produces approximately 95 percent of the USSR's raw cotton and cotton fibers, 15 percent of its vegetable oils, 100 percent of its machinery and equipment for cotton growing, more than 90 percent of its cotton gins, a large quantity of looms, and equipment needed for irrigation.[6]

Although cotton still predominates, research and geological discoveries of the 1950s and 1960s showed that Central Asia has much greater energy resources than previously believed. These discoveries, in turn, radically altered views about the region's potential economic development. In gas, oil, and hydroelectric power, Central Asia now ranks as one of the richest, most promising regions in the USSR. Subsequent exploration during the second half of the 1970s expanded the potential gas reserves significantly, especially in Turkmenia. When the new reserves are added to the deposits discovered earlier, Central Asia stands second only to Western Siberia in the volume of its holdings in natural gas.[7]

Thus, the traditional orientation of the Central Asian economy toward almost exclusive reliance on cotton no longer corresponds to the region's economic potential. Its rich energy potential would permit the development, alongside the cotton complex, of energy-intensive industries. Such development would, obviously, mean a dramatic rise in the industrial role and significance of Central Asia within the larger Soviet economy.

Central Asia's Role in the National Economy

Central Asia's place in the economy of the USSR is clear from Table 3.1, which reveals significantly lower indices per capita here than in the USSR as a whole. Soviet specialists on regional economies explain this phenomenon chiefly by alluding to two factors: (1) the legacy of economic backwardness from prerevolutionary times; and (2) the "demographic peculiarities" of the region (that is, "extremely high rates of population growth and increased proportion of the employable population that does not work in public production"). But history is more an excuse than explanation; after all, seven decades have elapsed since Central Asia came under Soviet control. The high proportion of nonworking population

Table 3.1 Central Asian Share of Soviet National Economy (1985)

Territory	5.7%
Population	10.9
National Income	4.0
Number of People in Labor Force	7.5
Basic Capital of Production Sphere	6.0
Capital Investments	6.4
Industrial Production	4.5
Agricultural Production	8.3*

*1984 data

Sources: *Narodnoe khaziastvo SSSR v 1985 godu*, 8, 12, 409, 390, 394, 48, 363, 93; *Narodnoe khoziaistvo SSSR v 1985 godu*, 229; *SSSR i soiuznye respubliki v 1985 godu* (Moscow, 1986), 88, 89, 221, 222, 237, 238, 270, 271.

is an effect, not a cause, and is a consequence of the economic development of the region as dictated from Moscow.

To judge from official statistics, Central Asia is developing with sufficient dynamism, particularly if compared with growth rates for the USSR as a whole (see Table 3.2). Although these data speak for themselves, it should be underlined that Kirgizia and Uzbekistan have had absolutely no growth in capital investment, even though these two republics account for more than two-thirds of Central Asia's national product.

Moreover, as the data in Tables 3.3 and 3.4 demonstrate, Central Asia's ranking in fixed capital is far below the region's ranking in population. When Central Asia is compared with two analogous regions—the Baltic and the Transcaucasus—one finds that the fixed capital in the Baltic region exceeds the population, whereas in the Transcaucasus the relationship is just the reverse. This discrepancy is particularly great and growing in Central Asia. It constitutes the region's main economic problem and has a decisive influence not only on the rate and character of economic growth, but also on social development.

Another indicator of Central Asia's relatively unfavorable economic situation is the disproportion between its share of population and its share of national income. If the regional statistics on national income are taken at face value, then the fact that the region's share of population is twice as great as its share of national income can be taken to mean that labor productivity is sharply lower in Central Asia. But let us look more closely at the region's labor productivity, both in comparison with the USSR as a whole and in comparison with our two control examples, the Baltic and Transcaucasus regions. As a measure of labor productivity, we use the ratio between a region's total income and the aggregate size

Table 3.2 Indices of Economic Growth in Central Asia and the USSR (1985 as a Percentage of 1984)

	USSR	Uzbekistan	Kirghizia	Turkmenistan	Tadjikistan
National Income	3.1	3.9	2.7	4.8	4.6
Ind. Production	3.9	7.3	3.7	2.0	4.3
Agr. Production	1.6	—	-4.3	2.8	2.2
Cap. Investment	3.0	0.2	0.1	4.0	4.0
Workers, Employees	0.6	0.8	2.2	3.3	2.1

Sources: SSSR i souznye respubliki v 1986 godu, 3, 88, 89, 221, 222, 237, 238, 270, 271.

Table 3.3 The Role of Central Asia in the Soviet Economy (as a Percentage of National Economy)

	1971–75	1976–80	1981–84
National Income	6.0	6.0	6.0
Industrial Production	4.0	4.0	4.0
Agricultural Production	8.0	8.0	9.0
Capital Investment	6.0	6.0	6.0
New Fixed Capital	6.0	6.0	6.0
Population (end of period)	9.2	10.0	10.7
Share of Population Growth	26.0	29.0	30.0

Note: Calculated on the basis of average annual indicators for the periods of the index and given in comparable prices. The 1984 data for Tadjik SSR and Turkmen SSR were interpolated.

Sources: Narodnoe khoziaistvo SSSR v 1984 godu, 56; *Narodnoe khoziaistvo Uzbekskoi SSR v 1984 godu,* 23, *Narodnoe khoziaistvo Tadzhikskoi SSR v 1982 godu,* 30, *Narodnoe khoziaistvo Kirghizskoi SSR v 1984 godu,* 13, 14.

of its labor force. As Table 3.5 illustrates, labor productivity is lower in Central Asia than in the USSR as a whole and in the other two national regions we are considering. This pattern, moreover, has remained constant for the entire period covered in the table. In 1970–1974, when labor productivity rose both at the all-Union level and among national economic

Table 3.4 Central Asian Share of Population and Fixed Capital Compared with other National Regions (in Percent)

Area	1975 Pop.	1975 Fixed Capital	1980 Pop.	1980 Fixed Capital	1984 Pop.	1984 Fixed Capital
USSR	100	100	100	100	100	100
Baltics	2.8	3.5	2.8	3.25	2.8	3.2
Transcaucasus	5.3	3.7	5.4	3.7	5.5	3.8
Central Asia	9.2	5.5	10.0	5.7	10.7	5.9

Note: Fixed capital is based on comparable prices from 1973.

Sources: Narodnoe khoziaistvo SSSR v 1984 godu, 61; *Narodnoe khoziaistvo Uzbekskoi SSR v 1981 godu,* 26; *Narodnoe khoziaistvo Turkmenskoi SSR v 1980 godu,* 44; *Narodnoe khoziaistvo Kirghizskoi SSR v 1980 godu,* 10; *Narodnoe khoziaistvo SSSR v 1984 godu,* 8.

Table 3.5 Labor Productivity in Central Asian, Transcaucasus and Baltic National Regions

	Nat. Income in Real Rubles 1	Share of USSR Nat. Income (%) 2	Ave. Annual Workers 3	Share Ave. USSR Workers (%) 4	Labor Produc. (103 rubles/ person) 5	Coeff. Lab. Prod. Activ. (2:4) 6
1970						
USSR	289.9	100.0	106.8	100.0	2.7	—
Baltics	10.1	3.5	3.3	3.1	3.1	1.13
Transcaucasus	10.2	3.5	4.1	3.8	2.5	0.92
Central Asia	15.2	5.2	6.2	5.8	2.4	0.90
1975						
USSR	363.3	100.0	117.2	100.0	3.1	—
Baltics	12.7	3.5	3.6	3.6	3.6	1.14
Transcaucasus	14.0	3.8	5.0	4.3	2.8	0.88
Central Asia	20.7	5.7	7.4	6.3	2.8	0.90
1980						
USSR	462.2	100.0	125.6	100.0	3.7	—
Baltics	14.9	3.2	3.8	3.0	3.9	1.07
Transcaucasus	22.3	4.8	5.7	4.5	3.9	1.07
Central Asia	27.4	5.9	8.6	6.8	3.2	0.86
1983						
USSR	548.1	100.0	129.9	100.0	4.2	—
Baltics	17.8	3.2	3.8	3.0	4.6	1.07
Transcaucasus	26.3	4.8	6.0	4.6	4.4	1.04
Central Asia	33.6	6.1	9.4	7.2	3.6	0.85

Sources: Narodnoe khoziaistvo Uzbekskoi SSR v 1982 godu, 188, 194; Narodnoe khoziaistvo Kirgizskoi SSSR v 1970 godu, 126; Narodnoe khoziaistvo Kirgizskoi SSR v 1980 godu, 154; Narodnoe khoziaistvo Kirgizskoi SSR v 1984 godu, 99; Narodnoe khoziaistvo Kirgizskoi SSR 1982 godu, 159, 170; Narodnoe khoziaistvo Tadzhikskoi SSR v 1982 godu, 178; Narodnoe khoziaistvo Turkmenskoi SSR v 1976 godu, 129; Narodnoe khoziaistvo Turkmenskoi SSR v 1982 godu, 128, 137; Narodnoe khoziaistvo Turkmenskoi SSR 1924-1984, 144; Narodnoe khoziaistvo Estonskoi SSR v 1984 godu, 144, 154; Narodnoe khoziaistvo Litovskoi SSR v 1984 godu, 144, 152; Narodnoe khoziaistvo Latviiskoi SSR v 1984 godu, 210, 226; Narodnoe khoziaistvo Gruzinskoi SSR v 1984 godu, 172, 165, 103, 107; Narodnoe khoziaistvo Azerbaidzhanskoi SSR v 1970 godu, 221; Narodnoe khoziaistvo Azerbaidzhanskoi SSR v 1984 godu, 145, 151; Narodnoe khoziaistvo Armianskoi SSR v 1980 godu, 151, 169; Narodnoe khoziaistvo Armianskoi SSR v 1984 godu, 227, 213, 146, 154.

Data for a few missing years have been interpolated or extrapolated.

regions, this growth was smallest in Central Asia. Table 3.5 also presents an index called "coefficient of labor activity," which correlates the region's share of the total national income with its share of total population. This indicator likewise suggests that the "level of labor activity" in Central Asia is less than that in the two other national economic regions.

However, although statistics on the labor force create no problems, the other constituent of our index of labor productivity is more difficult to establish; Soviet methods of calculating these indices distort the true magnitude of a region's national income. It is important to determine how significant these distortions are and how they affect data on the national income produced in Central Asia.

The main difficulty in computing national income for particular regions is that many products are finally used outside the regions in which they are produced. There are also problems in determining a republic's national income that are due to the turnover tax. According to present methods, regions that have more industry of the so-called B type (that is, production of consumer goods) and therefore produce goods subject to the turnover tax, have accordingly a higher index for national income. Under these conditions, the region's share of the total national income in the USSR is artificially inflated. Conversely, regions that produce more intermediate products (serving as raw materials or semifinished components for final products manufactured in other regions and subject to the turnover tax) find themselves disadvantaged. It is precisely to this last category of regions that Central Asia belongs.

In Central Asia, especially among cadres from the indigenous peoples, it is widely believed that their region makes a much greater contribution to Soviet national income than that depicted in the official statistics. They blame the underassessment on distortions caused by the system of price-setting, methods of adding on the turnover tax, and the existing economic relations between Central Asia and other regions and republics. In their view, Moscow's methods of calculating national income and interregional economic relations place Central Asia at a disadvantage and mask the significance of its role in the economy of the USSR. For example, the director of the Institute of Economics at the Tajik Academy of Sciences, Rashid Rakhimov, contends that if the national income were computed on the basis of intersector balances, "it could turn out that currently dominant conceptions of the relative and absolute levels of the production of national income in the Tajik republic would be corrected." Rakhimov adds (with due circumspection) that the revised data could lead to changes "in assessments of the region's level of development and in *demands for the development and distribution of its productive forces*" [emphasis added].[8]

Until now, however, the region's productive capacity has been defined exclusively by the production and export of cotton and its by-products. Approximately 96 percent of the raw cotton produced in Uzbekistan is shipped out for processing and manufacturing to the RSFSR, the Ukraine, Belorussia, and other republics, to Eastern Europe, and elsewhere. The industrial processing of one ton of raw cotton yields 3,400 meters of cloth, 94 kilograms of vegetable oil, 6 kilograms of soap, and so forth. But Central Asians benefit little from this. The main reason is the rate of turnover tax imposed at the various stages: 410 to 600 rubles is assessed on one ton of raw cotton, whereas 1,260 to 1,700 rubles is added to the products obtained from the industrial processing of each ton of raw cotton.[9] Obviously, if a more significant part of the cotton raised in Central Asia were also processed there, the region's national income as well as its share in the total national income of the USSR would be greater.

How much greater? Enough to raise its labor productivity significantly in comparison with other national economic regions and the USSR as a whole? According to calculations by the Uzbek economist Z. Solokhiddinov,[10] the real volume of national income produced by Uzbekistan in 1976–1980 was 7.8 percent higher than that reported in official statistics. Moreover, Uzbekistan's share of the national income of the USSR should be corrected to read not 3.80 percent, but 3.86 percent—that is, it should be increased by 0.06 percentage points. This correction can probably be extended to the entire region, for Uzbekistan accounts for about 70 percent of the national income in Central Asia. Still, although the revised data improve the picture slightly, Central Asia nevertheless continues to lag behind the indices for other national regions and the USSR as a whole.

Another distinctive feature of Central Asia is the structure of national income—that is, the relationship of current consumption to accumulation. Unfortunately, data are not available for the entire region, but only for Uzbekistan; similarly, data are unavailable for some republics in the Transcaucasus and Baltic regions. Hence, one is limited to a comparison of certain republics (Uzbekistan, Azerbaijan, Estonia) with the USSR as a whole. As these data demonstrate, the share of consumption in the national income of Uzbekistan has remained lower than that in the USSR as a whole and the other two national regions.

Capital Investment

The investment quotient allocated for Central Asia, in the course of the entire Soviet era, has undergone considerable change, as the data in Table 3.7 indicate. For the entire period of Khrushchev's experiment

Table 3.6 Percentage Share of Consumption in National Income (in Prices of Corresponding Years)

	1970	1975	1980	1984
USSR	70	74	76	73
Uzbekistan	65	73	72	70
Azerbaijan	74	75	73	71
Estonia	74	—	80	76

Sources: *Narodnoe khoziaistvo SSSR v 1970 godu*, 535; *Narodnoe khoziaistvo SSSR v 1975 godu*, 565; *Narodnoe khoziaistvo SSSR v 1980 godu*, 380; *Narodnoe khoziaistvo SSSR v 1984 godu*, 426; *Narodnoe khoziaistvo Uzbekskoi SSR v 1984 godu*, 232; *Narodnoe khoziaistvo Azerbaidzhanskoi SSR v 1984*, 152; *Narodnoe khoziaistvo Estonskoi SSR v 1984 godu*, 155.

with *sovnarkhozy*, Central Asia's share in Soviet investment remained in the range of 3.6 to 4.1 percent. Then came the dramatic spurt in the 1960s. That increase can be explained by increasing investment activity by the *sovnarkhozy*, which gained control over the distribution of investments within their territories. The growth of the late 1960s (after

Table 3.7 Central Asia's Share of Capital Investment (Based on Prices for the Given Period)

Period	Share
1921–1928	3.6%
1928/29–1932	3.8
1933–1937	3.7
1938–June 1941	4.1
1941–1945	4.0
1946–1950	3.7
1951–1955	3.9
1956–1960	3.9
1961–1965	5.3
1966–1970	6.5
1971–1975	6.1
1976–1980	6.3
1981–1985	6.6
1984	6.6
1985	6.3

Sources: *Kapital'noe stroitel'stvo v SSSR* (Moscow, 1961), 74; *Narodnoe khoziaistvo SSSR v 1970 godu*, 488; *Narodnoe khoziaistvo SSR v 1975 godu*, 513; *Narodnoe khoziaistvo SSSR v 1980 godu*, 343; *Narodnoe khoziaistvo SSSR v 1985 godu*, 369.

the dismantling of the *sovnarkhozy*) resulted from the heavy investment supplements made to overcome the devastation resulting from the 1966 earthquake in Tashkent. The increase in capital investment can be further traced to the development of gas and petroleum industries in the region.

As a result of all this investment, the construction capacities of the region were augmented significantly, which encouraged a number of production-branch ministries in Moscow to look favorably on further investments in Central Asia in subsequent years. This outlook apparently explains why the region's investment quota did not fall in later years. Nevertheless, it has ceased to rise since the middle of the 1960s and hence has remained virtually unchanged. This investment quotient is only half of the region's share of total population in the USSR.

In the five-year plan covering the early 1980s, growth in investment in Central Asia was smaller than in the USSR at large and less than in any other region in the country, except Kazakhstan (which had the same rate of growth). Between 1980 and 1985, investment increased by 19 percent for the entire Soviet economy, 18 percent in the RSFSR, 18 percent in the Ukraine, 26 percent in Belorussia, 34 percent in the Baltic region, 39 percent in the Transcaucasus, but only 16 percent in Central Asia (in adjusted prices).

In 1985 (the first year under Gorbachev's leadership) investment in Uzbekistan fell by 4 percent (from 7.145 to 6.811 billion rubles).[11] In the same year in Central Asia as a whole, investment dropped by 1.5 percent, while for the USSR as a whole it rose by 3 percent.[12] Hence, the end of the preceding five-year plan heralded a worsening of the investment situation for the Central Asian economy. Seen against the general background of investment in the USSR, Central Asia's situation has deteriorated.

No less important than aggregate investment is its distribution among sectors of the economy. The data in Table 3.8 show the breakdown for Central Asia and compare that region with other areas of the USSR. The table shows that Central Asia is distinguished by a most unusual type of investment policy: (1) the investment share for industry is the lowest and that for agriculture the highest, thus perpetuating the bias toward the region's agricultural sector; (2) the share allocated for transportation has declined substantially; (3) the quota for construction is less than that for the RSFSR, the Transcaucasus, and the Baltic regions; and (4) allocations for the social sphere are exceedingly low.

In short, investment allocations within the region continue to subordinate economic development to one overarching goal—cotton. All other areas of the economy are sacrificed to increase the cotton output. No other region of the USSR is bound so completely to a one-sided strategy of economic development. Further, Central Asia has the lowest

Table 3.8 Distribution of Capital Investment per Economic Sector (Percentage, Based on Adjusted Prices)

	Industry	Agriculture	Transportation and Communication	Construction	Social Sphere
Central Asia					
1971–75	28.2	29.5	10.5	3.6	28.2
1976–80	28.2	31.5	9.4	3.1	27.8
1981–85	28.5	33.2	8.3	3.2	26.8
Caucasus					
1971–75	37.0	17.7	10.2	3.8	31.3
1976–80	38.0	18.8	10.9	3.7	28.6
1981–85	39.5	19.3	11.4	3.7	26.1

Baltics					
1971–75	26.6	29.1	9.2	2.7	32.4
1976–80	26.9	27.5	9.4	3.4	32.8
1981–85	30.1	23.5	8.9	3.4	32.8
Belorussia					
1970–75	32.6	27.5	7.1	3.2	29.6
1976–80	32.7	27.5	9.4	3.3	28.5
1981–85	32.2	25.3	9.2	3.2	30.1
RSFSR					
1970–75	39.2	11.7	12.4	4.2	32.5
1976–80	38.9	12.4	14.3	4.4	30.0
1981–85	38.9	11.9	15.2	4.0	30.0

* Housing, health services, recreation, science, and education.

Sources: *Narodnoe khozaistvo Kirgizskoi SSR v 1984 godu*, 113; *Narodnoe khozaistvo Turkmenskoi SSR v 1984 godu*, 129; *Narodnoe khozaistvo Tadzhikskoi SSR v 1982 godu*, 170; *Narodnoe khozaistvo Uzbekskoi SSR v 1984 godu*, 209; *Narodnoe khozaistvo Gruzinskoi SSR v 1984 godu*, 149; *Narodnoe khozaistvo Armianskoi SSR v 1984 godu*, 185; *Narodnoe khozaistvo Azerbaidzhanskoi SSR v 1983 godu*, 104; *Narodnoe khozaistvo Litovskoi SSR v 1980 godu*, 129; *Narodnoe khozaistvo Litovskoi SSR v 1984 godu*, 124; *Narodnoe khozaistvo Latviiskoi SSR v 1984 godu*, 186; *Narodnoe khozaistvo Estonskoi SSR v 1984 godu*, 127; *Narodnoe khozaistvo Belorusskoi SSR v 1984 godu*, 121; *Narodnoe khozaistvo RSFSR v 1984 godu*, 222; *Narodnoe khozaistvo SSSR v 1984 godu*, 378.

Some figures, for which direct data are unavailable, are based on the author's calculations.

(and steadily declining!) investment quotient for the social sphere, although it has the highest rate of population growth in the USSR.

Published statistics provide only one basis for analyzing the structure of the Central Asian economy: fixed capital. Table 3.9 compares the distribution of fixed capital among economic sectors in Central Asia with the distributions in the USSR as a whole and in the Baltic and Transcaucasus regions. The data reveal clearly that the share devoted to industry, transportation, and communication in Central Asia is small, whereas agriculture's share is large. This distribution reflects, of course, Central Asia's concentration on the production and processing of cotton.[13]

The Decline of Soviet Cotton Exports

As mentioned above, cotton from Central Asia is one of the most important exports of the USSR, which ranks among the world's leading exporters of this staple. (In 1983, Uzbekistan alone produced almost as much cotton as the entire United States.) The USSR exports cotton to more than 30 countries. For the period 1965–1983, the Soviet share of the world's production of cotton fiber rose from 15 to 21 percent.[14] According to data for 1983, the largest producer in the world was China, followed by the USSR, with the United States in third place.

In the early 1980s, however, the volume of cotton exported by the USSR declined sharply: whereas cotton exports had risen by 55 percent in the 1970s, they fell 25 percent between 1980 and 1985.[15] Production, too, declined, but not so drastically; in Uzbekistan, for example, output fell by only 6 percent.[16] Given the Soviet Union's demand for hard currency (heightened by the reduced production of oil and its falling price on the world market), it is clear that the nation cut back its cotton exports—one of its most popular goods on the world market—only from dire necessity. Several factors help to account for the reduction in cotton exports.

First, in the mid-1980s, the USSR suffered a fall in the production of raw textile materials generally—not just cotton, but also chemical fibers. As a result, it could not easily cut its domestic consumption of cotton and divert the difference to sustain its export level.

In recent decades, cotton's share of the textile market in Western countries has declined (with a concomitant increase in chemical fibers). But, significantly, in the early 1980s the pressure from synthetics abated slightly and the demand for cotton increased. That change was due to several factors, including an improvement in the quality of cotton, changes in the relative prices that favored cotton over synthetics, and recognition of the superior hygienic properties of cotton textiles.

Table 3.9 Distribution of Fixed Capital by Economic Sector (as a Percentage of Total Fixed Capital)

Sector	Year	USSR	Baltics	Transcaucasus	Central Asia
Industry	1970	29.6	24.0	29.5	22.6
	1975	30.6	25.1	29.5	23.6
	1980	31.8	26.0	31.0	24.8
	1984	32.2	26.0	30.7	25.1
Agriculture	1970	12.3	18.3	14.3	21.8
	1975	13.3	19.6	14.6	22.8
	1980	13.7	20.2	15.1	23.2
	1984	13.8	20.3	15.5	23.5
Transportation and Communication	1970	13.6	14.5	13.4	11.5
	1975	13.6	14.0	14.3	12.4
	1980	13.6	13.4	14.0	12.7
	1984	13.6	13.3	13.9	12.6
Construction	1970	2.6	2.0	3.0	4.7
	1975	2.8	2.1	3.2	4.5
	1980	3.2	2.3	3.5	4.3
	1984	3.4	2.5	3.8	4.4
Social Sphere	1970	42.0	41.0	39.4	39.3
	1975	39.6	39.2	39.1	36.4
	1980	37.8	39.1	36.5	34.9
	1984	37.0	37.8	35.8	34.3

Note: Data based on comparable prices from 1973.

Sources: Narodnoe khoziaistvo SSSR v 1970 godu, 58, 60, 61; Narodnoe khoziaistvo RSFSR v 1960 godu, 18; Narodnoe khoziaistvo RSFSR v 1965 godu, 38; Narodnoe khoziaistvo RSFSR v 1975 godu, 27; Narodnoe khoziaistvo RSFSR v 1980 godu, 27; Narodnoe khoziaistvo RSFSR v 1983 godu, 27; Narodnoe khoziaistvo Ukrainskoi SSR v 1980 godu, 29; Narodnoe khoziaitsvo Ukrainskoi SSR v 1983 godu, 20, 21; Narodnoe khoziaistvo Litovskoi SSR v 1980 godu, 25, 39; Narodnoe khoziaistvo Litovskoi SSR v 1983 godu, 32; Narodnoe khoziaistvo Litovskoi SSR 1984 godu, 20; Narodnoe khoziaistvo Latviiskoi SSR v 1980 godu, 39; Narodnoe khoziaistvo Latviiskoi SSR v 1983 godu, 32; Narodnoe khoziaistvo Latviiskoi SSR v 1984 godu, 35; Narodnoe khoziaistvo Gruzinskoi SSR v 1975 godu, 26; Narodnoe khoziaistvo Gruzinskoi SSR v 1981 godu, 26; Narodnoe khoziaistvo Gruzinskoi SSR v 1984 godu, 22; Narodnoe khoziaistvo Azerbaidzhanskoi SSR v 1983 godu, 13, 14; Narodnoe khoziaistvo Azerbaidzhanskoi SSR v 1984 godu, 25, 26; Narodnoe khoziaistvo Armianskoi SSR v 1975 godu, 25; Narodnoe khoziaistvo Armianskoi SSR v 1980 godu, 29; Narodnoe khoziaistvo Armianskoi SSR v 1984 godu, 36; Narodnoe khoziaistvo Uzbekskoi SSR v 1980 godu, 22; Narodnoe khoziaistvo Uzbekskoi SSR v 1982 godu, 19; Narodnoe khoziaistvo Uzbekskoi SSR v 1984 godu, 28; Narodnoe khoziaistvo Tadzhikskoi SSR v 1975 godu, 20; Narodnoe khoziaistvo Tadzhikskoi SSR v 1976 godu, 20; Narodnoe khoziaistvo Tadzhikskoi SSR v 1981 godu, 25, 26; Narodnoe khoziaistvo Tadzhikskoi SSR v 1982 godu, 28; Narodnoe khoziaistvo Kirgizskoi SSR v 1975 godu, 17; Narodnoe khoziaistvo Turkmenskoi SSR v 1976 godu, 30; Narodnoe khoziaistvo Turkmenskoi SSR v 1980 godu, 44; Narodnoe khoziaistvo Turkmenskoi SSR v 1982 godu, 18; Narodnoe khoziaistvo Turkmenskoi SSR v 1984 godu, 24.

The USSR ranks significantly below the world level in both the production and consumption of synthetic fibers, and hence cotton still dominates in its mix of raw materials for textiles. As a result, it could not compensate for the downturn in cotton production by increasing its output of chemical fibers. Indeed, growth rates in the production of the latter have been inconsequential and, in 1985, production actually declined.[17] In the mid-1980s, therefore, the only way that the USSR could sustain its old export level was by cutting domestic consumption. This is evidence of the tremendous strain on Soviet fiber production.

Second, conditions on the world market changed with China's rise to leadership. Beginning in the late 1970s China adopted a variety of measures to stimulate greater cotton production and an improvement in its quality. That country's enormous labor reserves, its abundant state subsidies, its favorable climatic conditions in a number of regions, and the strong material incentives to make quantitative and qualitative improvements put China in a separate class from the other competitors. China's entry into the world cotton market brought a sharp intensification of competition, for buyers soon began to show increasing interest in Chinese cotton. Demand for the inferior Soviet cotton fell accordingly. The results were a decline in the Soviet share of the world cotton fiber market and a reduced proportion of production for export (from 30 to 24 percent of total output in the 1980–1985 period).[18]

As the reverses on the world market suggest, the quality problem of Soviet cotton is extremely serious. The assortment of raw cotton has deteriorated, and the yield and quality have declined. Thus, the share of harder-to-grow superior varieties in the total harvest declined from 77 percent in the early 1970s to 58 percent by the early 1980s. The share of the most inferior varieties, by contrast, rose from 14 to 29 percent.[19]

The Crisis in Cotton Production and Its Causes

Since the early 1980s, cotton production has been in the throes of crisis. The harvest of raw cotton in 1985 was 12 percent less than in 1980; yield (output per hectare) declined by 17 percent.[20] Such a downturn is utterly without precedent in the history of Soviet Central Asia.

The scale of the cotton crisis is abundantly clear from a close examination of the region's major cotton-producer, Uzbekistan.[21] Between 1975 and 1980, Uzbekistan's harvest of raw cotton increased by 25 percent, and its yield (output per hectare) by 17 percent; but the output of cotton fiber increased by only 5 percent.[22] For many years, to judge from statistical data, the total harvest of raw cotton and per-hectare yield substantially exceeded the production of cotton fibers. And this gap is steadily widening. Obviously, the industrial end-product is the cotton fiber, not raw cotton. But for the cotton-growing kolkhozes (collective farms) and sovkhozes (state farms), the final product is only the raw cotton that they deliver to state procurement centers; and all that matters is its quantity, since plan fulfillment is judged on a quantitative rather than qualitative basis. In accordance with this same principle, the employees at cotton-processing plants have no material incentives to store the cotton properly and give it higher-quality processing. The entire system of material incentives is geared toward achieving the quantitative goals of production.

It is imperative to evaluate performance and establish remuneration according to qualitative indices, a change that should involve several measures. Most obvious, state procurement payments should shift from raw cotton to fibers and by-products, taking into account their quality. Moreover, the pricing of fibers and by-products should take into account the work of cotton-processing plants—their expenditures for the treatment of the raw cotton, the quality of the processed product, and the yield in fibers. Finally, procurement centers and cotton-cleaning plants must store and process raw cotton from each producer separately.

But other, more technical problems have also played a role in causing the current crisis in cotton production in Central Asia. To improve the quality of cotton, it is above all necessary to develop and introduce only high-yield, disease-resistant, and fast-growing varieties with a large fiber output. Until now, attention has focused on a single characteristic—high yield. By default, the other properties—in which the producers had no material interest—have been ignored. Hence, the tasks now are to develop new varieties with a superior combination of characteristics and to put them into production. It is particularly important to achieve maximum volume in the production of thin-fiber varieties.

The cultivation and harvesting of the cotton plant is an extremely protracted and labor-intensive process. Cotton is, in general, one of the most labor-intensive of all agricultural crops. Thus, whereas the direct expenditure of labor for the production of one centner (100 kilos) of cereal is 1.6 man-hours, it requires 36 man-hours to produce one centner of cotton.[23] Despite the favorable demographic conditions in Central Asia, cotton production has encountered steadily mounting problems of insufficient labor. The primary reason is that the rural population in Central Asia has been migrating to the cities in recent years; secondly, the population that remains prefers other employment to the cultivation of cotton. Hence, it has become routine for cotton farms to recruit auxiliary labor to work the cotton fields by mobilizing significant contingents of people from other sectors of the economy as well as school children and students—with prolonged diversion from their regular work and studies.

The only solution is to increase the level of mechanization in the production process. Approximately 1,000 man-hours are currently expended on each hectare, but mechanization could reduce this to 600 man-hours.[24] Not all kinds of mechanization, however, lead to an improvement in the quality of the cotton grown. The technology of the machines used for cotton cultivation lags behind contemporary requirements. As a result, mechanized harvesting under adverse weather conditions increases the humidity and impurities in the cotton.

Contemporary technology, however, makes it possible for machines to bring in up to 95 percent of the entire yield. But this is possible only if the harvesters make five or six passes, which makes the soil less arable and hence reduces the next harvest.[25] Consequently, the scale of mechanized harvesting can be expanded only (a) if a new cotton harvester is developed that minimizes the number of passes required; and (b) if new varieties of cotton are developed that simultaneously lend themselves to mechanized harvesting and preserve the desired biological characteristics of the cotton fiber.

Another important means to reduce the labor required is to mechanize the watering system. The transition from watering by hand (which is now widely practiced in Central Asia) to mechanized systems would eliminate the onerous work of the workers engaged in watering. But this requires the creation and production of watering machines of a new design.

Greater use of mechanized harvesters will lead to a bottleneck at the next stage, when the cotton is cleaned and processed. Indeed, there is already an imbalance between the level of mechanized harvesting and the technical capacities of cotton-processing plants. The latter have proven unprepared to handle the massive volume of machine-harvested cotton, which contains more moisture and impurities than hand-harvested cotton.

To raise the quality of cotton processing (and hence fiber quality), two problems must first be solved. First, the difficulty in processing very moist and impure cotton can be overcome only by increasing the capacity of cotton-processing plants by 25 to 30 percent.[26] The increased capacity would reduce the processing periods and thereby limit spoilage and damage to fiber quality. The second task is to outfit procurement centers with additional machinery to dry the cotton and to construct additional closed drying platforms. But the main objective must be to raise the technological level of cotton-processing plants by creating more efficient machinery and by constructing larger enterprises that can quickly handle large volumes of cotton.

So far we have looked only at the machinery and equipment needed for cotton cultivation and harvesting. But irrigation presents another problem that must be solved if the cotton crisis in Central Asia is to be overcome.

This problem is not new but became more critical when Moscow tabled plans to divert rivers to serve water-deficient areas in this region. Now, more than ever, it is vital to increase the return and efficiency of existing irrigation systems and to put more effective methods of watering into operation. If these methods are exploited, they can substantially alleviate this region's water problem. But that requires, in addition to improved organization and administration, the outfitting of irrigation systems with modern watering equipment, which could substantially reduce the water consumption per unit of production. Hence, whereas Central Asia as a whole uses 570 cubic meters of water to produce one centner of cotton, and whereas Khorezm oblast consumes water at the rate of 700 to 800 cubic meters (because of the high salinity of the soil), the picture is radically different in the Golodnaia Steppe. There, the irrigation system is much more technologically advanced, with the result that water consumption is only 400 cubic meters per centner of cotton.[27] Water conservation could be further achieved by expanding the use of modern sprinkler systems.

Problems in the Central Asian cotton sector cannot be corrected by mere "organizational measures"—a favorite Moscow panacea for fundamental economic problems. Rather, it is plainly necessary to make enormous investments and to optimize their distribution within the sector. But, to judge from the tendencies in investment policy, that kind of radical turnaround is highly improbable. An increase in the investment quota for the cotton-growing complex depends on Moscow, not on the authorities in Central Asia; and Moscow has other priorities for its sectoral and regional allocation of resources.

The "Tragic Experiment" of Cotton

The struggle to produce more cotton has involved enormous costs. Until the era of glasnost, Soviet writers, sensitive to Third World (especially Islamic countries') perceptions of developments in Central Asia, rejected claims that cotton is responsible for serious problems in society. Countless Soviet publications, aiming to smash "bourgeois conceptions of the economic development of Central Asia," inveighed against the proposition—widely shared in Western scholarly studies—that the Central Asian economy should be analyzed in terms of an agrarian-colonial model. Soviet propagandists were especially sensitive to this accusation and expressed the greatest indignation over the thesis of a "superspecialization in cotton" in Central Asia. Outraged by the injustice of such an accusation, Professor Akhmed Ulmasov at the Tashkent Institute of Economics wrote in 1985 that the proposition of "a superspecialization in cotton-growing" in Central Asia is "a method of falsification by Sovietologists." He asserted that cotton growing in Central Asia was "a contemporary dynamic branch of production, based on a constantly expanding application of achievements in science and technology." "How can one speak of superspecialization in cotton," exclaimed Ulmasov emotionally, and then went on to accuse "bourgeois theoreticians" of resorting to "fabrications and inventions at any price."[28]

At the end of the 1980s, however, Soviet writers themselves began to recognize many of the problems which Ulmasov claimed were invented by Western Sovietologists. One such blunt recognition appeared in the Moscow weekly *Literaturnaia gazeta* in early 1987:

> Specialization should be reasonable. In Uzbekistan it has degenerated into the dictatorship of a single crop, indeed one so highly specific as cotton. It first became a monoculture in a psychological sense, when it drove all the other needs of the region from the minds of certain leaders. Then it crowded the normal crop rotation from the fields and pushed everything else out of the plan. By being transformed into virtually one great cotton plantation, Uzbekistan embarked on a long, tragic experiment—to determine the capacity of a monoculture to corrode not only agriculture, but also industry, education, health, and finally public morality.[29]

The cotton economy's "corrosion" of agriculture, industry, education, health, and public morality was reinforced by the cumulative effect of changes which occurred during the Brezhnev era. It was still possible to keep pace with cotton plan targets in the 1960s and, apparently, even in the first half of the 1970s by expanding the sown areas, raising the yield ratio, or other "honest" means. But not thereafter: excessive exploitation of the soil—by ignoring proper crop rotations, by making excessive use of harvesters, and by overusing pesticides—finally began to take its toll. Fertile soils had been depleted, and the acreage under cultivation had reached its absolute outer limits, given available water supplies. Yet Moscow, operating as ever on the principle that one must surpass the "attained level," constantly raised the plan targets. There remained but one alternative: inflation of the data. After the death of the Uzbek "grand vizier," Sharif Rashidov, when first Andropov and then Gorbachev launched purges of cadres, the terrible consequences of the grandiose cotton affair came to light. Virtually the entire *nomenklatura* (power elite) of Uzbekistan was involved. In the words, once again, of *Literaturnaia gazeta*:

Cotton, to which everything was sacrificed (including the normal life of townspeople, who were incessantly dispatched to work on cotton), had the same harvest in 1984 as in 1969. Only the production costs had increased. And how they had increased, warping the economy of the entire republic! To this very day the return on capital continues to decline; the construction of new housing is being cut back. After beginning with cotton, the leprosy of inflated reports permeated the entire republic, spread to the social sphere, and did not pass by culture and law enforcement organs. It is said: Make no idols. But they made one here: cotton, and cotton alone. It degenerated into a deception of society and themselves, into false honors, into bribery.[30]

After 1983 Uzbekistan was swept by a massive wave of arrests. Hundreds of leaders in kolkhozes and sovkhozes, ordinary employees as well as top figures in the economy (including ministers) and in the party apparatus—all were put in the dock and brought to justice. The majority of cadres were ethnic Uzbeks who had found that the only way to protect their positions and careers was to collaborate in the deception, the cheating, the violation of laws that had taken hold in the republic. This was a major catastrophe for the republic, involving not only the elite *nomenklatura* but also entire strata of the population. But the root cause was not the Uzbeks' cupidity; it was Moscow's economic policy.

Falsification was rampant from the national level down to individual farms. The heads of kolkhozes and sovkhozes simply bribed the procurement inspectors to inflate the amount delivered, both on the delivery receipts and in reports to their superiors. Another type of deception was to expand the area under cultivation and then to conceal this from both the planning and statistical offices.

The role of the central Soviet press in "uncovering" Central Asian (especially Uzbek) corruption was strongly resented by leading members of the local intelligentsia. According to the Uzbek writer Timur Pulatov, "The central newspapers, especially *Komsomol'skaia Pravda*, brought public opinion and the attitude of the country towards the Uzbek people to such a point that Uzbek children at the Orlyonok Pioneer Camp [a national camp for some of the elite members of the Pioneer children's organization] were isolated by fellow campers who told them, 'You are the children of thieves and bribe-takers. Go home.' "[31] In defending their people against what they understood as unjustified blackening of the Uzbek people's honor, the Central Asians maintained that the corruption was a natural response to unrealistic targets sent down from Moscow; in their view, those *most* responsible for the crimes were the accomplices in high places.[32]

Among the other major costs of the cotton economy has been severe damage to the natural environment. Academician Mirza ali Mukhamedzhanov blames the monoculture for putting the soil in Uzbekistan into the same condition as a gravely ill person. Thus, cotton has been cultivated on many fields without interruption for some fifty years which has exhausted the nutrients in the soil. Tractors cross a field up to thirty times a year. Cotton machines mercilessly compress the soil, destroying its microorganisms. And because cotton has a low immunity to disease and infestation, massive quantities of pesticides are used, killing every living thing in the fields. Norms for crop rotation have also been violated; cotton's share of sown acreage reaches 85 percent, whereas it normally should compose only 50 to 60 percent.[33]

From earliest times, Uzbek peasants rotated alfalfa with cotton cultivation. Alfalfa improves the structure of the soil and enriches it with nitrogen, thereby creating favorable conditions for high yields of cotton. Alfalfa made it possible to keep livestock, which, in turn, provided organic fertilizer for the cotton fields. But under constant pressure from Moscow to increase production at any price, it was impossible to let the soil rest. The classic cycle—cotton, alfalfa, manure, cotton—was broken. According to another Uzbek scholar, Favaris Kaiumov, in 1940, when the crop rotation was still practiced, alfalfa was planted in almost half of all land sown to cotton. But now alfalfa sowing is insignificant, and previously fertile soils are being exhausted.

Among the most seriously affected natural resources is water. In part because it was free to farmers, this precious commodity was used inefficiently, and enormous amounts were lost in poorly constructed and poorly maintained irrigation canals. This contributed to reduced flows in the region's rivers, and ultimately to the shrinking of the Aral Sea. As the sea dries up, harmful particles from its bed are becoming become airborne and are carried over great distances.[34]

The health problems associated with cotton go far beyond those immediately attributable to the shrinking Aral. Millions of men, women, and children who work in the cotton fields have been exposed to high doses of poisonous insecticides, defoliants, and other chemicals. Attempts to prohibit the use of such substances have often failed due to the pressure to meet planned production targets. When the dangerous defoliant "butifos" was banned, in some places it was replaced with equally dangerous substitutes.[35] A study of Akkurgansk raion (Tashkent oblast) in the 1970s found that inhabitants who lived in areas of the raion where cotton was planted were 60 percent more likely to suffer from disorders of the nervous system than those who lived in other parts of the raion.[36] The high incidence of acute intestinal disorders and jaundice in children also has been linked to cotton.[37] In a speech to the USSR Congress of People's Deputies, Adil Yaqubov, head of the Uzbekistan Writers' Union, compared the Soviet regime unfavorably with 19th-century slaveowners in the United States. At least in the United States, Yaqubov emphasized, the slaveowners were savvy enough to make sure that their slaves were well fed and strong.[38]

The sowing of cotton has also pushed out the other agricultural crops traditional to Central Asia, including fruits and vegetables, and pasturelands for livestock were cut back. Even the trees around peasants' houses were cut down to make way for cotton—and that amidst the scorching sun of Central Asia. Uzbek writer Otkir Hashimov complains that peaches which sell for three rubles per kilogram in the stores of Siberia cost five rubles at the market in Tashkent. This, he feels, is a result of sacrificing Uzbekistan's orchards to cotton. Hashimov points out that residents of the republic's rural areas where fruit might be grown today have to travel to towns simply to buy apples or melons.[39]

Still another harmful consequence of cotton has been the widespread use of children in agricultural labor. For example, children in 3 raions of Turkmenia were found to be working between 56 and 68 school days per year in the cotton fields.[40] When more regulations prohibiting child labor in the cotton fields were first introduced, local officials found ways to work around regulations or else simply ignored them. An administrator in Osh oblast's Public Education Department (Kirgizia) even defended the practice, saying that this was "not detrimental to [the children's] school work."[41] Nevertheless, the long periods which Central Asian children spend engaged in agricultural labor have been cited as one of the major factors contributing to the region's poor educational system. One local journalist who contemplated the fate of children who spend half of their childhood in dilapidated schools and the other half in the cotton fields caustically asked, "Will they become cosmonauts?"[42]

Central Asia's Exclusion from Textile Manufacturing

Although Central Asia is the cotton base of the USSR, it plays only a minor role in the manufacture of cotton textiles. Uzbekistan produces some 70 percent of the nation's cotton fiber, but it has a negligible share in textile output—just 2.7 percent in 1940, 3.7 percent in 1960, 2.8 percent in 1970, 2.7 percent in 1980, and approximately 4 percent in 1984.[43] Only 4 to 5 percent of the region's cotton production remains there;[44] the rest is shipped to the European part of the country, where more than 70 percent of the USSR's output of cotton textiles is produced.[45]

For more than a half-century, the Central Asian planners have attempted, in vain, to lessen this disproportion. Opponents of such demands argue it is more advantageous to ship cotton fiber than textiles. A typical expression of this view was advanced in the 1960s by E. Pospelova and E. Slastenko:

> The basic principle that should determine the placement and distribution of textile production is its proximity to the consumer. Proximity to the source of the raw material does not have the significance for the textile industry that it does for machine building or metallurgy. It has been well known for a long time that *the shipment of raw cotton is more economical than the shipment of textiles* [emphasis added]. Therefore, based on the opportunities [offered by] a high concentration, *it is far from expedient to create everywhere new districts of textile industry* [emphasis added].[46]

Obviously this passage refers to Central Asia, since no other regions in the USSR have the raw material to create such textile centers.

The above assertions are not, however, supported by any concrete calculation. The purported advantage in transporting cotton fiber rather than finished textiles is based merely on the lower rail tariffs set for the shipment of fiber. But the difference is not great and in any event simply reflects state tariff policy, which reflects not economic reality but the state's policies to regulate the development of various regions. Indeed, the shipment of cotton fiber over such immense distances is very costly and compounds the acute difficulties that already beset the aging and overloaded railway system. If to that are added the costs of reshipping textiles back to Central Asia and Kazakhstan to clothe the population there (approximately 50 million inhabitants), the entire Moscow argument proves specious.

Moreover, the largest textile factories in Central Asia (in Tashkent and Fergana) have significantly better economic indices than analogous plants in the Moscow, Ivanovo, and Vladimir oblasts of European Russia. Central Asia's abundance of labor, increased by the large number of people outside the official labor force (especially among the female population), constitutes an important argument in favor of establishing textile mills in the region. Indeed, providing employment opportunities (especially for the population of small towns, where industry is completely absent) is a critical economic and social desideratum for the region. According to data compiled by Nikolai Bedrintsev, a member of the Uzbek Academy of Sciences, in the 1970s the work force of Uzbekistan grew by 250,000 persons a year, whereas the number of jobs (outside of kolkhozes and sovkhozes) increased by only 100,000 a year (of which only 25,000 were in industry).[47] Under the circumstances, it would seem expedient to expand the most labor-intensive production, which includes the textile industry. Although this industry seems ideally suited for

Central Asia, Moscow has refused to modify its policy and expand that sector.

The indignation of the Central Asian establishment at this refusal sometimes comes through on the pages of the local press. Here, for example, is the statement by one of the leading Central Asian economists, I. Iskanderov:

> Is it not clear that the majority of enterprises manufacturing cotton in this country are detached from both the sources of raw material and the consumer? Most distressing of all is the fact that central planning organs [Gosplan in Moscow] have become inured to this situation and do not notice the disproportions in the distribution of production in cotton textiles. *Moreover, economists have come forward to try to legitimize the existing territorial structure of production of raw materials and finished products* [emphasis added]. In my view it is unwise to ignore any longer the exceptionally favorable conditions in Central Asia, especially in Uzbekistan, that would permit the manufacture of cotton textiles with the lowest production costs. Is it not time to reconsider long-range plans with an eye toward increasing Central Asia's share in the national production of cotton textiles with the calculation that they might completely satisfy all its own needs as well as those of Kazakhstan, Siberia, and the Far East?[48]

Those lines appeared in 1966. Two decades later the policy had basically not changed, and in 1986 Iskanderov was still trying to persuade Moscow to alter its policy:

> It is urgently necessary to prepare concrete proposals to create a gigantic center of textile industry in Uzbekistan, based on the favorable economic and natural conditions at hand, and also on the surfeit of labor resources. At the present time approximately 94 percent of the cotton fiber is exported out of the Uzbek SSR at the cost of great transportation expenditures. Part of this raw material is then returned to the republic in the form of finished cloth. This two-way shipping wreaks enormous economic harm on the economy of the country. Hence the creation of a large center of textile industry in Uzbekistan (to provide for the needs of the republic and eastern regions of the country for the basic types of textile products) is economically advantageous in every sense.[49]

But as Iskanderov wrote those lines, there was still little evidence that Moscow would revise the pattern of one-sided regional specialization that it had so systematically developed over several decades.

Aside from any economic concerns which may have prevented Moscow's development of a more balanced economy, political ones have undoubtedly also played a role. Soviet leaders have certainly understood that a more balanced economy (and, potentially, greater economic self-sufficiency) could serve as a basis for greater political autonomy.

Whereas until the middle of the 1980s Central Asians' arguments about the desirability of developing the textile industry in their regions were generally phrased in terms of what was good for the USSR as a whole, the reasons stated publicly at the end of the decade showed an important shift. Increasingly, Central Asians began to assert that the current economic arrangement may, in fact, be advantageous to other parts of the USSR, but that it was certainly disadvantageous to Central Asia. Increasingly, they implied that Central Asia had been and indeed still was treated by Russia as a colony.

In part, the change in the debate reflected the broadening of glasnost, the overall decline in the Soviet economy, and every Soviet geographic region's attempt to prove that it was pulling more than its "fair share" of the national economic burden. But this does not diminish the Central Asians' belief that their arguments are correct.

Adil Yaqubov, head of the Uzbek Writers' Union and deputy to the USSR Congress of People's Deputies, has been one of the most ardent defenders of Central Asian interests. In demonstrating how unfairly Uzbekistan was being treated, Yaqubov cited a world market price of 5,000 American dollars for one ton of raw cotton. Basing his calculation on the rate for Western tourists purchasing rubles in the USSR (one dollar purchased six rubles and thirty kopecks), Yaqubov estimated that one ton of raw cotton should sell for over thirty thousand rubles. Yet the Soviet government purchased this commodity in Uzbekistan for only eight hundred rubles per ton.[50]

Another prominent Uzbek writer, the poet Muhammad Salih, claimed that the terms on which Moscow purchased cotton were far more disadvantageous to Central Asia than those in effect under the last Russian tsar. According to Salih, in pre-revolutionary Russia an Uzbek peasant received enough payment from a kilogram of cotton to purchase a cow; today he receives only enough to buy fifteen boxes of matches.[51] Moreover, another Uzbek writer stressed that in recent years the injustice of the situation was becoming worse due to rising prices for fertilizer and other inputs.[52]

Within months after these two complaints, a modest price increase was announced for cotton harvested in 1989 in Uzbekistan, with an additional price increase due to take effect in 1990. Significantly, according to the new plan the price paid was in part to be determined by the quality of the cotton.[53] However, these increases do not appear to have curbed Uzbek criticism. The director of the Central Asian Scientific Research Institute's Agricultural Economy rejected the boost as far from sufficient, even without consideration of price increases, which will take effect in the near future, on many inputs into cotton cultivation.[54]

In emphasizing the urgency of their problem, the Uzbeks take care to refute the stereotype of the "easy" or "plentiful" life which they feel distorts the view of their region held by people in other parts of the country. They cite statistics, for example, that annual meat consumption in the USSR as a whole was 64.1 kilograms in 1987, whereas in Uzbekistan it was only 29. They cite analogous figures for dairy products: 190 for Uzbekistan and 341 for the USSR as a whole.[55]

The Central Asians' emphasis of cotton price readjustment, however, is just a part of their broader demand for a reorientation of their region's economy. Inasmuch as cotton remains a major crop, they boldly insist that *for the interests of Central Asia* the processing must increasingly take place in the region. They also demand that other crops—especially food crops, which they claim would yield a much greater profit—replace much of the cotton.[56] Pointing to the Japanese and South Korean success in employing millions of people despite scarce natural resources, some Central Asians also dream of developing high technology industry.

Given the severe economic problems which Moscow is facing today, it is most unlikely that the all-Union government will magnanimously accede to Central Asian demands to realign the economic relationship which has not fundamentally changed since tsarist days. However, with Central Asia's increasing political assertiveness and the center's decreasing ability to enforce its own economic will, the cotton economy and the colonial relationship which it dictated may finally be about to undergo fundamental change.

Notes

1. N. Khamraev and Zh. Borozov, "Problemy razvitiia narodno-khoziaistvennogo khlopkovogo kompleksa," *Izvestiia Akademiia nauk SSSR, Seriia ekonomicheskaia*, no. 1, 1986, p. 113.

2. These oases of Central Asia include the following: the Turan Lowland, the Golodnaia Steppe, the Zeravshan Basin, Surkhandarya, Chirchik, Murgab, Tedzhen, and the lands of the middle and, in part, the lower course of the Amu Darya.

3. *Sredne-aziatskii ekonomicheskii raion* (Moscow, 1972), p. 148.

4. *Sredne-aziatskii ekonomicheskii raion*, p. 7.

5. Ibid., 8.

6. Ibid.

7. V. Popov, "Mineral'no-syrevye resursy strany, ikh ispol'zovanie," *Planovoe khoziaistvo*, no. 4, 1981, p. 34. In addition, Central Asia is rich in nonferrous and rare metals, such as zinc ores, tungsten, and gold.

8. R. Rakhimov, *Problemy razvitiia narodno-khoziaistvennogo kompleksa Tadzhikskoi SSR* (Dushanbe, 1977), p. 67.

9. Z. Salokhiddinov, "Otsenka effektivnosti kapital'nykh vlozhenii v usloviiakh otkrytoi ekonomiki," *Ekonomika i zhizn'*, no. 10, 1985, p. 17.

10. Ibid.

11. *Narodnoe khoziaistvo SSSR v 1984 godu*, p. 385, *Narodnoe khoziaistvo SSR v 1985 godu*, p. 369.

12. *Narodnoe khoziaistvo SSR v 1985 godu*, p. 363.

13. In addition, these data demonstrate that Central Asia has a remarkably low share of fixed capital in the social sphere—housing, culture, education, trade, science, recreation, and services. Indeed, this share has undergone a significant decline. Even though the reduced share of capital in the social sphere is characteristic of the entire Soviet economy, its effect is disproportionately greater in Central Asia, whose population is growing so much faster than that in other areas of the USSR. Between 1970 and 1984, the Central Asian population grew by 44 percent, while its share of fixed capital in the social sphere shrank from 39.3 to 34.3 percent.

14. "Mirovoi rynok khlopka," *Ekonomika i zhizn'*, no. 5, 1985, pp. 61–62.

15. *Vneshniaia torgovlia SSSR, 1978*, p. 28, *Vneshniaia torgovlia SSSR, 1980*, p. 28, *Vneshniaia torgovlia SSSR, 1983*, p. 28.

16. *Narodnoe khoziaistvo SSSR v 1978 godu*, p. 176; *Narodnoe khoziaistvo SSSR v 1983 godu*, p. 180.

17. *Narodnoe khoziaistvo SSSR v 1985 godu*, p. 146.

18. *Vneshniaia torgovlia SSSR, 1985*, p. 28.

19. E. Rakhimov, "Reshaiushchii faktor intensifikatsii khlopkoproizvodstva," *Kommunist Uzbekistana*, no. 9, 1983, p. 51.

20. *Narodnoe khoziaistvo SSSR v 1980 godu*, p. 232; *Narodnoe khoziaistvo SSSR v 1985 godu*, p. 210.

21. I analyze the causes of the cotton crisis with respect to Uzbekistan, the primary producer of cotton in Central Asia. Uzbekistan's share of both the population and fixed capital in Central Asia is about 60 percent.

22. *Narodnoe khoziaistvo SSSR v 1975 godu*, pp. 287, 367; *Narodnoe khoziaistvo SSSR v 1980 godu*, pp. 184, 232.

23. I. Iskanderov, "Ekonomika respubliki v ramkakh edinogo narodno-khoziaistvennogo kompkleksa strany," *Ekonomika i zhizn'*, no. 2, 1986, p. 9.

24. Rakhimov, "Reshaiushchii faktor," p. 51.

25. N. Khamraev and Zh. Bozorov, "Problemy razvitiia," p. 116.

26. Ibid.

27. Ibid., p. 117.

28. A. Ul'masov, "Burzhuaznye kontseptsii ekonomicheskogo razvitiia respublik Srednei Azii," *Ekonomicheskie nauki*, no. 3, 1985, p. 96.

29. *Literaturnaia gazeta*, Feb. 11, 1987, p. 12.

30. Ibid.

31. *Komsomol'skaia Pravda*, Apr. 1, 1988.

32. Among others, see the comments by Uzbek writer Muhammad Salih in *Yash leninchi*, Feb. 25, 1988 and Otkir Hashimov, "Avladlarga nima deymiz?" *Sharq yulduzi*, no. 2, 1988, p. 155.

33. *Literaturnaia gazeta,* Feb. 11, 1987, p. 12.
34. Of course, the fishing industry which once thrived in areas around the Aral is also dying, and climatic changes have also been observed. For a detailed discussion of the water crisis in Central Asia, see Philip P. Micklin, "The Water Management Crisis in Soviet Central Asia," Final Report to the National Council for Soviet and East European Research, June 1989.
35. *Yash leninchi,* Jan. 10, 1989.
36. *Pravda Vostoka,* Mar. 4, 1989.
37. *Yash leninchi,* Nov. 11, 1988.
38. *Pravda Vostoka,* June 11, 1989.
39. Otkir Hashimov, "Avladlarga nima deymiz?" p. 157.
40. *Trud,* Oct. 1, 1988.
41. *Izvestiia,* Oct. 6, 1988, translated in FBIS SOV 99-198, Oct. 13, 1988, p. 60.
42. *Yash leninchi,* Nov. 11, 1988.
43. *Narodnoe khoziaistvo SSSR v 1984 godu,* p. 195; *Narodnoe khoziaistvo Uzbekskoi SSR v 1984 godu,* p. 79.
44. N. Chumanova and M. Tadzhimuratov, "Sovershenstvovanie osnovnykh proportsii vosproizvodstva v Uzbekistane," *Kommunist Uzbekistana,* no. 8, 1983, p. 52.
45. *Narodnoe khoziaistvo SSSR v 1975 godu; Narodnoe khoziaistvo RSFSR v 1975 godu,* p. 110.
46. I. Iskanderov, "Eshche raz o vtoroi tekstil'noi baze strany," *Ekonomika i zhizn',* no. 3, 1966, p. 25.
47. K. Bedrintsev, "O nekotorykh regional'nykh problemakh Uzbekistana," *Ekonomika i zhizn',* no. 4, 1973, p. 12.
48. I. Iskanderov, "Eshche raz," 25.
49. I. Iskanderov, "Ekonomika respubliki," p. 9.
50. *Yash leninchi,* Jan. 1, 1990.
51. This argument was presented at a plenum of the board of the USSR Writers' Union. Salih's claim was subsequently rejected by an official of Uzbekistan's Environmental Protection Society who said that before the revolution a kilogram and a half of cotton could purchase only a kilogram of meat (*Sovet Ozbekistani,* Feb. 10, 1989).
52. See Otkir Hashimov's discussion in *Yash leninchi,* May 16, 1989.
53. *Pravda Vostoka,* Sept. 27, 1989.
54. *Pravda Vostoka,* Nov. 14, 1989.
55. *Yash leninchi,* Dec. 27, 1989.
56. According to one Tajik's calculation, the profit from grapes would be six to eight times more than that from cotton, and the profit from citrus fruits fifty to one hundred times more! (*Komsomolets Tadzhikistana,* Oct. 29, 1989).

PART TWO
Politics

4

Power and Politics in Soviet Uzbekistan: From Stalin to Gorbachev

Donald S. Carlisle

Introduction

Through the decades of Communist rule in Central Asia, one of the most critical factors relevant to the Party's hegemony there has been Moscow's ability to control the region's leadership. The power to mandate who would serve in what posts, and to remove those who no longer suited the center's needs was a key factor in Moscow's ability to dictate policy and to control its implementation.

Moscow did not exercise this power over personnel in the same way throughout all periods in Soviet Central Asia's history. Rather, there appear to have been general cycles or recurring patterns which are reminiscent of Toynbee's thesis about the "action/reaction" or "stimulus/response" syndrome in the life cycle of civilizations. In relations between Moscow and the region's republics, there appeared a similar "attack/retreat" pattern as the center tried to impose its policy priorities on a recalcitrant Muslim traditional society. Since the 1920s, there have been periodic direct assaults on the existing status quo (producing turmoil and upheaval) followed by the center's retreat and retrenchment as a new equilibrium took shape. The resulting accommodation registered Moscow's recognition of the need for some reconciliation in the wake of partial success, and sometimes in the face of abject failure.

This chapter begins with the late 1930s and draws attention to the "action/reaction" and "attack/retreat" patterns. It argues that these patterns are helpful in understanding the significance of recent events. The focus of this analysis is on Central Asia's largest republic, Uzbekistan. While the history of the "action/reaction" pattern there has its own distinguishing characteristics, analogous phenomena appear in other Central Asian republics.

The top echelon of Uzbekistan's native political elite will be examined and some attention given to the Slav/Russian component of the republic's ruling elite. Initially, a novel framework is proposed which treats the native leadership in terms of its geopolitical or regional components. The paradigm is based on a division of Uzbekistan into intra-republic regions or natural geopolitical subsets. The chapter adopts a generational (both chronological and political) approach to leadership politics, but one of its major arguments is that regionally-based and locally-oriented groups within the native elite must also be identified. A geopolitical approach provides perspective on major ignored cleavages within what has conventionally been viewed as a homogeneous "Uzbek" national elite.

This analysis also evaluates the changing interaction between Moscow and Uzbekistan, i.e., the "center" and the major republic at its Central Asian periphery, and gauges the impact of different leadership cohorts and their policies. It argues that the dramatic domestic upheaval after the 1983 death of Sharaf Rashidov, Uzbekistan's long-time first secretary, is best explained as a concerted effort by Moscow to impose its priorities and to re-establish tight control over the republic's internal politics. The post-Brezhnev leadership was confronted with a republic which had achieved quasi-independence and autonomy during Rashidov's reign. Consequently, it launched a purge and anti-corruption campaign which served as a pretext for the de-Rashidovization offensive and as cover for the re-centralization effort.

This was the deeper meaning and subliminal impulse behind the recent Moscow-instigated offensive. The long-secure elite of the Rashidov era was the main target. In this endeavor—as in previous similar enterprises—the center relied primarily on recently promoted native cadres to implement the disruptive policies. It also orchestrated the campaign from behind the scenes through a revamped and replenished local Slav/Russian contingent operating in tandem with new native personnel.

In this chapter the cycles of "attack/retreat" from 1938 to 1990 in Uzbekistan are treated by tracing the changing historical landscape and examining the rise and fall of leadership generations. The analysis begins in the wake of the 1937 Stalinist bloodbath after Akmal Ikramov (secretary of the Party from 1925) and Faizulla Khodzhaev (the chairman of the Sovnarkom since 1925) were suddenly removed, tried publicly in Moscow, and summarily executed in March 1938. It ends in 1990, when the region was still reverberating from events set in motion by the deaths of Brezhnev in November 1982 and of Sharaf Rashidov in October 1983 but with a new equilibrium at home in the making.

Special attention is given to this post-1983 phase of the "stimulus/ response" pattern, which began with an attack on the status quo both at the center and in Central Asia. The purge in the Uzbek SSR lasted for five years and overlapped with the innovations Gorbachev introduced into the Soviet political system. Many political reputations were destroyed, including that of Brezhnev's son-in-law, Churbanov, who was implicated in the "Uzbek Cotton Affair." He was tried, found guilty, and sentenced for taking bribes to cover up corruption.

As might have been anticipated, there has been a backlash from the Uzbek side and Moscow's assault has weakened rather than strengthened its capacity to control local events. In fact, the assault has had a boomerang effect, producing a "defensive nationalism" in Central Asia and crystallizing an Uzbek national identity that previously existed only subliminally, in a diffuse and non-threatening form.

By the late 1930s in Uzbekistan a stable configuration had emerged that I have labeled the "dual society" or the "two-tiered system." In the Stalinist era, the center's accommodation with traditional Muslim society—after vigorous efforts to transform it—lasted for a generation or more. The more recent assault on Uzbek society has once more been followed by the regime's retreat and retrenchment. This has brought unintended and unexpected consequences for Moscow. As in the 1930s, this assault is being followed by the establishment of a new—but increasingly unstable—equilibrium between the USSR's center and its Central Asian periphery.

A Regional Perspective on Uzbek Politics

From one angle, the tale we shall tell is that of a struggle between Stalinists and anti-Stalinists in Uzbekistan. In more recent times, since the 1983 death of Sharaf Rashidov, it is the story of a fierce contest between Rashidovists and anti-Rashidovists. It is an account of the making and breaking of political careers. Many factors and forces are involved and many variables combine to make up a reliable framework for making sense of these factional struggles within the Uzbek native "Power Elite."[1] In these pages we adopt the perspective of generational analysis. An individual may be considered part of a larger generational cohort whose members share a similar chronological and/or "political" age. The cohort is thus distinguished from groups that precede and follow it. Members of a political generation usually share common origins, characteristics, formative experiences, and career patterns. In addition to the generational perspective, we also employ a neglected but relevant analytical prism of regional loyalties and geographic power bases. In fact, when dealing with native politics, we contend the "Uzbek" nationality label may be less helpful than regional identity in shedding light on intra-elite squabbles. The latter should be broken down into subsets or geopolitical categories which appear to be directly relevant to the active political contestants.

We suggest reconceptualizing Uzbek political terrain by subdividing it into regional or geographic categories. Some of these regional divisions are more oriented toward Moscow and closely linked with all-Union development patterns than others. The major intra-republic regions are based on a paradigm combining history, general location, differential socioeconomic conditions, and varying cultural traditions. They have functioned along with—and sometimes in place of—an "Uzbek" identity and provide a regional framework for identifying loyalty superior to rather than subordinate to Republic structures. Political struggle would naturally be confined within and channeled through the formal administrative structures of the Uzbek SSR. Likewise, participants would show deference to an Uzbek identity. However, this might mask the regional realities, subliminal loyalties, and geographic-based patriotisms that are in fact operative in the political game.

While stressing regional politics in Uzbekistan, one cannot ignore the contrasts and perhaps conflicts between Uzbeks and non-Uzbeks or between Central Asians and non-Central Asians. The various cleavages must be taken into account. Nor must we ignore the important internal divisions within the Russian/Slavic community in Central Asia. It is clear that all Russian inhabitants cannot be viewed as foreigners and "outsiders." Some have lived in Central Asia for generations. Many—indeed most—of the non-native cadres are drawn from such an indigenous yet non-Muslim local community. They must be distinguished from Slavs who have been "imported" to fill some of the most important posts and who, after a short tour of duty, leave the Republic.[2]

The following regional breakdown is submitted as providing the most important regional divisions in native politics. It offers a geopolitical framework for delineating loyalties in competition with the overriding but formal Uzbek national identity. The basis for this regional paradigm (but by no means the only grounds justifying it) is the pattern by which official Soviet analysis often geographically subdivides Uzbekistan.[3] Provided here is the Map of Salient Regions (Fig. 4.1) as abstracted from Soviet sources. The key contention is that it can also be viewed as a "political map" providing perspectives on the regional loyalties and geographic power bases of Uzbek politicians.

The Tashkent Region and the Fergana Valley
("North-Eastern" and "Eastern" Uzbekistan)

Although both regions have had their share of anti-Soviet activities (Fergana was the seat of the Basmachi movement), these areas have

Figure 4.1. The regions of Uzbekistan. (1) North-Eastern, (2) Eastern, (3) Central, (4) Southern, (5) Northwestern. *Source: Uzbekistan* (otv. red., L. N. Babushkin) (Moscow: Mysl', 1967).

always been the primary focus of Moscow's attention and the source of its most loyal and devoted native cadres. As the major Russian/ Soviet center, Tashkent oblast, and especially the city of Tashkent itself, has ranked at the top of the center's list of priorities. Tashkent per se is far less important in the natives' conception of their history for, among other reasons, it does not conjure up memories of past glories. The Fergana Valley is the major cotton region of the USSR and its development as such since 1929 has been the prime impulse behind Soviet economic efforts in the republic. That ambitious and mobile natives from these areas have hitched themselves to the Soviet wagon is an important regularity surfacing throughout the history of Soviet Uzbekistan.

Samarkand/Bukhara

These are the regional centers of past glory where the indigenous cultural and religious tradition is most firmly rooted. As an economic region, both during tsarist rule and in much of the Soviet period, it was of secondary importance to Moscow. Bukhara in particular suffered neglect throughout the first decades of Soviet rule. Symbolically, the main thrust of Soviet policies was evident in the fact that, while Samarkand was the original capital of the Uzbek SSR, in 1930 that role was transferred to Tashkent.[4]

Northwest Territories

The Northwest Territories, where the Khorezm Khanate once existed and which today include Khorezm oblast, clearly constitute a separate region. One also finds here the Karakalpaks, whose distinctive character was officially recognized with the formation of a Karakalpak Autonomous Republic which now functions within the Uzbek SSR.

Southern Region

In Surkhandarya and Kashkadarya oblasts at Uzbekistan's southern border, we find a historically and economically distinct region. For centuries it was part of the Bukharan Khanate. The Southern Region in ethnic terms is largely but not entirely Uzbek. Its inhabitants have traditionally been nomadic and raised cattle. This region contains some of the economically least developed areas of the republic.

These divisions have been clearly operative in Uzbek native factional politics. Later in this chapter, the regional framework will be tested in analyzing the tactics and power base of the long-time Uzbek Party First Secretary Rashidov as well as his successors and predecessors.

A close look at political history provides insight into "the rules of the game" Moscow and its local representatives used in manipulating and mastering national and regional politics. It has been suggested that the original impulse leading Moscow in 1925 to create the national republics of Central Asia was the need to divide its opponents and to undermine the regional unity of the Islamic community. A "divide and rule" approach recommended the establishment of national republics like the Uzbek SSR. The Soviet regime's opponents viewed this move as Moscow's creation of phoney political units based on artificial nationalities in order to play local ethnic groups against each other *within* and *between* republics. Thus, personnel cliques and factions, viewed as intra-republic groups, might be manipulated by Moscow so as to divide and re-divide native leadership. On the other hand, if these regional factions should crystallize into an Uzbek *republic* elite, this would complicate if not threaten Moscow's control.[5]

Stalinism in the Uzbek SSR:
The Double-Tier or Dual-Society Solution

In Uzbekistan, as elsewhere, Stalinism involved more than the police-state and the "cult of the personality." It provided unprecedented upward mobility for those initially mobilized by the five-year plans who, after 1937, stepped into the posts vacated by the punished and purged. We could say of Stalin's enterprise, as Fainsod observed in *Smolensk Under Soviet Rule* of the Bolshevik Revolution, it "tapped fresh talent from the lower depths of society and harnessed it to the revolutionary chariot."

In Uzbekistan the First Five-Year Plan brought an assault on traditional classes and created new social clusters. The early victims were the Muslim version of Russia's kulaks—that is, the *bai, manap,* and *kishlak* notables generally. But the Soviet kolkhoz order spawned its own novel version of the village economic notables. A Soviet-oriented rural aristocracy was imposed on the traditional order. Rural state and Party *nachal'niki* (managers or bosses) replicated in a new guise the time-honored elites of an older authoritarian order. Soviet "water lords," who controlled the irrigation system, represented a modern version of an ancient profession and practice. The Muslim religious elite—the *mullah*s and *ishan*s—also had been attacked in the Soviet regime's assaults on Islam "from above." The state's policies in the sensitive areas of education and, especially, women's issues had mobilized the religious elements in opposition. In the face of overwhelming force, *mullah*s and *ishan*s beat a hasty retreat. Much of the religious elite was destroyed, but, as a social factor, it seems not to have been eradicated, nor were the values it championed eliminated.

By the mid-1930s, Stalin's regime was pursuing a "Great Retreat" which involved a general socioeconomic stabilization. In Central Asia, this allowed the remnant of the traditional elites, if not to surface, then at least to function surreptitiously and to reassert its authority among the Muslim masses. The *dekhkan*s (peasants) continued to practice the old ways while meeting the state's economic requirements, for which the most productive were amply rewarded by high cotton prices. The regime's policies represented a prudent and temperate response to intractable problems. Although Stalinism was extremely intemperate in the political sphere, it proved to be careful and conservative in the socioeconomic realm.

In the Central Asian variant of the Great Retreat, the powers-that-be had learned that the essential economic goals of increased cotton production and state crop procurement could be achieved without trampling on or directly attacking traditional Muslim society. There was no immediate pressing need to attack deep-seated native mores and customs.

Indeed, the effort to do so during the First Five-Year Plan had proved counterproductive in economic terms. Consequently, by 1938 a kind of *modus vivendi* with traditional Uzbek society crystallized. There was, of course, a continued effort to locate and educate ambitious and talented natives who seemed attuned to modern ways and who were intent on upward mobility. The regime also promoted women's liberation programs so as to provide recruits for the labor force and to develop female Party and state cadres. But by the late 1930s these objectives were pursued less provocatively and more indirectly than earlier.

The ideological campaigns and open challenges to local customs—so evident in the late 1920s and early 1930s—were now conspicuously absent. By 1938, something like a two-tiered approach or a mass "demobilization" strategy seems to have been adopted. The upper tier was largely identical with the modern urban sector where the "Europeans" held sway. The lower tier comprised the native traditional world where the Uzbeks predominated. The regime sought to keep the two tiers or sectors separate although in touch and this strategy entailed a postponement of the effort to draw them together or to make them equal. The Stalinist strategy was to accept the continued co-existence of traditional and modern society for the long term. The acceptance of a dual society with a semi-permeable wall separating and connecting the Central Asian and European worlds was the Stalinist response to the dilemmas earlier created by too rapid modernization and too ambitious native communists' objectives.[6]

While terminating the assault on traditional society and abandoning rapid modernization, the regime did not remain passive in all other spheres during the heyday of Stalinism. Indeed from 1938 on there was evidence of an accelerated tempo of Russianization and Russification. But these problems were confined largely to the upper tier of the double-tier Stalinist structure. They *directly* affected only those natives who entered the communist elite or sought entry to "upstairs," that is, to the upper tier or the modern urban world. Those "downstairs," so to speak, or outside the urban centers, were mainly free to go their own way so long as the regime's paramount production and procurement needs were met. Thus, under "mature" or "high" Stalinism, the state's direct demands became confined largely to the economic sphere. It was only "upstairs"—in the higher reaches of the political stratosphere—that Stalinism in Uzbekistan required the injection of substantial Russian ingredients into the new brew that Moscow was concocting.

The Stalinist Generation: "The Class of '38"

The ambitious Uzbek *nachal'nik*s who had undergone Russification served as an essential buffer between the old and the new worlds. They had been uprooted and mobilized in the earlier phase of direct attack on traditional society. In 1937–38, they came to power. They played the role of mediators between the two worlds, as well as serving routinely as the "transmission belts" in Stalin's imperial mechanism.

This group—the Class of '38—provided the basic raw material for the post-World War II political generation that ruled in Uzbekistan, and some of its members lasted even beyond Khrushchev's 1964 removal. The de-Stalinization process in the Uzbek SSR and resistance to it from some of its elite can be viewed in perspective when we consider from whence these Uzbek leaders came and how totally dependent on Stalinism they had become.

The key native figures in the republic leadership were Usman Iusupov (who in September 1937 succeeded Ikramov as first secretary of the Party) and Abdudzhabbar Abdurakhmanov (who in 1938 became chairman of the Sovnarkom). In 1938 Iusupov was 38 years old and Abdurakhmanov only 31. They remained in their posts until 1950 when they were transferred to Moscow. They belonged to a new generation of Uzbek Soviet men whose emergence marked a distinct break with their predecessors, the *jadid*s. As members of "the class of '38" they were the pioneering models of the Uzbek Stalinist mold.

Among younger Uzbeks who now came onto the political stage were the former understudies and sometimes recent discoveries of Iusupov and associates, who had cast them for stellar roles in the Stalinist script. Especially noteworthy as representative of this native type that benefitted from Soviet rule, and from Stalinist mobility, were Sabir Kamalov and Sirodzh Nurutdinov.

In Uzbekistan as elsewhere in 1937–1938, both the Party and Komsomol organizations were decimated. Those who survived soon replaced the former leading Party cadres. The case of Sabir Kamalov illustrates the rapid upward mobility created by the Purge for the young, still somewhat inexperienced Uzbek Komsomolists. He was born in 1910 in Tashkent into a family of workers. As a youth, until 1929, he was employed in construction. Kamalov joined the Komsomol in 1926 and by 1930 was a Komsomol *apparatchik* serving in New Bukhara (Kagan). He entered the Party in 1930, and later became Komsomol secretary for the Karakalpak *obkom*. In 1936, he studied Marxism-Leninism at Tashkent and was sent first to a *raikom* and then to the Margelan *gorkom* secretariat. By 1938, he had risen to second secretary of the Fergana *obkom*. In 1939, he was propelled even higher, to the senior post of People's Commissar for Agriculture, and became a deputy chairman of the Uzbek Council of People's Commissars. All this Kamalov had achieved by the age of 29![7]

Another important example of this new Stalinist species was Sirodzh Nurutdinov. His career was long lasting and illustrates the spectacular rise of the Komsomol cadres in the immediate pre-war period when native personnel were at a premium. Nurutdinov's appointment proved not to be a stopgap measure for, unlike some others who enjoyed an exhilarating rapid ride to the political summit and a subsequent sudden trip down, Nurutdinov's career spanned Stalinist and post-Stalinist political generations. He remained a viable political figure in Uzbekistan through the 1950s.

A native of Tashkent, Nurutdinov was born in 1911 and, compared with his political peers (many of whom were orphans), he had something of an uneventful and even advantaged childhood. Nurutdinov completed primary and middle school between 1922 and 1929. He was the harbinger of a new type of Uzbek politician; he was one of the first Uzbek leaders who experienced what was to become the typical career pattern of the future—not that of the uprooted peasant, but an upwardly mobile Uzbek urban worker. He worked in a Tashkent factory for four years, acquired some skills there, and entered the Komsomol in 1930. In 1931 he was drafted into the Soviet army and in 1935, upon demobilization, he returned to his former employment at the Tashkent factory and served as a semi-skilled worker.

In Nurutdinov's case, as with other members of the "class of '38," Stalin's purge was the crucial turning point in his career. During 1937, as an aspiring *apparatchik*, he was named first secretary of the Tashkent Komsomol *gorkom*, and in 1938 he was transferred to the comparable *obkom* post. In 1938, he also entered the Party. Nurutdinov then was sent to Moscow to study at an industrial academy. On his return in 1941, the young apparatchik was named head of the Industrial and Trade Department of the Tashkent *obkom*. During World War II he again served in the Soviet army and was a key figure in the creation of Uzbek military units. He himself fought on the Stalingrad front. After demobilization, he was named a secretary of the Tashkent *obkom* and, in 1947, became its first secretary. This second wave in his career crested in 1949 when he became a member of the Uzbek Buro and was confirmed as a secretary of the Central Committee. He remained a viable figure and navigated through the shoals of early de-Stalinization.

The career of Amin Niiazov, who eventually became first secretary of the Uzbek Communist Party (1950–55), displays a slightly different pattern. Although not fully a member of the class of 1938 (having been born in 1903), Niiazov must have recommended himself to a regime desperately in need of those with links to the Uzbek masses and with some training and previous experience in running the state. In addition, his early army and Cheka credentials perhaps helped him to survive and to prosper when so many of his compatriots fell by the wayside. During 1939-40 Niiazov rose to visibility but not yet to prominence. For the latter outcome he had to await the 1950 exit to Moscow of Iusupov and Abdurakhmanov.

Mature Stalinism in Uzbekistan:
The Post-War Years

Like generational analysis, the geopolitical or regional paradigm provides perspective on leadership patterns and elite politics. During late or "mature Stalinism," the Tashkent/Fergana area was the principle source of native cadres. Not only was economic development—particularly cotton production and procurement—in these areas pushed, but the core contingent of the republic Buro and Secretariat was usually recruited from this Tashkent/Fergana axis. Samarkand, Bukhara, and other areas were relegated to secondary significance and their cadres largely excluded from top leadership positions.

The leaders who emerged at the political heights after 1937—the Iusupov clique, the "class of '38"and those who climbed to within sight of the summit, the Komsomol cadres—provided the personnel pool from which native leaders were drawn during the heyday Stalinism. As noted, the two most prominent native figures throughout this period were Usman Iusupov and Abdudzhabbar Abdurakhmanov, who were born in the Fergana Valley and Tashkent respectively. They were joined by Amin Niiazov and a few members of the pre-Purge political generation who had survived the bloodletting. Niiazov entered the Buro in 1946 and was appointed chairman of the Supreme Soviet in March 1947. Iusupov and Abdurakhmanov's transfer to Moscow in April 1950 triggered a game of political musical chairs that unfolded in several stages and in unexpected fashion over the next ten years.

The initially tame transition was accelerated and complicated by events which took place outside of the republic in Moscow. First came the death of Stalin in March 1953, which opened the succession struggle, the rise of Khrushchev, and his 1956 de-Stalinization campaign. The major ramifications in Uzbekistan were the meteoric rise (and equally sudden fall) of N. A. Mukhitdinov, the unexpected emergence of Sharaf Rashidov, and the latter's appointment in 1959 as first secretary.

With the 1950 promotion of Iusupov and Abdurakhmanov to Moscow, the two major native-held posts in Uzbekistan became open. In April, Niiazov stepped into Iusupov's role as the premier native apparatchik. Initially, A. Mavlianov became chairman of the Council of Ministers. Rashidov, who in 1949-50 was the chairman of the Writer's Union, then was named to Niiazov's former position as chairman of the Supreme

Soviet.[8] Niiazov and Mavlianov's appointments brought to power Uzbek politicians with largely the same profile as the Iusupov/Abdurakhmanov generation, but Rashidov's appearance signalled the emergence of a younger Uzbek type with weaker political credentials than his predecessor.

However, the most important career in the making during the late Stalin period was that of Mukhitdinov. He and Rashidov were born in 1917; this made them almost twenty years younger than the elder Uzbek Stalinists like Iusupov and nearly ten years younger than Kamalov and his ilk. Rashidov had joined the Party in 1939 and Mukhitdinov entered in 1942.[9] Both had taken the first major step in their careers either late in the war period (Rashidov) or after the war ended (Mukhitdinov). The authentic younger Stalinists like Sabir Kamalov and Sirodzh Nurutdinov were their seniors in length of Party membership and practical experience and had better *apparatchik* credentials and stronger claims to leading Party positions. Mukhitdinov began to climb the political ladder in 1947 as secretary for propaganda and agitation in the Namangan *obkom*. When his superior, A. Alimov, was promoted in October 1948, Mukhitdinov became first secretary of the *obkom*. His promotion to the republic Central Committee secretariat in 1950 (during the post-Iusupov transition) was his major political leap forward and shortly after, in September 1950, he became Tashkent oblast first secretary.

Rashidov's post-war career was politically less promising. He was transferred from the Samarkand organization (where by February 1945 he was cadres secretary) to a more visible but less politically potent post as editor of the republic's main Uzbek-language newspaper. Then, in July 1949, he became chairman of the Writers' Union, a sensitive post with responsibilities for the literary intelligentsia but certainly not a position portending future Party prominence.[10]

With the Abdurakhmanov and Iusupov 1950 transfers, Mavlianov and Niiazov stepped into the top government and Party positions. In August 1950, Rashidov was appointed to Niiazov's former position as Chief of State.[11] It was an appointment to a less powerful post, but it was nonetheless a promotion.

However, it was Mukhitdinov whose career displayed extraordinary promise. The two posts in which he had served within a matter of months during 1950—Central Committee secretary and then Tashkent Party kingpin—were crucial power bases. In 1951, he moved into the state apparatus for the first time. Mavlianov's tenure as chairman of the Council of Ministers proved shortlived. In April 1951, Mavlianov was replaced by Mukhitdinov.[12] Thus it was Niiazov, Mukhitdinov, and Rashidov who constituted the leading Party, government, and state trio in the last years of the Stalin era.

The Rise of Mukhitdinov

Stalin's death ushered in a period of political turmoil in Moscow from which Khrushchev emerged in 1954–55 as the leading if not yet the dominant figure. There were parallel processes at work in Uzbekistan. After Stalin's death, Iusupov returned to Tashkent. What position would he acquire or take? He opted for the government rather than the Party sphere, for in April 1953 he re-entered the Uzbek Communist Party Buro and became chairman of the Council of Ministers. Mukhitdinov had to be demoted and consequently was named first deputy minister. In 1953, Niiazov remained first secretary and Rashidov retained the largely ceremonial role of chairman of the Supreme Soviet—a post apparently of little appeal to ambitious Uzbek politicians. But Khrushchev's successful power drive soon changed things in Uzbekistan. Iusupov was the first major casualty. In November 1954, he was removed and his political career was abruptly brought to a close. Mukhitdinov replaced him and again became chairman of the Council of Ministers.[13]

What was clear at the center was soon reflected in the republics; the campaign for Party revival undertaken by Khrushchev breathed new life into the Party Secretariat, which in Stalin's last years had atrophied. As of 1955, the top Party post in Uzbekistan was still held by Niiazov, a holdover from the Iusupov era. This anomaly was not to persist for long. On his return in December 1955 from his Asian tour with Bulganin, Khrushchev stopped in Tashkent and there presided over a major power transfer. He had Niiazov removed and Mukhitdinov named the first secretary. Clearly Khrushchev had taken Mukhitdinov under his wing and a patron-client relationship became apparent. In February 1956, Mukhitdinov's rapid rise was certified by his being chosen a candidate member of the Presidium of the CPSU itself. Two years later, he was to be elevated to an even more important post at the political summit when he was named to the CPSU Secretariat and transferred to Moscow.

One must pause to reflect on Mukhitdinov's unprecedented appointments. No Central Asian politician in Soviet history had achieved anything comparable. While membership in the Party's Central Committee was commonplace for the republic Party leaders beginning with Ikramov, no Central Asian had previously achieved Politburo/Presidium status. True, in 1950 Iusupov had been named USSR Minister for Cotton, but admission to the Party's inner sanctum had been closed to Soviet Muslims. Even more startling than Mukhitdinov's entering the Presidium was his appointment as a CPSU secretary. Indeed, there is hardly any comparable case of such rapid mobility from the republic level to the center during the Khrushchev years. Mukhitdinov owed it all to Khrushchev and he became the latter's unvarnished supporter and his wholly dependent political client.

Mukhitdinov now emerged as the major Soviet Asian spokesman for Khrushchev's campaign to woo the Third World. He was given major political and diplomatic responsibilities and he travelled abroad for his mentor while simultaneously seeking to transform the Uzbek political scene. However, Mukhitdinov had too little time during his tenure as first secretary to remove rivals and promote supporters before proceeding to his more pressing and time consuming duties in Moscow. Consequently, his control in Uzbekistan was not fully consolidated.

Mukhitdinov's rivals remained in powerful positions and they included Stalinists of "the class of '38." Some, such as Nurutdinov, remained firmly entrenched in key Party posts and had solid career credentials and a claim to political prominence that pre-dated Mukhitdinov's. Indeed, three key figures of this Stalinist cohort rose to important positions or held onto key posts during Mukhitdinov's tenure in office as first secretary. They were Nurutdinov, Sabir Kamalov, and M. Mirza-Akhmedov.

Kamalov became chairman of the Council of Ministers when Mukhitdinov was named first secretary in 1955. He was a full member of the Uzbek Buro and could boast of a long career before 1938 as a Komsomol *apparatchik* and in numerous strategic Party posts. He was Mukhitdinov's main rival and the major local politician disadvantaged and pushed aside during his rise to prominence. Similarly disadvantaged by Mukhitdinov's emergence—and equally senior on all counts to him in Party service and experience—was Nurutdinov who by the mid-1950s controlled the Tashkent Party. He joined Kamalov on the Buro. Another rival of Mukhitdinov with equally superb Stalinist credentials and close ties to Iusupov was Mirza-Akhmedov. He was to follow Kamalov as chairman of the Council of Ministers when he succeeded Mukhitdinov as first secretary.

This is by no means the full cast of characters who had a vested interest in preserving the Stalinist era intact. Among Mukhitdinov's other rivals was Ia. Nasriddinova, who was married to Nurutdinov and who must have identified with his political friends and opposed his foes.[14]

Two other Uzbeks stand out as Mukhitdinov's allies in the political in-fighting. A. Alimov had been his political superior in Namangan and their subsequent rise and fall in unison is noteworthy. Rashidov was also a beneficiary of Mukhitdinov's efforts to orchestrate the removal of the Stalinist clique led by Kamalov. But Rashidov was not as directly dependent on Mukhitdinov for he had acquired the post of chairman of the Supreme Soviet *before* Mukhitdinov's rise and independently of his patronage. Because Rashidov's post was largely ceremonial and not as politically potent as other positions, it proved unattractive to ambitious Uzbek politicians. Consequently, Rashidov remained somewhat in the background and was not directly drawn into the vortex of the vicious political struggles that now unfolded. Nonetheless, in the end he emerged as *the* major beneficiary of the battle between Stalinists and anti-Stalinists in the Uzbek SSR.

De-Stalinization and Uzbek Politics

Mukhitdinov's effort to reconstruct the local leadership continued after his transfer to Moscow. Indeed, his service there seemed to give him more chips to play in the game and additional assets on which to call. The major planks of his strategy were pronouncements on nationality policy, accentuated "indigenization" or nativization of cadres, and embracing de-Stalinization. His particular tactic before and after his transfer to Moscow was managing de-Stalinization so as to undermine the local Stalinists of the Iusupov era. This resulted in the rehabilitation of the Uzbek leaders murdered in 1937–38, especially the former first secretary, Akmal Ikramov, who, along with fellow Uzbek Faizulla Khodzhaev, had been a defendant at the 1938 Moscow Show Trial.[15] Several native politicians still in power during the 1950s were directly or indirectly implicated in these events.

Iusupov, who was removed in 1954, was the main culprit in the Ikramov affair; but Abdurakhmanov (who had returned to the Uzbek SSR and been named chairman of the state planning committee) was a beneficiary of Faizulla Khodzhaev's fall and the 1937–38 bloodletting. Kamalov, Nurutdinov and Mirza-Akhmedov, as well as others in power, could also be implicated. Mukhitdinov launched the main salvo on the de-Stalinization front in October 1956 at the First Congress of the Uzbek Intelligentsia, and he was to hammer away at the theme in the years that followed.[16] Nonetheless, while Ikramov and others were soon rehabilitated, no local politicians were immediately removed.

In fact, Stalinists like Kamalov did not fall, but steadily rose. Kamalov became chairman of the Council of Ministers when Mukhitdinov took over in December 1955 as first secretary and he was then named first secretary in December 1957 when Mukhitdinov was promoted to the CPSU Secretariat and moved to Moscow. Then, in March 1959, he was abruptly removed without any warning and with no explanation. Others of his clique also quickly fell. Mirza-Akhmedov was replaced within several days. Soon Nurutdinov lost his Party post and was transferred to head the republic's trade union organization. Somewhat later, a short notice in the press announced that, because of health problems, Abdurakhmanov had asked to be relieved as minister.[17]

The 1959 purge brought Mukhitdinov's close associate Alimov to the post of chairman of the Council of Ministers. Rashidov was appointed first secretary in March.[18] Into Rashidov's vacated post as chief of state came Nasriddinova. She held this position for ten years and was to be removed in the wake of a major local scandal. Alimov's close ties to Mukhitdinov were confirmed by his fate. When in October 1961 Mukhitdinov was unexpectedly deposed, losing both the Secretarial post and his Presidium seat, Alimov also disappeared.[19] Rashidov's relation to him must have been less intimate, for Mukhitdinov's fall did not implicate him. In fact, Rashidov stepped into Mukhitdinov's seat, though as a candidate rather than a full member of the CPSU Presidium.

Rashidov as First Secretary

A striking feature of Rashidov's rise is the circuitous fashion in which he seemed to back into the post of first secretary. As one looks at his path to this post, it is noteworthy that two of the four individuals who served as first secretary in the 1950s had been chairman of the Supreme Soviet just prior to their appointment. Our understanding of Soviet politics generally would not have led us to expect this outcome. Chief of State had been considered a largely meaningless post, certainly not a launching pad for a major career. Yet two of the Uzbek first secretaries (Niiazov and Rashidov) did make such a career transition. Indeed, in 1983, this pattern would recur, for at the death of Rashidov, his successor—Inamzhon Usmankhodzhaev—also held the post of chairman of the Supreme Soviet immediately prior to his Party appointment.

The explanation for the Niiazov and Rashidov appointments may be rather simple and obvious. It is likely that in both instances the key figures leaving the post or orchestrating the power transition wanted weak successors who could be counted on to be subservient to their will. Iusupov preferred a Niiazov rather than a more potent political personality in the post. Mukhitdinov probably viewed Rashidov in the same light—not as a dangerous politician who might become a rival but as a figure with little or no local power base, an undistinguished past, and no chance for an independent political future. He was, of course, mistaken. Rashidov was to serve as first secretary for a much longer period than any of his predecessors.

The all-Union and republic Party congresses in autumn 1961 capped a very hectic and confused period in the life of Uzbekistan's Communist Party and Rashidov was reappointed first secretary in September. At the CPSU's Congress in October he was again elected to the Central Committee. With Mukhitdinov's unexpected and still unexplained ejection from the Secretariat, he also lost his seat on the Party's Presidium. In a major promotion, Rashidov was chosen a candidate member of the newly-constituted Presidium. He had benefited from Mukhitdinov's anti-Stalinist campaign and now he harvested the fruits of his predecessor's earlier efforts. But these prior events also had a negative fallout. Deep enmity must have been created between Rashidov and Ia. Nasriddinova, his successor as chairman of the Presidium of Uzbekistan's Supreme Soviet. Her husband, Nurutdinov, had been a prime casualty of Mukhitdinov's campaign from which Rashidov had profited more than any other politician. Their antagonistic relationship was to surface later during the 1969 Pakhtakor Affair. Khrushchev's continuing de-Stalinization campaign entered a new phase at the October 1961 Congress, and Rashidov had the opportunity finally to settle the score with his predecessor, Sabir Kamalov. For a brief time Kamalov had served as head of Fergana's *oblispolkom;* however, in January 1962, he lost this position and disappeared.

While Rashidov was now the most prominent Uzbek politician, he was by no means completely dominant. Besides Nasriddinova, his opponents and enemies with republic Party Buro status included Rakhmankul Kurbanov, chairman of the Council of Ministers,[20] and the young yet experienced secretary of the Tashkent *gorkom,* Kayum Murtazaev. His major allies were N. D. Khudaiberdyev,[21] K. Kamalov, N. Matchanov, N. Makhmudov, and perhaps also M. M. Musakhanov. Later they were joined by A. A. Khodzhaev, who was rising steadily in the 1970s.

Let us return at this juncture to the relevance of the regional paradigm outlined at the start of this study. Since 1937, Tashkent/Fergana personnel had dominated leadership positions. The victory of Rashidov radically changed that pattern. Now central and western Uzbekistan became the main source of leading cadres. Samarkand and formerly peripheral locales—in contrast to Tashkent—typically provided the personnel pool for Rashidov and his allies. The Rashidov contingent's emergence marked a shift in the geopolitical center of gravity in Uzbekistan.

De-de-Stalinization

The virtually complete subordination of the periphery (Central Asia) to the center (Moscow) was clear from at least 1938, yet Uzbekistan's politicians proved adept at manipulating issues raised at the center to their advantage locally. Mukhitdinov rode the de-Stalinization process to short-lived prominence in Moscow itself. Subsequently, Rashidov played the end of de-Stalinization to his advantage and used the fall of Mukhitdinov and Khrushchev to consolidate his position locally.

De-Stalinization had been a weapon used by Khrushchev for his political purposes and it had been picked up and wielded effectively locally by Mukhitdinov. The period after the Twenty-Second CPSU Congress was especially replete with rehabilitations and revelations about the worst excesses of the Stalin years. There was an Uzbek version of these rehabilitations and revelations. In 1962, the first official history of the Communist Party of Uzbekistan was published. It addressed these issues and listed many of the key Uzbek leaders killed in 1937–38. Of course, the rehabilitated Ikramov loomed large in the story as hero and victim and Usman Iusupov was for the first time singled out in an authoritative source as the main native culprit in the bloodletting.[22]

The removal of Khrushchev in October 1964 undercut, if it did not fully stop, de-Stalinization. What might be labelled "De-de-Stalinization" began to pursue its own special twists and turns in Uzbekistan. The most striking developments came to a focus on Faizulla Khodzhaev, the leading Uzbek state figure between 1925 and 1937. Following his arrest, Khodzhaev had been a principal co-defendant with Akmal Ikramov at the infamous 1938 Moscow show trial that featured Bukharin. Khodzhaev had not been among those rehabilitated after 1956. By 1962 Ikramov was a political hero but Khodzhaev remained (though no longer an "enemy of the people") what the new Party history termed a "factionalist" and "anti-Party" figure. A strange episode in 1964 suggested that he, too, had been on the way to rehabilitation but that Khrushchev's fall had sidetracked the process.[23]

There are indications of a struggle behind the scenes with regard to Khodzhaev's rehabilitation. Suddenly in 1966, short biographies marking the seventieth anniversary of Faizulla Khodzhaev's birth appeared in *Izvestiia* and *Pravda Vostoka*. The debate and struggle was ended and at last he, like Ikramov, was to be rehabilitated. In the following three years, numerous articles appeared in which Khodzhaev was restored to his legitimate place in Uzbek and in Bukharan history.

But in juxtaposition to the rehabilitation of Ikramov and Khodzhaev, the most extraordinary 1966 turn of events was the return to respectability of some of the Stalinists disgraced during Mukhitdinov's reign. That year brought a devastating earthquake to the Uzbek SSR but it also brought a political earthquake—the paradoxical rehabilitation of both the victims of Stalinism and the casualties of de-Stalinization. The treatment of Usman Iusupov at his death in May 1966 was clearly the turning point. Not only was his death marked by a prominent and laudatory obituary, but he was also posthumously honored by the Great Fergana Canal being named for him.[24] The irony was evident (and the message clear), since the Canal had borne Stalin's name until the 1950s. Apparently Stalin could not be rehabilitated but the Uzbek Stalinists could. The treatment of others whose Stalinist past had brought disgrace or obscurity confirmed that in Uzbekistan a novel amalgam of continued de-Stalinization and "De-de-Stalinization" was in effect. Nurutdinov also died in 1966, and he was given positive treatment similar to Iusupov. Meanwhile, without publicity, Abdurakhmanov—the major Stalinist still alive—received a ministerial post. The process of clearing and revarnishing the reputations of Uzbek Stalinists culminated in lavish praise of Abdurakhmanov when he died in 1975.

The motives behind this dual rehabilitation process remain obscure. We can speculate that a judgment was made that, even after the repudiation of Khrushchev, the future loyalty of the Central Asians would be better secured if they were given native Communists like Khodzhaev and Ikramov as heroes. Perhaps Iusupov and other Stalinists were promoted as heroes because Soviet Uzbek history had to be presented as a seamless web—as one continuous stream of success. The fundamental break marked by the bloodletting of 1937-38 had to be ignored or papered-over. The image of Faizulla Khodzhaev and Akmal Ikramov as loyal Leninists filled the need for past communist heroes—pre-1937 native figures that the native intelligentsia could look to with pride. Whether the local communist elite lobbied for Khodzhaev's rehabilitation, we do not know. However, it makes good sense to assume that Sharaf Rashidov would embrace Iusupov's cause as well as Khodzhaev's, which would help re-establish a seamless web of communist lineage and loyalty reaching back to the Revolution.

The "Pakhtakor Incident":
The Fall of Nasriddinova and Kurbanov

The role of independent, regionally based political machines appeared in the conflict between the Rashidov/Khudaiberdyev faction and the Tashkent/Fergana clique led by Nasriddinova and Kurbanov. The vicious struggle began in 1959 and surfaced with a vengeance in 1969. The curtain that hid the unsavory details of political machinations within the top-level republic Party elite was rarely raised during the Rashidov years. However, we are fortunate to have some emigré revelations, including details from an official who had served in Uzbekistan which confirm the bitter Rashidov-Nasriddinova conflict.[25] They also unveil nefarious dealings within the native elite, which culminated in Rashidov's victory over his long-time enemies in the republic Party Buro.

The events that brought Kurbanov's downfall, and Nasriddinova's removal and her transfer to Moscow, began with the so-called "Pakhtakor Incident" of 1969. This extraordinary and still unclarified incident brought the only known anti-Russian mass demonstration in Uzbekistan in more than a generation.[26] The 1969 native riot which followed a soccer match at Pakhtakor Stadium in Tashkent shocked the Uzbek elite and eventually brought Moscow's direct intervention in the republic's politics. In the course of the investigation, many unsavory details about the native elite surfaced. The subsequent major scandal came to focus on Kurbanov and his illegal activities. We are told that he (and others) were tried and found guilty; Kurbanov was sentenced to ten years in prison.

The main political consequence was Rashidov's consolidation of power following Kurbanov's ejection from his post and Nasriddinova's removal and transfer to Moscow. For a time she served there as chairman of the Nationalities Chamber of the USSR Supreme Soviet. Rashidov's close allies now moved into the vacated posts. N. D. Khudaiberdyev became chairman of the Council of Ministers; a Party official long linked to Rashidov, N. Matchanov, took over Nasriddinova's former role as chairman of the Presidium of Uzbekistan's Supreme Soviet.[27] Thus, by 1971, Rashidov and allies held the three key native positions in the leadership and it was only at this point that we can legitimately argue that he became the completely dominant Uzbek political figure. The Buro appointments announced at the 1971 and 1976 Congresses reflect this.

As to our geopolitical or regionally-based framework, one can say that now the Tashkent/Fergana cadre pool was relegated to a secondary role as a recruitment base for personnel, while those from what had been considered peripheral regions were promoted and brought to center stage.

End of the Rashidov Era:
The Emergence of I. B. Usmankhodzhaev

Evidence began to emerge during the 1970s that Rashidov was either grooming a successor or at least that a deputy in native Party affairs was emerging with all the necessary credentials to succeed him as first secretary. This individual was Asadilla A. Khodzhaev.[28] A turn of events in late 1978 suggested that some contrary political design had been set in motion and one perhaps not to Rashidov's liking. In December, Matchanov suddenly resigned "because of health." His replacement as chairman of the Supreme Soviet, Inamzhon B. Usmankhodzhaev, was an "outsider" to the republic's central elite in two ways. A native of Fergana, his background was in sharp contrast to that of the clique that had prospered under Rashidov's patronage.[29] Individuals from the Tashkent/Fergana regional axis were less prominent during Rashidov's reign. Not since the Kamalov/Nurutdinov (and Kurbanov) cadres had been displaced had a politician with roots in the Tashkent/Fergana region held the spotlight. Furthermore, I. B. Usmankhodzhaev was an oblast politician with no central Secretariat service in Uzbekistan to his credit. However, this promotion, his first appearance in the central republic power structure was to the least politically potent post. Therefore, aspiring Uzbek figures such as A. A. Khodzhaev or N. D. Khudaiberdyev seemed to have little to fear.

There were, however, two aspects of Usmankhodzhaev's career that might have prepared us for his surprise appointment in November 1983 as first secretary after Rashidov suddenly died. First, the post of chairman of the Supreme Soviet had indeed been held by first secretaries immediately prior to appointment to the leading Party position. Second, Usmankhodzhaev had served in Moscow between 1969 and 1972 as an instructor in the all-Union Party Secretariat. This service must have recommended him to those at the center and their local representatives who had special objectives in mind. Thus, his centrally-oriented credentials were in order; his family lineage also was superb, for he was the son of a leading Stalinist era official who for years was a political luminary in the Fergana Valley.[30]

If Russian patronage and central backing shed light on Usmankhodzhaev's unexpected promotion, other factors explain why he, rather than a more strategically-placed and locally prominent Uzbek was eventually chosen to succeed Rashidov. Most important was the mounting campaign to root out corruption launched by the Andropov regime upon Brezhnev's death. Despite the evidence of widespread corruption in Uzbekistan, the republic in 1982–83 remained immune to the "rooting out" and its leadership had remained untouched. This logjam was broken by the death of A. A. Khodzhaev in September 1983 and Rashidov's own demise several weeks later.[31] Subsequently, Usmankhodzhaev, with authoritative prompting from Moscow, unleashed a spectacular attack on local corruption and a wholesale purge of the republic's political elite. The main casualties were the leading figures of the Rashidov era.

Applying the regional paradigm, let us consider the turn of events soon after Rashidov died on October 31, 1983. The campaign unleashed against corruption struck the peripheral oblasts and outlying regions especially hard. It is certainly not by accident that the Dzhizak oblast, Rashidov's birth-place, home base, and favored fiefdom, was early singled out for special attack.[32] Similarly, the regional power bases of the political luminaries associated with Rashidov's reign were cleaned out, especially just prior to or in the wake of the June 1984 Plenum of the republic Central Committee. The tremors that followed that political earthquake continued to rock the republic throughout the 1980s. Many political heads rolled, the most prominent among them Musakhanov, Khudaiberdyev, and A. R. Khodzhaev—a long-time leading figure in the state administration.

What of those local politicians who at first survived the political earthquake and emerged to lead the native elite? As a result of the 1984–85 purge, the two figures who co-ruled with I. B. Usmankhodzhaev shared some common features of his political profile. His successor as chairman of the Supreme Soviet was A. U. Salimov, previously a Central

Committee secretary. Early in his career, Salimov attended Tashkent's Polytechnic Institute; he later taught there and eventually became pro-rector. Not coincidentally, this institute is where Usmankhodzhaev was educated. The new chairman of the Council of Ministers, G. Kh. Khaidarov also graduated from the Tashkent Polytechnic Institute.[33] It is of some additional interest that Anisimkin, then the senior Russian member of the Secretariat, had long been the director of the Chirchik Hydroelectric Complex. Located in the vicinity of Tashkent, this enterprise was where Khaidarov's whole work experience, as well as his administrative and Party career, unfolded before he was named in 1981 Head of the Heavy Industrial Department of the Party Secretariat. The ascendancy of Usmankhodzhaev, Salimov and Khaidarov (supported by Anisimkin and Second Secretary T. N. Osetrov) marked the return of the Tashkent/Fergana cadres to supremacy within the republic's elite.[34] It also strengthened Moscow's hold locally for it brought to power young, well educated and technically trained natives who were beholden to the center, linked career-wise to all-Union development priorities, and oriented principally toward Moscow.

The Anti-Corruption Campaign and De-Rashidovization

The status quo established in the wake of Rashidov's demise proved tenuous and temporary. Under pressure from Moscow, a widespread purge was launched to reassert control from the center. It took the form of an anti-corruption campaign that reached out to embrace various sectors of Uzbekistan's life. The watershed event proved to be the Sixteenth Plenum of the republic Party organization in June 1984. In its aftermath, the dismantling of the Party/state elite of the Rashidov era unfolded with a vengeance. By January 1985, 40 of the 65 oblast Party secretaries had been removed. The most salient statistic registering the purge's impact was the removal of ten of the thirteen *obkom* first secretaries (overwhelmingly Uzbeks). In addition, 260 city and raion secretaries were replaced. One-third of the chairmen of the oblast executive committees and their deputies and the chairmen of city and raion executive committees were removed in this period. Ninety new officials were also brought into the top echelon of the republic ministries and state apparatus. Late in 1985, a major kingpin of the Rashidov era fell as the long-time chairman of the Council of Ministers, N. D. Khudaiberdyev, was removed from office. Then, in January 1986, on the eve of the Party Congress, M. M. Musakhanov—the Tashkent *obkom*'s first secretary since 1969—"retired." A. R. Khodzhaev, a long-time fixture in the government, was publicly censured and removed.

The most sensational bombshell exploded at Uzbekistan's Party congress in January 1986. There Sharaf Rashidov was viciously attacked and singled out as the main culprit responsible for the amoral atmosphere and the systemic corruption uncovered. The main role in pillorying Rashidov fell to his successor Usmankhodzhaev. One surmises that the latter had been reluctant to personalize the anti-corruption campaign with a specific attack on his former boss. He had served with Rashidov on the republic Party Buro since 1978 and could not remain untarnished and plead total ignorance once Rashidov came under close scrutiny. Nevertheless, Usmankhodzhaev triggered the anti-Rashidov campaign from the rostrum at the Congress while seeking to minimize his own responsibility.[35]

The effect of the ongoing purge was evident in the make-up of the leading Party organs, announced at the conclusion of the 1986 Congress. Of the 177 full members of the 1981 Central Committee, only 34 were re-elected. The toll was even greater among the 85 originally elected as candidate members in 1981, for only 9 were retained. Consider also the reconstituted Buro, the Secretariat, and the latter's department heads: Of the 1981 Buro's full members, only two remained (I. B. Usmankhodzhaev and A. U. Salimov). All of the previous Buro's candidate members disappeared.[36] There had also been almost a clean sweep of the Secretariat and its respective departments. This was especially evident where a native had held the post.[37] In sum, a political tidal wave had swept away most of the elite's top echelon.

Yet another wave was subsequently to engulf even some who presided at the Congress. Within a year's time, the leading female politician, R. Abdullaeva—the Party secretary in charge of ideology and cultural affairs—was removed. Also startling was the fall of Chairman of the Supreme Soviet A. U. Salimov, who was a close ally of Usmankhodzhaev.[38] (Salimov had held the Supreme Soviet post since Usmankhodzhaev relinquished it upon appointment as Rashidov's successor.)

The most interesting new figure was Rafik Nishanov, who suddenly appeared and stepped into Salimov's vacated post as chairman of the Supreme Soviet, or Head of State.[39] This startling and unexpected development was nevertheless very much in tune with the ongoing anti-Rashidov offensive, for Nishanov was no novice but a veteran Uzbek politician who had been disgraced during Rashidov's climb to power.[40] His reappearance in Uzbekistan in this highly visible post provided impetus for the anti-Rashidov campaign which some, especially Usmankhodzhaev, would have preferred to see subside. Usmankhodzhaev had been reluctant to personalize the anti-corruption campaign by making Rashidov its main villain; Nishanov suffered from no such qualms. Indeed, he seemed to relish the opportunity to demolish the "Rashidov myth." In his first major address—the Lenin Anniversary speech—he vigorously and viciously attacked Rashidov.[41]

As Head of State Nishanov occupied the post which Niiazov, Rashidov and Usmankhodzhaev had held prior to their appointments as first secretary. By 1988, Usmankhodzhaev was the last major figure of the Rashidov era remaining in a high position. His future seemed dim with Nishanov positioned to replace him and in January he was removed. Nishanov was appointed first secretary. Subsequently Usmankhodzhaev was charged with corruption, tried, and found guilty.

A number of "Tashkenters" previously shunted aside during Rashidov's reign now re-emerged. Nishanov was not the only political casualty to reappear—Rasul Guliamov, Arif Alimov, and even Nurutdin Mukhitdinov also resurfaced publicly.[42] After his 1961 fall, Mukhitdinov had been posted to diplomatic work in Syria where he served for a considerable period. After 1969, Nishanov, too, had been politically exiled, also serving in the Middle East as the Soviet representative in Lebanon. Now Nishanov was raised to Head of State and leader of the Party, while Mukhitdinov had to settle for a much less potent post in his return to grace.[43] Alimov also had been resurrected and served as Minister of Fruit and Fruit Produce Industries. A precedent can be found in the protection and return of Rashidov's defeated opponent, Sabir Kamalov. He not only outlived Rashidov but occupied a series of minor posts in Uzbekistan during the Brezhnev era.[44] Who protected Kamalov during the Rashidov years remains an unanswered question.

Exit Rafik Nishanov; Enter Islam Karimov

Salient evidence of the effort to sweep away local politicians and to impose new, centrally oriented patterns at variance with local customs surfaced during the tenures of Usmankhodzhaev and Nishanov.[45] The crackdown they presided over—and the abrupt break with established ways under the guise of cleaning up local corruption—contributed to mounting local disorder and dissent.[46] It stimulated resistance to Moscow, created grievances to be exploited by opposition forces within the Uzbek intelligentsia, and reawakened restive religious feelings. Most importantly, it triggered the formation of an invigorated national consciousness that transcended the divisive and debilitating regional differences that were highlighted in this chapter. These deep-seated cleavages had hindered Uzbek national integration; they served Moscow's interests over the years as it played a "divide and conquer" game, cynically manipulating ethnic and regional divisions while paying lip service to national interests and unity.

In the wake of the assault on the Rashidov era, and as a result of Gorbachev's reforms, a new form of local politics surfaced outside of Uzbekistan's political establishment; something like a "defensive" or "reactive" national identity and consciousness was stimulated and a national elite crystallized in response to the derogation of the Uzbek people's reputation as a result of the "anti-corruption campaign" and the "Uzbek Cotton Affair."[47] Criticism of Moscow's long-time policy of treating the Uzbek SSR as a raw materials reservoir creating a local cotton monoculture served as the springboard for a counteroffensive by local Uzbek figures.[48]

As this counteroffensive developed, other important political changes were taking place. One was a major policy turnabout in the regime's long-time negative approach toward Islam.[49] The campaign of ideological assertiveness and atheistic propaganda in vogue during Nishanov's term in office was abruptly terminated. Since Nishanov's transfer to Moscow, Islam has been viewed more favorably and Muslim religious figures are now courted.

The Gorbachev era changes have yielded some ominous results. Among the most dangerous and dramatic have been the June 1989 riots in Fergana and, more recently, the Kirgiz/Uzbek violence in Kirgizia's Osh oblast.[50]

Evidence of new cadre policies and novel leadership profiles and career patterns appeared in the person of Nishanov's successor.[51] Nishanov's successor was Islam Karimov, a long-time government bureaucrat and something of a technocrat rather than a conventional party *apparatchik*.[52] Karimov had suffered a serious demotion during Nishanov's incumbency. While earlier he held a number of important posts, including membership on the Council of Ministers, under Nishanov he was unexpectedly transferred from Tashkent to the distant Kashkadarya oblast to serve as its first secretary. This was his initial Party professional post; while representing a demotion and career detour, it provided Karimov with necessary Party credentials when, in mid-1989, the Gorbachev regime felt it imperative to execute an abrupt about-face vis-à-vis Uzbekistan which entailed replacing Nishanov and rejecting his policies.

Karimov's appointment was surprising—even startling—since it broke with all precedents in terms of the career credentials necessary for the post of first secretary. Especially noteworthy was the fact that Karimov throughout most of his previous career had been an outsider to the Party *nomenklatura*. He had never been a member of the republic Party's Buro nor had he held a position in the central Secretariat—the normal personnel pool from which previous appointees came. The established practice of appointing the chairman of the Supreme Soviet to the senior Party post was also broken. That procedure had produced Rashidov,

Usmankhodzhaev, and Nishanov, and there is evidence that in 1989 the initial plan had been to replace Nishanov with the incumbent Supreme Soviet chairman, M. I. Ibragimov; however, dramatic events intervened to undercut that cadre arrangement, for Ibragimov was bypassed, and instead Karimov was elevated instead to Nishanov's post.

The key event producing the break with precedent and necessitating Ibragimov's rejection as Nishanov's successor was the Fergana Valley riots. They undermined the prestige and authority of the previous leadership. Perhaps the turmoil that had swirled around the emergence of a political opposition group, Birlik, and the appearance of religious restiveness, also contributed to Moscow's reevaluation. All this and more counseled rejection of the Andropov/Ligachev approach, especially the reliance on "outsiders" (cadres dispatched by the center) to govern Uzbekistan.

There have been policy changes since Islam Karimov's emergence and he has brought new personnel to the fore. In June 1990, the republic Party's Twentieth Congress chose a new Buro and Central Committee that portended the dawn of a new day. The membership that had been approved at the 1986 Congress was swept away. No one who served on the 1986 Buro or Party Secretariat remained;[53] of the 1986 Central Committee's total membership of 261, only 62 were retained by the 1990 Party congress. A mere four years separated the Congresses, yet the turnover rate in the Central Committee was 78 percent.

Islam Karimov's speech at the Party Congress was a kind of Magna Carta for the republic's political elite.[54] He listed a number of profound problems, documented grievances, and provided candid analysis of the present predicament. What Karimov described in his report was a republic-wide crisis in virtually all realms. He outlined his future agenda: republic "sovereignty" and locally based and oriented solutions. Most striking was his criticism of cadre control by "outsiders" and recently dispatched personnel who, he said, failed to understand local conditions. Further, he rejected the impression created in recent years that Uzbekistan and Uzbeks were corrupt and he sought to rehabilitate the reputation of both. In this regard the signal that the purge period was terminated surfaced in his quasi-rehabilitation of Rashidov. Karimov called for a more balanced view of Rashidov's many years of service and demanded an even-handed treatment of him that reflected both his positive and negative characteristics.[55]

Past and Present in Perspective

The turnover in Uzbekistan's political elite between 1983 and 1989 involved all organizational levels and reached into every realm of the power elite. During this period four individuals occupied the top post of republic Party first secretary. This represented unprecedented instability not only for the specific place and time; in fact, it was unmatched in the entire history of the USSR. Never had so many individuals held a republic's top Party post for so limited a time over such a short period. With the appointment of Islam Karimov in June 1989, the phase of wide-scale personnel turnover and political upheaval managed from outside Uzbekistan appeared to have ended.

Launched initially during Andropov and Chernenko's brief reigns (and managed thereafter by Ligachev and his associates), the anti-corruption campaign had sought to regain control for Moscow over Rashidov's virtually autonomous realm where he ruled for so long as communist khan. But by 1990, Moscow had found it necessary to revise fundamentally its nationality policies, and it jettisoned the radical interventionist and rapid integrationist approach. Ironically, the assault tactics, followed by Gorbachev's retreat, produced increased republic autonomy, unprecedented politicization and polarization, and unparalleled disarray within a demoralized and decapitated native elite.

Meanwhile, Uzbekistan's communist elite—weakened by Moscow's "continuous purge" since 1984—was largely paralyzed and increasingly polarized. It proved unable to deal with the mounting problems and to establish new priorities or to slow the momentum of the mounting national consensus against the political authorities in Moscow and Tashkent. Yet today environmental and economic issues have surfaced in new ways which complicate relations among Central Asians by exacerbating old rivalries and creating new national tensions. The violent ethnic explosions in Fergana, Andizhan, and Osh and the explosive demographic situation, generally, underline the importance of this unique juncture in Uzbek history. It is evident that Uzbekistan must redefine its relationship with the USSR and the rest of Central Asia—where a pan-Turkic or at least a regional consensus is building—as well as with the outside world.

Turmoil and disarray comparable to the 1984–89 phase had appeared in the Uzbek SSR during the 1930s. But unlike that earlier period, the more recent events have had results that were unintended and unexpected. The consequences are still unfolding in directions that are uncharted and in ways that are unpredictable; but the outlines of an emerging future are becoming clearer. The new relationship between Uzbekistan and a revamped USSR' will be fundamentally different. The republic's elite and the policies it espouses are becoming authentically national if not yet fully nationalistic. The terms "nation" and "nationalist" are now directly relevant to local politics; they are losing the superficial and fraudulent character they had for the most part since 1925, when an artificial national state–the Uzbek SSR—was established for a not-yet-existent nation—the Uzbeks. Today these are no longer empty analytical categories, but are reflective of empirical realities which are increasingly determining the character and content of political life in the republic.

For years, students of nationalism have debated the question, "What is a nation?" They have often neglected or ignored the equally salient issue, "When is a nation?" For nationalism does not suddenly emerge full bloom; like its constituent elements, it evolves. Content, Context, and Carriers, as well as the Clock and Calendar are relevant parameters in the emergence of the nation and nationalism. If they intersect and prove mutually reinforcing, a nation-state may be the outcome. Time and timing are crucial, for national identity does not reach all social strata simultaneously. The depth and extent—not to mention the intensity—of national consciousness is problematic; and as history repeatedly shows, whether members of a national intelligentsia become national leaders depends on their popular following.

The intelligentsia and middle class, and urban settings as opposed to rural locales, are the initial incubators for nationalism. But unless such restive elites have mass backing and their urban base expands into rural support, no powerful national amalgam emerges and no successful national movement can be born. Often local imperial/colonial masters, a foreign enemy, or an alien occupying power serve as the critical catalyst in the context of mounting problems and rising expectations. National consciousness is thus triggered and unity created in the face of common dilemmas and dangers. In Uzbekistan today—as in the USSR's other Central Asian territories—the answer to the "when" question regarding nationalism is probably "now," and if not "now," then in the very near future.

Where does this leave the regionally based paradigm introduced at the start of this chapter? Has it lost its relevance and been transcended by national integration? By no means. It should not be assumed that an Uzbek identity and an identification with Uzbekistan as a state have penetrated the personal sense of belonging of all strata of the population equally and now firmly integrate all regions of the republic. Quite the contrary. Sub-national identities (and trans-national Islamic and Turkic linkages) are likely to be invigorated—not eliminated—as the Uzbek nation is created.[56]

In the short run, as politicization and pluralism unfold, the most likely consequences are overlapping identities and compound allegiances. Thus, paradoxically, regional and parochial patriotisms will likely grow alongside the broader notion of "Uzbek nationhood."

Notes

1. An earlier version of this work included an extended treatment of the changing political elite in the Uzbek SSR. It provides lists of the Buro (1938-1981) and a detailed analysis of the Secretariat's departments. See Donald S. Carlisle, "The Uzbek Power Elite: Politburo and Secretariat (1938-1983)," *Central Asian Survey*, Volume 5, nos. 3/4, 1986.

2. For an analysis which stresses such distinctions, see Michael Rywkin, *Russia in Central Asia* (New York, 1963) especially chapters 7 and 8. For a recent updating of his argument, see his articles "Power and Ethnicity: Regional and District Staffing in Uzbekistan" and "Cadre Competition in Uzbekistan: The Ethnic Aspect"—both in *Central Asian Survey*, Volume 5, no. 1 (1985) and nos. 3/4, (1986) respectively.

3. There are numerous illustrations that could be cited. They would include virtually all cases of serious geographic and economic analysis where maps based on a regionalization scheme are presented. A source which suffices to document the point is the one-volume Uzbek Soviet Encyclopedia, *Uzbekskaia Sovetskaia Sotsialisticheskaia Respublika* (Tashkent, 1981), p. 560. It includes a physical geographic regionalization map which divides Uzbekistan into 10 zones or areas (p. 55). This volume also includes a division very similar to the one I have adopted, which results in 6 regions or subsets based on economic regionalization (see p. 237). The Soviet map adopted and reproduced in the text as Figure 4.1 is taken from the volume *Uzbekistan* which comprises one of the 22 volumes in the series *Soviet Union*. See *Uzbekistan* (otv. red., L. N. Babushkin) (Moscow: Mysl', 1967).

4. The transfer of Uzbekistan's government from Samarkand to Tashkent was noted but downplayed in the press in 1930. See *Pravda Vostoka*, Sept. 3, 4, and 5, 1930. Subsequently, for a generation or more, there was no reference in any Soviet publication that I have seen to the fact that Samarkand had once been the capital. Only in the late 1950s was this politically motivated omission corrected and Samarkand's earlier role as the Republic's capital cited again.

5. Moscow's ploy is very evident from a study of its role and tactics in Uzbekistan's internal politics between 1925 and 1941. It not only played sections of the native "Uzbek" elite against each other; it also imported non-Russian personnel so as to fuel the fires of ethnic rivalry within the Republic. Moscow also periodically reached into the local pool of natives and "exported" or transferred cadres to the center or other locales for training and political experience. Thus transformed, such seemingly loyal natives were returned to the republic and promoted to key posts. This process could be labeled "internationalization." It was obviously an attempt to undercut emerging national identification and to undermine local roots and allegiances. It also represented an effort to create new loyalties inclined to Moscow and more easily manipulable from the center.

6. See Donald S. Carlisle, "Modernization, Generations, and the Uzbek Soviet Intelligentsia" in Paul Cocks, Robert V. Daniels, Nancy Whittier Heer (eds.),

The Dynamics of Soviet Politics (Cambridge, MA: Harvard U. Press, 1976), chapter 13.

7. For a short biography of Sabir Kamalov, see *Bol'shaia Sovetskaia entsiklopediia* (Moscow, 1958), vol. 51, p. 139. The primary source from which biographical and career data for the 1930s and 1940s have been drawn is Uzbekistan's main Russian-language newspaper, *Pravda Vostoka*. Tracing Kamalov's (and many other individuals') path through every issue of the newspaper was a laborious but necessary task. Periodically, summary career profiles have appeared in *Pravda Vostoka*. They were especially abundant in late 1937, again in mid-1938, and once again in March 1950. However, to avoid voluminous citations, references will only be given for the salient points in an individual's career or when biographies were published in the press.

Obituaries published in *Pravda Vostoka* were an invaluable source. They were available for the earlier period this study covers only in the instance of premature deaths (and since so many of those were politically caused, only when the regime wished to publicize them). By the 1960s these obituaries of earlier prominent officials began to appear with some regularity as the Stalinist generation passed away.

Two official Soviet sources published in the Uzbek SSR are especially useful regarding prominent personalities of the Rashidov Era. These are the collection of biographies of the Deputies of the Uzbek SSR's Supreme Soviet for 1975 and 1980 (*Deputaty Verkhovnogo Soveta Uzbekskoi SSR* [Tashkent: Uzbekistan, 1976], and the same titled volume, published in 1981).

8. *Pravda Vostoka*, Aug. 27, 1950 announced that Rashidov's candidacy was presented by A. Alimov, who had been named Minister for Cotton on April 29, 1950. The key event re-aligning the elite was the Fifth Plenum of the Party. S. Kamalov and N. Mukhitdinov were made Buro members and named Party secretaries. Rashidov was also made a Buro member. (A. Mavlianov had been made a member and a secretary at the January 1950 plenum.)

A. Alimov—former first secretary in Namangan and then Samarkand, and soon to be appointed Minister for Cotton—was named candidate member to the Buro (*Pravda Vostoka*, April 25, 1950).

9. The first instance where I have found a reference to Mukhitdinov in the press was February 1947 when someone by that name was identified as secretary of the Komsomol Namangan *gorkom* organization. None of his biographies, however, refer to service in this Komsomol post (*Pravda Vostoka*, Feb. 2, 1947). By May 30, 1947, the secretary in charge of propaganda in the Namangan *obkom* is definitely our Mukhitdinov. He held that position until October 1948 when he was named first secretary of the *obkom*.

Mukhitdinov was born to a peasant family living in a rural region in the vicinity of Tashkent in 1917. He finished middle school and a *tekhnikum* in 1935. He received subsequent training in the field of economics and education and in 1939 was drafted into the Soviet army. There, we are told, "he was at Komsomol and political work." During the War years (1941-45) he participated in a number of campaigns and battles. He entered the Party in 1942. His key career step took place after demobilization for in 1946 he worked as a lecturer for the Central Committee of the Uzbek Party, thus bringing him to the attention of the Secretariat. Sometime after he was sent to Namangan where he served from at least May 1947.

The most detailed biography of Mukhitdinov appeared after he was elevated to power at the center in Moscow. It included a full-page photograph, an honor seldom granted an individual in such a prestigious Soviet source as the *Great Soviet Encyclopedia* (*Bol'shaia Sovetskaia entsiklopediia*, vol. 51, pp. 205–06).

10. For a short biography detailing his pre-War journalist activity, his wartime poetry, and his early post-War literary activity, see "Sharaf Rashidov" in *Istoriia Uzbekskoi Sovetskoi literatury*, (Tashkent, 1967), pp. 659–662.

11. Many biographical profiles of Rashidov have appeared but the first that I have located was published in 1950 (*Pravda Vostoka*, March 4, 1950).

12. Mukhitdinov's rising star was very visible at the Nineteenth Party Congress held in Moscow in October 1952. Only three Uzbeks were made full members of the Central Committee: Iusupov, Niiazov, and Mukhitdinov. The Russian watchdog in Uzbekistan—the second secretary, R. E. Melnikov—became only a candidate member. Sharaf Rashidov had to wait until the Twentieth Congress in 1956 to become just a candidate member of the Central Committee. It was not until 1961 that Rashidov became a full member.

13. Without a doubt, the key Stalinist figure who held the Uzbek SSR as something of a fief was Lazar Kaganovich. He acquired it, so to speak, in December 1937, when he made a "visit" to Tashkent. (In fact, in 1920-21 Kaganovich had similarly played a key role at Tashkent.) If during the Stalin era the Russians were labeled the "elder brothers"—with all that implied figuratively in asserting their dominant role—then Kaganovich literally had that position personally. He must have been Iusupov's patron at the center. In fact, Kaganovich had travelled to Tashkent in January 1950 probably to inform Iusupov and associates of their promotions and to prepare for the impending personnel transfer locally. In 1954 the key relationship became Khrushchev and Mukhitdinov.

14. The sole mention of their marital status that I have discovered surfaced when Nurutdinov died in June 1966. On *Pravda Vostoka*'s back page, three separate boxes appeared, sponsored by institutions and organizations, which offered condolences to Nasriddinova on the death of her husband (*Pravda Vostoka*, June 11, 12, 1966).

Iadgar Nasriddinova was born in 1920 and was orphaned. She joined the Party in 1942 after completing studies at the Tashkent Institute for Railway Transport Engineers. She immediately began a Komsomol career (and served as secretary of the Institute's organization 1942-46), rising to second secretary at the republic level during 1948-50. Transferring to Party work, she led Tashkent's Kirov *raikom* for two years. Then she was appointed Minister of Industrial Construction Materials in 1952, and from 1955 to 1959 served as deputy chairman of the Council of Ministers during the period when Kamalov and Mirza-Akhmedov directed its work. Like her husband, Nurutdinov, she became a Buro member; but in 1959, unlike him, she was not ejected and demoted but transferred to Rashidov's post when he became first secretary in March 1, 1959.

The only reference to her as an orphan in an official Soviet source appeared in R. Tuzmuhamedov, *How the National Question was Solved in Soviet Central Asia* (Moscow: Progress, 1973), p. 157.

15. For a detailed discussion of the rehabilitations of Akmal Ikramov and Faizulla Khodzhaev respectively, see my review articles in *Kritika* (Cambridge, Mass.), vol. 8, no. 1 (fall, 1971) for Khodzhaev, and no. 3 (spring, 1972) for Ikramov.

16. Mukhitdinov's speech not only initiates the de-Stalinization campaign. It also lays out the agenda that was to preoccupy Uzbek leaders over the next twenty years or more (*Pervyi s"ezd intelligentsii Uzbekistana, Stenograficheskii otchet* [Tashkent: Uzgosizdat, 1957] pp. 8-66).

17. On March 17, Alimov, then Samarkand's first secretary, was named chairman of the Council of Ministers. On March 20, Nurutdinov's transfer to the largely impotent post in trade unions was announced. Of course he, like Kamalov and Mira-Akhmedov, lost his Buro status. Nurutdinov was replaced as the Tashkent oblast secretary by R. G. Guliamov.

18. There was at this time a clash between Rashidov and Guliamov as to which should be named first secretary. Guliamov had *apparatchik* credentials superior to Rashidov. As early as 1944, he had a post in the central Secretariat's cadres division and by 1946 was a deputy director in the Secretariat's Propaganda and Agitation Department. On February 29, 1948, he became a deputy chairman of the Council of Ministers and in January 1951 was named chairman of the Tashkent *goriispolkom*. In August 1952, he was released for studies. The vital information on the disagreement within the Buro regarding Rashidov's appointment is recounted in Kamil Ikramov's article in *Literaturnaia gazeta* (June 10, 1987).

19. Mukhitdinov's fall was as meteoric and unexpected as his rise. One can speculate that it was somehow related to the collapse of Kirichenko's career in 1959-60. Kirichenko was CPSU Second Secretary in charge of cadres and heir-apparent to Khrushchev. By May 1960 he lost all his central posts and was demoted. A month later he suffered further political disgrace. Speculation has it that he was relatively liberal on nationality questions and that a retrenchment and crack-down on nationalism in the republics in 1959 undermined him.

20. Kurbanov, who replaced Mukhitdinov's ally Alimov in September 1961, had been first secretary of the Andizhan *obkom* and the beneficiary of its success recently as a cotton-producing area, for which it was singled out and lauded.

Kurbanov, born in 1912 and a Party member from 1940, had been "in leading Party work" between 1942 and 1946 and again from 1949 to 1961. In the interim he completed the Higher Party School—perhaps in Moscow itself—and then spent the period after 1949 in the Fergana Valley as a Party *apparatchik*.

Another rising star in the Party during the 60s was Rafik Nishanov. Born in 1926 and having joined the Party only in 1949, he constituted the next tier below Rashidov's cohort in generational terms. A Tashkenter for most of his career, Nishanov rose through the city's October raion Party organization. By 1961, at the age of 35, he was already chairman of the Tashkent *goriispolkom*. In 1963, he was made a secretary of the central committee and in 1966 a Buro member. In 1970, he was removed from his prestigious posts and ejected from the republic. Only fifteen years later did he return and begin to remake his career as chairman of Uzbekistan's Supreme Soviet and to take revenge on Rashidov for breaking his promising career.

21. Narmakhonmadi D. Khudaiberdyev is the counterpart to Murtazaev; they were the brightest stars of the younger echelon of the post-War generation, their paths crossing as the latter's prospects took a sudden and ultimately precipitous decline while the former enjoyed a meteoric ascent.

Khudaiberdyev was born in 1928, apparently in Dzhizak—Rashidov's home-base. Like Rashidov, he was educated in Samarkand, but at an agricultural institute. Completing studies in 1949, he remained on its staff until 1954. Then he spent a good part of the next six years in Bukhara, first as deputy chairman of the Bukhara *oblispolkom* and subsequently second secretary of the Bukhara *obkom*. Surely he was Rashidov's main ally during these years. With common origins in Dzhizak, and similar patterns of education and political maturation in the Samarkand/Bukhara nexus, this is a clear confirmation of the regional approach put forward earlier in this paper.

22. *Ocherki istorii Kommunisticheskoi partii Uzbekistana* (Tashkent: Uzbekistan, 1964), pp. 295-96. This key volume must be viewed as a Khrushchev era source. It was approved for publication in August and sent to press in September 1964. Khrushchev's fall temporarily halted publication, for the last page of the volume mentioned his removal and identified Brezhnev and Kosygin as having assumed his Party and state posts. The second edition of the Party history, published in 1974, dropped the passages implicating Iusupov in the Ikramov Affair.

23. This involved the printing of a doctored photo of Faizulla Khodzhaev with a beard added apparently to disguise him. Nevertheless, it represented his first photographic appearance in a Soviet publication since 1938. For an account of this bizarre event as well as the photo's original and doctored versions, see my detailed review article devoted to the Faizulla Khodzhaev matter in *Kritika*, cited above.

24. Iusupov died on May 7 and his death was announced on page one of *Pravda Vostoka* the next day. A detailed obituary appeared on page three. His funeral on May 9 was also given extensive coverage. For the renaming of the Canal in his honor, see *Pravda Vostoka*, May 20, 1966.

On October 29, 1974 it was announced that a Memorial Museum devoted to Iusupov's life opened at his birthplace in the Fergana valley. On the eightieth anniversary of Iusupov's birth, an article titled "Faithful Son of the Party" recounted his exploits (*Pravda Vostoka*, May 14, 1980). By July 1980, a raion in Kashkadarya oblast was named for Usman Iusupov.

Usman Iusupov—like his predecessor, Akmal Ikramov—was married to a Slavic woman. After his death, Iusupov's wife (Iuliia L. Stepanenko) served as director of a *kombinat* (industrial group of enterprises) named for her husband in Tashkent oblast's Yangi-Yul' raion. She died at the age of 63. (For her obituary, see *Pravda Vostoka*, April 29, 1972).

25. This individual was Boris Kamenetskii, whose family moved from Odessa to Tashkent shortly before World War II. He resided there until emigrating to

Israel in 1977 and had been a public prosecutor in the Uzbek SSR. The most detailed disclosure of unsavory aspects of intra-elite life appears in his article, co-authored with Aleksandra Aleksandrova, "Ispoved' zhenshchiny," *Kontinent*, 1984/5, pp. 209-220. Extended interviews with Kamenetskii in 1979 provided the basis for two studies "Crime and Corruption in Uzbekistan" and "Notes on Life in Uzbekistan" *Radio Free Europe-Radio Liberty Background Reports*, Oct. 19, 1979 and Oct. 26, 1979.

26. Besides Kamenetskii's treatment, the Pakhtakor events are also treated in Peter Reddaway (ed.), *Uncensored Russia* (New York: American Heritage Press, 1972), pp. 402-403.

27. Nazar Matchanov was born in 1923 and joined the Party in 1949. He was educated at the Samarkand Agricultural Institute. He spent some time in Namangan, but the greater part of his career was spent in Bukhara where he was a secretary of the *obkom*, chairman of the *oblispolkom*, and then first secretary of the *obkom*. From 1965 until 1970 he was a secretary of the Central Committee.

28. For his political career, see *Deputaty Verkhovnogo Soveta SSR (Desiatyi sozyv)* (Moscow: Uzbekistan, 1981), p. 147.

29. For biographies, see *Partiinaia zhizn'* (Tashkent), no. 12, 1983, p. 15, and *Deputaty Verkhovnogo Soveta Uzbekskoi SSR (Desiatyi Sozyv)*, p. 150.

30. Usmankhodzhaev represents the first instance of the son of a key figure from the Stalinist period rising to the political summit in Uzbekistan. His father—Buzrukkhodzha Usmankhodzhaev—was born in 1896 in a village in the Fergana Valley. He held many official posts in Fergana between 1918 and 1943. In that year he became chairman of the Fergana *oblispolkom*, a post that he held until 1952. Between 1952 and 1977 he was director of the main irrigation system of the Uzbek SSR—the Great Fergana Canal. A prominent native communist, Buzrukkhodzha was a delegate to all local Party congresses and was elected to the Central Committee. He died in 1977.

31. For A. A. Khodzhaev's death, see *Pravda Vostoka*, Sept. 18, 1983. There is no question that Khodzhaev had become the "second secretary" among native personnel; the posts he held, his prominence, and the publicity afforded him clearly confirm this. Then he suddenly died.

There are various rumors concerning the circumstances of Rashidov's death on October 31, 1983. One tale has him committing suicide after Moscow's agents confronted him with evidence of extensive wrongdoing under his auspices. Another story credits the official account of his heart attack, but suggests that it was triggered by the Andropov's regime's anti-corruption drive.

32. Dzhizak oblast did not exist as a separate administrative unit until it was officially created on December 29, 1973. Located in central Uzbekistan, there seemed no apparent economic or other grounds for it being singled out in this fashion—unless we postulate Rashidov's personal intervention. The Dzhizak oblast constituted 4.6% of the republic's territory and only 3.3% of its population. Its ethnic make-up was 75% Uzbek and 8% Russian. It contains no major cities or centers of republic-level importance.

33. Khaidarov was the clearest illustration of the emergence of the post-Stalinist generation at the power summit. He was born in 1939—the year

Rashidov joined the Party—and so was only fourteen when Stalin died. A Party technocrat whose early career was confined to the Chirchik region from 1970 he held subordinate posts in the central apparatus in Tashkent; then he led the Chirchik *gorkom*, and in 1979 returned to head the Department of Heavy Industry and Machine-Building of the Party Secretariat (*Deputaty*, 1981, p. 214).

34. Osetrov was to be retired "on a pension" (*Pravda Vostoka*, Jan. 10, 1986). Subsequently, he was arrested.

35. *Partiinaia zhizn'*, (Tashkent), no. 2, 1986, pp. 6-43 and 58-60.

36. For the 1981 and 1986 Buros, see the annual supplements of the *Bol'shaia Sovetskaia entsiklopediia*, *Ezhegodnik 1981*, p. 174 and *Ezhegodnik 1986*, p. 171.

37. Only one native—K. Tairov—reappeared in the same secretarial slot. In 1981 and 1986 he headed the General Department. Two non-natives were retained: V. I. Suskin, who headed the Water Department in both years, and S. A. Asriiants, who had led the Agricultural Machine Construction Department in 1981 and now was in charge of Heavy Industry and Machine Construction. However, two Uzbeks heading departments in 1981 had not been demoted but promoted. G. Kh. Khaidarov became chairman of the Council of Ministers and A. S. Ikramov was made a full secretary.

The two Russians who headed the strategic Organizational Party Work and the Administrative Organs Departments in 1981 (V. V. Okunskii and G. V. Arkhangelskii), were removed. They were replaced by P. V. Dogonkin and D. A. Usatov; Dogonkin was also named a Buro member.

The new second secretary was V. P. Anishchev, recently imported and at the time Moscow's key figure in the Republic. For an analysis of the 1981 departments, see Carlisle, "The Uzbek Power Elite," 125-26. For the 1986 departments, see *Partiinaia zhizn'*, no. 2, 1986, p. 64.

38. *Pravda Vostoka*, Dec. 5, 1986.

39. See his biography published upon his appointment in *Pravda Vostoka*, Dec. 6, 1986. At the Uzbek Party's Sixth Plenum in February 1987, Nishanov became a full member of the Buro—jumping over the candidate stage—and Salimov was dropped "in accord with his transfer to other work" (*Pravda Vostoka*, Feb. 15, 1987).

40. There is much irony in that Salimov had stepped into Nishanov's post in 1970 when he was disgraced! In 1986, the individuals involved were the same and the cause of the change identical. However, the roles of victor and victim were reversed.

41. *Pravda Vostoka*, April 24, 1987.

42. A new organization surfaced called "The Republic Council of Veterans of War and Labor." Its newly elected chairman was R. Guliamov. One of its deputy chairmen was none other than N. A. Mukhitdinov. Its Presidium included A. A. Alimov (*Pravda Vostoka*, March 17, 1987). Alimov turned seventy in April 1987 when he was identified as chairman of the Republic's Council for Environmental Protection.

43. Mukhitdinov's period of eclipse and exile was over. Between his earlier downfall and 1987, I was able to locate only four references to him in *Pravda Vostoka*. In 1969 when President Assad of Syria visited Tashkent, Mukhitdinov

was shown in the entourage accompanying the Syrian leader and identified in the related story (*Pravda Vostoka*, July 9, 1969.). When Assad made similar trips in 1974 and 1975, there was comparable treatment of Mukhitdinov. When his father died in 1976, on the newspaper's last page condolences were tendered (*Pravda Vostoka*, Nov. 16, 1976).

His return was explicitly signalled by the 1987 publication of his recollections, including memory of the impact on his father of Lenin's death in 1924 and some positive reflections on collectivization, as well as a reference to Stalin (*Pravda Vostoka*, May 10, 1987). Mukhitdinov was later identified as the chairman of the Presidium of the Governing Council for Preservation of Monuments, although it is unclear exactly when he was appointed (*Pravda Vostoka*, Aug. 7, 1987).

44. In 1973 Sabir Kamalov was deputy chairman of the Ministry of Procurement (*Pravda Vostoka*, March 21, 1973). He held the same post in 1980 when he was congratulated on his seventieth birthday and received an award (*Pravda Vostoka*, May 2, 1980). Kamalov died on June 6, 1990 (*Pravda Vostoka*, June 7, 1990).

45. Those "local customs" and the equilibrium disrupted are discussed in Nancy Lubin's, *Labour and Nationality in Soviet Central Asia*, (Princeton, NJ: Princeton U. Press, 1984). A pathbreaking study, it shed new light on native employment patterns and personal preferences. Lubin described the "affirmative action" policies and the system—subsequently labelled "corrupt"—that crystallized during the Rashidov years. For Lubin's discussion of "affirmative action" hiring practices and nepotism, see pp. 154–64 and 229–30.

46. Usmankhodzhaev stated that some ousted officials were giving a national or ethnic interpretation to what the regime wanted to be viewed as simply an assault on corruption.

47. Kamil Ikramov objected to the tendency to label it the "Uzbek Affair" and warned against thus inflaming national passions and feeding chauvinist tendencies. It is probably not by accident that Ikramov pointedly identified Osetrov and Orlov—two prominent Russians who had held high positions in Uzbekistan—as having been arrested along with leading Uzbek officials. See his very important article in *Literaturnaia gazeta*, June 10, 1987. For a detailed account of the corruption uncovered in Uzbekistan, see "Up Against the Mafia," *Moscow News*, no. 14, 1988.

48. For examples of the criticism of Moscow's policies which emerged at this time, see Boris Rumer's chapter in this volume.

49. In his 1986 address to the republic Party Congress Usmankhodzhaev linked the persistence of religious phenomena to nationalism and chauvinism. In contrast, Rashidov had largely ignored this topic in his speeches. In October 1986 there was a conference of the intelligentsia in which "remnants of the past" and religious-related phenomena were attacked. The Third Party Plenum signalled a new offensive in this direction. There, Usmankhodzhaev delivered a speech warning of their persistence and growth (*Pravda Vostoka*, Oct. 5, 1986). The paper's next issue was largely devoted to the discussion at the Plenum and elaborated in startling detail the depth and extent of the problem (*Pravda Vostoka*, Oct. 7, 1986). On October 18, *Pravda Vostoka* devoted a page to a discussion of

"atheism." Ayse Rorlich's chapter in this volume also notes that, in November, Gorbachev stopped in Tashkent on his way to India and delivered a speech which stressed the campaign for atheistic education (*Pravda Vostoka*, Nov. 25, 1986).

50. In June 1989, violent clashes broke out between Uzbeks and Meskhetian Turks in Uzbekistan's Fergana Valley. Just about one year later, a land dispute escalated into pogroms against Uzbek inhabitants of Kirgizia's Osh oblast. Although the Soviet central press largely blamed local nationalists and Islamic fundamentalists, many Central Asians believe that Moscow, through the KGB and other institutions, incited the violence.

51. Under the policy in effect since 1983, many cadres from the center had been posted to Uzbekistan. The first secretary of the Tashkent *gorkom* was B. F. Satin, who previously worked in the CPSU's Central Secretariat. He replaced a native. This was the first time a Slav held this post since just after World War II. (In 1990, Satin was replaced by an Uzbek.)

V. P. Anishchev, the republic Party's second secretary, previously was a secretary in the Voronezh city organization. V. G. Kretov, in charge of the Organizational Party Work Department, came from the Leningrad organization. Numerous other appointments could be cited, including that of the republic's chief prosecutor, Buturlin, formerly employed in the USSR's Public Prosecutor's office.

For a detailed study of cadre and recruitment practices, see the contribution in this volume by James Critchlow which follows. He presents the most probing and insightful treatment of the subject available.

52. Karimov was appointed on June 23, 1989. For his biography, see *Pravda Vostoka*, June 24, 1989. He was born in 1938 in Samarkand and grew up there. By 1960 he was employed in Tashkent. Between 1966 and 1983 he advanced up the bureaucratic ladder in the Ministry of Finances and in 1986 was named chairman of the republic's *Gosplan*. That same year he attended his first Party congress. His rapid rise is testified to by the fact that in 1986 he was chosen a full member of the Central Committee, leaping over the candidate member stage.

53. Pictures and short biographies of the Buro members were published in *Pravda Vostoka*, June 8, 1990.

54. For Karimov's report to the congress, see *Pravda Vostoka*, June 5, 1990.

55. The reference in Karimov's report to Rashidov appears in *Pravda Vostoka*, June 5, 1990, beginning with the bottom of column 2 on page 3.

56. An intriguing proposal by Abdukakhar Ibragimov, a Tashkent playwright, documents the continuing relevance of the regional paradigm stressed in this chapter. He suggested that Samarkand be renamed Uzbekistan's capital, thus returning the city to the prominent position it occupied from 1925 to 1930. (See *Yash leninchi*, July 26, 1990.) Could there be a connection between Islam Karimov's rise and this provocative proposal? As noted, Karimov was born and raised in Samarkand, and his brother still resides there. In 1986, Karimov's initial appearance at a Party congress was as a member of the Samarkand oblast delegation.

Even if Karimov had no hand in this startling suggestion of moving the capital, the proposal underlines the long-standing and continuing rivalry between Samarkand and Tashkent. Nor should one confine attention to these urban focal points. The emergence of Bukhara as a regional center and a renewed focus of local pride should not be underestimated. In addition, Kokand and other Fergana Valley cities provide potential foci for competing identities and regional patriotism.

5

Prelude to "Independence": How the Uzbek Party Apparatus Broke Moscow's Grip on Elite Recruitment

James Critchlow

Introduction

When in June 1990 the Uzbek Supreme Soviet declared the "political independence" of its republic, the event marked the culmination of a centrifugal process in relations with Moscow that had begun decades earlier. It focused attention on the Uzbek elite, the prime mover in the process, as a new actor on the Soviet and world scene—a force that could take Uzbekistan still further along the path of severing its ties with Moscow.

This chapter examines a crucial turning-point in the process, the defeat by the Uzbek elite of Moscow's campaign, launched by Gorbachev in February 1986, at the Twenty-Seventh Party Congress in Moscow, to reassert control over recruitment and promotion within the elite. The anatomy of that defeat is dissected here in an attempt to shed light on the goals, strategy, and tactics of the elite, today the leading force of Uzbek nationalism.

Although Uzbekistan and the other Central Asian republics appeared to lag behind others in challenging Moscow's authority in the perestroika period, as evidenced by the relative docility of speeches by their people's deputies at early sessions of the Congress and Supreme Soviet in Moscow, they had in fact begun to wrest autonomy from the center well before Gorbachev's accession. The decades after Stalin's death witnessed a quiet transfer of power in the region away from Moscow and into the hands of the republican Party organs. This shift had many facets, ranging from the political to the cultural, but none was more profound and far-reaching than the eventual erosion of Moscow's ability to control staffing of the Party and state *apparat*, especially at the crucial oblast and raion levels where policy is implemented.

Moscow's loss of control over recruitment, a process which was already well underway in the Brezhnev era, i.e. well before perestroika, culminated in the center's defeat in a pitched battle waged in the early Gorbachev years (especially 1986–87) in which the Moscow leadership tried, and largely failed, to reassert its authority in personnel matters. The stumbling-block was effective resistance by the local elites. A leading Moscow protagonist in the battle was Egor Ligachev, then CPSU secretary responsible for cadres. One can only speculate about the extent to which his lack of success in dealing with Uzbekistan may have helped lead to his removal to other spheres of responsibility.

It is the purpose of this chapter to retrace the conflict as it developed in Uzbekistan, and to assess the outcome and implications for the future.

Moscow's struggle to regain control of cadre policy in Uzbekistan will be examined here in the light of past practices of recruitment to the bureaucratic elite as they evolved under the posthumously disgraced Sharaf Rashidov, who dominated the republic as first secretary for nearly a quarter-century, from 1959 until his sudden death in October 1983. We shall attempt an assessment of failure by the Gorbachev administration to remedy the situation from its standpoint. Some of the measures used were common to the perestroika campaign being waged throughout the country, but the gravity and special ethnic nature of "negative phenomena" in Uzbekistan gave perestroika a unique local content, such as the concentration on eradicating ethnic and clan networks among officials.

The use of the term "elite" here is a broad one. Harasymiw has written that the "power elite" (members of republic and USSR central committees) is "roughly indicated by one's being advanced from a republic to the all-Union Party *nomenklatura.*"[1] We go beyond that to include in the "power elite" the lower-ranking oblast and raion Party organs, given their key responsibilies for recruitment into Party positions at those *nomenklatura* levels which they controlled. (In the light of subsequent changes, use of the term *nomenklatura* here may seem to some extent outdated; it should be recalled, however, that the *nomenklatura* was still the backbone of Party personnel procedures in 1986–87, the time of our principal focus.)

In addition to the "power elite," a considerable political role is played in Uzbekistan as in other Soviet republics by the "prestige elite," overlapping but not entirely co-terminous with the political elite as described above. This consists of primarily cultural figures—writers, artists, scholars—and scientists, who have a status within the national group which may transcend that conferred on them by their position within the official hierarchy. This prestige elite is ancillary to the "conveyor belt" function of the political elite in linking the leadership with the masses, but in performing that function is often found to pursue its own agenda. In Uzbekistan it has played an enormous role in rallying national opinion to oppose Moscow's policies and directives. The present discussion of recruitment will refer mainly to the political elite, but the interaction of indigenous elements of that elite with members of the national prestige elite is a factor of importance which should be borne in mind.

Various writers have discussed the emergence of the new indigenous elites in the Soviet republics as a product of Communist Party rule. Earlier assessments of the role of these elites tended to stress their commitment to Moscow. Bennigsen once wrote that, by 1939, the older generation of "national" communists "had yielded place to the rising generation of intellectuals, bureaucrats and technocrats—mostly of proletarian or peasant origin and of purely Soviet moulding—which to all intents and purposes, was without Islam and had pigeon-holed jadidism in a past that was over and done with."[2] Voslensky, perhaps viewing the nationality scene from the ethnic perspective of a Russian outsider, characterized those natives on the *nomenklatura* as "half-Russians" and people who "experience no national feelings."[3]

In the case of Uzbekistan, the leadership of the native elites in defending against encroachment on their national interests even before perestroika suggests that such demeaning dismissals are, at the very least, out of date. More fitting is the view expressed by Simon in his book-length study of nationalism and nationality policy in the Soviet Union: ". . . Since World War II the new national elites have become bearers of national aspirations and expectations. They are seeking a way to combine underlying loyalty to the Soviet system with the advancement of national ambitions."[4]

While the role of the Party, and the framework in which it operates, have been considerably altered since 1987 by Gorbachevian reforms introduced from the top, Moscow's defeat in its struggle with the Uzbek elites predates the most significant reforms. It was the result of the center's inability to overcome resistance within the republic, and remains today a pertinent illustration of the fact that national power in Uzbekistan had already increased independently of the perestroika reform.

Moscow Awakens to Its Problem

The post-Brezhnev scandals that erupted in the Central Asian Soviet republics, particularly in Uzbekistan, in the wake of Uzbek Party First Secretary Sharaf Rashidov's sudden death in 1983, brought home to the

Moscow leadership the disturbing truth that it was no longer fully in control of Party and state activity in those republics. In a plaintive allusion to the situation in his speech to the Moscow Party Congress in February 1986, Mikhail Gorbachev conceded that the leadership had been taken by surprise:

> The shortcomings in the republic did not occur all at once, they had been accumulating for years, small ones giving birth to larger ones. Uzbekistan was visited more than once by officials of Soviet organs, including Central Committee officials, who could not fail to notice what was going on.[5]

Concurrently, the scandals helped to focus the spotlight on the Soviet Union's gravest economic and environmental crisis, one that required resolute remedial action. Moscow's initial response was a series of measures designed to tighten its grip. In this, it relied on traditional authoritarian methods, operating through the Party chain of command. The ensuing campaign focused, in the spirit of "cadres decide everything," on reimposing central control of recruitment to the *nomenklatura*. Central control of recruitment had effectively been allowed to dissipate, particularly in the latter Brezhnev period, with Moscow's *de facto* abdication of personnel decisions to the Party organs at republican, oblast and raion levels, where local and ethnic considerations were dominant.

In his pointed remarks about Uzbekistan at the 1986 Party Congress, Gorbachev focused on the cadre issue at the primary Party level, declaring that "admission to the Party is in need of further improvement," that the Party must be shielded from "casual people, those who join it from careerist or other selfish motives." As to general cadre questions, he added:

> In the republican Party organization discipline has weakened, and those in honor have been the ones whose only principle was lack of principle, their own well-being and careerist considerations. There has been a spread of bootlicking and unrestrained adulation of "higher ranks". . . of various kinds of machinations, embezzlement, bribetaking, with socialist legality being crudely violated.[6]

Politburo Member Egor K. Ligachev, speaking as Central Committee Secretary responsible for cadres, went a step further and tied the problem of personnel directly to questions of nationality, complaining that parochial attitudes were causing difficulties. To remedy the situation, he called for "interrepublican exchange of cadres," i.e. importation of officials from other republics, presumably because they would be more pliable as instruments of Moscow's policies. At several points in his speech,

Ligachev made it clear that in this respect the Central Asian region was the paramount worry of the leadership, through his allusions to problems in Uzbekistan and neighboring Kazakhstan.

Ligachev referred approvingly to an earlier speech at the Congress by then Uzbek First Secretary Inamdzhan B. Usmankhodzhaev, who had conceded that "perversions of cadre policy" had taken place in his republic.[7] In retrospect, Usmankhodzhaev represents one of the great ironies of the CPSU's response to the situation in Uzbekistan, and symbolizes the defeat of its efforts to deal with it. Installed as first secretary to succeed Rashidov after the latter's death in 1983, and entrusted during his more than four years in office with leading responsibility for restoring order to the republic, he was himself arrested after being replaced in January 1988, and subsequently sentenced to twelve years in prison on charges of bribery and corruption. But in 1986–87, he was still Moscow's spokesman and the personification of its authority in the republic.

The Purge Begins

Details of "negative phenomena" in Uzbekistan made public both before and after the 1986 Moscow Congress suggested that the concerns of Gorbachev, Ligachev and other speakers were not idle. As more and more disclosures were made, Communists were being accused of incompetence and unreliability at all levels of the hierarchy in the republic, and in many cases charged with criminal behavior. At the very top level of power in the republic, former First Secretary Rashidov was posthumously denounced as a "latter-day Uzbek khan with Party card" and his body removed from its resting place of honor in Tashkent.[8]

A former Russian incumbent of the second secretaryship, the traditional proconsular post which is supposed to protect Moscow's interests in a national republic, was placed under arrest. Others arrested included an Uzbek former chairman of the republican Council of Ministers and a Russian deputy chairman, and the former first secretaries of five of Uzbekistan's then thirteen provincial Party committees (*obkoms*).[9] One of the *obkom* first secretaries was sentenced to death.[10] Against all of these men, the charges included embezzlement and bribetaking.

(Some doubt was cast on the legitimacy of these arrests when in 1988 it was charged that two of the principal criminal investigators assigned from Moscow, Tel'man Gdlian and Nikolai Ivanov, had used improper tactics to obtain evidence, including unsupported confessions extracted under duress.[11] However, these allegations have not deterred the courts from convicting and sentencing persons arrested by those investigators.)

At the middle level of the apparatus, embracing several hundred city and district Party committees (*gorkom*s and *raikom*s) and government executive committees, information about the extent of the purge was less precise, but there was an indication of the scope in the fact that three-quarters of the republican Central Committee—on which many of the leading officials of these committees were represented—changed in composition between the 1981 and 1986 Uzbek Party congresses. After 1986, the turnover continued, particularly at lower levels. Those remaining in office, from First Secretary Usmankhodzhaev on down, were harassed in the media—in all probability at Moscow's instigation—for unsatisfactory performance.[12] In particular, middle-level Party officials were censured for failing to deal properly with primary Party organizations, for which they had immediate staffing responsibility.

The purge penetrated deeply into lower levels. At a plenum of the republican Central Committee in February 1987, First Secretary Usmankhodzhaev, then in his heyday, announced that in the year 1986 alone—when the purge had already been running for at least two years—it had still been found necessary to replace approximately 750 persons in leadership positions, including 8 *obkom* secretaries, 100 secretaries of city and district committees, 40 chairmen of city and district executive committees and 18 ministers and other agency heads.[13] At another plenum the following month, it was revealed that during the same year 158 leaders had been expelled from the Party for unsatisfactory reports to meetings, and more than 2,000 had received reprimands.[14]

In a single oblast (Tashkent) "hundreds" were expelled from the Party for "crimes, bribes, speculation, and abuse of official position."[15] In another oblast (Kashkadarya) 88 percent of officials on the *obkom nomenklatura* and 75 percent on the *gorkom/raikom nomenklatura* were replaced; 366 "leaders" were dismissed for "negative motives."[16]

Information made public in July 1987 suggested that the net depletion of the Party ranks (expulsions and other terminations less admissions) may have been in the tens of thousands.[17] Given the pervasive influence of the Party in Soviet society and the lateral mobility of Party officials into and out of government organs, agricultural and industrial enterprises, and cultural institutions, the malaise of the Party infected the entire political elite. For example, it was reported that 90 percent of directors of state and collective farms in the republic had been replaced.[18]

Emergency measures taken by the leadership to cope immediately with lawlessness included "permanent" importation of Party and law-enforcement officials from other republics.[19] The USSR Chief Prosecutor, in an unusual article apparently written especially for the press of Uzbekistan, revealed that in order to strengthen law enforcement 70 percent of prosecutors in the republic, some of whom had themselves been accused of crimes, had been replaced. In all, it was revealed that more than 200 law-enforcement personnel who had compromised themselves had been dismissed. The USSR Prosecutor wrote that his office alone had assigned 85 staffers to reinforce the upper echelon in Uzbekistan, plus an additional contingent of more than 100 temporary investigators sent in to clean up pending cases during the summer of 1987. He reported that in the single area of cotton-raising and cotton-processing the number of persons guilty of crimes against the state was in the "tens of thousands," and that thousands of responsible officials had been called to criminal account. Meanwhile, in Uzbekistan crime had doubled over a five-year period.[20]

Rashidov's Cadre Legacy

From the pronouncements of senior republican officials taking their cue from the Moscow Party Congress, it became clear that the long-term solution to the situation in Uzbekistan was seen to lie not merely in actions against recalcitrant officials, no matter how widespread, but in a prophylactic revision of cadre policy aimed at restoring the center's control of recruitment to elite positions in Party, government, economic, and cultural institutions. Reform of cadre policy aimed at eradicating the pattern of abuses which had been allowed to grow during Rashidov's long term in office.

In the post-Congress period, speeches and articles by top Party officials charged with transmitting the Moscow line constituted a veritable catalogue of ways in which violations of recruitment and promotion policies had built up during the Rashidov years.

The center's chief instrument of control was supposed to be the sacrosanct *nomenklatura* system, those lists of offices, officeholders and candidates for office maintained by Party committees (more precisely, their organizational-party work departments) at the all-Union, republic, oblast, city, and raion levels. In theory, the *nomenklatura* gave each committee direct control over all relevant appointments at its level of jurisdiction.[21] The system also provided higher echelons with a mechanism for supervision of appointments through review of the lists. In practice, however, it was found that local officials had been circumventing the *nomenklatura* in various ways. One such way was direct defiance, through appointment of individuals not on the approved lists. Another common method of frustrating the system was failure to maintain an adequate "reserve" list of candidates, thus making it easier to appoint unknowns when vacancies occurred: in one raion in neighboring Kazakhstan, it was reported that of 109 *nomenklatura* vacancies filled, only 18 were selected from the "reserve."[22]

The Problem of Nationality

At first glance, demands for a more equitable sharing of positions among nationalities would seem to have little application to Uzbekistan, where Russians at the time of the 1979 census were less than 11 percent of the population but were overrepresented in the bureaucracy, as were Ukrainians with less than 1 percent. Of the 245 officials in leading positions elected as Supreme Soviet deputies in 1975, Russians comprised 14.3 percent and Ukrainians 4.1, more than their share of the republic's population as recorded in the 1979 census.[23] Yet the balance was shifting. In 1986, the year of the Moscow Party Congress, 71 percent of those admitted to CPSU membership in Uzbekistan were Uzbeks, compared with the Uzbeks' share of only 65 percent of those regularly employed in the republic.[24] The ascendancy of Uzbeks and other Central Asians as first secretaries of Party organs and leading chairmen of state and public organizations in the republic was even more marked.

The importance attached by the Soviet leadership to nationality in recruitment has been demonstrated by the time-honored practice of earmarking certain bureaucratic positions for a given nationality or cluster of nationalities (i.e. Europeans or Asians). This was generally interpreted by students of Soviet politics as rooted in the leadership's perception that some nationalities, e.g. Slavs, are more reliable than others. Thus, in the four Central Asian republics, Russians or Ukrainians had traditionally held the second secretary posts in Party organs and the deputy chairman positions in state bodies under native first secretaries and chairmen.[25] This was aimed at insuring central control of the apparatus while providing a sop to native pride. Some observers even dismissed the native incumbents of the top positions as mere figureheads: "The Second Secretary, far from being subordinate to the First, keeps him steady and under control."[26]

The Cult of "First Persons"

It was now obvious that in the post-Stalin decades, especially during the latter Brezhnev period, the native first secretaries in Central Asia, patrimonial figures like Rashidov, managed to consolidate a real measure of power, succeeding at the same time in neutralizing or co-opting their Slavic deputies. This turning of the tables by the first secretaries was echoed in recurring complaints by regime spokesmen who attributed the "negative phenomena" which had come to light in the aftermath of Rashidov's rule to a cult of "first leaders" or "first persons" that had allegedly been allowed to flourish.[27]

When one examined the incumbency of first-secretary positions in the light of the rising power of the incumbents, the point of demands

Prelude to "Independence" 139

for a nationality realignment became clear. A directory of high-ranking officials in Uzbekistan published in 1985 showed that in addition to the native first secretary of the republic, the incumbent first secretaries in eleven of thirteen oblasts (84 percent) were Central Asian natives.[28] This seemed to correspond roughly to the national composition of the republic, but in fact the two oblasts headed by non-natives, Navoi and Syrdarya, were small in size and population. At the next lower level, the city and district committees, the disproportion between native and European first secretaries becomes even more glaring. Thus, of 47 city and district first secretaries listed in the directory of 1975 deputies, only one was Russian (2.1 percent), and two were Ukrainian (4.3 percent), comprising a Slavic total of three (6.4 percent). All of the others (93.6 percent) were of Central Asian nationalities, with the predominant Uzbeks in the overwhelming majority (thirty-nine, or 83.0 percent, compared with their 68.7 percent share of the republic's population).[29]

Illicit Co-optation of Non-Natives

Implicit in Ligachev's call for "inter-republican exchange of cadres" was the assumption that mere nationality was no guarantor of a person's loyalty to the center. Prior to disclosure of the Uzbekistan scandals, plenty of Russians had been serving in the republic, and it became clear that many were enmeshed in wrongdoing (as were indeed Brezhnev's son-in-law and other non-Uzbeks in Moscow). In the light of this circumstance, it is instructive to look at the place which had been occupied by outsiders in Uzbekistan under Rashidov, and the kind of outsiders who were assigned there.

Once again, the directory of deputies to the republican Supreme Soviet elected in 1975, i.e., Rashidov's heyday, is a handy benchmark.[30] From this source, biographies of "Europeans" in positions at the oblast secondary level or higher, i.e., from *obkom* second secretary or *oblispolkom* deputy chairman upward, were selected. There were 23 Russians, 7 Ukrainians, 3 Armenians, and 1 Estonian. The "European" group included:

- the second secretary of the Uzbek Central Committee,
- the assistant to the republican first secretary,
- two deputy chairmen of the republican Council of Ministers and five ministers,
- the chairman of a republican state committee,
- two deputy chairmen of the Supreme Soviet,
- a republic-level Party secretary,

- the directors of three key Central Committee departments (administrative organs, organizational-party work, and agriculture),
- a deputy chairman of the republican KGB,
- a first deputy chairman of the republican People's Control Commission,
- a first deputy chairman of Uzbekistan's Gosplan,
- a secretary of the trade-union organization,
- eleven second secretaries of *obkom*s,
- a first deputy chairman of the Council of Ministers of the Karakalpak ASSR,
- a deputy *oblispolkom* chairman (Andizhan),
- a vice-president of the Uzbek Academy of Sciences.

It is reasonable to assume that these people were representative of the contingent on which Moscow had traditionally relied to protect its interests against the encroachments of nationality and local autarky. Significantly, 16 of the 34 individuals in this non-native group had received their higher education in Uzbekistan. Of the remaining 18, 12 had held three or more previous posts in the republic and four had held two there. Indeed, either local higher education or extensive local work experience seemed to be the channel through which non-native officials must usually pass in order to achieve high rank in Uzbekistan.[31]

Clearly, most of these high-level "Europeans" had had time to develop close ties with the native Establishment. If officials remained in Uzbekistan long enough to master a strange linguistic and cultural environment, the evidence was at hand that they, too, could be susceptible to temptation. This may help to explain why Russians and other non-Central Asians—judging from the record of arrests and dismissals—had been involved so extensively in "negative phenomena" in Uzbekistan. Indeed, there was a tradition of corruption among Russian administrators in Central Asia going back to pre-revolutionary times, blamed by one tsarist official on the power which they wielded, their separation from home, the heat, and the influence of Asian mores.[32]

Evidently, receiving one's higher education in Uzbekistan was a major factor in co-optation of non-Uzbeks into the elite network controlled by Uzbeks. During the Rashidov era, graduation from a *VUZ* in Uzbekistan was a prime "channel" of advancement, regardless of nationality. This is demonstrated by the fact that, in 1975, of a total group of 221 leading officials of *all* nationalities with completed higher education who were elected to the republican Supreme Soviet, 158 (71 percent) were graduates of *VUZy* in Uzbekistan, mainly those in Tashkent (121) or Samarkand (23).[33]

Subnational Networks

While identification of officials with Uzbekistan was clearly a major obstacle to Moscow's control of personnel matters, the picture was further complicated by the existence of secondary networks based on allegiance to the local *vatan* or homeland, and to kin and clan. Denunciations by Moscow spokesmen left little doubt that these remained strong in Uzbek and other Central Asian societies as a stumbling-block to implementation of "Leninist norms of recruitment, deployment and training of cadres." While the original tribal affiliations of the Turkic nomads from whom many of today's Uzbeks are descended once cut broadly across geographic boundaries, the more settled period of Soviet rule has provided ample opportunity for the development of territorial interests, whether along lines of localism, kinship, or clan and tribal identity.

Soviet media tend to be reticent about the specifics of vestigial tribal or clan consciousness, probably because publicity would tend to undercut the officially sponsored concept of "nationality" introduced to assist in the Sovietization of Central Asia. There is less reticence about nepotism in family relationships. In July 1987, a newspaper carried a story about a former head of Surkhandarya oblast's Administrative Organs Department (whose responsibilities included state security) discharged for obtaining forged work documents for his daughter.[34] At a meeting of social scientists in Uzbekistan, the republican second secretary, V. P. Anishchev, complained about nepotism in the scientific community, blaming it on poor "ideological-political work." He singled out a family named Pulatov:

> The father heads the Department of Philosophy; his son works in the same department as a senior instructor; in the Institute of Philosophy and Law, which includes the Department of Philosophy, his niece is working; in the same institute his daughter is studying as a graduate student. And such facts, unfortunately, are not few and far between.[35]

Mestnichestvo (localism) was also regularly condemned as an impediment to proper recruitment policies. Historically, identification with the locale has been more important than tribal or other allegiances among the sedentary populations of the urban oases. Even in rural areas, local identifications had no doubt been enhanced during the Soviet period by the socialization to oblast, city, and raion party and state institutions to which very few Soviet citizens had not been exposed.

Compartmentalization of recruitment by territory, a phenomenon that, paradoxically, appeared to be built into the nature of the *nomenklatura* system, doubtless assisted the growth of localism. The directory of 1975 Supreme Soviet deputies provides an opportunity to examine recruitment patterns for the first secretaryships of city and district party committees in terms of their relationship to the corresponding localities. These committees were the organs with direct "selectorate"[36] responsibility for staffing the republic's 22,000[37] primary Party organizations.

The key role in primary recruitment and promotion of the several hundred city and district committees (*gorkom*s and *raikom*s) in Uzbekistan was reaffirmed time and again in the course of the cadre-reform drive. There were also persistent complaints that in the past it was the *gorkom*s and *raikom*s that had been largely to blame for admission of "casual people" and "alien elements" to jobs in the Party apparatus, especially because of their failure to deal directly with the applicants and a "formalistic" approach to screening procedures; during the 1986-87 drive, these committees were apt to be the first to receive blame when recruitment mishaps occurred.[38] The city and district committees clearly bore much of the responsibility for such "perversions" as allowing ties of kinship, localism or personal devotion to be substituted for objective evaluation of the qualifications of applicants. In connection with the post-Congress cleanup, these committees received special attention.

Under Rashidov, cadre practices allowed officials at the *gorkom/raikom* level to spend much of their careers in the same oblast, facilitating development of a network of personal ties. The cohesion of personnel networks based on oblasts during the Rashidov period is made particularly striking by examination of the biographies of *gorkom/raikom* officials in the group elected to the republican Supreme Soviet in 1975. Previous employment in the same oblast had played a significant role in furthering advancement to their present positions. Of 47 in the group, nearly all had either been recruited from the oblast in which they were serving or had served in it at an earlier point in their careers. This lack of inter-oblast mobility was probably attributable to the role of the oblast committees in controlling the city and district *nomenklatura*. Whatever the case, it helped to pave the way for "localism" and lasting personal allegiances within the oblast. (Curiously, this lack of inter-oblast mobility as a factor in development of local attachments appeared to have received relatively scant recognition from those concerned with reforming cadre policy after the 1986 Party Congress.)

Even for positions at the oblast level, where the republic-level *nomenklatura* (i.e., the list of appointments controlled directly by the Uzbek Central Committee) was operative, there was a definite tendency to remain within the oblast of one's previous assignment. Of 31 oblast-level officials included in the 1975 Supreme Soviet deputies directory, 23 had held a previous post in the same oblast. While this may reflect a tendency to assign people to areas with which they were familiar, it also suggests that oblast interests were able to prevail even in Tashkent.

Not Enough Workers

The problem of low worker membership in the Uzbek Communist Party, a reflection of the small size of the native industrial proletariat, had plagued Moscow loyalists ever since the earliest days of Soviet rule. In the Rashidov period, the problem was compounded by a local tendency to favor not blue- but white-collar workers for admission to Party membership. The new cadre policy enunciated after the 1986 Party Congress aimed to eradicate the effects of past abuses, when white-collar bureaucrats eager for the privileges of party membership squeezed out workers and others employed in "the basic professions" (including specialists in health, education, and other "ideological" fields) from recruitment. Cases were reported of university graduates taking jobs as "workers" in order to gain admission to the Party, then quickly shifting to white-collar positions. Even real workers were said to seek quick promotion to white-collar status once in possession of a Party card.[39]

Not Enough Women

Emphasis on recruitment of women also went back to the early days of the Soviet regime; it was the object of continuing passive resistance in the traditionally Islamic society. While in recent times some women had come to occupy prominent positions in Uzbekistan, where that was once all but impossible, the limited scope of female recruitment to the bureaucratic elite was reflected in the fact that of the 245 persons in leadership or other elite positions elected to the republican Supreme Soviet in 1975, only 19 (7.8 percent) were women.[40]

Not Enough Youth

Similarly, with respect to youth, it is interesting to examine the situation in Uzbekistan under Rashidov. Among the above group of 245 Supreme Soviet deputies in senior positions, the average age attained in 1975, the year of their election, was 50; the median was 49. None of the group was under 35, and only 19 (including the 36-year-old first secretary of the Komsomol) were under 40. It should be noted that Central Asian society is one in which respect for elders is still strong, going back to the institution of *aksakals* (literally, "white beards") whose authority was great in the affairs of Turkic tribes. During the Soviet period, *aksakalism* was encouraged by local officials, through widespread deferential use of public pronouncements attributed to elderly males (identified as *aksakals*) in support of Soviet policies.

Moscow's Campaign to Restore Control

The overall strategy of cadre reform was clearly aimed at reducing the hold on the society of the existing personnel networks dominated by Uzbek males, networks that were typically linked through common roots in traditional allegiances, and at times by mutual complicity in "corruption." Ligachev at the Party Congress had clearly implied that this was to be done in part through replacement of Uzbek incumbents with persons brought in from other republics. At the same time, recruitment procedures within the republic were to be tightened, especially through more orderly use of the "reserve" in filling vacancies, in an obvious attempt to strengthen the hand of higher authority. To facilitate change, the social base of the reserve was to be broadened, expanding the pool from which the bureaucratic elite were recruited, with special reference to improving the representation of industrial workers, women, youth, and non-party members, as well as non-Uzbek nationalities.[41] Immediate expansion of the reserve was critical to enable the leadership to replace purged officials with more reliable incumbents.

At a meeting of the Tashkent *obkom* it was announced that during 1987 some thirty Party workers would visit the three Slavic republics, RSFSR, Ukraine and Belorussia, to get a better grasp of working with the cadre "reserve."[42] While stricter observance of *nomenklatura* procedures could improve the Moscow leadership's leverage in personnel matters, it remained to be seen whether the reforms proposed by the Gorbachev regime would eliminate the causes of past "abuses."

Other innovations were proposed as steps toward tightening central control by "improving the style of work with cadres." These sought to formalize personnel decisions and to make the decision-making more visible, rendering it more difficult for the informal ethnic networks to function. Among the measures were certification (*attestatsiia*), on-the-job training, interviews, rechecking of references, electability (*vybornost'*), "dynamic" vertical and horizontal transfers, replacement of officials who failed to meet plan goals by younger, energetic ones, and various forms of training. Those responsible for making decisions about recruitment, promotion, and other personnel actions were urged to abandon the practice of doing everything through paperwork without leaving their offices (*anketno-kabinetnyi stil'*), and to take the trouble to make personal contact with candidates.[43] In keeping with glasnost, decision-making was supposed in the future to be more open, with greater involvement of rank-and-file Party members and working collectives at meetings.[44] In general, Moscow representatives and their spokesmen in the republic were relentless in voicing demands for greater zeal and accountability at all levels.

To bolster cadre reform, attention was directed to the need for improved training of personnel to inculcate not only skills but loyalty. Training outside of Uzbekistan, especially in the RSFSR, was emphasized. This involved higher Party education and other forms of education at various levels of the hierarchy. As part of the crackdown on crime, new law-enforcement cadres were being trained at juridical faculties in the RSFSR.[45]

During the 1986–87 academic year, 5324 students from Uzbekistan (*Ozbekistanliklar*) were said to be studying at institutions of higher education (*VUZy*) in other republics; there was no indication of how many were Uzbeks, Russians, etc. According to the same source, more than 800 graduates of "central" *VUZy* had come to work in Uzbekistan in the school year just past.[46] First Secretary Usmankhodzhaev publicized the exchange by publicly congratulating a group of Party members from Uzbekistan who had completed higher Party schools in Moscow, Leningrad, Sverdlovsk and Saratov, as well as Tashkent.[47]

All of these measures had as their objective the disentrenchment of the Uzbek-dominated republican elite. It was with respect to nationality that the new cadre recruitment policy most directly threatened the status quo. Ligachev's call for "inter-republican exchange of cadres" constituted a repudiation of the policy of *korenizatsiia*, which had been introduced in the early Soviet period to encourage recruitment and training of native officials as "conveyor belts" to bring Communist ideology and organization to the Central Asian masses. This policy had been essentially abandoned by Stalin, one of its framers, with the purge of "bourgeois nationalists" in the 1930s, but then re-introduced after his death. It was based on recognition that only those who are at home in the languages and cultures could bridge the nationality gap effectively.

"Inter-republican exchange" obviously aimed to dilute the Uzbek composition of the elites by opening the door to more positions for Russians and other non-Central Asians. The demand for it was buttressed by complaints that Uzbeks had been excessively favored in recruitment over others, even over their kindred Central Asian nationalities from "neighboring fraternal republics." It was argued that the staffing structure should correspond more closely to the "national composition of the population," which would put the Uzbeks at a clear disadvantage vis-à-vis their present status. Apparently it was assumed that, in an Uzbek context, Kazakhs or Tajiks would be more tractable than Uzbeks, on the principle of *divide et impera*.

One concrete action which had grave implications for Uzbekistan was the naming, in the wake of the Party Congress, of a Russian, Gennadii V. Kolbin, as Party first secretary in neighboring Kazakhstan. Kolbin replaced the Kazakh incumbent Dinmukhamed A. Kunaev, who was subsequently removed from the Politburo. (Kunaev had been the only representative of Central Asia broadly defined.) The ensuing riots drew worldwide attention. In Uzbekistan, the most visible consequence of a parallel shift in policy was the designation of a Russian, B. F. Satin, to the important post of first secretary of the Party's Tashkent city committee, which had previously been headed by an Uzbek.

Ligachev's call for "interrepublican exchange of cadres" also appeared to address the problem of Russians who had lived so long in Central Asia that their reliability was in doubt. Importation from other republics of replacements uncontaminated by previous attachments, rather than relying as in the past on mere nationality as a guarantor of the loyalty of republican officials, would help to prevent illicit co-optation of Russians and other outsiders into the native networks. At the same time, this posed a dilemma for the center: would officials new to the republic, however faithful to Moscow's interests, know enough about the local scene to function effectively?[48]

In its effort to humble the Uzbek elites, Moscow tried to win grass-roots support in the republic. The masses were encouraged to use perestroika and glasnost to criticize officials and expose their shortcomings and misdeeds, in the name of "democratism."

In addition to "democratism," the slogan of "electability" introduced by Gorbachev also seems to have caused some anti-elite ferment in Uzbekistan. One collective was accused of "demagogic attempts to push to the surface their 'own' comfortable, undemanding leader." (This was, of course, before the 1988 Party Conference and the 1989 Congress proceedings in Moscow had given greater sanction to democratization.) At a champagne factory in Tashkent oblast, the workers rejected three officially endorsed candidates and elected a fourth, who was said to have been the defendant in a criminal trial and who had been expelled from the Party.[49] In one raion, workers and peasants voted out one of every five managers (although in this case with the sanction of higher authority, it appears).[50] In the Tashkent oblast city of Almalyk, members of the city Komsomol organization refused to elect a Party-endorsed leader with extensive Komsomol experience; the first secretary of the Party *gorkom*, in reporting this incident, said that it was "like a bolt from the blue" but that on looking into the matter he had decided that the decision of the members was correct.[51]

Speaking at the Uzbek Party plenum in March 1987, an *obkom* first secretary declared that some leaders were so frightened by "various processes and tendencies taking place among young workers" that they were diverted from making principled decisions.[52]

Pressure from the center also took the form of attacks on national and religious sentiments among the elites. A plenum of the Uzbek Party held in October 1986, censured Uzbek writers for "idealization" of the past through praise of such native figures as Tamerlane and Babur.[53] Party members were reprimanded for attending Islamic funeral ceremonies or placing Islamic emblems on their private automobiles.[54]

Elite Resistance

The cadre campaign provoked a storm of resistance. Those among the "outs" who had not been imprisoned were still in a position to make trouble: for example, it was reported in July 1987, that 1,450 dismissed secretaries of primary Party organizations were at large, working on collective and state farms.[55] More than three years after the leadership had fired its first major salvo in the war against "negative phenomena," at the June 1984 Uzbek plenum, a deposed city official in Navoi oblast organized a march of war veterans on a *raikom* and the *obkom* to protest the action taken against him. He also organized "a collective libel" of the *raikom* secretaries involved.[56] In Andizhan oblast, local interests were accused of using trumped-up charges to "settle scores" with a new oblast chief judge who had been assigned by the Central Committee in Moscow; his enemies succeeded in having a "stern reprimand" placed in the judge's Party personnel file.[57]

The campaign to replace corrupt or incompetent officials with fresh cadres was also vitiated, according to press reports, by the tendency of those ousted to resurface in other responsible posts. Sharp condemnation of this practice at the 1986 Party Congress did not succeed in ending it. The problem was mentioned in the June 1987 decree of the Central Committee in Moscow aimed at "serious shortcomings in the work of the Tashkent oblast Party organization on admission to the Party and strengthening of the Party ranks"; the decree called on Party organs not to permit re-admission to the Party of "persons expelled from it for bribery, embezzlement and padding reports." The Surkhandarya *obkom* Administrative Organs Department head mentioned above as having been fired for getting forged documents for his daughter turned up as a department head in the oblast trade-union organization despite his misdeed. That and a number of similar cases were attributed to the connivance of higher authority in concealing the true grounds for dismissal through the face-saving announcement "in connection with transfer to other work."[58] An *obkom* first secretary lamented that oblast, city and raion officials "often take up the defense of leaders who have compromised themselves."[59]

The revolving door through which dismissed officials were able to continue their careers in new positions was evidently due not just to skullduggery but also to the shortage of qualified replacement candidates. The intensity of the purge strained human resources. For example, in the Karakalpak ASSR, as of spring 1987, six state-farm directors had been in office less than a year, and five less than two years.[60] It was announced by the Uzbekistan prosecutor that, in view of the large numbers of people involved in corruption, only the most egregious perpetrators would face charges.[61] The effect of high turnover on cadre replacement was exacerbated by the inadequacy of the reserve pool of candidates, which had allegedly been kept deliberately small by local officials in order to frustrate higher authority. There was also the problem of insufficient training. In the Fergana Valley in 1987, ironically a center of massive unemployment, there were positions for 23,500 economists with higher education filled by only 7,500 incumbents, of whom 2,800 had already reached pension age, and replacements were being received at the rate of only 700 a year.[62] A *raikom* secretary in Tashkent claimed that by the time he could train instructors and department heads they were snatched away by higher authority.

In defiance of the ongoing purge, reports of bribery, thefts and nepotism by those in office were still appearing regularly in the press. A note of weariness had crept into speeches. In the words of one Party loyalist, an *obkom* first secretary, "Life has become more interesting, but it's harder to work."

Leading Party officials became vocally critical of the cadre reform. An *obkom* first secretary reminded participants in the March 28, 1987 plenum of the Uzbek Party that successful work with cadres was impossible without "stability." Instead of steady, painstaking work to train people, he noted, "we are allowing promotions and dismissals to be hasty." Another *obkom* first secretary asserted that realization of the Party's decisions depended "not on bawling out, not on crushing, not on nihilism in evaluating work," but on a more objective approach. He criticized the various commissions investigating his oblast which were trying to collect "as many negative materials as possible" and thus harming the cause by "breeding in officials a lack of confidence and faith in their own capabilities and possibilities." If leaders were to be encouraged to experiment, he added, then they must also have the right to make mistakes.

Doubts about the impact on the economy were also openly expressed. The first secretary of Surkhandarya oblast questioned whether anything had really changed for collectives who had adopted the new work style: "Based on our experience, you can say it hasn't." In March 1987, the chairman of the Uzbek Council of Ministers observed, "According to all basic indicators, Samarkand oblast has begun to work worse than at the beginning of last year." The first secretary of the Syrdarya *obkom* commented that in some places "rank-and-file working people are seeing that there is a perestroika in words but not in deed, that everything is as before." The head of an administration in Khorezm oblast was censured in the press for speaking up at an *obkom* plenum: "They should help us and not criticize. Otherwise there's no desire to work. What's happening is that perestroika is reduced to a settling of scores."[63]

The elites also fought back against Moscow's attempts to stir up the masses against them. There was criticism of "shouters" who, invoking the new slogan of "democratization," were saying that "life is changing," and had "harnessed criticism to settle their own affairs." A republican newspaper accused of blackmail six employees who, allegedly in a false spirit of glasnost, had written denunciations of their former superior; by sending telegrams to Moscow they were able to make trouble for local officials who tried to halt their campaign to discredit the officials.[64]

In the end, Moscow's efforts to use the Uzbek masses to pressure the elites from below was to backfire. They were thwarted by the elites' ability to appeal to the nationalist feelings of rank-and-file Uzbeks, to persuade them that the purge was also aimed at them. More and more, articles began to appear in the Uzbek media complaining that much of the criticism of the republic in Moscow newspapers was unjustified, an affront to Uzbek honor at all levels of the society. There was a particular outcry against the term "the Uzbek affair" which had been coined by Moscow officials and newspaper writers as a catchword for corruption; Uzbeks noted indignantly that corruption payoffs had ended up not in Uzbekistan but in Moscow. As a result, the cadre purge was perceived by Uzbeks as threatening not merely the officials involved, but the autonomy and integrity of their republic.

As much as rank-and-file Uzbeks had good reason to resent the conduct of their own corrupt officials, their chagrin at Moscow's intervention in the affairs of their republic seems to have been even greater. The wounded feelings of all Uzbeks at the supposed affront to their honor helped produce a national consensus of resistance to the center. The poet Muhammad Salih looked back on Uzbek bitterness at the center's anti-corruption and cadre campaign in a later newspaper interview:

> Let's say that if a journalist from the central press wants to write about the crime of padding accounts, then he naturally picks Uzbekistan and doubtless the "padder" Rashidov as the example. At the same time, that journalist well knows that in order to "pad" millions of tons of cotton in secret from the Politburo it takes not just Rashidov but two people. . . . They were taking money not just in Tashkent but in the George Hall (of the Kremlin). . . . In Uzbekistan 9 million people were living out their days below the poverty level. Before we could talk about this, we had to prove that those nine million people were not all thieves. . . . Usman-

khodzhaev, who was then the leader of our republic, suddenly announced that there were not enough cadres. He asked Moscow to send a few thousand leading cadres to Uzbekistan. Indeed, there were many empty slots. For the Gdlian and Ivanov group had been working with all its might. In the process of exposing criminals, thousands of guilty and innocent were thrown into jail. As Usmankhodzhaev's request was filled, the slots that had been emptied by Gdlian were filled one after the other.[65]

An even more sardonic view of the cadre campaign was expressed by another Uzbek writer, Timur Pulatov:

Nearly 300 officials of all ranks were sent to Uzbekistan to replace the disgraced locals. Unfamiliar with the "land of cotton's" economic workings, with the national character, the traditional way of life, and the language, many of the new people proved to be misfits and started to blame all their failures on "nationalists" who, in league with the local mafia, allegedly opposed the cleansing of the moral climate in Uzbekistan.[66]

Popular disgruntlement over the region's economic and environmental crisis, caused by the Moscow planners' ruthless expansion of cotton growing, also played into the hands of the elites. The true enormity of the situation caused by the cotton monoculture began, thanks to glasnost, to be a regular topic of Uzbek media. The litany of grievances was staggering, from desiccation of the Aral Sea leaving in its wake a vast salt desert, to a rise in infant mortality due to contamination of drinking-water sources with agricultural chemicals, to the stark fact that Uzbekistan's living standards placed it at or near the bottom rank of the Soviet republics, with only half the per capita national income of the country as a whole. All of this helped to rally Uzbek public support for the native elites in their confrontation with Moscow.

The Campaign Stalls

Initially, the top leadership's response to Uzbek resistance was to keep on the pressure. For a time, *obkom, gorkom,* and *raikom* officials continued to be singled out for censure at Party meetings and in the press. But gradually, as the resistance movement broadened from the bureaucratic elite to embrace the cultural intelligentsia and other strata of Uzbek society, the campaign slackened.

Despite Moscow's stress on improving the "style of work with cadres," there continued to be "misjudgements and mistakes" in recruitment, leading to a high rate of turnover of those in office. An indigenous official appointed to the key job of oblast executive committee chairman in Navoi oblast had to be dismissed only eight months later, a raion first secretary appointed in Bukhara oblast lasted only one month longer, and a *gorkom* second secretary in Tashkent oblast was kept for only three months. All of them were removed for "negative reasons."[67]

From the start, Moscow had failed to exhibit resolve to carry through its program of "interrepublican exchange of cadres" on a scale sufficient to cripple the native elites by replacing substantial numbers of Uzbek officials with other nationalities. There was similar indecision about taking measures to change the social base of the elites. As a result, "reform" seemed to be addressed more to the style of work than to the fundamental criteria of recruitment—perhaps in keeping with the vagueness of Gorbachev's pronouncements on cadre policy.[68] It appears that this hesitation may be attributable, at least in part, to disagreement within the Moscow leadership, given that the two Politburo members most visibly concerned with Uzbekistan were Gorbachev and Ligachev.

In the absence of firm criteria of selection, the reform lacked teeth. The Russian second secretary in Uzbekistan admitted that it was against Party policy to employ "arithmetical" quotas in implementing recruitment directives.[69] The measures adopted did little to affect the national and territorial bases of recruitment.

As a result of the center's lack of firmness and direction in the face of resistance, Uzbeks were able to hold on to their substantial plurality of first secretaryships and chairmanships at the various levels of the Party and government apparatus. Perhaps daunted by the Alma-Ata riots which had followed First Secretary Kunaev's replacement by a Russian in neighboring Kazakhstan, in Uzbekistan the leadership did not follow the change of nationality of the Tashkent *gorkom* first secretary with similar nationality shifts in other highly visible posts.

Three years after "interrepublican exchange of cadres" was proclaimed by Ligachev at the 1986 Moscow Congress, there were Slavs in prominent positions in the republic, but nearly all of their posts had been held by Slavs before the Congress, so that change was minimal. Central Asian incumbents retained their earlier slender majority of the Uzbek Party Buro and a majority of the new Party commissions created under the Gorbachev reforms of the Party apparatus. Perhaps the most striking evidence of Moscow's retreat was the fact that in 1989 those two important Central Asian posts that had been wrested from native control, the Kazakh first secretaryship and the first secretaryship of the Tashkent *gorkom*, were restored to native tenancy.

The preponderance of Uzbeks in *obkom* first secretaryships—that bulwark of the native elites—also remained unchanged. Indeed, a consolidation of oblasts put through in September 1988, was to reduce the number of non-indigenous incumbents of first secretaryships from two to one.

The most telling sign that day-to-day control of the Party machinery remained largely in Uzbek hands was at the level of the raion organizations, whose important functions include recruitment to primary Party organizations, a major determinant of the overall composition of the Party. No comprehensive list of incumbents was available, but in a tally of seventy-one urban and rural first secretaries whose names were gleaned from the press in the latter part of 1987, in 1988, and in the first part of 1989, sixty-one (86 percent) were identifiable by name as "Muslims," and only nine (13 percent) as Slavs, leaving one lone Armenian in neither of those categories.[70]

If large numbers of Party workers were really transferred "permanently" from the RSFSR and other republics, as had been promised, they did not appear conspicuously among holders of important assignments, except in police and prosecutorial areas, which had been clearly reinforced by outsiders. Indeed, even in those areas there were signs of a tendency for the importees not to stay in Uzbekistan. One of the most celebrated cases was that of General Eduard Alekseevich Didorenko, who was assigned to Uzbekistan as first deputy minister of internal affairs, one of the top law-enforcement posts. Didorenko created such a furor by making statements impugning the loyalty of residents of Uzbekistan, Russians included, that he was recalled and left the republic.[71] Another Russian who left the republic, reportedly under pressure from discontented Uzbeks, was the *Literaturnaia gazeta* journalist Vladimir Sokolov, who had written controversial exposés of "corruption" there.

As to fulfillment of the center's stated intention to broaden the social base of the Uzbek Party, and of the Party and state organs, detailed information is not available, but it is clear that here, too, resistance was stiff. In one incident, a Tashkent *raikom* first secretary spoke out against rejuvenation, protesting that a ceiling on the "age composition of the reserve" was a factor leading to the inexperience and lack of authority of some *raikom* officials. In the same context, he noted that 60 percent of secretaries of primary Party organizations in his raion had indicated, in response to a survey, that they were not receiving competent assistance from *raikom* officials.[72] As for women, there did not appear to be a significant change in the sex composition of leading Party and state jobs. There was one noteworthy exception, the election of a woman, Rimadjan M. Khudaibergenova, as first secretary of the Khorezm *obkom*, but whether this was done under pressure from Moscow or for purely local reasons is unclear. The mere fact that the levers of access remained largely in the hands of Uzbek male bureaucrats suggested that old patterns were not apt to change abruptly.

Implications for the Power Balance

The outcome of the cadre campaign demonstrated that Moscow, by using the law-enforcement organs to supplement its political power, was able to target individual offices for replacement of incumbents. But such actions had to be conducted on a scatter-shot basis, and at a high price in terms of the local resentment which they generated. The fundamental lesson of the failed cadre campaign was that Moscow lacked the capability to effect a general restructuring of the Uzbek apparatus by *political* means.

Resistance by the elites was not the only factor that thwarted Moscow's plans to reassert its control over elite recruitment. Hesitation and lack of decision on the part of the center also played a role, as did the emergence of a destabilizing economic and social situation in Uzbekistan. But it was clear that the Uzbek elites had stood up to Moscow and won.

The old Soviet Uzbek elites, whatever their shortcomings, helped the Party to maintain political stability while promoting economic development and a degree of social change in the face of challenges of many kinds, beginning with the "basmachi" rebellion and "national communism." These elites evolved over many decades in response to the Party's needs for an apparatus that could deal with a largely Islamic-traditionalist, nationalistic, elder-venerating, agrarian, male-dominated society with inherent hostility to change. Now the equilibrium of many years has changed.

Gorbachev's reforms of the electoral system may have helped to render moot the question of recruitment by weakening not only the center's grip but also that of the republican Establishment. New forces have been awakened in the society which threaten not only Moscow's control but also that of the Uzbek elite. Nevertheless, what emerges clearly from the record of this confrontation is that in its future dealings with the republic Moscow will have to reckon with Uzbek power, and proceed on a basis of bilateral negotiation, not of fiat. Given the central role of Uzbekistan in Central Asian politics, this swing in the balance of power could not fail to affect the other republics of the region.

Notes

1. Bohdan Harasymiw, *Political Elite Recruitment in the Soviet Union* (New York: St. Martin's Press 1984), pp. 32–33.

2. Alexandre Bennigsen, *Islam in the Soviet Union* (New York: Praeger, 1967), p. 161.

3. Michael S. Voslensky, *Nomenklatura* (Vienna: Verlag Fritz Molden), 1980, pp. 406–407.

4. Gerhard Simon, *Nationalismus und Nationalitätenpolitik in der Sowjetunion* (Baden-Baden: Nomos Verlag), 1986, p. 19.

5. "Political Report of the Central Committee of the CPSU to the XXVII Congress of the Communist Party of the Soviet Union: Report by CPSU Central Committee General Secretary M. S. Gorbachev, February 25, 1986," *Materialy XXVII S"ezda KPSS* (Moscow: Politizdat, 1986), pp. 80–81.

6. Ibid.

7. *Pravda*, Feb. 28, 1986 (both speeches).

8. *Literaturnaia gazeta*, June 6, 1987. The author was Kamil Ikramov, son of Akmal Ikramov, a former head of the Uzbek Communist Party who was one of the defendants executed together with Nikolai Bukharin following the famous purge trial of March 1938. His article was reprinted by *Pravda Vostoka* in Russian and *Sovet Ozbekistani* in Uzbek.

9. *Pravda Vostoka*, Mar. 29, 1987.

10. Ibid.

11. See Julia Wishnevsky, "The Gdlyan-Ivanov Commission Starts Its Work," *Radio Liberty, Report on the USSR*, June 30, 1989, p. 1.

12. See *Radio Liberty Research*, 162/87, Apr. 10, 1987.

13. I. Usmankhodzhaev, Report to Fourth Plenum of the Uzbek CP Central Committee," February 14, 1987, *Kommunist Uzbekistana*, no. 4, 1987, p. 38.

14. *Pravda Vostoka*, Mar. 29, 1987.

15. *Pravda Vostoka*, June 25, 1987.

16. *Pravda Vostoka*, Apr. 18, 1987.

17. Usmankhodzhaev revealed in a speech to the republican Party *aktiv* (*Pravda Vostoka*, July 12, 1987, p. 3) that 388,000 Party members, "i.e., about two-thirds of the republican Party organization," were living in the countryside. That put the total membership at somewhere above 582,000, compared with 640,000 at the time of the February 1986 Uzbek Party Congress. Expulsion from the Party is a necessary preliminary to prosecution of Party members.

18. *Pravda Vostoka*, Mar. 29, 1987, p. 2, col. 3.

19. Usmankhodzhaev, Report to the Twenty-First Congress of the Uzbek Communist Party," p. 11.

20. *Sovet Ozbekistani*, July 11, 1987.

21. Merle Fainsod, *How Russia Is Ruled*, Revised ed., (Cambridge: Harvard University Press, 1964), *passim*; Voslensky, *Nomenklatura, passim*.

22. *Partiinaia zhizn' Kazakhstana*, no. 1, 1985, p. 40.

23. *Ozbekistan SSR Aliy Sovetining Deputatlari (toqqizinchi chaqiriq) / Deputaty Verkhovnogo Soveta Uzbekskoi SSR (deviatyi sozyv)* (Tashkent: Uzbekistan, 1976), *passim*. These were the deputies elected on June 15, 1975 to the ninth session of the republican Supreme Soviet. Only deputies occupying leading positions (245 from a total of 470) were selected for the analysis. Population shares are from *Uzbekskaia SSR* (Russian-language volume issued by the Uzbek Soviet Encyclopedia), (Tashkent: 1981), p. 66.

24. "Report by Second Secretary V. P. Anishchev to Sixth Plenum of the Uzbek Communist Party," *Sovet Ozbekistani*, Aug. 12, 1987, p. 2.

25. In the few cases where Slavs have occupied the top position in Uzbekistan, their deputies have commonly been natives.

26. Hélène Carrère d'Encausse, *L'Empire Eclaté: La Révolte des Nations en U.R.S.S.* (Paris: Flammarion, 1978), p. 145.

27. Usmankhodzhaev, Report to the Twenty-First Congress of the Uzbek Communist Party.

28. Central Intelligence Agency, *Directory of USSR Officials: Republican Organizations*, (Washington, 1985).

29. *Ozbekistan SSR Aliy Sovetining Deputatlari* and *Uzbekskaia SSR*.

30. *Ozbekistan SSR Aliy Sovetining Deputatlari*.

31. For a discussion of the role of "channels" in recruitment, e.g. education as an "institutional locus," see Robert D. Putnam, *The Comparative Study of Political Elites* (Englewood, New Jersey: Prentice Hall, 1976), pp. 45 ff.

32. K. K. Pahlen, *Mission to Turkestan* (London: Oxford University Press, 1964), pp. 156–57.

33. *Ozbekistan SSR Aliy Sovetining Deputatlari*.

34. *Pravda Vostoka*, July 15, 1987.

35. Report by V. P. Anishchev to republican meeting of social sciences, Jan. 17, 1987, *Kommunist Uzbekistana*, no. 3, 1987, p. 76.

36. Vera Dunham, *In Stalin's Time: Middleclass Values in Soviet Fiction* (Cambridge University Press, 1976), pp. 53 ff.

37. *Sovet Ozbekistani*, July 11, 1987.

38. Anishchev report to Sixth Plenum, p. 3.

39. Ibid.

40. *Ozbekistan SSR Aliy Sovetining Deputatlari*.

41. This campaign was foreshadowed by Usmankhodzhaev's report to the Twenty-First Congress of the Uzbek Communist Party in February 1986, on the eve of the Moscow Party Congress, and was developed in speeches at various subsequent plenums of the Uzbek Central Committee.

42. *Pravda Vostoka*, Apr. 8, 1987.

43. See, for example, the speech by N. R. Radzhabov at the March 1987 plenum of the Uzbek Communist Party, *Pravda Vostoka*, Apr. 1, 1987, p. 5.

44. Anishchev report to Sixth Plenum.

45. *Sovet Ozbekistani*, July 11, 1987.

46. *Sovet Ozbekistani*, July 7, 1987.

47. *Pravda Vostoka*, July 4, 1987.

48. See Putnam, pp. 134 ff., for discussion of "elite-mass congruence" and information flow from and to elites and non-elites as factors in "elite-mass linkage." Effective linkage between elites and masses can reduce the need for coercion to maintain a political system.

49. *Pravda Vostoka*, Apr. 8, 1987.

50. *Pravda Vostoka*, Apr. 1, 1987, p. 5.

51. *Pravda Vostoka*, Apr. 1, 1987, p. 3.

52. *Pravda Vostoka*, Mar. 29, 1987.

53. *Pravda Vostoka*, Oct. 5, 1986. p. 2.

54. *Sovet Ozbekistani*, July 25, 1987, p. 3.

55. *Pravda Vostoka*, July 12, 1987, p. 3.
56. *Pravda Vostoka*, July 15, 1987, p. 3.
57. *Pravda Vostoka*, Mar. 29, 1987, p. 3.
58. *Pravda Vostoka*, July 15, 1987, p. 3.
59. *Pravda Vostoka*, Apr. 1, 1987, p. 5.
60. *Pravda Vostoka*, Apr. 7, 1987, p. 2.
61. *Ozbekistan adabiyati va san"ati*, Feb. 6, 1987, p. 2. Later on, Buturlin himself was replaced, under a cloud in Uzbek eyes.
62. Unless otherwise noted, the remaining references in this and the following three paragraphs are to speeches at the Fifth Plenum of the Uzbek Central Committee held March 28, 1987, as printed in *Pravda Vostoka*, Apr. 1, 1987.
63. *Pravda Vostoka*, Apr. 21, 1987.
64. *Pravda Vostoka*, July 15, 1987.
65. *Ozbekistan adabiyati va san"ati*, Dec. 15, 1989, pp. 4-5.
66. Timur Pulatov, "Corruption is Being Uprooted," *Moscow News*, no. 1, 1990.
67. Usmankhodzhaev report to Fourth Plenum of Uzbek CP Central Committee, Feb. 14, 1987, *Kommunist Uzbekistana*, no. 4, 1987, p. 38.
68. As an example, see Gorbachev's report to the CPSU Central Committee plenum held January 27, 1987, published in *Pravda* of the following day.
69. Anishchev report to Sixth Plenum.
70. See J. Critchlow, "Obduracy of Uzbek Cadres Casting Shadow on Nationalities Plenum," Radio Liberty, *Report on the USSR*, Mar. 24, 1989, pp. 21-22.
71. See J. Critchlow, "Furor over MVD General Exposes Political Divisions in Uzbekistan," Radio Liberty, *Report on the USSR*, May 5, 1989, pp. 13-15.
72. *Pravda Vostoka*, Apr. 1, 1987.

PART THREE

Identity and Religion

6

Ethnic Attitudes and Relations in Modern Uzbek Cities

Ronald Wixman

Introduction

Although at present one can find much literature on various aspects of Soviet nationality policy, until very recently little was published (either in Soviet or Western works) on actual ethnic attitudes toward different peoples or on interethnic relations. Because of such problems, Western scholars like Karklins attempted to gain insights through interviews with recent emigrés from the Soviet Union (especially ethnic Germans residing in the Federal Republic of Germany and Jews in the United States).[1] However, no studies appeared by Western social scientists based on field studies conducted in the USSR.

Yet, questions of ethnic attitudes and relations are of great relevance to the study of any multiethnic society. In the case of Soviet Central Asia, they are crucial to an understanding of developments in the late 1980s and 1990s. This is nowhere clearer than in the greatly accelerated exodus of Russians from Central Asia which is observable today.

This chapter, based on interviews carried out in Uzbekistan in the summer of 1985, attempts to provide a part of the very complex picture of ethnic relations and attitudes. The author, of course, recognizes this study's limitations. The number of individuals interviewed is relatively small (only a few hundred) and the observations were limited to three cities in only one republic. Moreover, it does not attempt to examine in detail such questions as relations between major indigenous nationality groups (e.g., Tajiks and Uzbeks), or relations among members of the same nationality group who are from very different regions. However, in the absence of any other studies of this nature on the subject by Western social scientists, it does provide insights into some aspects of ethnic relations and attitudes discernable among the inhabitants of three of Uzbekistan's largest cities (Bukhara, Samarkand, and Tashkent).

In the summer of 1985 I travelled to Bukhara, Samarkand, and Tashkent, where I was able to observe social interactions in a variety of settings between members of different ethnic groups (i.e. Central Asian and European peoples).[2] I also had the opportunity to interview individuals and groups of people under a variety of circumstances. The settings for observations included public places (markets, teahouses, restaurants, parks, and shops), housing developments and homes, a variety of workplaces, and on public transportation. The people were from disparate social groups, and included students, professionals (e.g. doctors and professors), housewives, shoppers, workers, farmers in markets, and children.[3]

Many individuals were very willing to share their feelings about ethnic relations and interethnic attitudes in Uzbek cities. This was especially true when talking to children, mothers in mixed marriages, university and technical school students, and shopkeepers in bazaars. The reverse was true when institute personnel were engaged in similar conversations. Their answers to questions on ethnic relations read like standard textbooks, as did those of government officials and hotel front desk-workers.

In addition to talking with people, I also spent a great deal of time directly observing everyday behavior and listening to others' conversations. In most cases Europeans and Central Asians sat and socialized separately. This general pattern was repeated every time I went to parks, *chaykhanas*, (teahouses) and other public gathering spots. Clearly, this is a good indicator of *actual* relations between Europeans and Central Asians; it is probably a better one than more easily cited Soviet literature on ethnic relations or official speeches by public officials.

Interethnic relations in urban areas of Uzbekistan, as everywhere else, are complex, contextual, and highly situational.[4] People who get along well under certain conditions may be virtual enemies under others. One can cite incidents of great harmony and great enmity between the same groups; both situations may represent accurate reflections of these relationships. One must be careful not to describe these relationships in exaggerated terms, or to overemphasize certain aspects relative to others. Generalities about these relations may be correct, but nonetheless mask many specifics. Thus, to say that Central Asians and Slavs do not get along well is absolutely true in some ways, yet totally inaccurate in others.

On the surface the various native peoples of Central Asia and European immigrants coexisted in apparent harmony, and interethnic relations could be described as cordial. However, underlying these superficially good relations were a variety of serious problems that surfaced under varying circumstances. These problems included overt and perceived ethnic prejudice, competition for jobs, promotions, positions and housing, and incompatible life styles heightened by peoples living in close proximity within an urban environment.

In order to describe interethnic attitudes and relations in contemporary urban Uzbekistan, a number of interrelated factors must be examined. Among these are: (1) attitudes based on actual social interaction; (2) attitudes and impressions stemming from biases, including perceived relative social positions, and attitudes toward intermarriages; and (3) attitudes based on reaction to official or perceived discrimination and competition. The three substantive sections of this study deal with each of these subjects.

Ethnic and Social Interaction

The single most important source of ethnic attitudes and relations (and, simultaneously, the most important influence on these attitudes and relations) is probably actual social interaction between or among the various ethnic groups. Positive and negative experiences in social meetings, at places of work, neighborhoods, or in general everyday life are the main determinants of interethnic attitudes. The degree to which people show respect (or disrespect) for one another as individuals or as culture groups has a major influence on the development of these ethnic relations.

In this section we will consider the social interaction between Central Asians and Soviet Europeans (Slavs, Balts, Germans, Ashkenazic Jews, etc.) as groups. We will look at the ways in which these groups interact in social situations, in particular in *chaykhanas*, *stolovaias* (workers' cafeterias), in the work place, and in parks. The degree to which these disparate groups interact is an excellent indicator of actual ethnic relations. When groups readily communicate and talk freely with each other, one can assume that relations range from reasonable to very good; on the other hand, avoidance patterns and openly expressed hostility are indicators of relatively poor relations.

In interviewing Europeans and Central Asians it became apparent that little socializing took place across traditional cultural lines. The lack of social interaction was especially clear in activities outside the place of work or study. Almost all adults and college students interviewed claimed to have colleagues at work or in school who were from the opposite groups (except those who worked in the bazaars or market places). But when asked about how often they went to the homes of these colleagues, went out to restaurants or theaters with them, or had them over as guests in their own homes, a different picture emerged. This situation is not unlike the pattern in American cities where people of different ethnic, religious, cultural, racial, or social backgrounds work together. Americans are cordial and talk to each other at work, but go their own ways after work and socialize primarily with people of their own backgrounds. Relations remain cordial as long as certain sensitive issues are avoided.

When I asked Uzbek and Tajik children how often Russian (or other European) adults came to visit their parents, most answered "rarely" and others "never." This was especially true of the inhabitants of the Old Quarter[5] in Bukhara and Samarkand. Slavs, on the other hand, sometimes had Central Asian guests, but infrequently. Even most Uzbek and Tajik *children* claimed that outside of school and school-related activities they did not associate much with Russian children. This was especially true in the case of those who attended native language schools. (This is not surprising, since almost no Russians enroll their children in Uzbek or Tajik language schools.)

In the old cities of Bukhara and Samarkand, I observed children playing in groups (four or more children) in areas near schools, in parks, and on streets. Here, in only 3 out of 38 groups of children did I observe any mixing of Central Asians and Europeans, and in none of these 3 were more than two Europeans present.[6] On the other hand, in the newer sections of these cities and Tashkent, ethnically mixed groups of children were commonly seen. However, even in these situations monocultural groups made up over 50 percent of the observed groups (32 out of 60); and rarely was there an equal distribution (only two cases).

Thus, even in the newer more ethnically mixed parts of the cities, the more common pattern was to see European children playing with other Europeans, and Central Asians with other Central Asians. In interviews with 30 Russian mothers in ethnically mixed parts of Bukhara and Tashkent, 22 actually expressed a desire to promote friendships of their children with other Europeans and to inhibit similar friendships with Central Asian children (especially those that live in the Old Quarters of the cities) because, as some said, the indigenous children are *"griaznye i dikie* (dirty and wild)." They said that Central Asian children were always fighting and that they lie; therefore, they did not want their children around them. These women (all of whom had lived in Uzbekistan for less than 20 years) also supported the view that Central Asian women are mistreated by their husbands and that they live in an oppressed state (*ugnetennoe polozhenie*). This was also voiced by various European Soviet tourists in this region. Many Russians felt that the social structure and system among the Central Asians is unacceptable to them. Slavs frequently expressed views that Central Asians are violent, not honest, mistreat their wives, and that they do not learn Russian well (a sign of their backwardness and inferiority).[7]

It is extremely difficult to judge to what extent the newer parts of these cities are ethnically mixed or segregated. Although virtually all Soviet sources at the time claimed that there was no discrimination in housing by ethnic groups and that there was no segregation (forced or voluntary) other than in the traditional or old sections of cities where "natives" formed the majority of the population, walks through different parts of these cities gave very different impressions. Unlike in the West where sociologists and geographers have done many detailed studies on settlement patterns of various ethnic, racial, and social groups in various cities, the Soviets were very slow to begin to publish this kind of data.[8] Only recently have any major works been published in the USSR that deal with ethnic identity and community interaction.[9]

One must also consider that individuals do not choose where they wish to live, but rather find housing, or are given housing, through housing bureaus or places of work. Therefore, one cannot determine to what extent housing segregation by ethnic or culture group would occur if individuals and families had more choice in selecting their place of residence.

Sometimes people living together encounter major problems that do not exist when they live separately. Central Asians and immigrant Slavs, too, sometimes find it difficult to live in such close proximity. One major problem that exists in more integrated areas in the Uzbek cities is incompatibility of cultures. In apartment buildings with mixed Central Asian and European families complaints commonly referred to food preparation. The Slavs complained about the smell of Central Asian cooking; for their part, the Central Asians complained not only about the smell of cabbage, but worse, about the "disgusting smell of pork cooking." A number of Uzbeks and Tajiks openly expressed deep resentment of having to inhale pork fumes. To more religious Muslims this is intolerable. However, one cannot simply change apartments in the USSR. Not infrequently this has led to arguments between neighbors, and a number of Central Asians used this as an example of the disrespect the Slavs had for their culture, customs, and food.[10]

The urban Slavs also complained about how noisy their Central Asian neighbors were and how often they had noisy guests. They often put this complaint in terms of the number of children the Central Asians had, and how noisy they and their friends were. Another common comment by Slavs was that the Central Asians, and in particular those coming from villages, did not know how to use the various amenities of an apartment building, and that they did "not know how to live s *drugimi* (with others)." The Central Asians often discussed how unfriendly their Slavic neighbors were and that they (the Slavs) were always complaining. Central Asians' response to this comment by Europeans was "If they don't like it here, why don't they go home?"

As with housing, the workplace also provides a setting for ethnic interaction. Unfortunately, it was not possible for me to enter factories and other places of work unaccompanied in the USSR. All description of relations at workplaces were obtained through discussion and interviews with individuals in public places, *stolovaias*, and outside places of work. I had discussions with 22 Russians, 8 Ukrainians, 6 Germans, 4 Ashkenazic Jews, 35 Uzbeks, 28 Tajiks, 8 Kazakhs, 6 Central Asian Jews, and 3 Crimean Tatars in Tashkent. Their comments paralleled those obtained in similar discussions in Bukhara. (No interviews were conducted in Samarkand.) In virtually all cases the individuals who worked in factories or large enterprises said that their places of work had people of various nationalities working in them. Relations at work tended to be cordial and friendly between the groups. All asserted they had friends of all nationalities at work. Only one, (a Tajik) claimed that ethnic relations at work were poor.

However, when I asked about the maintenance of these relationships *after* work or at lunch, a different picture emerged. Only 4 Uzbeks, 2 Tajiks, 2 Kazakhs, and 4 Central Asian Jews (among the Central Asians) socialized regularly with their European co-workers outside work. All Central Asians, on the other hand, socialized and had lunch with Central Asians of other nationalities on a regular basis. The pattern among Europeans was analogous. Only 3 Russians, 2 Ukrainians, and 3 Ashkenazic Jews socialized with Central Asians on a regular basis outside the work place, while all had strong friendships with other Europeans.

Because they were good locations to observe social interaction between different groups, I observed places of eating and drinking in Uzbekistan. In particular, I visited tea houses *chaykhanas*) in Bukhara, Samarkand, and Tashkent, where I observed a total of 836 people seated at 196 tables. The vast majority of the tables (187) were "monocultural," i.e., comprised solely of Central Asians or Europeans as culture groups. These accounted for 773 of the 836 people.[11] Obviously, the dominant pattern was monocultural socializing. It should be kept in mind, of course, that *chaykhanas* are traditional places of socializing among Central Asians and are not a part of Russian or other Soviet-European cultures. In these places tea and traditional Central Asian (not European) foods are served, and therefore one would expect the majority of people there to be Central Asians.

In order to ascertain why so few Europeans came to these *chaykhanas*, I asked 30 European residents of Bukhara and Samarkand whether they went to *chaykhanas* in general, and if so why (or why not) they went (or did not go). Twenty-eight replied they normally did not; 24 of them declared that the main reason they did not attend them was because they, in essence, "did not mix with the natives." They found them alien, and 4 claimed that the "locals do not like us there." When I asked Central Asians whether or not Europeans were welcome there, they seemed not to care one way or the other. It is perhaps relevant to point out that prior to engaging in conversation, I was ignored in *chaykhanas*. When in discussions I claimed to be Georgian, Moldavian, or Jewish, I was still basically ignored, but when I claimed to be American (i.e., foreign), the local Central Asians became openly hospitable. This tended to corroborate what the Europeans had said regarding their not feeling comfortable there.

On the other hand, much greater mixing took place in *stolovaias*.[12] Here, however, people tended to come and go as individuals and did not socialize as much. People took whatever seat was empty. Little ethnic segregation was visible. In *stolovaias* people did not tend to engage as much in conversation, but rather, ate, drank, and left. In general, however, relatively fewer Central Asians frequented these institutions. Perhaps this was related to the food served, but it was clear that *stolovaias* were primarily European with many Central Asians attending, and *chaykhanas* are primarily Central Asian with few Europeans going there.

Socializing patterns in parks were similar to those described in the housing situation and eateries. In general, people associated along cultural lines. Most often, Central Asians socialized with other Central Asians and Europeans with other Europeans. It is significant that large numbers of both Europeans and Central Asians used parks. Both enjoyed the tree-covered areas, flowers, open water, and other amenities provided by parks. In all, 110 monocultural Central Asian groups (of 3 or more people), 116 monocultural European groups, and 45 mixed groups were observed in the parks of these three cities.

Intermarriage patterns reflect similar ethnic relations. Until quite recently the Soviets touted increasing rates of intermarriage throughout the USSR, but these statistics are misleading as they reflect any and all ethnic intermarriages. Thus Russian-Ukrainian or Uzbek-Tajik intermarriages (which are quite common) and not viewed as intermarriages by the groups involved are not distinguished in the situations from Slavic-Central Asian ones. However, it is clear from the few studies that have been done on Central Asian (or Muslim)-Slavic intermarriages that such coupling is still relatively uncommon.[13]

It is important to note that intermarriage is not by definition a measure of Russification. While it is true that for most peoples outside their own republics the assimilation process represented by intermarriage with

Russians is primarily a form of Russification, this is not the case in Central Asia. Here it appears that most frequently intermarriage between Central Asians and Europeans results in a process of "Central Asianization" of the Europeans.

When testing the direction of assimilation one must look at the ethnic identification of the children as the primary indicator of the direction of assimilation trends. During my stay in Uzbekistan I went to the homes of children whose parents were of different origins (i.e., one Central Asian and one European). In all cases it turned out that the father was Central Asian in origin and the mother European. In all, I interviewed 23 European women (18 Russian, 2 Ukrainian, and 3 Ashkenazic Jews) who had married Central Asian men; 16 were married to Uzbeks, and 7 to Tajiks. Of these 23 women, all but 1 were either born in Central Asia themselves or had resided there since their youth. This is an important distinction, as I was told that the newer European immigrants tend to socialize less with Central Asians than those who have lived there for prolonged periods of time (or those who were born there).

Although these women are obviously exceptions to the general rule in that they actually married Central Asian men, and they come from the *older* European immigrant population (the majority of Europeans in Uzbekistan migrated to that area starting in the mid-1950s), their views are nonetheless valuable. Unlike the more recent immigrants (who described the Central Asians as violent, dishonest, backward, lazy, and wife abusers), when asked about why they married Central Asian (Muslim) men they (all 23 women interviewed) expressed the view that Central Asian men treat their wives and children *much* better than Slavs do. They commonly said, *"Oni ne piut i ne biut"* (they neither drink nor beat [their wives]). All but two complained that Slavic men, being drunkards, often come home and abuse their wives and children, something they found intolerable. In addition, they all stressed the fact that Uzbek and Tajik men loved their children, were generous, and helped more with chores like shopping and taking care of the children than did Slavic men.[14] A few European wives of Central Asian men discussed the fact that their husbands treated not only their own parents, but also the parents of their non-Central Asian wives with the greatest respect.

The number of children also appeared to be a major issue in these mixed marriages. The European women often felt that they wanted to have larger families than the usual one or two children common among contemporary European Soviets. That Central Asian men often wanted four was very appealing to them. Importantly, in all cases the children considered themselves as inheriting the nationality of their father (Uzbek or Tajik) and were at least bilingual (the father's native language and Russian) and often displayed the same trilinguality of other Uzbeks and Tajiks in Bukhara and Samarkand. I was informed that these children were listed in the census as having their father's nationality, but that most frequently Russian was put as their native language. Apparently it is more common for the mother's language (the language used in the home) to be listed as the child's native tongue. When I asked the children themselves what their native tongue was, they usually claimed multilingualism and could not answer it directly. Some of the younger ones claimed they used Uzbek (or Tajik) with their friends and family and Russian with their mother, her relatives, and in school.

In terms of their behavior, the children of these mixed marriages (i.e. of European women and Central Asian men) functioned as Central Asians. Most of their friends and associations were with Uzbeks and Tajiks, although they often had family ties to their mothers' families. A number of these children told me that their friends were mainly Uzbeks and Tajiks and that they were rejected and mocked by many of the Russian children, in particular by those of parents who recently came to the region.

The Russian and Ukrainian women who had married Central Asians unanimously admitted that their families opposed the marriages (to varying degrees) and still do. Two claimed to have been totally disowned by their families. The 2 Ashkenazic Jewish women interviewed said their families had moved to Central Asia from the Ukraine during World War II, and that they had become accustomed to the ways of Central Asians and felt more comfortable among them (the reason given why they never moved back to the Ukraine). Nonetheless, their families were upset at their marrying Central Asians. Each commented, however, that once the children came along, their parents accepted both their husbands and children, and that from that point on relations were excellent. They also claimed their own relatives openly socialize with their husbands' families. This was rarely the case among the Russians and Ukrainians interviewed.

The Slavic women felt that their Central Asian in-laws accepted them and their children much better than their own families had. This acceptance seems to lead to greater assimilation of these women and their children by the Central Asians. The basic rejection by their own families further pushes them in that direction. In addition, the surrounding Central Asian communities appear to accept them more readily than the surrounding Slavic ones.

In terms of relationships, attitudes, and intermarriage, the Central Asian Jews are more similar to their Muslim neighbors, and the Ashkenazic Jews are closer to the Slavs. Although they recognize each other as Jews and at least until the 1989 census were both listed as such in the census, their cultural values are more like the peoples among whom they live. I was told that whereas marriages between Central Asian Jews and Tajiks were becoming more common, it was rare for a Central Asian Jew to marry an Ashkenazic one. Similarly, Ashkenazic Jews more commonly marry Slavs than Central Asian Jews.

When I asked local Russians about their attitudes toward mixed marriages, they expressed a guarded disapproval. In conversations they basically said "some of my best friends are . . ., but I would not want my child to marry one." Many said that they would not marry a non-European, but that if others wanted to, that was their prerogative. Central Asians expressed a similar attitude on the subject. They, however, said that if an Uzbek (or Tajik) married a Slavic girl they would accept her and the children as Uzbek (or Tajik), but only as long as they (the wife and children) respected their (i.e. Central Asian) ways.

As a result of conversations with ethnic German emigrants from Central Asia, Karklins states that when Slavic women marry Central Asian men they become totally assimilated by the Central Asian culture group, learn the language, and become Muslims.[15] That they learn the language and become culturally assimilated to a great extent is true. This results from the integration of these people into the families of their husbands; however, they do not necessarily become Muslims. The men they marry tend to be modernized and not extremely religious. Two of the husbands laughed when I asked about religion and answered basically by saying "Were I religious, I would not marry an infidel." The real attraction seems to be traditional family views on the part of the Slavic or Jewish women and their rejection of the contemporary urban Slavic family situation where wife and child abuse and divorce are common.

Uzbeks and Tajiks interviewed in Samarkand and Bukhara saw little if any differences between themselves as ethnic groups (many maintaining that they are basically one people) and saw marriages across this line as normal; however, this was not the case in Tashkent. Here the Uzbeks and Tajiks were more distinct.

As can be seen from the above, intermarriages between Europeans and Central Asians are still not very common; moreover, according to Arutiunian (one of the Soviet Union's leading ethno-sociologists), the rates of intermarriage in Uzbekistan on the whole are now *declining*.[16] Among the cross-cultural marriages (i.e. involving a Central Asian and a European) the common pattern is for the male to be a Central Asian and the woman European. Rarely does the reverse occur.

It is clear that, in general, Central Asians as a group do not readily socialize with Europeans. They work together and are cordial in conversation (when they converse), but lead different lives. It could be said that in general, in Uzbek cities, Central Asians and Europeans live together, but separately.

Ethnic Attitudes

The social interactions between the immigrant European and indigenous Central Asian peoples reflect some basic ethnic attitudes held by each of them toward the other. Many of these stem from a perception of a colonial situation (by both groups), a situation until recently categorically denied in official Soviet publications. Others derive from both real and perceived situations of competition for positions, jobs, housing, etc. by these two groups. Also important are reactions to cultural prejudices held by the various groups.

One of the leading factors behind the perception of a colonial situation is the urban/rural distribution of the peoples inhabiting Uzbekistan. Although urban/rural distributions were not given in the 1979 census, according to one published ethnodemographic study only 28 percent of the Uzbeks living in the USSR were classified as urban in 1979.[17] The comparable figures for the other major Central Asian nationalities were: Tajiks—29.2 percent, Kirgiz—19.6 percent, Kazakhs—31.6 percent, and Turkmen—32.3 percent.[18] Undoubtedly, the levels of urbanization for each of these peoples registered within their respective republics were even lower than those registered on the all-Union level. The figure of only 29.2 percent of the Uzbek population being registered as urban in 1979 is strikingly low when compared with figures reported by the same author for 1913. In that year 24 percent of the population of Uzbekistan (and at that time few Europeans lived there) was classified as urban.[19] According to the census in 1970, 23.0 percent of the Uzbeks, 26.8 percent of all Muslims, and 88.8 percent of all Slavs living in the Uzbek SSR were classified as urban.

In contrast to the indigenous nationalities, the vast majority of Slavs in Uzbekistan—almost 90 percent in 1970—live in urban areas. Moreover, the majority of Slavs in rural areas are not actual farmers, but rather workers, administrators, engineers, teachers and other professionals. Arutiunian indicates, for example, that in the USSR only 6 percent of all Russians are classified as *kolkhozniki* (collective farm workers), while among Uzbeks the corresponding figure is 32 percent. (Among Tajiks it is 30 percent and among Turkmen 45 percent).[20] We must also consider that the data for Russians includes *all* Russians in the USSR; the corresponding figure for Russians in Uzbekistan would likely be much lower. Arutiunian also indicates that among Estonians in urban areas in 1970, 81 percent of the workers were classified as either skilled laborers or intellectuals and in rural areas 76 percent. (It is likely that analogous figures for Russians are somewhat lower.) However, in the case of Uzbeks, the figures are only 67 percent and 37 percent.[21] During my visit to Uzbekistan I encountered several rural Uzbeks who reported that they knew of a few rural Slavs who were farmers. Most of these Slavs, however, raised pigs for consumption by Europeans in the nearby cities; this, of course, did not lead to good relations in the rural areas, where the Muslim Uzbeks are more conservative than in the cities.

The above facts are important in that they affect the perceptions of the local Central Asians about their European neighbors. First and foremost, the Europeans occupy only what are perceived as the higher level positions (unlike in the European parts of the country, or Siberia, where Europeans are engaged in the full range of economic activities). In that sense, Europeans in Central Asia form a colonial class. Moreover, local Europeans tend to see all Europeans as being better educated, having higher status, and being superior to the Central Asians (something they would not see if they lived in their own territories where their own ethnic kinsmen sweep streets and live in villages). In addition, the situation encourages Europeans living in Central Asia to see the "natives" as conservative, poorly educated, backward, inferior, and "uncivilized" in Slavic terms.

The differences in standards and modes of living between Central Asians and European groups in Samarkand, Bukhara, and Tashkent are obvious. The marketplaces provide the most striking examples. Here rural Central Asians come into the cities to sell their wares; and here urban Slavs come into close contact with rural Central Asians—a situation that leads to many of the Slavic stereotypes of Central Asians and contributes to their impressions of the "backwardness" of these people. Urban Slavs also see these rural people browsing (albeit to a much lesser degree) in the state-run stores. In all of these cities the shopping patterns showed pronounced differences in behavior between the two groups. As I observed, the Europeans tended to shop in state run stores where the goods were oriented to the tastes of the local Slavic population (clothing, foods, etc.) and Russian was the main language used in commerce. Most native Central Asians (including Central Asian Jews), on the other hand, shopped primarily in or near the large open markets where the foodstuffs and clothing catered to Central Asian tastes, and where Uzbek and Tajik were the dominant languages. Although one can find many Central Asians in the state operated stores, the proportions are much smaller than in the markets. Modern urban Central Asians shop in both types of places.

Even more striking are the obvious differences in life styles between the almost exclusively native Old Quarter (with its adobe houses) and the more modern parts of town with their mixed European and modernized Central Asian inhabitants. Especially in the Old Quarters I observed most women with their heads covered, and wearing braids and colorful clothing based on traditional forms. Less frequently the men wore kaftans, or had beards and mustaches, which is common in rural areas.

Many Uzbek and Tajik men of all ages still wear the *tiubiteika* (skull cap).[22] These locals are fond of socializing outdoors in the many parks and *chaykhanas*, where they sit and talk for hours. Many immigrant Europeans base their stereotype of the "lazy" local people on this behavior.

These customs seem to be a problem especially in terms of European tourists coming to the area from other parts of the USSR. I frequently heard Russian tourists comment on the life styles of the native Central Asians while walking through the Old Quarters and around historical monuments. On a number of occasions I heard Russians start conversations with local Uzbeks and Tajiks in which they denigrated them and their culture. Among other things, they chastised them for being backward, conservative, religious, and dirty, as well as for mistreating their women and "multiplying like rabbits." On the other hand, I never saw a Central Asian approach a European and start *any* conversations. Although the Central Asians usually just walked away, on a few occasions they verbally retaliated by either defending themselves and their culture, or by telling the Europeans to "go back to Russia." The Central Asians were always more polite to the Russian tourists than the reverse. However, according to many Uzbeks and Tajiks, it appears that local Russians, and in particular those that have resided in this area since before, during, or just after World War II, in general do not display this behavior. A number of Uzbek students in Tashkent commented that relatively recent Russian arrivals (and rarely other Europeans) have the tendency to make such comments. Regardless of which Russian is saying it, the Central Asians resent these remarks and this leads to hostility.

The place where I observed the most uninhibited verbal confrontation was the *madrasah* (Islamic school) in Bukhara. Only there were the Uzbeks, Tajiks, and students of the *madrasah* openly hostile to outsiders (including initially to me). On two separate occasions in one day I saw a group of Central Asian men standing in front of the *madrasah* in an attempt to prevent a group of Russian tourists from entering the institution. Having struck up a conversation with a group of *madrasah* students I was eventually invited in and given a private tour and meeting with a group of students. Openly and even bitterly they complained that tourists were paraded through the school and thereby disrupted study and prayer. The students commented that these tourists not only showed *no* respect for their religion, school, or them as individuals, but that they actively interrupted them, laughed at them, and denigrated their religion. They also objected to women being taken into the religious institution at any time.

It was also quite shocking to see a placard with the quotas for Bukhara oblast with its list of meat, eggs, cotton, etc. (written in some language in the Arabic script, Uzbek, and Russian) hanging inside the *madrasah*. The students strongly objected to its presence, but they claimed there was nothing they could do about it. Two commented to me that they doubted that Muslims were paraded through Christian seminaries or that similar quotas would be found in them. Whether this is true or not, that is their perception of the situation. The students and other men in the *madrasah* were clearly anti-Russian, and most of all, anti-tourist.

I witnessed two shouting matches that almost led to fights between Russian tourists and these students. When I asked whether this was a common occurrence, the students said that it was "more frequent than was acceptable." Although most of the students seemed reluctant to discuss Christianity in the USSR, in private, two students made some important statements regarding this subject. One said that when he was in Moscow on a visit, he went into the Kremlin and was appalled by the "crosses over the crescent" (the symbol of Christianity's victory over Islam in tsarist Russia) so prominently displayed over the churches there. He felt that should not be allowed. He wondered what would happen if Muslims ever displayed a crescent over a cross. When I commented that these are historical and artistic monuments that perhaps should be kept the way they are whatever their original significance, he retorted that "in the Soviet Union no such attitude motivates the leadership." He also angrily commented, "We cannot revere our ancestors because they conquered Russia—is that not also a historical fact? Yet they may revere their ancestors who conquered ours!" Another student dealt with what he perceived as an intolerance for their religious-cultural customs, while the regime sanctioned Christian ways. Pointing to official denigration of circumcisions and burial in a shroud, and approval for burial in a coffin, he said this was the institutionalization of Orthodox Christian custom by the government. In the same conversation, another Uzbek (though not one of the *madrasah* students) sarcastically interjected, "As is well known, pork is socialist, while *palav* (an Uzbek rice dish) is not."

Some Western scholars, among them Bennigsen, Carrère-d'Encausse, and Wimbush, have explained the retention of traditional customs as statements of religious piety and anti-Soviet in nature.[23] In my own earlier works on the North Caucasus I also held this position.[24] However, I have greatly revised my own views. It appears that one of the major problems in terms of ethnic relations in Central Asian cities is the situation regarding religiously based ethnic customs. The position of such religiously derived customs as circumcision, marriage and burial customs, pork avoidance, head coverings (and in particular men wearing the *tiubiteika,*) and the respect for elders (*aksakal*) are seen differently by Russians on the one hand and Uzbeks and Tajiks on the other. In interviews with me, many Russians and other Europeans (in line with the official position of the Soviet regime) indicated to me that they saw many of these phenomena as religious holdovers (*perezhitki*); because they represented a backward past, they felt they should be eliminated from Central Asian life. Yet Uzbeks and Tajiks saw the situation quite differently. They viewed these phenomena as legitimate components of their culture and society, and integral parts of their modern ethnicity. Modern Uzbeks, even totally secularized ones, do not see pork avoidance, circumcision, traditional burials, and marriage (and here I refer specifically to *traditional* and not necessarily *religious* ones) as backward, negative, or religious acts of faith, or as anti-communist.

Many formerly religious customs become part of the modernized cultures. This is true of the various peoples of Soviet Central Asia and the Russians as well. These customs and events are seen as expressions of one's ethnicity and often are major social occasions where family members (both immediate and extended), friends, neighbors, and "fellow ethnics" get together to celebrate various customs. This is not to say religion is not important, as it most certainly is among the peoples of Central Asia. When asked, the vast majority of even modern Uzbeks professed a belief in God, but they were quick to stress the ethnic character of these formerly primarily religious customs. Especially significant are those customs that involve social gatherings, which in themselves are extremely important in the culture of Uzbeks, Tajiks, Central Asian Jews, and other peoples of the region.[25]

This observance of "religious" practices by non-believers is similar to what can be observed in the United States. Here the vast majority of modern, secularized Americans are still inclined to have a religious ceremony at their marriage and burial. Many are also buried on hallowed grounds of their respective religions. To a great extent, they view holidays like Christmas and Easter as important family-oriented secular occasions and enjoy religious services or rituals because of their beauty, spirit, or social aspects. These social aspects also explain the continued celebration of the *bris* (ritual circumcision of male children) and *bar mitzvah* among otherwise secularized American Jews, or baptism among secularized Christians.

Circumcision is an *extremely* important part of Uzbek, Tajik, and Central Asian Jewish society. Even a number of Communist Party members and intellectuals from among these groups maintained that a male cannot be an Uzbek, Tajik, or Jew, (and equally importantly a member of Uzbek, Tajik, or Jewish society), unless he is circumcised. All people interviewed, regardless of age, sex, or social position from among these three groups said that their male children would be circumcised. They also disagreed with the official Soviet position on this issue and maintained that the practice would be continued regardless of the "state's position." On a number of occasions, I started discussions on this subject in mixed company (where both Muslim and Slavic people were present). The Slavs always maintained circumcision was an utterly barbaric custom that should be eliminated; they saw Central Asians' continued practice of this custom as a sign of their persistent "backwardness."

That circumcision is commonly practiced in the United States shocked the Slavs and delighted the Central Asians. When I commented that it is now common practice even for Christians to circumcise their male children, and that it is considered hygienically better to do so, the Central Asians of Muslim and Jewish background immediately started discussing this with me and were eager to tell their relatives and friends. The response of the Slavs was quite the opposite. Some said that I was lying and being a provocateur; others were simply stunned and said nothing; 2 Russians even claimed that this was true only because "the Jews control America." The Central Asians continued to maintain that regardless of origin or function of this custom it was important to do this in order to be part of their own societies. The social aspect of this ritual in terms of family and neighborhood gathering is still very important. To Christian Slavs, however, it is an abhorrent custom under any circumstances.

Similarly, the wearing of a *tiubiteika* by a male or the covering of the head of a married woman, respect for elders, and pork avoidance were seen as ethnic rather than religious by even the most modern Uzbeks.[26] The term "respect" came up over and over when discussing these types of behavior. That ethnic Russians do not respect this attitude on a social level, and worse, that Russians openly criticize these customs creates hostility on the part of the Central Asians. That Soviet government officials push the use of coffin burials and refer to pork avoidance as backward clearly shows the lack of awareness on their part of the Christian-Russian nature of the "Soviet" ways. As one Uzbek put it, "Why is it communist to be buried in a coffin but not in a shroud?"

The mixture of the social and the religious was also demonstrated in discussions I had about Sufism and Sufi orders. Both at the Bukhara *madrasah* and at other places Central Asian Muslims pointed out that some Sufi groups were actually social organizations or burial societies that saw to it that "proper" burials were performed. They also mentioned that these groups raise money for weddings, burials, and circumcision parties—all ethno-social customs frowned upon or openly discouraged by Russian and other European Soviets (albeit not by Central Asian Party members). According to my informants, Central Asians, even Party members, commonly associate with these Sufi societies—often for these reasons and less frequently for totally religious ones. These organizations also help in the arrangement of marriages and in inter-family relations. When I asked about the role of such "brotherhoods" in the procurement of jobs, positions, housing, services, etc., I was told basically that it was the duty of a member of the "society" to help his fellow member. This is not to imply that Sufi groups with a purely religious basis do not exist. Indeed, all Uzbek and Tajik informants plainly admitted that they did. However, many function also as burial societies, organizations to raise communal funds for socio-religious activities, and "mutual help" societies.

Many young university-educated Central Asians are proud of their past and express a desire to maintain their people's cultural characteristics. Accordingly, the study of Central Asian history and literature and the restoration and preservation of historical monuments have become important to urban Central Asians. Many young Uzbeks and Tajiks I met proudly reported that they had donated money and time to restore old monuments such as *madrasahs*, mosques, and tombs.

A number of Russians, Ukrainians, and ethnic Germans in these cities saw this in a totally different light. They not only viewed Central Asians as conservative and backward, but openly expressed anger at the fact that, "after all *we* have done for them" and "with all the money *we* have given them . . . they waste it on *that* (the rebuilding and restoration of old buildings)." Paradoxically, these same Europeans lauded the Soviet regime for helping restore old churches and sometimes felt it should do even more to restore *their* old buildings and monuments.

In conversations in the newer parts of Samarkand and Bukhara, and even more so in Tashkent, Russians often displayed the attitude that "we (Russians) brought them (Central Asians) civilization." I discussed this common Russian belief with local Central Asians. Young Central Asian students often pointed to this or that monument and commented that the Russians were still "forest-dwelling barbarians" when Central Asians' ancestors were scientists and had a very high civilization. It is clear that Central Asians do not feel inferior culturally to their European, and in particular, Russian, neighbors.

During discussions on the role of Russians and other Europeans in Uzbekistan, Russians frequently used the pejorative term *chechmek* to refer to the Central Asians.[27] This term came up most frequently when they discussed Central Asians' "ingratitude" for all the Russians had done for the local population. Rarely did urban Russians actually speak of the *chechmeks* as equals, but rather as younger (less advanced) brothers.

The concept of the ethnic Russians as the *starshie brat'ia* (elder brothers) of all Soviet peoples is also problematic. Until recently, Soviet literature on ethnic relations portrayed Russians as the elder brothers and implied that the Russians had the right to subordinate other peoples to themselves. Soviet works abound with this theme and there is hardly a Brezhnev-era book or article on the subject of ethnic relations between the Russians and the minorities, or on the general subject of ethnic relations in the USSR, that does not extol the Great Russian "elder brother," his culture, language, generosity, and leadership qualities.

Many young Uzbeks and Tajiks expressed feelings ranging from distaste to open anger over this idea of the first among equals. When asked what role the Russians played in Soviet society, in helping other peoples of the Soviet Union, and in World War II, most of the Uzbeks and Tajiks interviewed agreed that the Russians were the dominant people in the country and therefore logically had a leadership role to fulfill. They also said that the Russians had helped other peoples in the Soviet Union, and that they (the Russians) had suffered greatly during World War II. However, they also said they were tired of constantly having to read and hear about it. A number of Uzbeks also eventually commented that the Jews were slaughtered en masse (and often with the help of Slavs), and that proportionately the Belorussians, Latvians, and others had lost more than the Russians, but the Russians ignore these facts. A few resented what they considered the downplaying of their (i.e., Central Asian) role in the War. In essence, the overkill bothered them. Some even commented that this was just part of the propaganda to justify Russian dominance and colonialism throughout the USSR.

When dealing with the nationality situation, Westerners need to be especially careful in assessing the role of the nationalities of the Soviet Union in World War II. The Soviet stress on the solidarity of the Soviet peoples during the War is, in fact, by and large correct. Similarly, it is also true that literally millions of Soviet citizens openly supported the Nazis in their initial invasion into then-Soviet territory. That Soviet citizens of all nationalities fought against the Nazis does not, however, imply that they were doing so out of a love for Stalin, the Soviet system or state, or for the "elder brother Russians." This is a complex matter indeed and displays the high degree to which ethnic relations are situational.

The importance of *the situation* can also be illustrated with the American experience during World War II, when Whites and Blacks from officially segregated communities in the South (and unofficially segregated Northern areas as well) found themselves defending one another's lives, fighting, eating, and living together in the American military units in Europe and the Pacific. At home, however, these same men would never have considered living, eating, or socializing together, or in extreme cases even using the same toilets. Similarly, Whites and Blacks fought together in Vietnam even when at home there was a great deal of racial strife.

Central Asians, particularly the better-educated ones, seem tired of the praise of the Russians and their language, culture, and roles in Soviet society. This aggrandizement of Russians is interpreted by Central Asians as a down-playing of their own cultures, languages, and role in Soviet society. Yet, virtually every young Central Asian whom I approached spoke Russian well. The Uzbeks and Tajiks at times even expressed a pride in doing so. In Samarkand and Bukhara virtually all Uzbeks, Tajiks, and Central Asian Jews are trilingual (Uzbek, Tajik, and Russian) and see this as a norm. In Tashkent, Russian was clearly the language of the city and all Uzbeks I met there (with the exception of rural dwellers and some elderly people) spoke it well.

The reverse, however, is not at all true. Few Russians, Ukrainians, or Germans living in Tashkent can speak Uzbek well (if at all). In Samarkand and Bukhara, a significant number of Russians who have lived there since before or during the Second World War did know either Uzbek or Tajik. These people (i.e., the longer-term residents) tended to have a lower level of education than the newer arrivals and to be far more accepting of Central Asian customs and people, and appeared to be more integrated into Central Asian society. Both the Central Asians and Russians that I spoke to distinguished between the majority of Russians (i.e., more recent immigrants) and those who have lived there for long periods of time. Many of this latter group's children speak Uzbek and Tajik well.

Central Asians (and in particular many younger Central Asians) resented the fact that Slavs live in their southern homeland for years and do not learn any of the local languages. Uzbeks and Tajiks were especially critical of Slavs who flaunt this linguistic ignorance. Many Central Asians felt that inasmuch as the government demands that they all learn the Russian language, *respect* would dictate that the immigrants should learn Uzbek. Several Uzbek university students in all three cities commented about the constant call in the Uzbek press for Uzbeks to master the Russian language; however, there was no similar call for Russians living in Uzbekistan to learn any Uzbek. Such examples of cultural bigotry make it easy to understand the enthusiasm with which Uzbeks supported the October 1989 law making Uzbek the republic's official language.

When discussing aspects of attitudinal situations among the various peoples of Central Asian cities, some basic patterns emerged. In general, Central Asians perceive most European groups (and Russians in particular) as something of an alien and colonizing or quasi-colonizing population. (Germans and Tatars, on the other hand, seem to be perceived as "deportees" rather than as colonizers.) Central Asians feel that the aliens do not show enough respect toward the local people or their languages, cultures, and traditions. Immigrant Europeans tend to view native *rural* Central Asian groups as backward, conservative, dirty, and wild. These same Europeans view "modernized" Central Asians as "elevated" or "civilized" people, but rarely as equals.

Discrimination and Competition

Of all issues discussed with young Central Asians (18–35 years of age)[28] and Europeans of virtually all ages, the one that appeared to be the most important was *perceived* discrimination and competition for positions, jobs, and housing. The competitive aspect of ethnic relations was far more visible in Tashkent than in the two more traditional cities. As the center of administration, commerce, industry, and education, not only for Uzbekistan, but all the rest of Central Asia as well, Tashkent has many of the "best" jobs, schools, and housing in the republic. As Central Asians indicated, it is also the Central Asian "modern" showcase city for students from Asia and Africa.

While Central Asians saw this issue very differently from the local Europeans, both groups were in some ways correct in their assessment of the situation. Central Asians complained that the immigrants had the best housing and jobs not only in Tashkent but in all other urban centers in Uzbekistan as well. They perceived that Europeans were taking housing and jobs away from Central Asians. It appears that as they apply to higher educational institutions, graduate from them, and begin to seek jobs and housing opportunities, Central Asians see Europeans occupying places and positions that they themselves want. Modern urban Central Asians were quick to tell me that they now have enough native educated people working as administrators, technicians, laborers, teachers, doctors, scientists, engineers, and writers to staff all necessary positions in the republic. They also felt that many natives could not move due to a housing shortage. A few commented that rural Uzbeks and others could not find places to live in the cities because "no space" existed for them. Thus, the presence of Europeans in these cities created the image that space is in short supply because these immigrants had taken the available housing.

Interestingly, Europeans saw discrimination working in the opposite direction. In their eyes there seemed to be an active policy of "affirmative action" whereby Central Asians received preferential treatment regarding government positions, jobs, housing, places in school, and the like. Many Russians and Ukrainians commented that Central Asians obtained jobs "even when they are not qualified for them." The Slavs saw this as evidence of nepotism and corruption. In a few cases the Russians living in Tashkent viewed Tashkent as a Russian city and bemoaned the immigration of *chechmeks* from the countryside. The local European residents saw the Central Asian elites as inferiors who got there through nepotism or affirmative action. This attitude is not unlike the attitude of some White Americans toward Black doctors, lawyers, professors, and students in the United States today.

Many Russians cited cases of nepotism and corruption in Uzbekistan. Uzbeks, on the other hand, angrily retorted that nepotism and corruption were far worse in Moscow and Leningrad. One Uzbek even said, "If you want to see nepotism, look at Brezhnev's son-in-law." Central Asians seemed aware that Russians and even foreigners stereotypically view them (Central Asians) as black marketeers. In this regard many young Central Asian students commented that one does not make as much selling melons in the market as fixing televisions and cars privately in Moscow. They readily admitted that black marketeering is a way of life, but stressed that it was the Russians more than anyone else who benefitted.

When questioned about corruption among political leaders in Uzbekistan, students answered that (regardless of corruption) they disliked many of the local political leaders, but they still preferred these individuals to Russians. In this way they are very much like other nationalities who prefer to be ruled by one of their own kinsmen (regardless of quality) rather than by an outsider. (The Russians have an expression for this situation—"*plokho no nash* [bad but ours].") The Uzbeks felt that they could criticize, and even call for the removal of "their own" corrupt local leaders; however, under no circumstances did they want that person replaced by the non-native (regardless of how good the replacement might be). This kind of feeling was graphically shown by the riots that occurred in Kazakhstan when Kunaev (a native Kazakh) was replaced as Party boss by Kolbin (a Russian brought in from outside the region). The Uzbek replacement of Rashidov from Uzbekistan, on the other hand, was not accompanied by violent protest.

Urban Central Asians in Uzbekistan were very much aware of this trend and openly commented on it. On a number of occasions they proudly informed me that Central Asia (the republics of Uzbekistan, Tajikistan, Kirgizia, and Turkmenistan together) had surpassed the Central Industrial Region (centered around Moscow) in population, and that it had become the most populous of the 19 economic regions of the USSR. They all, however, doubted that this would affect Soviet policy making in any significant way. They felt that control was firmly in the hands of those in the Moscow area and would remain so even if the population of Central Asian nationalities continued to grow. Today, in 1990, there is no doubt a different sense among Uzbeks regarding these levels of control.

For obvious reasons, Central Asia's demographic trends are viewed with much apprehension by the Russians living in Uzbekistan. Whereas Russians in the RSFSR and other European areas may read at a distance about demographic trends among Muslim peoples, it is those living in Central Asia (and less so in the Caucasus) that most often confront the masses of children and their parents daily. It is much the same in the United States where Whites living in major urban centers or southern states perceive the higher rates of natural increase of Blacks and Hispanics with much greater concern than those living in states like Oregon, Minnesota, or North Dakota.

To Russians in urban Uzbekistan, this high rate of natural increase coupled with a significant urban migration from rural areas poses a threat. Many Russians commented that although life in Uzbekistan had certain advantages (e.g., climate, food, housing, and other amenities), they were either leaving the area or were thinking about it. In assessing the significance of this, one must also consider that the majority of Russians in Central Asia did not come from places like Moscow or Leningrad, which have fine cultural institutions and relatively good living conditions, but rather from smaller provincial towns and cities in which supplies in general are lacking and cultural facilities few and of a poorer quality.

The higher birth rates of native Central Asians than Europeans in the cities of Uzbekistan, coupled with a substantial in-migration of rural Central Asians and a concomitant out-migration of Europeans, ensures a greater nativization of these cities in the immediate future. This situation will undoubtedly result in a stronger native culture in these same cities and a relative diminution of European (i.e. Russian) influence in them. A similar situation existed in the Transcaucasian republics of Azerbaijan, Armenia, and Georgia from the 1950s to the 1960s, and has continued at an increasing rate. In those republics, the use of native languages increased in the cities with such nativization. If this same trend continues, one should expect to see an even greater sense of security and self assurance on the part of Central Asians (and in particular Uzbeks) in the cities of Uzbekistan.

Conclusion

Modern Uzbeks and other Central Asians living in the cities of Uzbekistan are self-assured and confident. They see themselves as well educated and capable of carrying out all tasks of a modern nation. Moreover, they are extremely proud of their own cultural heritage. They cherish their language, culture, and history in the same way that other modern nations do. Similarly, they feel they have the right to preserve many traditional cultural customs as an integral part of their modern culture and identity. Hospitality, reverence for their elders, and strong nuclear and extended family ties are very important to them. Many of their values derive from religious rites and practices. Most important, they feel that this situation should be respected by other nationalities. In their view, they do not tell Russians what to keep or discard from their culture, nor how they should live in Russia itself; they would like that same courtesy returned.

What appears to be a key element in contemporary relations between native Central Asians and immigrant Europeans, especially Russians, is the attitude of European immigrants toward the above-mentioned situation. The inability and/or unwillingness of ethnic Russians living in Uzbekistan to recognize and respect the heritage of the Central Asians and their contemporary cultural attitudes has led, and is leading, to greater Central Asian hostility toward the Russian presence. It is the incipient racism of these Europeans, their anti-Islamic and anti-Central Asian attitudes, that is the basis for contemporary anti-Russian feelings among Central Asians. On a higher level, years of official attacks on Central Asian culture by the Soviet regime have led to a growing anti-Russian attitude among younger, well-educated Central Asians.

Arutiunian, who considers language and interethnic communications important in the development of better interethnic relations and general social development in the USSR, states that it is important both for non-Russians to learn the Russian language and for the Russians living in the various republics to learn those languages.[29] Yet, as noted above, while many Central Asians make a concerted effort to learn the Russian language and, in general, feel positively toward that language, the reverse is not at all true.

In urban Uzbekistan during my visit there appeared to be a superficially cordial relationship between the various ethnic groups living there. As long as the wrong topics were not discussed or the wrong things said, this cordiality was maintained. These groups worked together, rode the same buses, and often lived side by side in relative harmony. Some of this superficial calm changed at the end of the 1980s. But even at the time of my visit, Central Asians and Europeans lived quite apart from one another and infrequently socialized across the major cultural lines. They lived together, but separately. The cordiality rapidly broke down when things were said or done that were irritants to one or the other group, or following expressions of disrespect for the other's culture.

The major problem of perceived competition for jobs, positions, and housing seems to be getting worse. Central Asians, and in particular Uzbeks, demand preference on the grounds that Uzbekistan is *their* homeland. In the eyes of many, and in particular young Central Asians, the Russians (along with Russian language and culture) have been favored over the indigenous people. At the beginning of the Gorbachev era, Uzbeks perceived the regime in Moscow as continuing to promote colonization in the name of the "friendship of nations," the "brotherhood of peoples," and the obligations of the "lesser brothers" (the minorities) to serve their "elder brother" (the Russians). The local Russians, on the other hand, saw the Central Asians as backward and inferior, but nonetheless favored by both the regime and even more so the local officials (through corruption and nepotism) in a policy of affirmative action. They also saw Central Asians as not properly grateful for all that the Russians had done for them and the sacrifices that they (the Russians) had made; this attitude is reminiscent of the British and French when they were being pushed out of their former colonies.

The accelerated out-migration of Russians and other Europeans from Central Asia reflects the general dissatisfaction with living in that region and even fear which has now gripped many of Uzbekistan's inhabitants. Given that most of the Russians whom I interviewed claimed that the material living conditions were better in Central Asia than in the Russian areas whence they came, one must conclude that either there is something drawing them to these other areas that outweighs these amenities or that deteriorating ethnic relations with Central Asians are pushing them out. The unwillingness of Central Asians to move out of Central Asia can, to a great extent, also be explained by their antipathy toward living among Russians and other Europeans. As Fierman's chapter in this volume makes clear, this is not the only reason; but it was one of the major ones mentioned by Central Asians when I asked about why they had not chosen to seek residence or employment in regions outside Central Asia.

In essence, the urban Uzbeks and Tajiks in Uzbekistan look at the ethnic situation in the following way. They feel that they are the hosts and the Russians the guests. They see hospitality as very important in their culture toward their guests, while also recognizing the reality of the fact that they have been a colony of Russia. They feel, however, that the Russians are poor guests who do not return this hospitality with proper behavior and respect. They return this hospitality with contempt for their hosts, look down on them, and denigrate their culture. One group of Uzbek students in Tashkent suggested that it had reached the point where many Central Asians felt the Russians were "overstaying their welcome." The evidence available today about thousands of Russians seeking to leave Uzbekistan suggests that Russians (and other Europeans) are now keenly aware of this.

Notes

1. Rasma Karklins, *Ethnic Relations in the USSR* (Boston: Allen & Unwin, 1986), pp. 2–3.

2. "Central Asians" includes Uzbeks, Tajiks, Karakalpaks, Kazakhs, and Central Asian Jews; "Europeans" includes Russians, Ukrainians, Ashkenazic Jews, Germans, Estonians, and Latvians. Of course, in situations of mere observations it was often not possible to distinguish either the various Central Asians from each other, or the Europeans.

3. For obvious reasons the names of individuals interviewed are here withheld. In most cases individuals' names were not solicited as their ethnicity was all I wanted to know. This trip was followed by one to Transcaucasia (Azerbaijan and Georgia) in the summer of 1987 where similar observations and interviews were conducted to verify, compare, and contrast the findings of the study conducted in Uzbekistan two years earlier.

4. So important is the contextuality of ethnic situations to attitudes and relations that Karklins divides her book into chapters based on contextual concepts and situations.

5. Many Central Asia cities have an "old quarter" which is predominantly inhabited by members of indigenous nationalities. By contrast, the population of these same cities' "new quarters," has a large (and sometimes numerically dominant) population of European nationalities.

6. One must consider that these observations were made during the summer when schools were closed. In addition, it was not determined whether these Europeans lived in the Old or New Quarters.

7. This sounds remarkably parallel to comments made by Anglo- (and other) Americans about Mexicans, Puerto Ricans, and other Hispanics in American cities today.

8. The first work of this type was V. O. Ruvavishnikov's "Etnosotsial'nye aspekty rasseleniia v gorodakh Tatarii," *Sovetskaia etnografiia*, no. 1, 1978, pp. 77–89. In this article the author indicates that the Tatar and Russian populations are not evenly distributed in the cities of Kazan and Almetevsk.

9. In the middle of the 1980s a number of works began to appear in the USSR relevant to ethnicity, multilingualism, social behavior, and various attitudes.

These provide important information by nationality, sometimes with data that were not published with official census results. Among the works are the following: Institut etnografii im. Miklukho-Maklaia, *Natsiia i kul'tura* (Tallin: Akademiia nauk Estonskoi SSR, Institut istorii: 1985) with important contributions by Iu. V. Arutiunian, L. M. Drobizheva, I. A. Grishaev, and A. A. Susokolov; and *Etnosotsiologiia: tseli, metody, i nekotorye rezul'taty issledovaniia* (Moscow: Nauka, 1984).

10. An interesting situation parallel to this has been noted by Laquian in the Malaysian capital Kuala Lumpur. The Malaysian government subsidized middle income housing there in hopes of creating an environment where Muslim Malays and non-Muslim Chinese would live in mixed or integrated environment. However, among other things, the Malays found the smell of pork coming from Chinese homes unbearable. Thus, in spite of the best intentions on the part of the Malaysian government, the incompatibility of cultures led to open hostilities between the two groups they were trying desperately to integrate (Aprodicio A. Laquian, "Urban Tensions in Southeast Asia in the 1970s," in *Population, Politics, and the Future of Southeast Asia,* ed. W. Harold Wriggins and James F. Guyot [New York: Columbia University Press, 1973], p. 137).

11. In Bukhara, I observed 80 tables where 355 individuals were seated. Of the tables, 79 (with 351 people) were monocultural. In Samarkand, 62 of 64 tables (with 236 of the 248 individuals) were monocultural. Even in Tashkent, 46 of the 51 tables (with 186 of the 233 people) were monocultural. It was not possible to interview individuals about their ethnic identities, so they were classified either as Europeans or Central Asians.

12. I observed 161 tables with 906 people seated at them. Thirty of the tables (with 215 people) were in Bukhara, 46 (with 225 people) were in Samarkand, and 85 tables (with 466 people) were in Tashkent.

13. For a discussion on such intermarriages see Rasma Karklins, "Islam: How Strong Is It in the Soviet Union? Inquiry Based on Oral Interviews with Soviet Germans Repatriated from Central Asia in 1977," *Cahiers du Monde Russe et Soviétique,* 21, no. 1 (1980), pp. 72–73.

14. This contradicts a statement by Arutiunian where he indicates that in Tashkent only among 5 to 6 percent of the Uzbek families do the husbands help the wives with household chores, etc. See Iu. V. Arutiunian, "Sotsial'no-kul'turnaia obshchnost' sovetskikh natsii: nekotorye itogi i perspektivy razvitiia," in *Natsiia i kul'tura,* p. 26. This, however, may show how different the Uzbek men who marry non-Muslim women are in their behavior from those who do marry Muslim women (i.e., they are not traditional).

15. Rasma Karklins, "Islam," pp. 72–73.

16. Iu. V. Arutiunian, "Sotsial'no-kul'turnaia obshchnost'," p. 27. He further indicated a similar trend in Azerbaijan and Tajikistan.

17. Viktor Kozlov, *The Peoples of the Soviet Union* (Bloomington: Indiana University Press, 1988), p. 66.

18. Ibid.

19. V. I. Kozlov, *Natsional'nosti SSSR* (Moscow: Statistika, 1975), p. 77.

20. Iu. V. Arutiunian, "Sotsial'no-kul'turnaia obshchnost'," p. 17.

21. Ibid., p. 19.

22. Wearing turbans is common in the city primarily among rural Uzbeks and Tajiks who come to the market or to visit or shop in the city. It is unusual for an urban Uzbek or Tajik to wear one, except among the elderly.

23. See, for examples, Alexandre Bennigsen and S. Enders Wimbush, *Mystics and Commissars* (Berkeley: University of California Press, 1985) and Hélène Carrère d'Encausse *Decline of an Empire* (New York: Newsweek Books, 1979).

24. See for example Ronald Wixman, *Language Aspects of Ethnic Patterns and Processes in the North Caucasus* (Chicago: University of Chicago Press, Geography Research Series No. 191, 1980), pp. 198–200 and Ronald Wixman, "Ethnic Nationalism in the Caucasus," *Nationalities Papers*, Vol. X (2), Fall 1982, pp. 149–50.

25. Drobizheva provides an excellent discussion of the differences in the components of the ethnic identities of a variety of peoples of the USSR (including Uzbeks) in L. M. Drobizheva, "Natsional'noe samosoznanie i dinamika kul'tury," *Natsiia i kul'tura*, pp. 48–63.

26. Drobizheva indicates that the wearing of the *tiubiteika* is an important visual symbol of ethnicity among Uzbeks, and that silk embroidered with ethnic ornaments or *tiubiteikas* are also important gifts among Uzbeks (Ibid., pp. 54 and 56).

27. The term *chechmek* appears to be a pejorative term used by Russians for Asians or Muslims. This term has no inherent meaning, but seems to the Russian ear to be a mimicking of the sound of Turkic languages.

28. I found much greater ethnic tension among the younger, modernized, and well-educated Uzbeks and Tajiks than among the older or more conservative members of these groups. The more religious and conservative ones tended to ignore or avoid the European immigrants on the everyday level, or had little occasion to have contact with them. (Frequently the lack of knowledge of the Russian language precludes close interaction between them.) In general, ethnic relations were far less an issue to them than to the more educated and secularized ones probably because they came into less contact with these Europeans, and were not in competition with them. In addition, unlike the younger, more educated population, they did not read the press that deals with political, technical, or ideological issues. It is the younger, more educated, and secularized Central Asians who come into daily contact with these problems and encounter the Great Russian chauvinism so constantly expressed in the press and on the streets. Being of university age, they are also more prone to express their views, as are urban-educated intellectuals. For an excellent discussion of the labor force and ethnic competition in Uzbekistan, see Nancy Lubin, *Labour and Nationality in Soviet Central Asia: An Uneasy Compromise* (Princeton: Princeton University Press, 1984).

29. Arutiunian, "Sotsial'no-kul'turnaia obshchnost'," p. 27.

7

Islam and Atheism: Dynamic Tension in Soviet Central Asia

Azade-Ayse Rorlich

Introduction

Following the October Revolution, the Bolsheviks sought to achieve the triple goals of forging a Soviet state, building a Soviet society, and molding a Soviet man. As they embarked on the road toward these goals, Russia's new leaders recognized the potentially disruptive effects of competing ideologies and loyalties. Consequently, already in 1918 they proceeded to move against political rivals and religion. Because the exclusivist nature of the Marxist-Leninist ideology that guided the Soviet leadership left no room for ideological, political, or cultural pluralism, religion—recognized as a major hindrance to social engineering—became the target of a long series of anti-religious and atheistic campaigns. Although the approaches to eliminating religion changed over the ensuing decades, the Communist Party persistently sought to eliminate religion.

In this context, the 1977 Constitution, which introduced a shift from "antireligious" to "atheistic" propaganda, represented a major policy shift. The use of the latter term projected an image of a church-state relationship free of the militantly adversarial quality of the earlier years and resting on education (rather than coercion) as the most appropriate means to achieve full acceptance of the atheistic creed.

According to the official pronouncements of the Brezhnev era, religion had all but disappeared and the nationalities question had been solved. In reality, the unimaginative atheistic propaganda and the bureaucratic approach (which often offended the national pride and the dignity of believers and unbelievers alike), had been partly responsible for the resilience of religious beliefs and practices, and the sharpening of the national awareness of the peoples of the Soviet Union.

The emergence of M. S. Gorbachev gave impetus to the efforts of those interested in economic and political reform and added boldness to the requests of those who pursued a national or religious agenda. For 1987 alone, the Council for Religious Affairs received more than 3,000 complaints from citizens who reported abuses and arbitrariness ranging from decisions to keep mosques under lock and key to those prohibiting the ringing of church bells in certain areas.[1] These citizen reports reflect the active involvement of Christians and Muslims alike in the process of glasnost, while also suggesting their willingness to work toward bringing about a new approach to the state-church relationship.

The present chapter will focus on the Muslims of "Central Asia." Because the term "Central Asia" is used in a cultural sense, its meaning is somewhat broader than in the other chapters of this volume. Here it will include Kazakhstan; moreover, the term "Central Asians" will also include the Kazakhs. Thus defined, at the time of the last complete census, in 1989, Central Asian Muslims numbered some 35,423,042 people.[2] These figures are based on the contention that the sum-total of those ethnic groups which had traditionally been part of the Islamic *umma* (community of believers) could be viewed as the accurate indicator of the size of the Islamic community of the region. This view is supported by a 1973 *khutba* (sermon) delivered by the *mullah* (Muslim cleric) of Tashkent's Shaykh Zaynutdin Mosque. In the *mullah's* word's, "only he who will publicly declare in front of all believers, in the mosque, that he no longer accepts Allah's commandments will cease to be considered a Muslim."[3] In fact, this implies that in the Central Asian context, anyone who does not consider himself a Muslim cannot claim a Central Asian ethnic identity.

Central Asia's incorporation into the Russian empire and its subsequent isolation from the Muslim *umma* prompted the Muslims to engage in a reevaluation of their identity. Isolation brought about an enhanced regional identity. It was this regional identity, still comprising Islam as its main attribute, that evolved into a protonational identity under the conditions of Russian rule.

The political and administrative catalysts of the Soviet period were conducive to a rapid transition from the protonational to the national form of identity among Central Asians. In this way, Islam still represented an important, even if no longer the main attribute of identity.

Official and Parallel Islam

One of the catalysts affecting the evolution of the identity of Central Asian Muslims and their relationship with the Soviet state was the organization on October 20, 1943 (in Tashkent) of a Muslim Religious

Board which is called The Spiritual Directorate of the Muslims of Central Asia and Kazakhstan. From the state's perspective, the major task of the Central Asian as well as of the other three Muslim Religious Boards (two for the Caucasus, one for the European regions of USSR and Siberia) has been to coordinate and guide that segment of religious life revolving around the functioning mosques, registered *mullahs* and officially recognized religious communities. This constitutes "official Islam." It exists against the background of a thriving network of religious communities which have no official recognition, numerous Sufi brotherhoods, and a growing number of unregistered, "self-appointed" or "itinerant" *mullahs*. These represent the "unofficial," or "parallel" Islam. No discussion of Islam in the USSR can be complete without considering its role in Islam's resilience and current resurgence.

In the case of "official Islam," by the mid-1980s, Central Asia had some 230 functioning mosques. (This represented almost two-thirds of the USSR's total functioning mosques.)[4] It is likely that the region also accounted for the bulk of the USSR's total 751 registered Muslim communities.[5]

Along with these registered communities, there were at least 1,800 unregistered ones.[6] Indeed, some scholars have challenged this latter figure as far too low. S. Muslimov, a candidate of philosophical sciences and a docent at the Daghestan State University, maintained that "how many 'parallel' mosques [exist] is known only to Allah. . . . [T]he figure of 1,800 cannot be accurate even if one takes a simple logical approach to the topic."[7]

Muslimov's contention is supported by the results of surveys and studies conducted by propagandists of scientific atheism and by other scholars, as well as by the declarations of some Party officials. In a conversation with foreign journalists in 1987, First Secretary of the Tajik Communist Party Makhkamov admitted that in his republic "Islam is still a great power, and over the past few years, the number of believers has even increased."[8] He made no effort to hide the fact that such a situation was causing great concern for the Party.

A similar situation seems to exist in Kirgizia, particularly in Osh, in the eastern Fergana Valley. In this area young people between the ages of seventeen and thirty represent 30 percent of the Islamic community; 5,000 exclusively religious marriages were conducted between 1984 and 1987, and the concept of secular funerals does not even exist.[9] According to one report, people are "proud" that prayers from the Koran are said at funerals, and "when four people meet, they begin talking about God." In fact, even members of anti-religious teams assist "all the time" with religious funerals.[10]

Some Kirgiz atheistic propagandists explain the high religiosity of people in this part of their republic by the fact that Islam penetrated the area very early, and as a result, by the time of the revolution, it had a numerous clergy and a rich spiritual life that sustained many important religious centers.[11] Indeed, from the tenth to thirteenth centuries this part of Kirgizia was part of the Karakhanid state, which adopted Islam in 960.

In Kazakhstan, consternation about the increase in religiosity was strong enough to prompt special attention in the report of the Kazakh Party Central Committee to the Fifteenth Party Congress (February 1981).[12] Likewise, the subject was extensively covered at the Uzbek Communist Party Central Committee held in October 1986. More recently, Uzbek Communist Party Central Committee secretary M. Kh. Khalmukhamedov recognized a stabilization or even revival of observance of religious traditions and rituals among young people, Komsomol, and even Communist Party members. According to Khalmukhamedov, at issue is not "the struggle with the believers, but the emancipation of their consciousness from the narcotic of religion which is partly forced [upon the people] by the clergy under the cover of national [tradition]."[13]

The Native Officials and Islam

At least until recently, according to CPSU doctrine, religious believers and those who observed religious practices were unfit to take leading roles (including Party membership) in Soviet society. Nevertheless, there is considerable evidence that in the 1980s many Party and soviet officials were condoning or even promoting Islam.

In some cases, tacit support apparently came from oblast or even republic level officials. Thus, when Turkmen Party First Secretary Niiazov gave a speech in July 1988 at the CPSU Nineteenth Party Conference, his sketch of perestroika's tasks related to improving public morality in Turkmenistan included the elimination of such evils as embezzlement, over-reporting, window dressing, corruption, and the demoralization of leading cadres.[14] However, notably absent from his list was religion. Just a couple of years previously, religious observance had regularly been included in such inventories of transgressions.

Although this tolerance or support at the very highest republic levels may be quite recent, there is evidence that lower rank officials were at least tacitly aiding religion somewhat earlier. Thus, one "exposé" published in 1986 reported that Party organizations of five Tajik sovkhozes (state farms) carried out no atheistic propaganda for two years and their members protected those who observed religious rituals.[15] Similarly, other Tajik farm officials are alleged to have tacitly supported the *ad hoc* transformation of their guest houses into prayer houses and permitted nine "tea shops" to serve the same function.[16]

Similar stories appeared in the other republics. In Uzbekistan's Dzhizak oblast, communists were said to have spent 500,000 rubles to restore a mosque; in Bukhara oblast, A. Karimov (the first secretary of the Bukhara oblast Party committee for many years) was charged with sponsoring construction of mosques and holy tombs and using state funds to pave the roads leading to them.[17] In another instance, some native officials in the Kirgiz village of Atabay (located in the foothills of Ken-Tau) cooperated with religious believers by failing to take action on a raion government decision to open an ethnographic and historical museum in the eighteenth-century mosque of Shamet Ishan.[18]

Although changes in Soviet policy toward Islam have made it easier for officials at all levels (at least tacitly) to promote Islam, some members of the bureaucracy still oppose this "softening." Indeed, they go out of their way to link Islam with unwholesome activity. At the end of 1989, when Tashkent oblast Party committee secretary E. I. Fazylov argued that the revival of Islam in Central Asia might be the result of support from high-ranking Party members, he implied that such people represented anti-perestroika forces favoring inertia. Moreover, to document the link between Islam, social conservatism and even moral corruption, he referred to the file of B. E. Sviderskii (the prosecutor in some of the most famous corruption trials of Central Asia) and argued that two of the most famous personages of the trials—the "cotton lord" Adylov and the Bukharan Party secretary Karimov—had protegés among the clergy whom they generously endowed with funds.[19]

Religious Believers and Leaders

In recent years there have been many manifestations of an increase of religiosity in Central Asia. These include the rise in the number of believers and changes in their age and occupational profile, a rise in the income of religious organizations, stepped-up efforts to build and renovate mosques, and changes in the age and educational profile of the clergy. Observances of ritual obligations and pilgrimages to holy places have also increased, and there have been many more overt statements of religiosity (e.g., wearing religious symbols and using them as decorations).

One of the most important facts is that believers are no longer largely rural inhabitants of venerable age. Results of sociological surveys indicate that in the republic of Tajikistan as a whole, 45 percent of the people considered themselves believers, while in some areas, 22 percent of the adults, one-third of the young people, as well as one-third of the children in the sixth and seventh grades openly claimed to be believers.[20] In Kirgizia's city of Osh, a survey discovered that 37 percent of the inhabitants openly declared themselves believers.[21]

As noted, religiosity is particularly high in southern Kirgizia. This should be seen in its historical context. In the case of Atabay (whose officials described above cooperated with believers), the village had been a center of learning with five *madrasahs*. It also had numerous mosques and a cemetery reserved only for the descendants of the Prophet, Imam Ali, and Ahmad Yasawi. In the twelfth century, the latter had founded the Sufi brotherhood of Yasawiya.[22] This order played a major role in the Islamization of the nomadic tribes and, despite its decline after the emergence of the Sufi order of Nakshbandiyyah in the fourteenth century, it continued to attract followers throughout the centuries. One of them, A. Satybaldyev, founded the underground order of Hairy Ishans in the Fergana Valley. This order still functions as an authentic secret society, mainly among the Kirgiz. It is quite openly anti-Soviet.

But today religiosity is on the increase in other parts of Kirgizia as well. This is particularly remarkable because, in contrast to southern Kirgizia, the Islamization of the rest of what is today Soviet Kirgizia was completed only in the nineteenth century.[23]

Throughout Central Asia, the number of *mullahs* (especially young ones) is increasing, and they are frequently well educated.[24] In his report to the ideological workers of Tajikistan in August, 1986, republic First Secretary Makhkamov pointed out that some graduates of the Faculty of Oriental Languages in Dushanbe join the ranks of *mullahs*.[25] Articles by atheist propagandists express special alarm about the growth in the number of "pseudo-*mullahs*."[26]

Better educated believers and *mullahs* will be more likely to probe the spiritual boundaries of Islam and search for religious fulfillment beyond the observance of ritual. Such a development may soon invalidate some of the survey results which indicated that, at least in Turkmenia, only 3 percent of those who prayed daily were acquainted with the dogma.[27]

Indeed, recent developments in Central Asia suggest that the intelligentsia is making its contribution to the eradication of "religious illiteracy" and the emergence of "thinking believers." On October 20, 1989, the Kazakh literary weekly *Qazaq adebiyeti* published a chart of the Arabic alphabet and the two most important *suras* (chapters) of the Koran: "Al-Fatiha" and "Al-Ihlas." These were rendered both in the original Arabic and Cyrillic transliteration. They were followed by a Kazakh translation and commentary. Subsequent issues of *Qazaq adebiyeti* published lessons teaching the Arabic alphabet. A two-record album containing fourteen selected *suras* of the Koran were made available to the Kazakh public in October, 1990.[28] The first issue of the Kirgiz literary weekly *Kirgizstan madaniyati* for 1990 launched a new page entitled "Dil sabagi" (Language Lesson). Most striking about the lesson was that the editor ignored the alphabetical order and chose the word *iyman* (*iman*), which means "expression of faith," for its inaugural entry. The lesson was the contribution of the *kazi* (judge) of the Muslims of Kirgizia, S. Kamalov, who in his discussion of *iman* emphasized the role which expression of faith plays in the life of the Muslim believer; he also provided the text of the prayers that, as manifest acts of worship, buttress *iman*.[29]

Increasingly, Central Asian *mullahs* who graduate from Islamic institutions of higher education see their duties extending far beyond sermons and rituals. Instead, they are "community leaders" who are receptive to the needs and problems of the believers. The Talhatan Baba Mosque in Turkmenia was renovated thanks to the efforts of Imam (spiritual leader who leads Muslims in prayer) Annamuhammed Annaberdi, a graduate of the Al-Bukhari Islamic Institute.[30] The *imam* of the Kazakh city of Chu, Abdurassulkhan Kasym, a graduate of the Mir-i Arab Madrasah of Bukhara, led the efforts of the population to build a new mosque, which opened its doors to worshippers in 1983.[31] In another case, a Tajik *mullah* organized help for a family which had lost its house in a fire.[32]

The new generation of *mullahs* seems to have attracted not only graduates of institutions of higher education, but also former Komsomol and Party members. In his remarks regarding Islam in Kirgizia, Moldokasymov critically noted, "In the past, they lectured on atheism but now they wear turbans and have become *mullahs*."[33]

Mullahs who have taken the initiative to open mosques illegally, to build new mosques, and to restore old ones are being assisted by the mass of believers and by some individuals high in the Party and soviet hierarchies. These individuals take a risk in doing so, as did I. Kurandykov, former deputy chairman of the Samarkand oblast soviet. Help also comes from the underground Sufi brotherhoods.

Patterns of Observance

Fulfillment of ritual obligations has always been regarded as a mark of at least attachment to religious traditions, if not outright religiosity. Thus, most studies (both Western and Soviet) of Central Asian Islam identify observance of religious rituals as an important criterion in determining the level of attachment to religion. In the case of Central Asian Islam, the ceremonies connected with the life-cycle rituals of marriage and death, as well as those marking the ritual of circumcision, the celebration of the feast of sacrifice (*Kurban Ait* or *Bairam*), observance of the month of fasting (*Ramadan*), and the feast following it represent the most commonly observed traditions. In addition to these, communal prayers (*mawlud*) marking the birth of the Prophet also appear to be increasingly common.

Soviet Central Asians follow a "double track" calendar according to which they celebrate secular Soviet holidays as well as participate in the observance of religious ones. This fact is confirmed by the results of a survey among Turkmens.[34] Atheist propagandists complain about this phenomenon and say that the rural Uzbek and Tatar youth (who obviously attend Soviet schools) "so often are present in those places where religious ceremonies are held."[35] The fact that educated people, teachers and Party members observe religious rituals reflects the increasing appeal which religion has for educated Muslims. Among this group, even in the 1970s Soviet scholars recognized that the level of religiosity was 10 to 15 percent higher than among the same group of the non-Muslim population.[36]

Most Central Asians perform the rite of circumcision and choose to supplement a Komsomol wedding with a religious ceremony. Marriages outside their religion are rare, despite the fact that they are actively encouraged by the government. When, indeed, these "international" marriages do occur, they are newsworthy and become the focus of journalistic and official attention.[37]

Observance of the month of *Ramadan* is also increasing among Central Asians; during the last few years, children and youths, as well as adult members of the Party and intelligentsia, have engaged in the complete or partial fulfillment of this Muslim ceremonial obligation. Observance of *Ramadan* by school children and students led to a drop in cafeteria attendance, and negatively affected the sales of food-catering establishments.[38]

The feast that concludes the month of *Ramadan* is celebrated widely by young and old who gather at mosques for the communal prayers. Absenteeism from work at holiday time, however, seems to be widespread only among women whose bosses choose to look the other way. Some Party members have noted with concern that during *Ramadan* and the feast that follows it "the activity of the Muslim clergy intensifies and the number of observant Muslims increases, particularly among the youth, but also among children of school and preschool age." Some attribute this to "shortcomings in the atheistic education of the young generation."[39]

As for observance of rituals connected with death—the most widely observed rites in Central Asia—age, social status, educational level, political affiliation are irrelevant. This perhaps is due to the fact that death emerges as the ultimate "emancipator," which renders meaningless the contractual obligations and pressures of society that might inhibit religious observance. According to press reports, even prominent communists are bid farewell in Islamic funerals.[40] More significant than the endurance of religious funerals and the proliferation of religious inscriptions on gravestones (for which the leaders of enterprises producing them are blamed) is the emergence of cemeteries as centers of religious activity and as mirrors of the complex relationship between ethnicity and religion. Segregated along religious, national, and even tribal lines, cemeteries are becoming "centers" of religious celebrations and festivals. Geographically removed from the confines of social and political life and endowed with a measure of immunity by their very nature, cemeteries seem to make possible a freer expression of religious feelings than the mosque; in addition, they preserve the advantages of communal worship that the mosque offers.

Party and government officials have expressed concern over the fluid boundary between a religious festival and a nationalist gathering. This problem was serious enough to prompt the Presidium of the Uzbek Supreme Soviet in 1985 to issue a decree concerning the institution of an annual "Memorial Day" on the last Sunday in March. The decree was aimed at providing a secular replica to the religious traditions and thus build a pantheon of new traditions; it was also intended to "centralize" and bring under state control memorial celebrations, thus preventing their metamorphosis into nationalist gatherings.[41]

As indicated above, overt manifestations of religiosity are not confined to observance of rituals. According to Tajik Party First Secretary Makhkamov, some believers choose to make a public statement regarding their allegiance to Islam by wearing religious symbols and amulets and by decorating their cars with verses from the Koran. Others give newborn babies names with a clear Islamic resonance. In 1988, Makhkamov suggested that historians and philologists join efforts in preparing lists of patriotic, non-religious names.[42] This idea is very similar to a proposal of I. Beliaev (made in *Literaturnaia gazeta* in 1987) to change Central Asian place names in such a way as to eradicate any reminders of Islam.[43]

Observance of Islamic rituals is so widespread that Rafik Nishanov, secretary of the Uzbek Party addressing the Party plenum on January 30, 1988, noted the complexity of the religious situation in the republic, where for many communists the Islamic code of morality was more authoritative than the Party norms and rules of socialist morality. He also pointed out that many communists had "withdrawn from the struggle with Islam."[44]

Recognizing the tenacity of religious observance, republic Party organizations attempted to create new institutions to encourage Soviet (atheistic) rituals and traditions. For example, the Council for Perfecting the Soviet Way of Life was formed under the Uzbek Communist Party Central Committee; the Commission for Establishing New Rites and Customs was formed by the Tajik Academy of Sciences; and in Turkmenia, a new Council for Scientific Atheism and Progressive Traditions was created.

Nevertheless, the sanctions imposed on those who observe religious rituals have relaxed in recent years. At the beginning of the Gorbachev era, it was common for communists to be expelled from the Party for Islamic observances.[45] Indeed, in the past, religious practice sometimes was sufficient to send scholars to labor camps.[46] In Uzbekistan, as late as 1986, raion Party secretaries, school and factory directors, and soviet officials were still being dismissed for religious observances.[47] By the end of the 1980s, however, the policy toward religious observance was substantially more relaxed.

New Scholarship and Modernization of Islam

One of the responses to the religious resilience of Central Asians and the growth of religiosity which they exhibited since the 1970s was an increase in attention to Islam in scholarly debates and in general a growth in scholarship on the subject. Until 1989, most Soviet scholarship on Islam focused above all on the dogmatic concepts of Islam, on criticizing the "modernization" of Islam in the USSR, and identifying the harmful aspects of its social doctrine. For example, a study published in 1975 takes a strong position against the "internationalist" quality of the *umma* concept and argues that "those who attempt to prove the 'internationalism of Islam' on the basis of the *hadiths* (prophetic traditions) and the Koran cannot go further than reiterating the statements of the petty bourgeois nationalists on this issue."[48] Nevertheless, by contrasting Islam with socialist internationalism (defined as the community of the ideas and interests of the working class), the author demonstrated that he considered the "internationalism" of the *umma* a compelling force to be reckoned with.

The unity of the *umma* was similarly challenged in a volume published a decade later on the national and international dimensions of the socialist way of life of the Soviet people. Its authors reiterated the old argument regarding the incompatibility of ethnicity and religion and argued that national consolidation was inevitable and Islamic unity would eventually be destroyed by it.[49] The fallacy of this argument rests in the fact that its authors equate Islamic unity with political unity, whereas for the

Muslims, Islamic unity is first of all the spiritual unity of the community of believers, a unity that transcends race and political systems.

Soviet authors have also viewed Islam as an enemy of social harmony in a society whose *weltanschauung* rests on the twin pillars of class loyalty and loyalty to a secular ideology. Hence, K. Kocharli and R. O. Kurbanov point out that Islam "hinders the rapprochement of peoples, the unity and mutual assistance of workers of various nationalities by the sheer fact that it identifies the religious community with the ethnic."[50]

The concept of brotherhood in Islam was also attacked by V. V. Naumkin in an essay "On the Issue of '*Hassa*' and '*Amma*' " (traditional concepts of the "elite" and "masses" in Islam), and by N. G. Prusakova in her analysis of "The Concept of 'Islamic Nation' and 'Islamic State' in the Ideology of the Movement for the Formation of Pakistan."[51]

Despite these attacks, Central Asian Muslims have continued to emphasize the concepts of equality and brotherhood in Islam and attempted to prove the "compatibility of socialism and Islam." Indeed, the strategy of "constructive coexistence" and even "integration" adopted by the Muslim leaders has made a "frontal attack" on Islam extraordinarily difficult if not altogether impossible. Within this context, Nugman Ashirov's essay *Musul'manskaia propoved'* (The Muslim Sermon) emerges as one of the most open, sophisticated, and learned attacks on "modernizing Islam." Notwithstanding Ashirov's contention that modernization of Soviet Islam was a "sign of the crisis which it is experiencing," his analysis of the role of *khutba*s (sermons) in maintaining the unity and vitality of the *umma* is perceptive and demonstrates an attempt to enable antireligious propaganda to overcome the handicaps of crude generalization and to draw more on the theoretical and factual documentation which scholarship can provide.

Ashirov views *khutba*s as vehicles of "modernization" in Soviet Islam. What one learns from his analysis, however, is that these vehicles of modernization are rooted in the pre-revolutionary *jadid* tradition as proved by the articles published in the Tashkent paper *Hurshid* in the early twentieth century.[52] He argues that today both the length and content of *khutba*s illustrate their importance as instruments of "modernization," and as vehicles capable of unifying the community and "socializing" even its "alienated" or less active elements.

The use of such *khutba*s has more recently been demonstrated by Mufti Muhammad Sadiq Muhammad Yusuf, head of the Religious Board of the Muslims of Central Asia and Kazakhstan since March 1989. On numerous occasions the Mufti has emphasized the importance of *khutba*s for the education of Muslims and stressed the contribution *khutba*s make in teaching respect for others, encouraging high standards of morality and work, and fighting the ills of drugs, alcoholism, and prostitution.

Recently the Mufti provided a "model" sermon, the first of what might become an entire series of *khutba*s disseminated through the print media. On January 5, 1990, the Uzbek literary weekly published Muhammad Yusuf's sermon on the role of men as husbands and family heads. The Mufti amply punctuated his statements with references to the Prophet and the Koran. This first sermon was to be followed by another one dealing with the image of women in the Scripture.[53]

In his *Musul'manskaia propoved'*, Ashirov calls the attention of those involved in atheistic propaganda to the fact that criticism of "modernizing" Islam is a difficult task and that in order to be successful at their work, propagandists have to study the sources of religious resilience. Moreover, according to Ashirov, "modernization" of Islam is dangerous because it misleads people as it tries to prove the compatibility of Islam and communism. Ashirov cites as an example the following statement by the *imam* of the Talhatan Baba Mosque in Turkmenia: "We Muslims, having become acquainted with the project of the new constitution of the USSR, have become convinced that many of its articles correspond to the teachings of the Holy Koran and the Prophet Muhammad. . . ."[54]

Not surprisingly, the *khutba*s which Islamic religious leaders have recently addressed to congregations have emphasized personal and social morality, warned against the use of alcohol and tobacco, and urged modesty in dress. This makes it rather difficult for propagandists to attack Islam, particularly when the statements of the Mufti emphasize the fact that the moral values of Islam are in harmony with the goals of perestroika.[55]

Even Ashirov recognized that the legitimacy of certain "Soviet traditions" is enhanced when reinforced by religious ritual. He deplored the fact that celebrations of many secular holidays, life cycle rituals, release from the army, and moving into a new house are accompanied by a *"mawlud"*—a group prayer which not only puts the "communal seal of legitimacy" upon that particular event, but also becomes a "mini-course" in religious teachings.

The most interesting function of *khutba*s seems to be their emergence as *ad hoc* classes of religious education. "Serialized" *khutba*s have become common. These are like "religious crash courses" which address topics relating to the dogma as well as rituals. For a community which is still deprived of religious education, it is this function of the *khutba* which is perhaps the most responsible not only for the endurance of the community, but as of late, for transforming the believers from "Muslims by virtue of birth and tradition" into "thinking" and even practicing Muslims.

In the early Gorbachev era, authoritative statements indicated serious Party concern over efforts aimed at modernizing Islam so that doctrinal purity would be safeguarded while the observance of ceremonial, ritual obligations was adapted to the imperatives of the Soviet milieu. According to a 1986 editorial in *Sovet Turkmenistany*, this was a particularly dangerous phenomenon because "religious believers and especially present-day Islamic modernists are promoting the idea of Islam as a democratically principled religion, concerned with the well-being of the people, characterized by a high level of morality, and supporting the material and cultural development of the Soviet people."[56]

The "modernization" efforts of the religious leadership and the rank and file clergy are aimed at "emancipating" Islam from an adversarial relationship with the state, integrating it, and contributing to its growth within the system by addressing the real and the seeming contradictions between its social doctrine and dogma and the socio-political principles that guide the Soviet state. When the "modernized" Islam of Central Asia accepts science as proof of God's power, seeks credit for peace and prosperity, and claims scriptural justification for the changed position of women, the task of the atheist propagandists becomes even more difficult.[57] The Party leadership of Kazakhstan was less than jubilant when Khazret Gil'manov, the representative of the Kazakh republic to the Spiritual Directorate, presented social progress as the result of divine providence, and the *imam* of the Chimkent mosque, Sh. Mukhametzhanov argued that certain Islamic practices which contradict contemporary conditions should be changed and then "Islam will continue to exist in Communism as well."[58] The sermons of those *imams* who believe in the predestination of science and technology by God are perceived as equally dangerous.[59] They prompt sharp responses in the pages of literary and socio-political publications which have argued for a long time that Islam is opposed to scientific progress.[60] The difficulty which "modernizing" Islam creates for those interested in the success of atheistic propaganda is especially clear in a 1988 attack on the Muslim Spiritual Directorate of Central Asia and Kazakhstan for its attempts to "modernize" official Islam.[61]

Changing Perception of an Islamic "Threat"

Soviet discussions of Islam have traditionally identified the religion's militancy as one of the main reasons for the adversarial relationship between Islam and the Soviet state. In this regard they often point to the concept of *jihad* (holy war) as the main mark of Islam's exclusivism.

Recently, however, there has been an attempt—even if only in the scholarly literature—to move away from the old simplistic explanations of *jihad* and to provide a more well-rounded discussion of this complex concept. A particularly interesting example of this newer treatment is an article by A. Sagadeev, who seeks to refute the theses of those who, biased by their own faith, have a very parochial view of the world. Sagadeev argues that a simplistic approach to religion erroneously leads to the classification of the people of the world into peaceful and bellicose, solely on the basis of their religious affiliation. In the process of developing his analysis, however, Sagadeev also addresses the issue of the roots of Western hostility toward Islam and notes that negative attitudes which were shaped by illustrious thinkers such as Thomas Aquinas grew into axioms that dominated Western thought for centuries.

Sagadeev's discussion of *jihad* extends beyond the standard popularizing explanation of its meaning as holy war. He analyzes the nuances and the substantive differences between the concepts of "*jihad* of the heart" (*jihad an-nafs*), "*jihad* of the tongue" (*jihad al-lisan*), "*jihad* of the hand" (*jihad al-yadi*), and "*jihad* of the sword" (*jihad as-sayf*), and backs his interpretation with Koranic texts. Sagadeev also concludes that there is nothing in the Islamic dogma per se which could provide reason for labeling Islam a religion of violence. Pointing to the fact that "even in conquered lands, Muslims did not impose Islam with the force of weapons," Sagadeev argues that "Islam of the sword" was a choice presented to pagans alone, and it never represented the lot of "people of the Book" (Christians and Jews). Sagadeev's discussion of *jihad* within the context of contemporary politics identifies it as the banner under which people can rally to fight colonial oppression, as well as the standard under which the "democratic" forces of Afghanistan could fight for the achievement of their goal.[62]

Some scholars have demonstrated a reluctance to accept such a favorable view of *jihad*. N. M. Vagabov concentrates on *jihad's* meaning of holy war (*ghazavat*) and concludes that *jihad* is one of the more vivid manifestations of Islamic exclusivity.[63] His 1985 analysis of the social ethos and ideological essence of the concept of doctrinal exclusivity in Islam is not a purely intellectual exercise. It is aimed at highlighting the inherent features of Islam which act as hindrances to acculturation and "internationalization."

In more recent times, however, prominent Soviet scholars have insisted that whatever problems or danger Islam may pose to the Soviet state, these are not the result of the inherent features of Islam, but rather stem from the ill-conceived and misguided policies of the Party and government leadership. Speaking to a reporter of the Leningrad paper *Smena*, M. Prozorov, the head of the Islamic Studies Group of the Institute of Oriental Studies of the USSR Academy of Sciences, argued that the main prerequisite for a successful approach to Islam in USSR is for

Soviet scholars and political activists to achieve emancipation from "Islamophobia." When he referred to the Muslims of Central Asia as "a critical mass capable of exploding any minute," Prozorov identified the roots of the Muslim discontent in the inequities they experienced and noted that "Budenny's campaign in Central Asia, Stalin's repressions of Muslims, and the destruction of both mosques and manuscripts [have all played their role]."[64]

Attempts to Exploit Islam in Foreign Policy

Studies of Soviet Islam point to a genuine paradox in the relationship between the Soviet state and official Islam: until recently the state has taken a negative view of the modernization of Islam which was aimed at forging a more amicable *modus vivendi* with the state; meanwhile, Muslims, at least those belonging to "official" Islam, promoted modernization as the means to forge a truly peaceful coexistence and a harmonious *modus vivendi* with the state.

This relationship was further complicated by the fact that the Soviet establishment pursued a dichotomous policy with regard to its Muslims. Within the context of domestic policy, Muslims were treated as bearers of a backward religion; in foreign policy, they were projected into the role of bridge builders with the countries of the Third World. Leaders of Soviet Islam acted as emissaries of good will, messengers of peace, and public relations personnae. Furthermore, the Soviet establishment transformed the capitals of the Muslim republics into centers of international meetings and Third World cultural events.

Between 1970 and 1980, seventeen international Islamic conferences were held in Central Asia. However, after the Soviet invasion of Afghanistan in December, 1979, the relationship of the Muslim Spiritual Directorate with foreign Muslims ebbed for several years. The 1980 Tashkent Conference was attended only by 27 countries. By the mid-1980s, however, the situation had markedly improved.

Delegations of the Spiritual Directorate of Central Asia and Kazakhstan took part in numerous international gatherings in the second half of the decade. Among them was the Ninth International Conference on Islamic Thought organized by the Algerian Ministry of Islamic Affairs (July 4-9, 1985). They also participated in conferences and roundtables in Moscow (May 20-23, 1986), Baku (October 1-3, 1986), and again in Moscow (March 1987). The common denominator for all was the struggle for peace, and the concern of the Muslims of the world with disarmament and moral-ethical values in the nuclear age.[65]

The Baku Conference, attended by 600 representatives of Muslim organizations from sixty countries and by delegates of the World Muslim

League, was dedicated in its entirety to "The Struggle of Muslims for Peace."⁶⁶ Shamsuddin Babakhan, who was the Mufti of Central Asia and Kazakhstan at that time, presented a report entitled "Islam and Peace in the Nuclear Age." It was no accident, perhaps, that the Mufti was awarded the Ibn Sina Medal and Prize for 1986. The prize was instituted in 1981 by Novosti Press Agency, Soviet social, cultural, religious, and scientific organizations, and by their counterparts in countries of Asia and Africa. The award was in recognition of an individual's contribution to the cause of peace and friendship among peoples.⁶⁷

There is no doubt that the concerns for peace voiced by the Central Asian Muslim religious establishment were genuine, but its desire to underline the confluence of interests between Islam and the Soviet state encouraged it to push the existing tension with the regime into the background. Thus, at times, religious leaders became spokesmen for Soviet foreign policy. In one such instance, relying on the *hadiths* of the Prophet on the subject of peace and friendship, Muslim leaders called upon all people to live in peace and friendship, and criticized the United States for using outer space for military purposes.⁶⁸

The Soviet government's use of the "Muslim card" was not confined to conference attendance and cultural events. It also included Muslim representation in the Soviet diplomatic corps, joint scientific missions, and involvement of foreign Muslims in activities that add to the prestige of the participants at a minimum economic cost and significant political gain for the USSR.

Sometimes use of the "Muslim card" in foreign policy backfired or entailed unexpected costs for the Soviet government. The 1980 Tashkent conference dedicated to the advent of the fifteenth Islamic century (held in the aftermath of the invasion of Afghanistan) was boycotted by many Islamic countries. And although speakers at the September 1979 symposium held in Dushanbe to discuss the "Contributions of the Muslims of Central Asia, Volga, and the Caucasus to the Development of Islamic Thought, Peace, and Progress" stressed the loyalty of Soviet Muslims to their country, they did much more to emphasize the pride which Central Asians took in the legacy of al-Bukhari, Ibn Sina, and al-Biruni.⁶⁹

The Problem of Sufism

As noted above, in recent years there has been an increase in Soviet literature on Islam. Along with other aspects, this also certainly applies to the study of Sufism in its various manifestations and dimensions. Sufism, a mystical doctrine aimed at achieving personal union with God, was born in the first centuries of Islam in reaction to the formal legalism of the dogma. The journey of a disciple (*murid*) on the path (*tariqa*) toward God was led by a spiritual master called a *sheikh, pir, ishan, murshid,* or *ustad*. When in the twelfth century Islam was threatened for the first time by invaders of other faiths (the Crusaders in the West and the Qara Khitai in the East), Sufis assumed the role of defenders of the faith and emerged as a mass movement of organized brotherhoods (or *tariqat*) of disciples who submitted to the code of secrecy and strict discipline imposed by the master. At that time, Central Asia offered a most fertile soil for Sufi expansion and even emerged as the birthplace and cradle of three of the most celebrated *tariqat*: the Yasawiya and Kubrawiyya of the twelfth century, and the Nakshbandiyyah of the fourteenth century. From its inception, the popular, grass-root dimension allowed Sufism to offer itself as an alternative, a "parallel path" to the legalism of Islamic doctrine.[70]

Today, Sufism still remains a "parallel Islam." It has its own structure, which is the sum-total of the structures of the brotherhoods, but since it is not recognized by the government, it is free of the "jurisdiction" of official Islam. In fact, however, a Sufi is under two "jurisdictions." As a Muslim, he is under the jurisdiction of the Tashkent Muftiate. Moreover, he also falls under the "jurisdiction" of his brotherhood, or, to be more precise, under that of his *sheikh* or *pir*.

Most observers feel that the recent increase in publication of literature about Sufism has accompanied an upsurge in Sufi activity.[71] According to Beliaev, these activities include active Islamic propaganda aided by an "Islamizdat" or underground publications.[72] Given the strict discipline, the code of secrecy, and the organizational infrastructure which the brotherhoods offer, such a contention is more than plausible.

Atheistic literature abounds with citations and vilifications of "holy men" and "itinerant *mullahs*" who congregate around holy places and preach publicly. It can be assumed that these are the members of various Sufi brotherhoods. Bearing similarities with the pre-Islamic model of the Indian *sadhu* sages, the cynic philosophers of the Hellenistic period, and the "Fools in Christ" of the Christian era (all of whom challenged the monopoly of "official religion" and practiced an asceticism of a highly public nature), the Sufi "holy men," who traditionally had enjoyed the prerogative of publicly reproving evil-doers, today seem to confine their roles to those of teachers and "keepers of the faith."

Some of the Sufi holy men have become directly involved in addressing the social, moral, and educational needs of their fellow Muslims. Points in case are *ishan*s Dzhamalov, Dzhuraev, and Zakirov, who were found operating two religious schools in Tajikistan; the holy men of the Uichinsk raion (Uzbekistan), on the other hand, were responsible for collecting the funds necessary to build a prayer house in a cemetery.[73]

The ubiquitous presence of *ishans, sheikhs,* and *murids* in holy places which attract large numbers of visitors speaks indirectly of the public nature of their asceticism and the tremendous influence they can have on believers. It also explains the merciless campaign against holy places and pilgrimages conducted by the government until 1989. Many of the holy places of Central Asian Muslims have been "secularized" and transformed into libraries, homes for the elderly, dining halls, cultural centers or museums.[74] To discredit the itinerant Sufi *mullahs,* officials have villified them as opportunistic seekers of riches who use the road of religion to accumulate wealth.[75]

As a place of ritual pilgrimage, a holy place offers an opportunity for socializing, dissemination of ideas and recruitment. Against the background of the nature of the Sufi *tariqat,* the government perceived these holy places as so dangerous that it closed many of them and in 1987, oblast commissions were instructed to begin issuing "passports" for those that continued to function.[76] Yet Sufism is a widespread phenomenon. The special care which Demidov took in villifying Sufism by calling it "alien to Islam" and associating its leaders and adherents with the "bandit regiments of the *basmachi*" indicates that the Soviet establishment perceives Sufism as a more serious threat than "official Islam."[77]

Sufism does, indeed, represent a more serious threat because it cannot be controlled through a government-sanctioned organization or framework. The Sufi's code of secrecy, and the organizational framework of the brotherhoods, could be used to mobilize Muslims and build a "political infrastructure." Such sobering realities in the wake of developments in Iran and Afghanistan have focused more attention not only on Sufism but also on Central Asia's own *mujahideen* of the 1920s and 1930s—the *basmachi*—who are popular subjects now in novels and scholarly monographs alike.[78] And while until 1988 Sufi brotherhoods were mentioned only so that they could be vilified, in 1990 the founder of one of them—Yasawiya—was honored with an anniversary article published in *Qazaq adebiyeti.*[79]

Changes in the Promotion of Atheism

During most of the 1980s, the state's predominant response to the perceived threat of Islam was the intensification of atheistic propaganda and atheistic education. Throughout Central Asia, scientific atheism departments of philosophy faculties, people's universities, and houses of atheism became very active. These and other institutions organized countless lecture series and "days of atheism" through which, until 1989, the regime crudely combatted religiosity and sought a gradual eradication of Islam. Yet, by the admission of atheistic propaganda organs themselves (particularly candid in the climate of glasnost), the results of this campaign were dismal. The main culprits included the acute shortage of qualified cadres, lack of a sophisticated understanding of Islam, and failure to devise a methodological approach which would match the complexity of the task. Meanwhile, Soviet Islam began to exhibit greater dynamism and militancy. Believers attained higher educational achievements, and some emerged as more savvy "politicians" than the propagandists who sought to convince them.

At the very end of the 1980s, Soviet anti-Islamic propaganda began to be informed by a much more nuanced understanding of the religion. One scholar who contributed to this trend was I. A. Makatov, deputy director of the Uzbek branch of the Institute of Scientific Atheism of the CPSU Central Committee Academy of Social Sciences. Among other things, Makatov took issue with the results of surveys which sought to assess the strength of Islam in Central Asia without basing this on sound sociological criteria. He pointed out that often religiosity was defined in terms of observance of rituals rather than in terms of the existence of a belief in the supernatural. Moreover, stressing the need to distinguish among types of religiosity and atheism, Makatov provided a typology of the contemporary Muslim clergy. He offered three main categories: officially registered, unregistered (so-called "self employed"), and those sanctioned as religious leaders by the community from among the leaders of the *ishan* and *murid* groups.

Since the end of the 1980s, the efforts of atheistic propagandists and of the Party and government establishment seem to be directed at bringing activities of the unregistered members of the clergy under control by registering them. Official Islam seems to be assisting the establishment in this task because, in addition to the self-serving enhancement of its own prestige, it may help eliminate one of the reasons for the attacks on Islam. Makatov acknowledged the fact that the unregistered segment of the clergy represented a real power, since it waged an uncontrolled campaign on behalf of religion and, in the process, fulfilled the ritual needs of the believers. He warned, though, that singlemindedly targeting this group for criticism was a mistake. Moreover, he urged scrutiny of the ideological positions of the registered religious centers without, however, antagonizing those leading organizations which have stated their support for the policies of the Soviet government.

Makatov pointed out that those involved in atheistic propaganda should be able to draw a distinction between the political line pursued by religious organizations loyal to the policies of the CPSU and the Soviet government and the religious ideology which the same organizations promoted in mosques, churches, and synagogues. He thus suggested that atheistic propaganda support the political line advanced by the clergy, while working to bring about the demise of the religious ideology the clergy promoted.

Makatov addressed issues relating to the pitfalls of atheistic propaganda as well as to the "windows of opportunity." He argued that, as propagandists intensify the propaganda against Islamic beliefs and practices as well as against Islam as a theological and ideological system, they need to bear in mind the specific qualities of Islam as a religion and the imperatives of the freedom of conscience guaranteed by the constitution.

Makatov's most interesting suggestion, however, concerned the Sufis. He criticized the atheist workers who resisted the registration of various *murid* groups, indiscriminately relegating all of them to the category of extremist groups. Emphasizing legality and constitutionality as the most important principles of the antireligious struggle, Makatov argued that the anti-*murid* campaigns should seek to reeducate less extremist individuals and isolate them from the extremists. According to Makatov, atheistic campaigns in the traditionally Islamic areas should be subtle, their aim should be the education and "conversion" of the believers, and great care should be taken so as not to hurt believers' feelings. He condemned crude atheistic campaigns which could be harmful and even counterproductive.[80]

Makatov's warnings were probably prompted by his thorough knowledge of the abuses which, paradoxically, continued to exist side by side with the pronouncements on glasnost and perestroika. For example, a Russian propagandist named Baranov launched a crude attack on Islam in a local Turkmen paper just as the Baku Muslim Congress was concluding its activities in October 1986. Baranov labelled Islam the religion of plunderers and conquerers.[81]

More puzzling than Baranov's attack was the 1987 verdict delivered by A. Tursunov, a doctor of philosophical sciences and a Muslim by background. Tursunov challenged the claim of the Muslim ideologists who regarded Islam as a civilizing religion.[82] The strident nature of Tursunov's 1987 attacks on Islam is especially noteworthy against the background of the preparations for the celebration of the millennium of Christianity in Russia. During this period the Soviet press highlighted the organic link between Russian culture and Orthodoxy and extolled the virtues of the religion which gave Russia a special place among the nations of the world.[83] Muslims must have wondered about the meaning of equality in the family of Soviet peoples when they learned that nine new saints of the Russian Orthodox church were glorified in the summer of 1988 in Zagorsk; meanwhile, Muslims still had to request passes to visit the tombs of their own saints. Such perceptions of inequality were somewhat alleviated when in August 1989, the Muslims of Central Asia took part in the festivities in Kazan and Ufa that marked 1100 years since the adoption of Islam by the ancestors of the Volga Tatars.[84]

By 1989, while remaining true to the goal of weakening the hold of Islam on Central Asia, Tursunov had adopted a much more sophisticated approach in his critique of "modernizing" Islam. Distancing himself from the simplistic verdicts he had offered in the past, Tursunov argued that, because of their focus on the political dimension of Islam, Soviet scholars had remained oblivious to the emergence of an Islamic scientific methodology and gnoseological system; he thus implied that these phenomena represented a real asset for "modernizers."[85]

Ironically, in some ways atheistic education seems to have contributed to a growing interest in religion. A Turkmen radio journal entitled *Adam ve din* (Man and Religion) became very popular with believers, most likely for the same reason that in Tatarstan attendance at atheism classes was "motivated by the interest of the students in religion."[86] In atheism classes, lectures aimed at vilifying Islam started with a review of the pillars of Islam and ceremonial obligations and addressed the issue of holy places. Thanks to this, readers and listeners ultimately learned more about religion than atheism.[87]

One atheist official has complained, "We must have the Koran in Kirgiz. How can we fight against the Koran if we don't know what it contains?" Interestingly enough, his cries are not at all dissonant with the demands put forth by the participants at the Fourth Congress of the Religious Board of the Muslims of Central Asia held in March 1989.[88]

Atheistic education has always played an important role in the antireligious campaigns of the Soviet government. However, until as late as 1989, the failure of atheistic propaganda prompted some members of the Central Asian Party leadership to call for a more thorough study of the experience of the 1920s and 1930s in search of ways to address issues of interethnic relations and religion. In early 1988, Uzbek Communist Party secretary Kh. Khalmukhamedov made such a suggestion during a roundtable discussion at the republic Party Institute of History. His idea was endorsed by many participants. It is disturbing that this proposal relied upon policy models from a period in Soviet history associated with frontal attacks on religion and nationalism.[89] At the Uzbek roundtable, however, Khalmukhamedov's simplistic approach was offset by the more sophisticated view of A. S. Chamkin, senior scholar at the Institute of History. Chamkin argued that discussions of nationalism and religiosity could not be limited to examinations of abstract categories. He therefore proposed the organization of a republican Center for the Study of Man which would focus on the interdisciplinary study of the individual in his/her undiluted complexity.[90]

Given not only the fluidity of the era of glasnost and perestroika but the developments of 1989 and early 1990, it can be argued that atheistic propaganda will not return to the practices of the 1920s and 1930s. At best it will attempt to achieve a level of sophistication so that the process of eradicating religion through the acculturation of believers may become plausible sometime in the future. Given the recent dynamism of religious life in the Soviet Union, this might be a distant future indeed. The October 1990 USSR law on religion provides for recognition of churches as legal entities. It also offers a formula for religious education, simplifies the organization of parishes, and allows the opening of more churches. Such proposals give grounds to believe that in the USSR atheism may be in greater danger than religion.[91]

Assertive Islam and the Emergence of a New *Modus Vivendi*

The survival of Islam in Central Asia is rooted in the nature of the religion itself. It bears witness to the force of the unique relationship between ethnicity and religion contained in it. Thus, the dynamism of Islam in Central Asia today should be viewed as more than the result of a "defensive backlash" to atheism or as a response to the stimuli of Iranian fundamentalism and Afghan resistance. Moreover, while both of these factors are important, the growth of tensions rising from unsolved social problems may have been an equally important catalyst of the dynamism that Islam now exhibits. Today Central Asians' multifaceted problems exist in a socioeconomic and political context that embodies a tension between center and periphery and epitomizes the we/they dichotomy. Central Asians perceive many of today's problems as the result of inequities perpetuated by the center. As a result, their sense of being wronged is often translated into an expression of loyalty to religious, national, and even tribal particularism.

There is evidence that developments in Iran and Afghanistan have contributed to the radicalization of Islam in some areas of Soviet Central Asia. For example, it is reported that Turkmen children sing religious songs learned from the Iranian "Radio Gurgen." Likewise, the events in Iran and Afghanistan may have a special impact on Tajikistan. Besides geographical proximity, Tajiks share tribal and ethnic kinship with Afghans and Iranians and so they are likely to be more receptive to the influence of the neighboring countries. Moreover, as an Iranian people, Tajiks seem to feel overwhelmed by the predominantly Turkic environment of Soviet Islam.[92] Noteworthy in this regard is the publication of an illegal newspaper, *Islamskaia Pravda*, in Tajikistan. The paper so far has featured speeches of Khomeini, the Pakistani leader al-Maududi, and excerpts from the works of Al-Afghani.[93]

A Tajik named Saidov (born in 1947) has publicly proposed the establishment of an Islamic state. Saidov is said to have learned the Koran by heart already at an age when other children were first learning to read. Saidov's father, a self-styled *mullah*, had once been a sovkhoz (state farm) director and a Party member; upon retirement, he returned his Party card and proclaimed that religion was more important. Saidov called for an armed struggle in order to achieve establishment of an Islamic state on the territory of Tajikistan. However, he was also willing to probe legal channels, such as when he presented this demand to the CPSU Twenty-Seventh Congress in 1986.

Saidov's arrest in August 1986 provoked violence in the town of Kurgan Tiube, not far from the Afghan border. When the people of Kurgan Tiube (including teachers and Party members) took to the streets, they were joined by residents of neighboring raions who gathered near the office of the ministry of internal affairs to request Saidov's release.[94] This incident reveals not only the willingness of the believers to make a public statement regarding their religiosity, but speaks of Saidov's popularity, as well as of the existence of a well-organized network (probably that of a Sufi brotherhood) that conveyed the news of his arrest. In other words, it could be viewed as yet another testimony to the strength of Sufism in Central Asia. In the aftermath of the ethnic clashes that swept through Central Asia in the summer of 1989 and in the winter and early summer of 1990, it has become more urgent than ever to resolve the dilemmas presented by the active network of Sufi brotherhoods.

Given the complexity of the social and ethnic tensions of recent years, and given the failure of atheistic propaganda (both in its crude and more sophisticated forms), the Soviet leadership seems to have discarded its discriminatory policy toward Islam. Now the regime seems to be seeking accommodation with it.

The policy shift came in the aftermath of events in the early months of 1989. On February 3, 1989, the large number of Muslims who had participated in the Friday prayer at the Tilla Shaykh Mosque of Tashkent marched to the main square of the city, toward the building that houses the Uzbek Council of Ministers. After performing the afternoon prayer in the square, the demonstrators asked to be received by the president of the council, Kadyrov. The purpose of the march, however, was clear even before Kadyrov received the delegation of the marchers, since the crowd held posters that read, "Mufti Babakhanov is a product of the period of stagnation; the Mufti should be elected by the Muslims, not appointed by the Party leadership." When Kadyrov finally received the spokesmen for those gathered in the square, the latter demanded the resignation of Mufti Shamsuddin Babakhanov and put forth the candidacy of Muhammad Sadiq Muhammad Yusuf, the 37-year-old rector (president) of the Tashkent Al-Bukhari Islamic Institute.[95] Because the delegation cited Babakhanov's failure to meet the standards of morality befitting his position, at the time the media and even Western scholars labelled this an act of religious fundamentalism. In fact, however, this was a political act, through which the people demanded a voice in the decisions affecting the religious life of their communities. This contention is supported by the fact that Muslims in Andizhan, Fergana, and Namangan affirmed the will of their communities by ousting the imams appointed by the old Mufti and electing their own new religious leaders.[96]

It seems that believers' ire due to their powerlessness to appoint their own religious leaders (from the Mufti down to *mullahs* of village mosques) was equal to the callousness of the policy of the USSR Council for Religious Affairs on this issue. According to K. M. Kharchev, former president of this council, "*Mullahs* were often selected on the principle 'the worse, the better;' the rationale for this atheistic approach was that 'people will not follow incompetent religious leaders, and as a result, the influence of religion will weaken.' "[97]

If the election of the new Mufti was a first major affirmation of "people power," it was soon to be followed by a second victory, as seven religious leaders, the Mufti among them, were elected USSR People's Deputies. Their election is proof that, at least for the time being, the political establishment of the Soviet Union has decided that co-optation is a better alternative to confrontation in dealing with Islam. The appointment of Ratbek Nysanbayuly as Mufti of the newly elected Religious Board of Kazakhstan in January 1990 is, on the other hand, proof of a parallel, growing trend toward decentralization in the administration of religious affairs.[98]

The new *modus vivendi* between the Soviet state and the Muslims of Central Asia was officially launched in March 1989, at the Fourth Kurultay (Congress) of the Muslim Religious Board, when one of the six copies of the Koran authorized by the Caliph Osman was transferred from the Tashkent museum where it had been kept since 1918 to the library of the Religious Board. (In 1918, in a gesture of good will toward Muslims, Lenin had authorized the Koran's removal from St. Petersburg [where it had been brought after the Russian conquest of Central Asia] and its return to the Muslims.)

No less important in marking the beginning of the new *modus vivendi* was the speech which Kharchev delivered at the Kurultay. He quoted from Lenin's December 3, 1917 "Appeal To the Toilers of the East," in which the Bolshevik leader addressed "all those whose customs and prayer houses were destroyed, and whose customs and beliefs were trampled by the tsars and oppressors of Russia." Lenin had assured his listeners that "from now on your beliefs and customs, and [your] national cultural institutions are proclaimed free and inviolable." By his reference to this speech, Kharchev pointed out that the religious freedom of perestroika represented a return to Leninist principles. Equally important, Kharchev signaled that the Soviet leadership would give Islam the same treatment as the Russian Orthodox Church.[99]

The emergence of a new era of tolerance toward Islam is further attested to by several developments that have unfolded since early 1989—the opening of new mosques, changes in the official pronouncements of the Party leadership on religion, and a media campaign aimed at correcting some of the damage done by past biased representations of Islam. As for mosques, in his Kurultay remarks Kharchev stated, "New mosques are being opened, many have already been opened, and many more will be opened." This fact was confirmed by other Kurultay participants who provided various concrete examples.[100] Indeed, by the middle of 1989, more than sixty mosques had been opened in Central Asia, and repair and construction of others were proceeding apace.[101] The emphasis which average Muslims and religious leaders alike place on the need to have more mosques is rooted not so much in their role as places of worship as in their potential to be social centers and nuclei for the moral regeneration of the Muslim communities.[102]

The new *modus vivendi* between Islam and the Soviet state is reflected in the statement on religion which the Uzbek Communist Party included in its December 1989 election platform. The platform stated: "The republican Party organization actively favors the freedom of religion and the legal rights of the believers, [as well as] cooperation with religious organizations."[103]

This platform is in harmony with the recent media campaign's tone. Today the aim of the press with regard to religion is to inform and educate rather than chastise. The Soviet journal *Nauka i religiia* (Science and Religion) has played a leading role in accomplishing this task so far. In its January, May, and June issues for 1989, it published a series of articles on the life of the Prophet Muhammad; the June issue also featured an article on the *haj* (pilgrimage); issues in the second half of 1989 offered a Russian translation of 24 *suras* (chapters) of the Koran. Similarly, Uzbekistan's literary journal *Zvezda Vostoka* (The Star of the East) has also been publishing the Russian translation of the Koran in installments.[104]

In addition to its broad scope, what is remarkable about the new *modus vivendi* is the belatedness and suddenness of its arrival. These last characteristics suggest that the Party and government leadership may have been forced by the imperatives of glasnost to discard the approach to religion which resulted in different kinds of policies toward Christianity and Islam respectively. Yet the leadership seems to have followed this bifurcated approach until 1989.

It was perhaps the growing awareness of the explosive nature of the tensions that had accumulated in Central Asia that prompted the Party and government leadership to soften their stand on Islam and even to co-opt it in pursuit of the goals of perestroika by enlisting the help of the Muslim religious establishment. The events of 1989 and 1990 provide ample evidence to support this contention. Following his election to the post of Mufti in March 1989, M. S. Muhammad Yusuf was highly visible, for example, in press interviews and as a member of the "peace-making delegation" that traveled to the Fergana Valley in the aftermath of the ethnic violence that rocked Uzbekistan in the summer of 1989. The Mufti's public statements emphasized the harmony between the goals of perestroika and those of the Muslims.[105] He also pointed out, however, that danger to interfaith and interethnic harmony could come not from the "mainstream" Islam, but from splinter groups. This is a clear reference to the Sufi groups that are not sanctioned by "official Islam." In fact, the government and Party leadership seems to have found common ground on which to forge a working relationship with the Muslim religious leaders in their shared apprehension of this elusive dimension of Islam—the parallel "house" of the Sufi brotherhoods.

The apprehension of the Muslim religious establishment stems from theological considerations, while that of the government is rooted in political concerns. The Muslim religious establishment disagrees with the conservative interpretations of the dogma provided by "splinter groups" such as the self-styled "Wahabis"; for the government, however, it is not the dogma but their militancy that is the main source of concern.

Participants at the Fourth Kurultay voiced concern over the existence of splinter Muslim groups that translate their puritanism into requests for the abolition of coeducational schools, discarding of European clothes and hair fashions for women, and removal of male doctors from maternity wards. According to the testimony of some of the Kurultay delegates, "Wahabis" at Samarkand University warned the female students at that institution that if they refused to switch to their national dress for the May Day demonstration, they would be killed. "Wahabis" seem to have gained followers even among women in some areas, since in Namangan some 300 women organized a demonstration demanding that a separate mosque for women be opened. This can be viewed as a clear statement of the "Wahabi" response to the problem of mosque attendance by women.[106]

The pronouncements of conservative splinter groups on the issue of women stand in sharp contrast with the concerns voiced by the delegates of "mainstream" Islam at the Fourth Kurultay. A. Vasiev, for instance, called the attention of those gathered to the sorry state of health care and to the serious health problems of Central Asian women. Vasiev proposed that the Religious Board demand some concrete action from the republican government. When he spoke of the tragedy of self-immolations, Dzh. Yuldashev identified their roots in existing social problems, not in religious imperatives, which were usually seen as the culprits in the atheistic propaganda.[107] This indicates that mainstream Islam, and not splinter groups, may have a better understanding of the socioeconomic, cultural, and political problems that confront the Muslims of the USSR today. As a result, this mainstream can become a reliable partner in the new *modus vivendi*. However, this seems likely to happen only if and when the Soviet government moves to correct past inequities in all spheres of life and only if it is ready to respect the commitment of Central Asians to Islam as a theology, as well as a way of life.

Notes

1. K. Kharchev, "Establishing Freedom of Conscience: The Seventieth Anniversary of the Adoption of the Decree 'On the Separation of Church and State and School and Church by the Soviet of People's Commissars of RSFSR,'" *Izvestiia*, Jan. 27, 1988, p. 3.

2. The population figure cited is based on census data published in Ann Sheehy, "Ethnic Muslims Account for Half of Soviet Population Increase," Radio Liberty, *Report on the USSR*, Jan. 19, 1990, pp. 16–19.

3. N. Ashirov, *Musul'manskaia propoved'* (Moscow: Politizdat 1978), p. 52.

4. It is believed that until 1988–89, there were 150 mosques in the Uzbek republic, 30 in the Kazakh, 25 in the Kirgiz, 15 in the Tadzhik, 4 in the Turkmen, and 5 in the Karakalpak republic (A. Bennigsen and S. E. Wimbush, *Mystics and Commissars. Sufism in the Soviet Union*, [Berkeley: University of California Press, 1985], pp. 60, 70, 81, 90, 101, 108, and 112). For an estimate of the total number of mosques, see I. Beliaev, "Islam i politika," *Literaturnaia gazeta*, May 13, 1987, p. 13.

5. The figure of 751 was given by Kharchev in an interview with I. Achildiev, "Garantii svobody," *Nauka i religiia*, no. 11, 1987, p. 23.

6. I. Beliaev, "Islam i politika." If the unregistered communities are distributed proportionally among the Soviet Muslim population, then there were over 1,100 in Central Asia and Kazakhstan.

7. S. Muslimov, "Prismotrimsia k sebe povnimatel'nei," *Nauka i religiia*, no. 7, 1988, p. 6.

8. See Werner Pirker's report from Dushanbe in *Volksstimme* (Vienna), May 9, 1987, p. 3.

9. *Sovetskaia Kirgiziia,* Mar. 16, 1987, and Sh. Bazarbaev, "Kayra kuruu zhana ateistik ish," *Kirgizistan Kommunisti,* no. 10 (Oct.), 1987, pp. 58–62.

10. S. Urkunbaev, "Batadan baary bashtalat," *Leninchil zhash,* Aug. 20, 1987.

11. "Praktika, opyt, problemy," *Voprosy nauchnogo ateizma,* no. 31, 1983, p. 217.

12. A. I. Artem'ev and K. Sh. Shulembaev, "Partiinoe rukovodstvo ateisticheskim vospitaniem," *Voprosy nauchnogo ateizma,* no. 31 (1983), p. 183.

13. "Aktual'nye problemy mezhnatsional'nykh otnoshenii i internatsional'nogo vospitaniia mass. Zasedanie za kruglym stolom v Institute istorii partii pri Ts. K. Kompartii Uzbekistana," *Kommunist Uzbekistana,* no. 5, 1988, p. 83.

14. *Pravda,* July 2, 1988, pp. 11–12.

15. *Tojikistoni Soveti,* June 11, 1986.

16. T. Karatygina, "Po ateisticheskim siuzhetam," *Kommunist Tadzhikistana,* no. 11, 1986, p. 7.

17. E. Iusupov, "Narodnye traditsii i predrassudki Islama," *Sovetskaia kultura,* Dec. 18, 1986, p. 3.

18. In. Petrash, "Ostryi signal. Byt'ili ne byt' narodnomu muzeiu," *Nauka i religiia,* no. 12, 1987, p. 11.

19. O. Brushlinskaia, "V chem koren' zla?" *Nauka i religiia,* no. 11, 1989, pp. 12–15.

20. Bess Brown, "Tajik Survey Reveals Extent of Religious Belief Among Young People," *Radio Liberty Research* 150/88, Mar. 31, 1988 and E. Kublitskaia, "Obshchestvo massovogo ateizma glazami sotsiologa," *Nauka i religiia,* no. 1, 1990, pp. 34–35.

21. *Leninchil zhash,* Aug. 6, 1987 and A. M. Masaliev, "Uluchshit' patrioticheskoe i internatsionalisticheskoe vospitanie rabochego kollektiva—glavnoe uslovie dlia uskoreniia sotsial'no ekonomicheskogo i dushevnogo razvitiia," *Propagandist-Agitator Kirgizistana,* no. 2, (Jan.) 1988, pp. 2–16.

22. On Yasawiya, see Bennigsen and S. E. Wimbush, *Mystics and Commissars* pp. 33–36.

23. In the part of Kirgizia which was Islamized later, Islam was introduced as the bearer of sociopolitical ideas able to satisfy needs for internal cohesion rather than a theological school aimed at satisfying purely spiritual needs. Having embraced the Islamic *weltanschauung* at different times in history, the Kirgiz of the North and South became the architects of a House of Islam that thrives on the tension between its prerogatives as a theology and its quality as a bearer of sociopolitical ideas. For a detailed analysis of the dimension of Kirgizia's Islamization, as well as of the relationship between religion and ethnicity, see Guy Imart, "The Islamic Impact on Kirghiz Ethnicity," *Nationalities Papers,* nos. 1–2, 1986, pp. 65–88.

24. *Sovet Turkmenistani,* Jan. 4, 1986; *Pravda Vostoka,* Mar. 24, 1985, Masaliev, "Uluchshit' vospitanie"; and Alimov, Dziuba, Lepikhov, and A. Shlienkov, *Izvestiia,* Jan. 17, 1986, p. 3.

25. For Makhkamov's report see *Agitator Tadzhikistana,* no. 20 (Oct). 1986, p. 11.

26. Along with numerous places in other republics, reports note their presence in Turkmenistan's Vekilbazar, Tagta, Tel'man, Bairamali, Il'ianli, Kalinin, and Murgab raions.

27. F. N. Il'iasov, "Religioznoe soznanie i povedenie," *Sotsiologicheskie issledovaniia*, no. 3, 1987, p. 54.

28. A. Debisaliev, "Quran haqinda," *Qazaq adebiyeti*, Oct. 20, 1989, p. 14; Nov. 3, 1989, p. 14, and Nov. 24, 1989, p. 16; also T. Zhaksybaeva, "Zvuchit Koran," *Kazakhstanskaia Pravda*, Oct. 16, 1990.

29. "Zhangi atalma: Dil sabagi. Iyman," *Kirgizstan madaniyati*, Jan. 4, 1990, p. 13.

30. A. Abdullah, "La second naissance de la mosque 'Talkhatan-Baba,' " *Les Musulmans de L'Ouest Sovietique*, no. 3, 1986, pp. 12–13.

31. A. Mussabek, "Il y a une mosquee dans la ville de Tchou," *Les Musulmans de L'Ouest Sovietique*, no. 1, 1986, pp. 22–23.

32. Brown, "Tajik Survey."

33. *Leninchil zhash*, Aug. 6, 1987.

34. *Mugallimlar gazeti*, July 5, 1985.

35. *Lenin bairaghi*, Aug. 7, 1986.

36. For the level of religiosity among university and high school students, see T. Saidbaev, *Islam i obshchestvo: opyt istoriko-sotsiologicheskogo issledovaniia*, (Moscow: Politizdat, 1978), p. 181.

37. Among the Turkmens, for instance, 61 percent perform circumcision. See F. N. Il'iasov, "Religioznoe soznanie," p. 54. Fifty-five percent of the Uzbeks in the cities and 58 percent of these in the villages observe the rituals of circumcision, religious marriage and burial. See L. A. Tul'tseva, " O nekotorykh sotsial'no-etnicheskikh aspektakh razvitiia obriadogo-prazdnichnoi kul'tury v Uzbekistane," *Sovetskaia etnografiia*, no. 5, 1984, pp. 15–24. On international marriages, see In. Kuz'mina, "Vstrecha s Nurekom," *Nauka i religiia*, no. 2, 1986, pp. 24–30.

38. See Makhkamov's report in *Agitator Tadzhikistana*, no. 20 (Oct). 1986, p. 11 and Brown, "Tajik Survey."

39. *Yash leninchi*, June 10, 1986; and T. Osipova and T. Iskanderov, "Konstitutsionnye garantii svobody sovesti," *Kommunist Uzbekistana*, no. 11, 1989, p. 65.

40. *Sovet Ozbekistani*, July 30, 1985.

41. On funerals see *Satsialistik Qazaqstan*, June 10, 1984 and July 25, 1985, p. 4; *Sovet Ozbekistani*, July 30, 1985; with regard to cemeteries as religious and nationalist statements in Kazakhstan, see A. Rozanov, "Chei obychai?" *Nauka i religiia*, no. 5, 1987, pp. 16–18.

42. "New Uzbek Leader Speaks on Religion," *Central Asian Newsletter*, May 1988, p. 14.

43. I. Beliaev, "Islam i politika" (part 2), *Literaturnaia gazeta*, May 20, 1987, p. 12. Talib Saidbaev, Director of the Institute of Philosophy and Law of the Uzbek Academy of Sciences, took issue with Beliaev's suggestion and argued that for the sake of equity, such changes should be implemented everywhere, not just in Muslim areas (T. Saidbaev, "Rezonans. Islam i politika," *Literaturnaia gazeta*, June 10, 1987, p. 14).

44. *Central Asian Newsletter*, May, 1988, p. 14.
45. See K. M. Makhkamov's report in *Agitator Tadzhikistana*, no. 20 (Oct.), 1986, pp. 1–15.
46. O. Brushlinskaia, "V chem koren' zla?"
47. *Sovet Ozbekistani*, Nov. 4, 1986.
48. N. Ashirov, *Islam i natsii* (Moscow: Politizdat, 1975), p. 92.
49. Ts. A. Stepanian and A. K. Karypkulov, eds., *Internatsional'noe natsional'noe v sotsialisticheskom obraze zhizni sovetskogo naroda* (Moscow, 1985), 283.
50. F. K. Kocharli and R. O. Kurbanov, "O reaktsionnoi sushchnosti kontseptsii musul'manskogo natsional'nogo kommunizma," *Voprosy filosofii*, no. 12, 1982, p. 111.
51. These essays were published in *Islam v istorii narodov Vostoka* (Moscow, 1981), pp. 40–51 and 100–123, respectively.
52. N. Ashirov, *Musul'manskaia propoved'* (Moscow: Politizdat, 1978), p. 9.
53. M. S. Muhammad Yusuf, "Fan. Turmush. Ailadagi yar," *Ozbekistan adabiyati va san"ati*, Jan. 5, 1990.
54. Ashirov, *Musul'manskaia propoved'*, 18.
55. M. S. Muhammad Yusuf, "Islam i vera, i obraz zhizni," *Zvezda Vostoka*, no. 12, 1989, pp. 138–39.
56. *Sovet Turkmenistany*, Jan. 4, 1986.
57. S. Dorzhenov, *Qazaqstan Kommunisti*, no. 9, 1985, pp. 47–53.
58. A. I. Artem'ev and K. Sh. Shulembaev, "Partiinoe rukovodstvo ateisticheskim vospitaniem," *Voprosy nauchnogo ateizma*, no. 31 (1983) p. 185.
59. N. Kh. Saidov, *Sistema nauchno-ateisticheskogo vospitaniia v usloviiakh razvitogo sotsializma* (Tashkent: Fan, 1982).
60. See the article on Muhammad published in *Adabiyat va sungat*, Mar. 18, 1988.
61. *Kommunist Tadzhikistana*, no. 2, 1988 and Brown, "Tajik Survey," p. 2. For criticisms of "modernizing" Islam also see articles by Zh. Bekbaev in *Madaniyat zhana turmush*, no. 1, 1986, p. 18, and by I. Jabbarov in *Ozbekistan adabiyati va san"ati*, July 5, 1985.
62. A. Sagadeev, "Dzhikhad," *Nauka i religiia*, no. 6, 1986, pp. 24–25. Another recent study of contemporary Islam is by A. Akhmedov, *Islam v sovremennoi ideino-politicheskoi bor'be* (Moscow, Politizdat, 1985).
63. M. Vagabov, *Musul'manskii konfesionalizm v proshlom i nastoiashchem* (Makhachkala, 1985).
64. This is cited by Paul Goble, "Islamic 'Explosion' Possible in Central Asia," Radio Liberty, *Report on the USSR*, Feb. 16, 1990, pp. 22–23.
65. On participation in international conferences, see R. Nisanbaev, "Soviet Ulema Participants in the 'Islamic Thought' Conference in Algeria," *Muslims of the Soviet East*, no. 1, 1986, pp. 6–7; Mufti Chamsouddin-khan, "Le desarmement est l'imperatif du temps," *Les Musulmans de L'Ouest Sovietique*, no. 4, 1986, pp. 6–7; Ann Sheehy, "International Islamic Conference meets in Baku," *Radio Liberty Research* 372/86, pp. 1–6; and *Izvestiia*, Mar. 23, 1987, p. 3.
66. On the Baku Conference, see "Communique," *Les Musulmans de L'Ouest Sovietique*, no. 1, 1987, pp. 3–5.

67. "Mufti Chamsouddin-khan est laureat du prix ibn Sina," *Les Musulmans de L'Ouest Sovietique,* no. 1, 1987, p. 18.

68. "Des Hadiths du Prophete au sujet de la paix et de l'amitie," *Les Musulmans de L'Ouest Sovietique,* no. 4, 1986, p. 5; "Extraits des discours des participants a la conference de Baku," *Les Musulmans de L'Ouest Sovietique,* no. 2, 1987, pp. 3-6; and E. Ridvanova, "Yadro teliukesine yol bermemiz," *Lenin bairaghi,* Sept. 9, 1986. Tashkent, the sister city of Seattle, launched an appeal to the people of this American city to join hands to defend the cause of peace. See *Lenin bairaghi,* Aug. 30, 1986 and Sh. Y. Shakir, "Meetings in America," *Muslims of the Soviet East,* no. 1, 1986, p. 8.

69. V. A. Kuroedov, *Religiia i tserkov' v Sovetskom gosudarstve* (Moscow: Znanie, 1981), 220-29.

70. For a detailed study of Sufism in Russia and the USSR see A. Bennigsen and S. E. Wimbush, *Mystics and Commissars.*

71. The following of these studies should be particularly noted: V. N. Basilov, *Kul't sviatykh v Islame* (Moscow, 1970); S. M. Demidov, *Sufizm v Turkmenii. Evoliutsiia i perezhitki* (Ashkhabad, 1978); S. M. Demidov, *Turkmenskie ovliady* (Ashkhabad: Ylym, 1976); Kh. D. Dodykudoev, *Mazhabho-yi Musulman* (Dushanbe: Donish, 1967); S. B. Dorzhenov, *Islam bugunku kundo* (Frunze: Ilim, 1980); A. Khaiydov, *Din hem edebiyat. Magtimgulining dorejiliginde sufizm ideialari* (Ashkhabad: Ylym, 1978); S. Mambetaliev, *Sufizm zhana aning Qirgizstandagi agimdari* (Frunze: Ilim, 1972); E. Sharipov and E. Bazarov, *Muqaddas jailar toghrisida haqiqat* (Tashkent: Fan, 1977); and *Sufizm i sufiiskaia literatura* (Moscow: Znanie, 1965).

72. See Beliaev "Islam i Politika" (part 2).

73. *Pravda Vostoka,* Mar. 24, 1985 and Karatygina, "Po ateisticheskim siuzhetam," p. 7.

74. On holy places and the relationship of believers to them, see *Ateizm i religiia. Voprosy i otvety* (Moscow: Politizdat, 1985); *Sovvetik Qirgizstan,* July 31, 1984, *Sovet Ozbekistani,* Dec. 3, 1983; and G. Alimov *et al.,* in *Izvestiia,* Jan. 17, 1986, p. 3.

75. *Sovet Ozbekistani,* Nov. 4, 1986, 3. For criticism of holy places see Iu. Kudratov, "Eskilikke karshi amansiz kuresheik," *Lenin bairaghi,* May 17, 1986; and S. Ashirov, "Mukaddes er tirile," *Lenin bairaghi,* June 3, 1986, p. 4.

76. *Sovetskaia Kirgiziia,* Mar. 16, 1987.

77. S. M. Demidov, *Sufizm v Turkmenii,* pp. 4 and 132.

78. Two novels are S. Omurbaev's *The Storm* and K. Yashen's *Khamza.* Among the monographs are E. Iu. Iusupov, *Basmachestvo. Sotsial'no-politicheskaia sushchnost'* (Tashkent: Fan, 1984) and V. Abylgaziev *Krakh politicheskogo banditizma* (Frunze: Kirgizstan, 1984).

79. S. Iztileuuli, "Uli zhibek zholimen," *Qazaq adebiyeti,* Sept. 19, 1990, p. 3.

80. I. Makatov, "Aktivno perestraivat' ateisticheskuiu rabotu," *Kommunist Uzbekistana,* no. 6, 1988, pp. 58-65.

81. This is reported in the *Central Asian Newsletter,* no. 6 (Dec.) 1986, p. 6.

82. A. Tursunov, "Voprosy teorii: 'Ateizm i kul'tura,'" *Pravda,* Jan. 16, 1987, pp. 2-3.

83. On the Millennium celebrations and the relationship between religion and culture, see "O natsional'nom chuvstve," *Nauka i religiia*, no. 5, 1988, pp. 3-6; the interview with Patriach Pimen in *Izvestiia*, Apr. 9, 1988, p. 3; and *Izvestiia*, May 20, 1987, p. 2.

84. "Islam dinen kabul ituebezga 1100 el," *Kazan utlari*, no. 10, 1989, p. 191.

85. A. Tursunov, "Islam i nauka," *Nauka i religiia*, no. 5, 1989, pp. 6-8 and no. 7, 1989, pp. 24-25.

86. Werner Pirker's report *Volksstimme* May 9, 1987 and *Sovet Turkmenistani*, Feb. 5, 1986; and G. R. Baltanova, "V nerazryvnom edinstve," *Vestnik vysshei shkoly*, no. 7, 1987, p. 63.

87. R. Astakov, "Klas sagadinda ateistik terbie," *Turkmenistanin khalk magarifi*, no. 1, 1986, pp. 44-46; M. K. Dzhabarova, "Nekotorye rezul'taty issledovaniia otnosheniia molodezhi k ateizmu i religii (po materialam Tadzhikskoi SSR)," *Voprosy nauchnogo ateizma* no. 34 (1986), pp. 167-175.

88. *Leninchil zhash*, Aug. 6, 1987. A similar request came from a Russian teacher who proposed that the Bible and the Koran be made available in the series "Literary Texts." See *Komsomol'skaia Pravda*, May 13, 1988, p. 2. The last edition of the Koran was published by the Spiritual Directorate in 1984. See also, "Le Kouroultai (Congres) des Musulmans d'Asie Centrale et du Kazakhstan," *Les Musulmans de l'Orient Sovietique*, nos. 2-3, 1989, p. 13.

89. "Aktual'nye problemy mezhnatsional'nykh otnoshenii i internatsional'nogo vospitania mass. Zasedanie 'za kruglym stolom' v Institute istorii partii pri Ts. K. Kompartii Uzbekistana," *Kommunist Uzbekistana*, no. 5, 1988, p. 73; the volume G. M. Lifshits, *Ocherki po istorii ateizma v SSSR: 20-30 gody* (Minsk: Nauka i tekhnika, 1985) represents a collection of essays on atheism written by one of the most active atheistic propagantists of that period.

90. *Kommunist Tadzhikistana*, no. 5, 1988, p. 79.

91. See S. Kaufmann's interview with K. Kharchev, Chairman of the USSR Council for Religious Affairs (Paris, July 1, 1988) in *Le Monde*, July 3-4, 1988, p. 3.

92. E. Naby, "Tajiks Reemphasize Iranian Heritage as Ethnic Pressures Mount in Central Asia," Radio Liberty, *Report on the USSR*, Feb. 16, 1990, pp. 20-22.

93. *Mugallimlar gazeti*, Mar. 23, 1986; V. Rabiev, "Ateisticheskie siuzheti: V shkolu s . . . Koranom," *Kommunist Tadzhikistana*, Jan. 31, 1987, p. 3.

94. V. Rabiev, *Kommunist Tadzhikistana*, Feb. 12, 1987.

95. For a biography of the new Mufti, see M. S. Muhammad Yusuf, "Islam i vera, i obraz zhizni," *Zvezda Vostoka*, no. 12, 1989, p. 137.

96. Brushlinskaia, "V chem koren' zla?" pp. 16-17.

97. This is quoted from Brushlinskaia, "V chem koren' zla?" pp. 18. For Kharchev's release from the presidency of the Council for Religious Affairs, see Oxana Antic, "Kharchev Replaced as Chairman of Council for Religious Affairs," Radio Liberty, *Report on the USSR*, Aug. 4, 1989, pp. 1-3.

98. "New Muftis in Kazakhstan and North Caucasus," *Central Asia and Caucasus Chronicle*, Mar., 1990, p. 24.

99. See *Les Musulmans de l'Orient Sovietique*, nos. 2-3, 1989, p. 13.

100. Ibid., p. 14.

101. T. Osipova and T. Iskanderov, "Konstitutsionnye garantii," 47–48.

102. *Zvezda Vostoka*, no. 12, 1989, p. 144; K. Rakhimov, "Makhallia, nachalo nachal," *Nauka i religiia*, no. 9, 1989, pp. 28–29.

103. *Pravda Vostoka*, Dec. 7, 1989.

104. V. Panova and Iu. Vakhtin, "Zhizn' Muhammada," *Nauka i religiia* no. 1, 1989, pp. 52–55; no. 5, pp. 56–59; no. 6, pp. 56–61. For the Koran see no. 7, pp. 36–37; no. 8, pp. 34–35; no. 9, pp. 30–31 and 65; and no. 12, pp. 54–56. The first installment in *Zvezda Vostoka* appeared in no. 1, 1990, pp. 142–163.

105. M. Muhammad Yusuf, "My za dobro i spravedlivost'," *Nauka i religiia*, no. 11, 1989, pp. 15–21.

106. Brushlinskaia, "V chem koren' zla?" pp. 16–20.

107. *Les Musulmans de l'Orient Sovietique*, nos. 2–3, 1989, pp. 16–18.

8

Forging a Soviet People: Ethnolinguistics in Central Asia

Isabelle Kreindler

Introduction

As demonstrated in diverse settings throughout the world, language is a major force which can help or hinder governments' efforts to unite peoples living under the same political system. Faced with a population speaking many dozens of languages, the Soviet government has long attempted to promote Russian as the primary means of communication among members of different nationalities. At least since the middle of the 1930s, Moscow has sought to encourage the integration of Central Asians into Soviet society through promotion of teaching Russian language skills.

Moscow did not promote Russian simply as a channel which, by serving as a lingua franca, would facilitate communication. Rather, it also saw Russian language as a primary "cultural integrator" which could play a central role in helping to merge the diverse populations of the USSR into the "new historical community—the Soviet People."

The present chapter will examine the way in which the Party used Russian language instruction in its attempt to bridge the cultural and geographic distance between the Soviet Union's Slavs and the Central Asian peoples. This campaign reached its height during the Brezhnev era, when Russian was routinely referred to as non-Russians' "second mother tongue." The way in which this campaign was conducted may at least partly explain the linguistic self-assertiveness which manifested itself in Central Asia in the late 1980s.

The drive on behalf of the Russian language, first launched in the late 1950s, accelerated into the mid-1980s with few signs of abatement until it was derailed by Gorbachev's "revolution." The October 1978 decree "On Measures for Further Improving the Study and Teaching of the Russian Language in Union Republics" was followed by that of June 1983 "On Further Measures for Improving the Study of the Russian Language" and by the School Reform of 1984, which called for still more vigorous measures to "insure a mastery of Russian by all secondary school graduates."[1]

The special preparatory classes for teaching Russian to six-year-olds, first introduced experimentally in Kirgizia in 1965, spread to all republics (albeit with considerable delay to Armenia, Estonia, Latvia, Lithuania, Tajikistan and Uzbekistan and with an interesting twist in Georgia and Azerbaijan, where the classes were at first used to teach the national language only). By 1979, all republics had preparatory classes and all were teaching Russian according to a model program drawn up by the center. The 1984 School Reform, which lowered the age of first-graders from seven to six, theoretically insured that all six-year-olds would begin to study Russian. At the same time, Russian lessons first introduced experimentally in non-Russian kindergartens in 1973, were rapidly expanding not only in kindergartens but also in nursery schools.[2] In addition, intensive Russian language classes on the primary as well as secondary level along with numerous Russian elective courses in the upper levels continued to proliferate in all republics.[3]

Special directives (backed, of course, by financial allocations) were issued to split Russian language classes whenever the number of students reached 25. In small village schools where three grades are often taught simultaneously by one teacher, Russian was the only subject which could not be taught to more than one grade at a time.[4] The extraordinary position of Russian in schools was also reflected in the lavish supply of technical teaching aids and the requirement that every non-Russian school be equipped with a special Russian Language Resource Center (*kabinet russkogo iazyka*). Even the use of computers for teaching Russian began to receive considerable attention.[5] Extracurricular activity programs, including "Russian Festivals," "Russian Fridays," "Russian Mornings (or Evenings)," Russian language contests, festive meetings with Russian language schools, and travel to other republics continued to expand.[6] Teacher training and retraining programs were constantly reexamined, expanded, and improved; numerous and frequent seminars, workshops, and conferences were held on the all-Union and various local levels; and there was a marked increase in the publication of new textbooks and grammars, various dictionaries, and other teaching materials and aids.[7]

All this enormous effort on behalf of teaching Russian to the non-Russians was justified on the grounds that it was the language of cross-nationality communication and that its mastery furthered "the strengthening of the political, economic, and spiritual unity of the Soviet People," while failure to master Russian caused "a perceptible loss to state interests."[8] Russian in the Soviet Union was said to be not only a lingua franca, but also "the powerful instrument for spiritual unification . . . the most important factor in the consolidation of the historical community."[9] "Mastery of the Russian language," according to the editorial in *Sovetskaia Kirgizia* which had welcomed the 1983 decree on further improving the teaching of Russian, "promote[d] the ideological-moral formation of the students in a spirit of friendship and unity."[10] Or, as the Soviet linguist Mikhailovskaia put it, "Russian promotes a single socialist culture of the new social and international community—the Soviet people."[11] "The question of studying the Russian language in the national schools," as explained by the then USSR Minister of Education Prokofiev, was "being viewed above all from the standpoint of the drawing together of nations."[12]

Language as an Instrument of Acculturation

The double mission placed on the Russian language, to act both as the language of cross-nationality communication and as the instrument of spiritual integration on the basis of Russian culture called for two contradictory approaches. For the purpose of communication, the quickest and most efficient approach would have been to teach a "basic Russian" that stressed everyday, useful, practical vocabulary. Non-native pronunciation and even "varieties" of Russian, as long as mutual comprehension was preserved, also could have been tolerated. This is exactly what has happened with English in its role as international lingua franca. As the African writer Chinua Achebe put it, "the price a world language must be prepared to pay is submission to many different kinds of use."[13] Such an approach, however, could not promote the second mission, that of spiritual integration through the Russian language. For, as Academician Bromlei explained, though the common Soviet culture was developing in the Russian language, this did not imply any "loss of *samobytnost'* (distinctiveness)."[14] The beauty, the uniqueness, the national character of the Russian language had to be preserved. Safeguarding the purity of the Russian language was in fact seen as "an all-Peoples' cause."[15] Thus, it is not at all surprising that while, in the words of Professor Allworth, "the central political forces push[ed] to reduce the significant cultural, artistic and social variations among the non-Russians," teachers in non-Russian schools were instructed to stress the uniqueness of Russian and Russian culture.[16] In singling out the Great Russian people and their language, a teacher did not need to worry about the usual injunctions against "national narrow-mindedness" or "national conceit." Tchaikovsky's lines in which he expressed his passionate love for "the

Russian person, for Russian speech, for the Russian frame of mind, for the beauty of Russian faces, for Russian customs" were, for example, recommended for teaching the accusative declension.[17] Lomonosov's praise of Russian as the language which alone has "the greatness of Spanish, the liveliness of French, the strength of German, the tenderness of Italian and, in addition, the richness and brevity of Greek and Latin," was recommended for its "patriotic and truly objective (sic) comparative evaluation." (His Ode to Empress Elizabeth was also highly recommended for its ability to "awaken patriotic feelings.")[18] Gogol's *Dead Souls'* digression on the Russian troika, which only "a clever people" could have invented and which like Rus' is flying into the future while "other peoples and states step aside to let her pass," was taught in order to impart Gogol's "fervent faith in the great qualities of the Russian people, in the blossoming of [their] national genius, and in the universal-historical destiny of Rus'."[19]

In the teaching of Russian literature, there were no problems with what Allworth has termed "truncated historical development."[20] Not only Russian classical literature, but also selections from pre-19th century works, including parts of the 12th century "Slovo o polku Igoreve" (the latter presented with a very different point of view from Suleimenov's), was to be read in the original. Works by Lermontov, Tolstoy, Tiutchev and others were carefully combed for expressions which carry special meanings in Russian culture and in Russian *byt* (everyday life). Special dictionaries were then produced and teaching methods devised on how best to impart the national Russian connotations. In teaching Pushkin's *Captain's Daughter*, for example, such words as *golubushka, krasnaia devitsa, kumushka, kniaginiushka, baryshnia*, and *sviaschchennik*—all terms no longer in use in modern Russian and representing a cultural and therefore semantic void in non-Russian languages—were lovingly explained against "an emotional background" created by the teacher. Otherwise, it was claimed, "the national-historical reality pale[d], and the emotional frame [became] lifeless. . . ."[21] "Historicisms and archaisms," as an author of the revised 1981 curriculum for Kirgiz language schools put it, "increase[d] the ability to penetrate into the richest artistic world of Russian classics and promote[d] the acculturation to the lasting spiritual values of the Russian people."[22]

Russian historical literature was not subject to any tampering, even when it clashed with the "friendship of peoples" theme. Lermontov's poem "Borodino" for example, has a line about the retreating French in which they are called *"basurmany"*—a term Kirgiz youngsters immediately recognize as the native Kirgiz *"busurman"*—Muslim, by which they as well as other Muslims of Russia were known. But in the poem, the word is used as a synonym for "enemy!" (It was advised however, to take some "prophylactic" measures in order to prevent laughter [nervous?], as had apparently occurred in some classes.)[23]

Customs and associations connected with the Russian Orthodox religion were also never ignored, for anything related to the Russian people and its milieu was deemed important for the New Historical Community—the Soviet People. The teacher was called upon to explain the roles of *pop* and *popad'ia* (Russian priest and his wife), the institution of *kum* (baptismal relative), and the ceremony of *obvenchanie* (church wedding). Ironically, while native Russian authors were at times taken to task for their fascination with churches and bells (Brezhnev personally was supposed to have complained that there was too much bell ringing on Soviet television), a multimedia campaign to introduce "the Bell" in Central Asian schools was launched which almost approached the intensity of the birch tree campaign which had been launched earlier. For the bell, it was argued, forms "an essential and a profoundly national link in Russian culture, without which it is difficult to create an integral picture of Russian history, of the life of the Russian people."[24]

All this was of course very far from teaching a practical lingua franca. Precious time was spent on outdated Russian customs and what is a largely useless, or at best a passive Russian vocabulary. Clearly, one could be quite effective in the economy or the army without ever having heard of a *luchina* (a wooden splinter used by Russian peasants for light) or a *domovoi* (a Russian house spirit). Having the "right association" with *izba* (a Russian peasant's hut) or *vechernii zvon* (ringing of the bells in the evening) is not really essential for a manager or an engineer, even in an enterprise where Russian is the only language of communication. Obviously, this was not a cost-effective approach to teaching Russian as the language of cross-nationality communication, the lingua franca of the Soviet Union!

But this approach did make sense if the goal was national integration through socialization to Russian culture. For then not only did the Russian language have to be uniform for all, but it also had to carry the same associations and connotations as for the native Russian speakers. As Mazipov, a well-known Russian language teacher and pedagogical methods specialist in Kirgizia put it, "a language can become a second mother tongue only when it is grasped emotionally . . . when behind its every word there stands an image, when it awakens a whole swarm of images."[25] To do this, the Russian language teacher could not simply teach a mastery of Russian; rather, in the words of two other Kirgiz methods specialists, he had to "immerse" the students into the Russian spiritual world, promoting thereby "a gradual *sblizhenie* (coming together) and ultimately also the integration within the framework of a common socialist culture."[26] Or, as N. M. Shanskii, the head of the central

Research Institute for teaching Russian to non-Russians and M. V. Cherkezova, author of the model program for teaching Russian literature in all non-Russian schools insisted, "all students must be socialized to the ethical and esthetic riches of the Russian classical and Soviet literature and through it to the history, the culture, the spiritual wealth of the Russian people, to the distinctiveness of their national character."[27]

Such socialization, however, was not easy to achieve. Sheer expansion in the teaching program and increasing standardization of content and teaching materials could not insure an identical reception. People's esthetic appreciation for nature, for example, is always closely connected with geography. There are areas where winter carries only the unpleasant association of dampness and rain, and not of white, sparkling snow, or where due to a near absence of trees, autumn carries no associations of the adjective "golden." Even more troublesome are associations and connotations in the domain of values, of humor and above all of national symbolism.

A new discipline, *etnokul'turovedenie*, had appeared in the middle of the 1970s to help overcome the national "barriers" of viewing Russian words through a national prism. *Etnokul'turovedenie* is a difficult term to translate, but it can be roughly described as "linguistic ethnopedagogy" or "ethnolinguistics." The discipline is actually a take-off from *lingvostranovedenie*—linguistic cultural geography of a particular country, first introduced by Vereshchagin and Kostomarov in teaching Russian to foreigners.[28] Vereshchagin and Kostomarov's goal is to explain "sovietisms" and to impart an understanding and an appreciation of the Soviet way of life in the process of teaching the Russian language to foreigners. In the case of teaching Russian to non-Russians in the Soviet Union there was of course no need to teach "sovietisms," or to explain the Soviet way of life. Here the emphasis was on "russianisms," the unique and specific elements of the Great Russian culture, which many Soviet nationalities lack. For such peoples as the Central Asians (who are so culturally different from Russians), the task of teaching "russianisms" was especially difficult. Nevertheless, as explained by one of its leading exponents, L. A. Sheiman, *etnokul'turovedenie* aids the Russian teacher in accomplishing the major task of socializing the students "to the culture of the Russian people under the conditions of a shared socio-cultural community, chiefly through their [the Russians'] vivid language."[29]

The Kirgiz Republic had in fact taken the lead in this new teaching approach. As early as 1978, its Pedagogical Research Institute organized a special group to study ethnic reception of Russian literature under Professor B. S. Meilakh. In addition to Sheiman, who edits the journal *Russian Language and Literature in the Kirgiz School* (*Russkii iazyk i literatura v kirgizskoi shkole*) and heads the Russian literature section in the Kirgiz Pedagogical Research Institute, there are numerous other experts in the field, such as N. M. Varich, T. V. Romanevich, and F. D. Borisov. Specialists in *etnokul'turovedenie* in other republics included M. M. Abduvalieva and B. A. Khodzhibaeva in Tajikistan, V. G. Smoliakova in Uzbekistan, as well as prominent researchers and curriculum developers working in the center, such as I. Kh. Maiorova and M. V. Cherkezova. All of these pedagogues and researchers studied and analyzed possible points of cultural interference and difficulties of reception of Russian language sources; they also sought to devise methods and teaching materials which would help bring Central Asians' views, values, and tastes closer to those of the Russians.

Russian language and literature teachers who were instructed to impart the beauty of the Russian winter or the "Golden Autumn" were urged to be both enthusiastic and tactful. They were taught to be even more sensitive and careful in matters of personal esthetics.[30] Teachers encountered problems like the following: To a Kirgiz, *ai* (the moon) is a standard symbol of beauty and "a face like the moon" is a common cliché image of a beautiful face. In Russian however, one meets quite different moon images such as for example Pushkin's description of Olga in *Eugene Onegin*:[31]

Krugla, krasna litsom ona,
kak eta glupaia luna
na etom glupom nebosklone.

(Her face is round and red
like the stupid moon
in the stupid sky.)

There is also the problem of hair and eyes: light-haired and light-eyed Russian heroines usually stir little emotion among Central Asian students whose ideal beauty has black hair and black eyes. Teachers had to work very hard indeed to overcome the aversion to the concept of a blonde, blue-eyed beauty. Even artistic representation was of little help. A teacher who used art as an aid discovered that Kirgiz sixth-graders found Botticelli's representation of spring as a beautiful young maiden "not at all pretty," but rather "pale, blue-eyed, light-haired, [and] too lifeless."[32] First-year students at the Kirgiz Women's Pedagogical Institute found Esenin's poetic image of his beloved "with hair like a stack of oats" (*so snopom volos svoikh ovsiannykh/ oposnilas' ty mne navsegda*) "not only not beautiful, but simply horrible."[33]

It was equally difficult for teachers to break the automatic association of *kok koz* (blue or grey-eyes) with negative characteristics. It was noted that Kirgiz pupils consistently avoid describing one of Gorky's positive heroes as "grey-eyed," or even change the color of his eyes to black.[34] Teachers also had to explain such symbols as the wolf which had clashing connotations for different nationalities. While generally negative in Russian culture, the wolf is a heroic figure in cultures of Turkic background. It was even more difficult to attempt to break down the firmly entrenched family values according to which Turgenev's Bazarov in *Fathers and Sons* is viewed with great disapproval because of his lack of respect for elders, or Russian tragic heroines such as Katerina in Ostrovsky's *Storm*, who are seen as getting their just rewards for their infidelities. Sometimes, as in the case of church bells, the concept itself is missing in the culture; in other cases, the connotation which existed was "all wrong." An example of this is a 16th century account of the fall of Constantinople to the Turks:[35]

When full quiet was restored
instead of the ridiculous ringing of the bells
the pleasant voice of the *muezzin* was heard.

Kirgiz pupils do not find the haggling in Gogol's *Dead Souls* at all funny, nor do they see the humor in Saltykov-Shchedrin. Curiously, even a modern *Krokodil* cartoon poking fun at food in Soviet cafeterias— it pictured a man with a clothespin on his nose in an attempt to avoid smelling the terrible-looking spaghetti on his plate—was completely misunderstood. The pupils thought the man pinched his nose to prevent dripping into the food, but it hurt so badly that the spaghetti turned blue in his eyes.[36] (Could this mean that food in Kirgiz cafeterias is not so bad, or that most Kirgiz simply do not eat in them?)

But the greatest effort was directed toward acculturating the Central Asians to the purely national symbols of Russia such as *Rus'*, *Moskva*, *troika*, *izba*, and of course, the bell and the birch tree. For help in solving these kinds of problems, teachers were advised to read articles with such titles as "Variations on the Theme of the Birch Tree," "The Bell in Russian Life," and "There is the Smell of Rus' There." Some of these articles gave pedagogical hints and suggested holding special programs and extracurricular activities in order to evoke the correct and emotionally charged associations with these symbols.[37]

Effectiveness

How effective was this ethnocultural approach? Taught by a talented teacher who approached the subject with great tact and (above all) an intimate knowledge of the students' national culture, it could have resulted in breaking down some cultural barriers and establishing a closer rapport with the Russians. Sheiman gave as an example of successful acculturation the case of Kirgiz eighth-graders who greeted the girls coming late to the Russian class from gym, with the following expressions typical of Old Russia: *"Vot oni nashi golubushki,"* *"Net, oni nashi krasnye devitsi."* (Here are our dears. No, they are our young beauties.)[38] A 1983 study in Kirgizia claimed that the more experienced the reader, the less negative his attitude to blue or grey eyes: sixth-graders, the study purported to show, reacted negatively to all blue or grey-eyed heroes even when these were positive characters; eighth-graders, while not enthusiastic, were no longer hostile; and students at a philological faculty (at Kirgiz Women's Pedagogical Institute) were said to have outright favorable reactions.[39] Of course, this may not necessarily have been a case of radical change, but simply a reflection of being more experienced in knowing what one was expected to answer. Many teachers used to cite their students' compositions about "Beautiful Birches" or "Birch Groves" as proof of their success in overcoming the cultural barriers. But again, it is unclear whether this was more a reflection of socialization to Russian values or a desire to get a good grade.[40]

On the other hand, the ethnocultural linguistic approach (especially in the hands of a less competent or not too tactful teacher) may have been quite irritating; perhaps it even helped to stimulate a livelier interest in the student's own traditional national esthetics, values, and symbolism. One wonders, for example, if it was only a coincidence that in Chingiz Aitmatov's legend of Raimaly-aga in *The Day Lasts More than a Hundred Years*, the aging freedom-loving bard is finally stopped from his wandering only when he is tied to a tree—a birch tree![41]

Indeed, during the Gorbachev era, a great deal of evidence has accumulated which suggests that the all-out Russian language campaign in general and the emphasis on Russian cultural values in particular were counterproductive. Probably, the most spectacular proof of this has been the language protests which effectively launched the movement for redressing the linguistic balance between the various native languages and Russian, including a revival of the Arabic alphabet.[42] The concept of Russian as the "second mother-tongue" is now openly admitted to be not just "unrealistic and psychologically mistaken, but even insulting."[43]

While a trickle of articles on the ethnocultural linguistic theme still continues (indeed, in 1989, the Institute for Teaching Russian to Non-Russians was supposed to have finally completed the *Dictionary of Obsolete Vocabulary in Works by 19th Century Russian Writers*), the tone has become much more subdued. In a recent article on "The Rearing of Patriots-Internationalists," the author specifically cautions against the use of Russian literature which emphasizes "love toward Russia, its nature, customs, and *byt* . . ." since "it may not succeed in its purpose."⁴⁴ On the other hand, articles have appeared specifically calling for the minimizing of obsolete vocabulary and discontinuing the teaching of old Russian proverbs, or for totally shifting the emphasis in the teaching of Russian poetry. In the case of Esenin, for example, rather than stressing his birch trees and Russian huts, a recent article advised teachers to focus on the Oriental features of his poetry.⁴⁵ Another poet, the quintessentially Russian Pushkin (whose works though very difficult were until recently considered essential in the non-Russian schools), has now been revealed as most unpopular in Central Asian republics. A recent study of Kirgiz eighth- through tenth-graders shows Pushkin's poetry in the very last place, while among adult Central Asians, protests against Pushkin, or rather against his place-names seem to crop up with growing frequency.⁴⁶

Notes

Abbreviations

   RIALKSH—*Russkii iazyk i literatura v kirgizskoi shkole*
   RIAKSH—*Russkii iazyk v kirgizskoi shkole*
   RIANSH—*Russkii iazyk v national'noi shkole*

1. For a discussion of the 1978 decree see Roman Solchanyk, "Russification to be Stepped Up," *Soviet Analyst*, Jan. 9, 1980, pp. 7–8, and *RIANSH*, 1979, no. 1, 1979, pp. 2–5; on the 1983 decree, see *RIALKSH*, no. 5, 1983, pp. 7–9, "In the Politburo of the CPSU CC," translated in *Current Digest of the Soviet Press*, 35, no. 21, 1983; on the 1984 reform, especially as it pertains to the teaching of Russian, see *RIANSH*, no. 4, 1984, pp. 3–25.

2. For a discussion of preparatory classes see Roman Solchanyk, *Radio Liberty Research* 11/80, Jan. 2, 1980. In June, 1984 it was announced that more than 1 million six-year-olds would begin studying Russian in September 1984, while younger children would be learning in kindergartens according to the recently issued standard program (*RIANSH*, no. 3, 1984, pp. 11 and 15–17).

   However, at the all-Union Conference in Moscow (September 1986) calls to evaluate the teaching of Russian to six-year-olds provoked a "lively" discussion with regard to when it should begin. (Early echoes of glasnost'?) (*RIANSH*, no. 3, 1987, pp. 61–62.) Parents' objections in Estonia were carried in *Russkii iazyk v estonskoi shkole*, no. 2, 1987, pp. 3–4.

3. The special intensive (more literally, "deeper study" *uglublennye*) Russian classes and Russian electives (*fakul'tativnye*) began on an experimental basis in several republics in the early 1970s and were institutionalized on the all-Union level by 1979 (*RIANSH*, no. 3, 1975, pp. 83–84; no. 1, 1979, p. 2; and no. 6, 1982 pp. 32–33). For details of more recent programs see, for example, *RIANSH*, no. 5, 1983, pp. 26–30, 63–66, and 70–72; or *RIALKSH*, no. 2, 1987, pp. 1–9.

4. *RIANSH*, no. 1, 1979, p. 2; no. 3, 1983, p. 69.

5. *RIANSH*, no. 2, 1976, pp. 37-39; *RIALKSH*, no. 3, 1984, pp. 1-3. In 1986 alone, 3 all-Union conferences on the use of computers in teaching Russian and other languages were held (*RIANSH*, no. 2, 1987, p. 61).

6. Azerbaijan was one of the first republics to stress extracurricular activities. See, for example, *Russskii iazyk v azerbaidzhanskoi shkole*, nos. 1, 3, 6, and 7, 1972. For a later description of activities in the Kirgiz republic see *RIALKSH*, no. 1, 1986, pp. 8-18.

7. In 1975 a special five-year program to train Russian teachers for non-Russian schools was introduced in all pedagogical institutes (*RIANSH*, no. 6, 1976, pp. 4-7).

8. *RIANSH*, no. 5, 1985, p. 7; no. 3, 1987, p. 16.

9. *RIANSH*, no. 2, 1985, p. 91; *RIALKSH*, no. 1, 1985, p. 51.

10. *Sovetskaia Kirgiziia*, June 21, 1983, as quoted in *RIALKSH*, no. 6, 1983, p. 2.

11. N. G. Mikhailovskaia, ed., *Kul'tura russkoi rechi v usloviiakh natsional'no-russkogo dvuiazychiia* (Moscow: Nauka, 1985), p. 3.

12. Cited in Roman Solchanyk, "Language and Education in Soviet Schools," in *The Changing Status of Russian in the Soviet Union*, ed. Isabelle Kreindler (International Journal of the Sociology of Language, no. 33 [1982]), p. 116.

13. Chinua Achebe, "English and the African Writer," quoted in Ali A. Mazrui, *The Political Sociology of the English Language, An African Perspective* (Contributions to the Sociology of Language, vol. 7) (The Hague: Mouton, 1975), p. 222.

14. Iu. V. Bromlei, "Dukhovnaia kul'tura i etnicheskie protsessy," in Bromlei et al., eds., *Sovremennye etnichesktsie protsessy v SSSR* (Moscow: Nauka, 1975), p. 377. See also V. G. Kostomarov, "Russkii iazyk i burzhuaznye kontseptsii mirovogo iazyka" (*RIANSH*, no. 7, 1986, pp. 9-17) where he argues against any Russian "varieties."

15. *RIANSH*, no. 3, 1982, p. 84.

16. Edward A. Allworth in a paper delivered at the Conference "Central Asia: The Decades Ahead," Munich, August 1985.

17. " 'Kruglyi stol' redaktsii," *RIANSH*, no 3, 1981 p. 67.

18. I. S. Stepanenko, "Vospitatel'nye vozmoshnosti kursa," *RIANSH*, no. 1, 1984, p. 46.

19. A. P. Seliverstova and N. I. Sharina, "Vyrazitel'noe chtenie khudozhestvennogo teksta kak sredstvo esteticheskogo vopitaniia," *RIAKSH*, no. 5, 1976, pp. 13-14.

20. Edward A. Allworth, at the Conference on Central Asia, Munich, August 1985.

21. T. V. Romanevich, "O nekotorykh priemakh etnokul'turovedcehskogo kommentirovaniia leksiki khudozhestvennogo teksta," *RIALKSH*, no. 4, 1983, p. 40.

22. M. I. Zadorozhnyi, "Slovar'naia rabota na urokakh russkogo iazyka po novoi programe," *RIALKSH*, no. 4, 1981, p. 4.

23. F. D. Borisov, "Kirgizskie shkol'niki i komicheskoe v russkoi literature," *RIALKSH*, no. 1, 1982, pp. 29-30; E. N. Kurbatova, "Materialy k urokam po

stikhotvoreniiu M. Iu. Lermontova 'Borodino' v VII klasse," *RIALKSH*, no. 5, 1982, p. 47.

24. L. V. Mikhailova and Ia. R. Chmonina, "Kolokol v russkoi zhizni," *RIALKSH*, no. 4, 1983, p. 50.

25. R. G. Mazipov, "Istoriko-bytovoi, stranovedcheskii i etnokul'turovedcheskii kommentarii na urokakh russkogo iazyka," *RIALKSH*, no. 1, 1982, p. 16.

26. M. I. Zadorozhnyi and V. P. Kaipova, "Priobshchenie k dukhovnym tsennostiam russkoi kul'tury na zaniatiiakh po russkomu iazyku (Variatsii na temu o russkoi bereze)," *RIALKSH*, no. 6, 1983, p. 19.

27. N. M. Shanskii and M. V. Cherkezova, "Russkaia literatura v natsional'nykh shkolakh soiuznykh respublik," *Sovetskaia pedagogika*, no. 4, 1982, p. 75.

28. E. M. Vereshchagin and V. G. Kostomarov, *Iazyk i kul'tura: lingvostranovedenie v prepodavanii russkogo iazyka kak inostrannogo. 2 izd.* (Moscow: Russkii iazyk, 1976).

29. L. A. Sheiman, "O natsional'no-kul'turnom aspekte shkol'nykh russkoiazychnykh kursov," *RIANSH*, no. 3, 1987, p. 13.

30. Isabelle Kreindler, "Teaching Russian Esthetics to the Kirgiz," *Russian Review*, no. 3 (July) 1981, pp. 333–338. This is how, for example, a Russian winter is taught in sunny Turkmenia: "In School No. 37 the Russian lesson usually begins with a report by the pupil on duty. 'Today is February 12, Thursday. It is now winter,' he informs his fifth grade. 'Is our winter like the winter in Russia?' asks the teacher. The pupil explains that here it is warm, but in Russia it's freezing and snowing. Weather is also the opening topic in the first grade. The teacher: 'What season of the year is it now?' 'Winter,' answers the first-grader on duty. 'And what falls (*idet*) in winter?' Getting no response, she hints, 'white flakes, what are they?' After deep deliberation, the pupil comes up with an answer: 'a girl comes.' After one of the classmates corrects him, the teacher calls upon visual aids and drills them in producing sentences. 'This is snow. This is winter. The children are building a snowman. The boys are skating.' Then the whole class recites the poem 'Winter,' which all have learned by heart. . ." (A. P. Grachev, "Uspekhi i problemy rusistov sel'skoi shkoly," *RIANSH*, no. 9, 1987, pp. 16–21.)

31. L. A. Sheiman, "O tipologii etnokul'turnykh obraznykh sootvetstvii v kursakh russkogo iazyka i literatury dlia nerusskiikh," *RIAKSH*, no. 1, 1977, pp. 10–14.

32. L. A. Sheiman, N. M. Varich, "O natsional'nykh kartinakh mira," in *Voprosy prepodavaniia russkogo iazyka i literatury v kirgizskoi shkole. Vyp. 6.* (Frunze: Mektep, 1976), pp. 92–93.

33. N. M. Varich, "Etnokul'turovedcheskii kommentarii na urokakh literaturnogo chteniia (okonchanie)," *RIALKSH*, no. 6, 1983, p. 29.

34. *RIAKSH*, no. 1, 1977, p. 11.

35. L. A. Sheiman, "Problemy etnokul'turovedcheskogo obespecheniia russkoiazychnoi literaturnoi kommunikatsii v natsional'noi shkole," *RIALKSH*, no. 4, 1983, pp. 3–4.

36. F. D. Borisov has been working on ways of imparting Russian humor to the non-Russians since the mid-1970s. For some of his articles, see *RIALKSH*,

no. 2, 1981, pp. 47-52; no. 3, 1981, pp. 9-19; no. 1, 1982, pp. 23-31; no. 3, 1986, pp. 9-14; no. 6, 1986, pp. 16-19.

37. *RIALKSH*, no. 4, 1983, pp. 17-24 and pp. 50-53; no. 6, 1983, pp. 19-28 and 37-42.

38. L. A. Sheiman, "O natsional'no-kul'turnom aspekte shkol'nykh russkoiazychnykh kursov," no. 3, *RIANSH*, 1987, p. 16.

39. N. M. Varich, "Etnokul'turovecheskii kommentarii na urokakh literaturnogo chteniia," no. 6, *RIALKSH*, 1983, pp. 28-29.

40. For sample compositions see *RIALKSH*, no. 6, 1983, pp. 26-27.

41. In an article published in *Voprosy literatury*, Aitmatov specifically pointed out the importance of preserving "the national peculiarities and distinctiveness of cultures as a guard (*zaslon*) on the road to universal unification." (Chingiz Aitmatov, "Byt' ekhom mira," *Voprosy literatury*, no. 3, 1986, pp. 4-13).

42. By the end of 1989 all Central Asian republics, including Kazakhstan, had drafted laws granting the native language official state status, adding provisions for encouraging the study of the Arabic alphabet.

43. V. M. Solontsev, "Natsional'no-iazykovye otnosheniia (Kruglyi stol)," *Voprosy istorii*, no. 5, 1989, p. 46.

44. "O slovare-spravochnike ustarevshei leksiki v proizvedeniiakh russkikh pisatelei 19 v.," *RIANSH*, no. 8, 1987, pp. 24-26. M. V. Cherkezova, "Vospitanie patriotov internatsionalistov," *RIANSH*, no. 6, 1987, p. 33.

45. E. V. Grinval'd, V. I. Zimin, "Istoriko-etimologicheskoe kommentirovanie russkikh poslovits i pogovorok," *RIANSH*, no. 8, 1988, pp. 7-9; V. I. Osminina, "Vospriiatie 'orientalii' poezii Sergeia Esenina inoiazychnoi auditoriei," *RIALKSH*, no. 1, 1986, pp. 32-34.

46. See L. A. Sheiman and G. U. Soronkulov, "Probuzhdenie interesa k chteniiu russkoi liriki," *RIANSH*, no. 7, 1988, p. 35; *Radio Liberty Research* 309/88, July 12, 1988; and James Critchlow, "Uzbeks Demand Elimination of Non-Native Place Names," Radio Liberty *Report on the USSR*, Jan. 20, 1989, p. 19.

PART FOUR

Socioeconomic Issues

9

Women and Society in Central Asia

Martha Brill Olcott

Introduction

Seventy years of Soviet rule have failed to fully integrate women into Central Asian life. Central Asian society has changed, but the role of women within that society largely has not. Even today a woman's place is generally still predetermined at birth. This is true despite the fact that the Bolsheviks promised a social revolution that would parallel their political one, and that for more than seventy years the Soviet regime has sponsored social, political, and economic policies designed to place women on the same footing as men.

A female born in an urban setting can expect to receive virtually the same education as her male counterpart, but she still is almost definitionally precluded from fulfilling leadership roles in her society. Particularly if she lives in a large city, where both employment and daycare are available, she can expect to have a career of her own; but her principal function is familial, to be a good wife and mother.

A female born in a rural setting—and this is where the overwhelming majority of most Central Asians still live—can expect a far more circumscribed existence than her male counterpart. She will likely receive less education and have virtually no opportunity for occupational or geographical mobility. This means that more often than not she will spend her life engaged in seasonal agricultural labor. But her main task will be to marry early and raise as many children as nature grants her.

In the Khrushchev and Brezhnev years, and even through the mid-1980s, Party officials and social scientists in Moscow and in the various Central Asian republics publicly heralded the demise of Islam and the creation of a modern socialist society in Central Asia. But the reality of the situation is almost exactly the opposite of what official Soviet rhetoric long maintained.

As the chapter in this volume by Ayse Rorlich illustrates, Central Asia remains a traditional Islamic society. The amount of formal religious training that most Central Asians receive is less than that of their co-religionists in other parts of the Muslim world. But particularly in rural areas, their lives are as much shaped by traditional customary practices as are the lives of Muslims who live outside of the Soviet Union. In some ways the restrictions on the dissemination of religion imposed by the Soviets may have even led to the preservation of traditional society. Cut off from the more formal teachings of Islam, many Central Asians have had to depend upon the preservation of traditional practices as the sole means of demonstrating respect for their faith.

As Islam is honored if the ways of the ancestors are kept alive, women are expected to make their contribution by tending to the nurturing of the next generation. Most of the social problems relating to women derive from this expectation. By the standards of a developed society, they marry too young and have more children than they are able to bear and raise in healthy conditions.

The career opportunities of women are sharply restricted by their family obligations, and this in turn has further retarded the economic development of Central Asia. The economy is thus doubly stricken. Denied the potential of skilled female labor, Central Asia is further crippled by the economic burdens posed by the high birthrate of the indigenous population.

Moreover, the perpetuation of a traditional Muslim society is at odds with the development of an industrial society. As elsewhere in the USSR, the economic achievements of Soviet rule, though real, have been much overstated in Central Asia. What is worse, the much heralded new communist morality never emerged, and the Central Asians' own culture has been unable to bridge the social and moral gap which has developed between the old and new worlds. Here, too, Soviet policy makers deserve to be faulted, as the official anti-religious policy made it impossible for a new Islamic infrastructure to develop and bridge the gap.

This unbridged gap creates severe social problems in Central Asia. Alcoholism, drug addiction, and juvenile delinquency are all epidemic in the region. However, they are only insignificant problems among the indigenous female population of Central Asia, because most women seem to philosophically accept their fate. A minority do break out from the confining roles assigned them. Some do it positively by training for careers and leaving home; a small minority become sociopaths, in some cases by becoming prostitutes; and still others cope by trying to end their lives.

Until a few years ago the Soviet press simply denied that there were serious problems related to the integration of Central Asian women.

Now the existence of these problems is not only admitted, but their severity is often highlighted. Nonetheless, few suggested remedies have been forthcoming. Furthermore, even if remedies could be identified, implementing them would likely prove beyond the means of the financially strapped Central Asian republics. Moreover, the discrediting of communist rule could lead to the exacerbation of some of these problems, as traditional Islamic society may be uncritically embraced as a way to reject the tainted communist present.

Childbearing in Central Asia

The woman's role as childbearer is the key to the preservation of the community. The high birthrate in the area is a direct result of Islamic teachings, which forbid abortion and are generally understood to be against the practice of contraception as well.

As Nancy Lubin's chapter illustrates, Central Asia has the highest birthrates in the Soviet Union, and women there expect to give birth to large families. However, according to a study conducted in 1985, they actually bear far fewer children than they expect. This survey asked how many children married women ages 18-44 expected to bear. The average figure nation-wide was 2.5, whereas Turkmen women reported that they expected to bear 6.3 children, Tajik women 5.9 children, Kirgiz and Uzbek women 5.6 children, and Kazakh women 4.3 children. For every thousand women nation-wide only 51 said that they wanted to have 6 or more children, whereas 593 Turkmen women, 510 Tajik women, 437 Uzbek women, 430 Kirgiz women, and 231 Kazakh women responded positively to this question.[1]

Not surprisingly, the same study revealed that women with more education have fewer children. Unfortunately the data are available only by republic and not by nationality, and in each case the birth rate for the republic as a whole is lower than that of the titular nationality.[2] However given that the overwhelming majority of the population of Tajikistan, Turkmenistan, and Uzbekistan are indigenous Central Asians the data from these three republics is of particular value. In Tajikistan women with only primary education had an average of 5.3 children, those with incomplete secondary education 4.0 children, and those with higher education 1.7 children. In Turkmenistan the respective averages were 4.7, 4.0, and 1.8 respectively; and in Uzbekistan 5.0, 5.0, and 2.0.[3]

These data support the conclusions of early studies, most particularly the research of the Uzbek demographer O. B. Ata-Mirzaev, whose research from the late 1970s showed a clear correlation between the educational level of an Uzbek woman and the number of children that she bore. The average number of children borne by Uzbek women in his sample with higher education was 2.3 children, compared to 5.1 by women with only primary or incomplete secondary education.[4]

Some scholars suggest that the strict correlation between education and family size may not hold for the younger generation. A study of Tashkent by V. V. Koroteeva, drawn also from a 1985 sample, showed that for Uzbek women under thirty there was no relationship between education and desired family size.[5] Until the publication of the full 1989 census it will be difficult to know whether her findings reflect a general population trend.

Until recently, most Soviet scholars explained the dramatic increase in the size of the Central Asian population as an example of the triumph of Soviet medicine. Thus, leading Soviet ethnographer S. P. Poliakov has argued that declining infant mortality rates are the primary cause of the population increase, and that birth rates have remained largely unchanged since the pre-revolutionary period.[6] Poliakov, professor of ethnography of Moscow State University, has travelled throughout Central Asia for over thirty years, and has lived in rural as well as urban regions of all four republics for extended periods.

But other data may indicate that Soviet medical care, rather than deserving praise for a high Central Asia birthrate, is actually an obstacle to women's achieving their ideal family size. In the past several years there has been an unending series of exposés about the deplorable state of Soviet medical care and the generally poor sanitary and health conditions of Central Asia in general and rural Central Asia in particular.

Although infant mortality rates have certainly declined over the past seventy years in Central Asia, they are still significantly higher than the national average. In 1987, the infant mortality figure for the USSR was 25 per 1000, compared to 38 per 1000 in Kirgizia, 46 per 1000 in Uzbekistan, 49 per 1000 in Tajikistan, and 56 per 1000 in Turkmenistan.[7] In 1988, the infant mortality rate in Turkmenia was 58 per 1000 compared to 19 per 1000 in the RSFSR.[8] Official figures for 1989 show slight declines. But a recent article in *Soiuz* suggests that this is because physicians are manipulating the statistics, reporting the deaths of underweight babies as miscarriages. One of the doctors quoted in the article, a female obstetrician from Tajikistan, alleges that severely underweight babies are denied food by hospitals and upon their deaths, listed as "miscarriages."[9]

The highest infant mortality figures occur in the area around the Aral Sea; in Karakalpakia in 1988 there were 111 infant deaths per 1000 live births.[10] In this region the pollution from the dying Aral Sea and poisons from the local cotton economy have led to the contamination of all the available drinking water.

A spring 1990 Soviet television special, "Save the Aral Sea," vividly portrayed the grief of the local population confronted by what seems to be the inexplicable pending demise of their people. The camera panned rural cemeteries, which had gravesites covered by cradles. The commentator explained that the people who lived in the region hoped that in this fashion they might appease whatever evil spirit was killing off their children.

Even in the cities of Central Asia the infant mortality rate is much higher than in European Russia. The highest urban mortality rate in the USSR for 1988 was recorded in Ashkhabad, 53 per 1000, compared to 38 per 1000 in Dushanbe, 29 per 1000 in Frunze, and 28 per 1000 in Tashkent, while in Vilnius and Riga there were 11 deaths per thousand live births.[11] The real picture may be far worse, given the repeated complaints that many hospitals simply fail to report their mortality statistics.[12] The noted Uzbek poet Muhammad Salikh has publicly claimed that in Uzbekistan the actual mortality figure is 100 per 1000.[13]

The miserable conditions in Central Asian hospitals and health care facilities and the poor health of Central Asian mothers go a long way towards explaining the high infant mortality rates. According to one account, 90 percent of all hospitals in Central Asia and Kazakhstan lack sewerage, 65 percent are without hot water, and 20 percent lack all running water.[14] Moreover, throughout the region there is an acute shortage of maternity beds, and many women who experience difficult labors have to be driven considerable distances over bad roads in order to reach a facility with even a minimal surgical capacity.

It is very hard to find precise figures on the mortality rate of women in childbirth, but it appears to be well above the all-Union level. One Turkmen official noted that half of all women who undergo surgery in the course of childbirth in Tashauz oblast die,[15] while another Turkmen official alleged that two out of every three maternal deaths in the republic in childbirth could have been prevented.[16]

In the past few years teams of physicians from the RSFSR, Belorussia, and the Ukraine have been sent to Central Asia to try to improve prenatal and infant health care. But these teams report that they can make few improvements in the conditions that they encounter, and that they are unprepared to perform surgery in hospitals without water. Moreover, they see no way to help prevent infections when a local hospital, a "well-supplied" one at that, receives only 2000 diapers monthly for 700 births.[17]

One of the greatest problems that doctors from European Russia confront in Central Asia is the low level of education about health and hygiene. Local women generally do not know how to take proper care of themselves while pregnant or how to tend to their newborn children.

Folk remedies like blood-letting are still resorted to for treatment of such common conditions as acute diarrhea. Simple ignorance kills many children, such as in the case of the Turkmen child placed in the refrigerator to reduce his fever. The Russian physician who detailed the circumstances to a *Komsomol'skaia Pravda* reporter noted that this same woman had already lost six of her thirteen children to various childhood diseases.[18]

All of the Central Asian republics have passed legislation designed to provide better prenatal and infant medical care, but they have found it difficult to allocate the necessary resources to finance these programs. Thus, in early 1990, Tajikistan's government reported that during the previous year it managed to add less than a quarter of the planned new beds in maternity hospitals.[19]

High infant mortality and maternal death rates are also caused by the poor physical condition of many women before and during their pregnancy. Some reports indicate that nearly a third of all pregnant women in Central Asia are anemic, and one study from Osh oblast in Kirgizia reported that 80 percent of all pregnant women in the region have severe dietary deficiencies.[20]

The typical diet in rural parts of the region, which consists of flat bread and tea, helps account for many of the health problems that pregnant women experience. It also explains the high incidence of premature births, the problem of low birth-weight of children, and the high incidence of rickets and other diseases caused by dietary deficiencies.[21]

In July 1990, President Islam Karimov of Uzbekistan signed a presidential decree mandating better health care of pregnant and anemic women, promising free food for school children and for pregnant and nursing mothers in poverty-stricken rural regions.[22] But to date there has been little follow-up in the press to indicate that the planned program has been implemented on a mass scale.

Many of the region's massive health problems are a result of the catastrophic deterioration of Central Asia's environment. For example, currently there is no potable drinking water in the Karakalpak ASSR and four oblasts of Uzbekistan (Kashkadarya, Khorezm, Bukhara, and Navoi oblasts).[23] Recent studies have revealed that 80 percent of all young children in these regions suffer from serious illnesses. Although the contaminated water supply is said to be the cause of the health problems, the area is not expected to have an uncontaminated source of water until 1993 or 1994. The problem of contamination is so severe, that women in the area have been advised against nursing their children because their own milk is toxic. However, because those who use infant formula often prepare it using contaminated water, the incidence of severe infant diarrhea continues to rise. Moreover, the acute shortage of even contaminated water has further increased the incidence of infection because, especially in summer when the temperature rises to 120 degrees and women are fearful of "wasting" precious water on bathing babies or washing diapers.

The health of women and their unborn children is also adversely effected by their employment. This is particularly true of women who work in the cotton fields and those who cultivate tobacco. Doctors who travel to the region have complained of "chemical curtains" which hang over the fields. Despite official efforts to restrict employment, pregnant women still cultivate both crops.[24] Consequently, most women have already developed chronic health problems from handling chemical defoliants well before their first pregnancy.[25] Women who work in rice fields are at risk as well, as aircraft sometimes spray phosphoric chemicals on the fields where pregnant women are working.[26]

The health risks for women employed in the cultivation of tobacco are especially severe, and not only pregnant women, but also young girls continue to harvest tobacco. One study from Tajikistan reported that these women are six times more likely to give birth to underweight or vitamin-deficient children than those who live in other parts of the republic. Moreover, during the prime harvest season, August and September, local rates of infant mortality double.[27] Similar statistics have been published in other republics.[28] Moreover, at least one Tajik physician has claimed that the USSR Ministry of Health has long deliberately concealed the severe health risks for women that are associated with Central Asian agriculture, in order to avoid a decrease in agricultural productivity.[29]

Some scholars believe that traditional marriage practices also account for some birth defects in Central Asia. Endogamous marriages are still common, and it is said that between 20 and 40 percent of all marriages in Central Asia are between relatives; this allegedly further increases the incidence of genetic defects.[30]

For the moment, while everyone agrees that more must be done to improve the conditions under which women give birth to and begin to nurture their children, most admit that the magnitude of the task that local officials confront is well beyond the current resources at their disposal. Consequently, while health conditions in Central Asia continue to deteriorate, the birth rate in the region remains virtually unchanged.

Childrearing and Family Life in Central Asia

Virtually without exception, the Soviet histories and guidebooks applaud the emancipation of Central Asian women that has occurred during the decades of Soviet rule. To be sure, viewed from the outside, the Central Asian society of today little resembles that of seventy-odd years ago. Women are equal to men before the law, and there is at least token female presence in all spheres of public life.

Nonetheless today, as was true earlier, childbearing and childrearing remain the central tasks of a woman's life. Virtually all Central Asian women marry. The 1970 census reported that 94 percent of Central Asian women between the ages of thirty and forty were married, and this figure does not reflect those marriages that are unregistered by Soviet law.[31] For example, official marriage statistics do not include marriages of women who are living as second or third wives. Yet polygamy is not uncommon, especially in rural areas. This conclusion is well substantiated in the conclusions of the field research of Sergei Poliakov, who, until the late 1980s was unable to publish uncensored versions of his findings.[32]

Women often are married before their sixteenth birthday. Although these unions are almost always consecrated according to Islamic law, parents generally wait to register the marriages of under-age children until after the birth of a male child. Sometimes they even wait until several children are born, and only then go to the ZAGs (civil registration hall) and record the union.

Central Asian informants report that almost all marriages in rural regions are still arranged, and even in urban areas it is common for relatives to assume responsibility for finding spouses for marriageable family members. The press campaign against the practice of female self-immolation makes repeated reference to the pervasiveness of arranged marriages.[33]

The initial negotiations in the arrangement of marriages are carried out by the mothers of the young people, with the mother of the prospective groom generally taking the initiative to find a suitable bride for her son among relatives or neighbors. If the two women decide that a match is possible, then their husbands begin formal negotiations to determine the size of the *kalym* (bride price) which will have to be paid for the wedding plans to go forward. The size of the *kalym* varies according to the prestige of the two families involved.

The tradition of paying the *kalym* remains widespread throughout the Fergana Valley region in Uzbekistan, in southern Kirgizia, in western Tajikistan, and throughout Turkmenistan. Typically the bride price is three to four thousand rubles, paid in money, land, or livestock. A girl's "value" reflects her family's rank in traditional society. For example, Poliakov found a young satin factory worker in Dushanbe whose parents collected a *kalym* of twelve thousand rubles because she was the descendant of a clan leader, and he writes of daughters of "holy" families in Turkmenistan who have reportedly fetched up to forty thousand rubles.[34]

For their part, the bride's family is expected to fully outfit the new wife with all of her clothing as well as the necessary household goods. Families, even among the educated urban elite, begin to accumulate the necessary items when their daughters are young children. When consumer goods started to disappear in the late 1980s, Central Asian women began to hoard household goods, fearing that the needed items would not be available in the years to come. Thus household items were quickly added to the list of deficit of consumer goods, as future mothers-of-the-bride busily used contacts and bribery to obtain the cotton-flower tea services that all young brides receive, as well as china, silverware, clothing, and cloth to be used in making bedclothes and blankets.

As much of a girl's trousseau as possible is made in her home, and she begins to help her mother with the fine embroidery and weaving once she is nine or ten. In fact, a girl spends most of her childhood preparing for her wedding. She begins to learn how to do basic household chores like baking and cleaning at age six or seven, and then as she gets older she learns the more specialized tasks she will be expected to perform as a young bride, including sewing, weaving, spinning wool, and tending livestock, as well as minding babies and young children.[35]

The trousseau items are put on display just before the wedding—a practice that continues to be widespread even among Europeanized families in the republic capital cities.[36] Poliakov estimates that the average dowry is worth about six thousand rubles, and he maintains that the high cost of the trousseau is resented by many fathers. This, he believes, helps explain the parental neglect that many girls experience in childhood. Fathers, he writes, try to spend as little additional money on their daughters' education and upbringing as possible. They also try to get girls to make a direct contribution to the family's income as early as possible, because their contribution will be lost at an early age.[37]

Virtually the only way that the payment of the bride price can be avoided is if the bride is "stolen." A girl sometimes arranges her own "kidnapping" in order to avoid the match that her parents have planned for her. Sometimes it is agreed to by both parties because the *kalym* cannot be met. But the traditional community usually shuns those who are married by kidnapping, because this practice undermines the perpetuation of traditional marriage practices.[38]

Local informants report that even today most rural brides have had little or no contact with their future husbands prior to their weddings. Sometimes a girl is allowed to walk along the other side of the road from her future husband to get a glimpse of him; other times she is shown his picture. But Poliakov reports that it is common practice for the picture of a handsome man to be substituted for that of an unattractive groom.[39]

The continued practice of arranged marriages is commonly cited as one of the prime causes of female suicides. In the past several years there has been a great deal of press attention to the problem of self-immolation of young Central Asian women in Tajikistan, Uzbekistan and Turkmenistan.[40] Uzbekistan's government has even set up special commissions to study the problem. But self-immolation is only one form of suicide practiced by Central Asian women. Suicides by ingesting poisoned vinegar potions and by drowning are also said to be common. One report from Uzbekistan indicates that suicides by self-immolation account for only about 40 percent of all female suicides.[41]

Because families and hospitals both tend to conceal unsuccessful suicide attempts, it is hard to know how many young Central Asian women try to take their lives each year. Investigators from an official commission appointed by Uzbekistan's government admit that in that republic alone there were 270 female deaths by self-immolation in 1987, 280 in 1988, and 310 in 1989.[42] Turkmen officials report that there were 34 such deaths in 1987, and 22 deaths in the first few months of 1988 alone.[43]

Given the unreliability of the data base from which information about female suicides in Central Asia is drawn, as well as the limited data available about suicides nation-wide, it is hard to know the comparative severity of the problem. Concern for the "high" incidence of self-immolation of women in the region initially came from journalists in the center, at a time when Moscow was openly writing about Islam as a major detriment to the social and economic development of the region. Yet even in 1989, when the historical role of Islam was being reevaluated throughout Central Asia in much more positive ways, there was still keen official concern over these suicide attempts by women.[44]

The reasons why women attempt suicide vary. Poliakov argues that the underlying reason is marital difficulties, as suicide is the only means available to most women who want to end an unhappy marriage.[45] Central Asian culture is generally not supportive of the idea of divorce, and the area's divorce rate remains the lowest in the USSR, with the lowest incidence of divorce occurring in Tajikistan, where only 1.5 per 1000 marriages end in officially granted civil divorce annually.[46] Nonetheless, a man can receive a religious divorce simply by repeating the phrase "I divorce thee" three times, while a Central Asian woman can almost never successfully sue for a religious divorce.

The most common cause for divorce is infertility. A woman is not considered to have fulfilled her responsibility as a wife until she has borne her husband a child. Many husbands will not divorce an infertile wife, but choose instead to take a second wife. A man who does neither is considered to be besotted with love for his wife. Most women will go to drastic lengths to "remedy" their infertility. They generally prefer treatment by religious healers to that of physicians; this is because infertility is usually regarded as a form of divine retribution for spiritual uncleanness. Poliakov claims that religious "treatments" for infertility account for the bulk of the money collected at major Central Asian pilgrimage sites and infertile women make up the majority of all pilgrims.[47]

Many of the Central Asian females who commit suicide are infertile women who have been cast out or beaten by their husbands for their failure to bear children. A "cast out" rural woman has few social and economic options. Her own family need not take her back, and they will not if it leads to their own social disgrace. If she has technical training she can find a job in a town; if she does not, then she may face a choice between prostitution and suicide, with the latter seeming the less frequent option.[48]

A more common cause of suicide is harsh treatment by mothers-in-law. A newly married woman is turned over to the supervision of her husband's mother. Some women gently initiate their young daughters-in-law, while others do so cruelly. Either way, a young bride has little choice but to accept her fate, for the community grants her no privileges, while the matriarch of a household enjoys absolute communal respect.

The bride remains a sort of apprentice homemaker until the next marriage in the family takes place or until she moves into her own home, which is sometimes not for another decade or so. But the bride of the youngest son will remain under the direct tutelage of her mother-in-law indefinitely, if the youngest son, as is true in most traditional households, chooses to continue to live in his parents' home.

Some of the most vivid accounts of female suicides describe women who tried to end their lives rather than submit to harsh treatment by their mothers-in-law. The suicide attempt of a 25-year-old Tajik school teacher was singled out by *Sel'skaia zhizn'* in Tajikistan for comment. The wife of a youngest son who lived in a household of some twenty people, she was reprimanded by the chairman of her local soviet when she asked for a divorce after enduring years of repeated beatings.[49]

Two studies done in Uzbekistan conclude that suicide attempts occur among women of all ages and all social classes. One from Samarkand reported that the 52 female suicide victims from that oblast in 1988 ranged in age from 14 to 77, and included women who took their lives because of their infertility, to end systematic beatings, and to end lives centered around husbands whom they despised.[50] A second study from Kashkadarya oblast, which drew on data from 1987, reported that the 67 victims in that region included women of all occupations.[51] Some Soviet analysts have concluded that women who work in industry or the service sector are more likely to take their lives than those who engage in agriculture, because the need to adhere to traditional social roles is a greater burden for the more modern woman.[52]

Despite all the publicity around the self-immolation of women in recent years, Central Asian society is still harsh in its judgement of the "failed" suicide victim. As with unhappy wives who try to flee their homes to return to their natal families, the community's sympathy is apt to lie with the abandoned husband and not the wife, who will often be forced to return to the home that she ran away from.

The traditional Central Asian community remains unforgiving of those who violate its values. Women are expected to serve their husbands and families. If they derive personal happiness from this, they are fortunate women. If they do not, they are truly unlucky. Their individual satisfaction is not the concern of the community, nor is it something that they are expected to concern themselves with.

The Employment of Women

For decades Central Asian Party leaders and educators have filled Women's Day speeches with praise for the success of Soviet rule in integrating women into the regional labor force on terms roughly equal to those of men. However, in reality, the situation in Soviet Central Asia with regard to the employment of women is not appreciably better than that of other Muslim societies in South Asia.

Women make up the largest category of unemployed and underemployed people in Central Asia. Precise information on female unemployment is fragmentary. One study from Kashkadarya oblast in Uzbekistan reports that over 70 percent of the unemployed in the region are women, whereas another source from Turkmenia asserts that less than 20 percent of all women in most rural regions are employed.[53]

Most women view employment for pay as secondary to their family responsibilities, and so they are free to do only those jobs which are compatible with child bearing and child raising. Moreover, culture restricts their employment as well. Even urban intellectuals believe that it is unseemly for women to occupy leadership positions because this means that they would exercise authority over men.[54]

Women's occupational mobility is further limited by the norms of proper social conduct. A woman from a traditional family can work but not travel freely, even within her home region, let alone to other regions of the USSR, or worse yet, to foreign countries. These restrictions place very real limits on the types of careers most Central Asian women contemplate. Most men opt to spend their lives working close to their place of birth, but a man who chooses to work outside of Central Asia is not considered disgraced by this decision. His female counterpart is. Moreover, restrictions on the social interaction of men and women further affect the specialties women train for, as they prefer receiving higher education in those subjects, like education and nursing, where they will have few male classmates.

The 1989 census statistics on levels of education by nationality are not yet available, and older statistics lack information about the field of study and the type of institution completed. The materials from the 1979 census do not show significant differences between the levels of educational attainment of men and women for primary school through specialized secondary education. However, there are significant differences in the numbers of men and women completing higher education, especially among those living in rural areas. In general, very few rural Central Asians complete their higher education, and only about a third as many women as men complete advanced education.[55]

Official statistics are misleading because they do not provide the kind of information that is necessary to document how education generally reinforces the restricted occupational mobility patterns of women. For example, one study from Tajikistan reported that girls made up only 15 percent of all vocational-technical school students, and it is precisely this kind of education that is necessary for women to be employed in the industrial workforce.[56] Moreover, those women who do attend vocational high schools disproportionately train for white collar jobs in the service industry, education, or health care.

Official statistics on occupation present data for the percentage of women in the total workforce by sector, rather than the percentage of all women employed. Moreover, they present material by republic and not by nationality. Yet even the available statistics clearly document the underemployment of women. For example, in 1987, women accounted for 51 percent of all workers and service sector employees in the USSR as a whole. But in Uzbekistan women accounted for only 43 percent of these workers, in Turkmenistan 41 percent, and in Tajikistan 38 percent; in Kirgizia, where about 40 percent of the population is European, they accounted for 48 percent. The figures include women in all branches of the economy.

Moreover, official statistics conceal the underemployment of women. Women engage in seasonal agriculture, but they are almost always employed as hand laborers. They are charged with harvesting the cotton, fruit, vegetables, and tobacco, while men drive the farm machinery, or work as brigade leaders and administrators of the collective and state farms. Women also provide the bulk of the labor in the second economy, cultivating the produce that is raised for trade. However, the management of that economy is carried out by men. Similarly, statistics on the number of female workers are also misleading, as most female "workers" are engaged in traditional handicraft production, like weaving rugs, and work in exclusively female factories or workshops.

There have been several studies done on patterns of female employment in Tajikistan which document the underemployment of women. Two studies, completed in 1986 and 1990 respectively, showed almost identical conclusions. Both reported that only 38 percent of all Tajik women were employed, as opposed to 50 percent of all women nationwide. Moreover, 40 percent of all employed women worked in agriculture, and, of these, 65 percent worked at jobs which required no specialized training. In fact, over 91 percent of all unskilled agricultural labor in Tajikistan was performed by women. Moreover, in the years under study (1965–1987), the sex-linked patterns of employment became more rather than less firmly established. Thus, at the end of the period, the proportion of Tajik women employed in construction had dropped, while the percentage employed in agriculture had increased.[57]

Even when women do work, they often do not control their earnings. Poliakov reports that throughout rural Central Asia women are able to keep only the money they make on the side, from the sale of a handicraft which they produce. However, money earned from labor on the collective farm, or from the sale of produce through the second economy, belongs to the family and is turned over to the male head of the household. Moreover, it is the husband who is in charge of household expenditures. But as women generally work at unskilled agricultural labor, their financial contribution is small, only about sixty or seventy rubles on average per month, and those pensioned off only about thirty rubles.

Besides lack of suitable training, the acute shortage of child-care facilities (especially in rural areas) is another reason why women are underemployed in the Central Asian economy. According to data from the mid-1980s, 56 percent of all Soviet children under age six were in state child care facilities, but only 28 percent of those in Uzbekistan, 29 percent of those in Kirgizia, 28 percent of those in Turkmenia, and 17 percent of those in Tajikistan. Data from 1988 give evidence of considerably lower figures for children in day-care facilities in rural regions; 13 percent in Turkmenia and 4 percent in Tajikistan.[58] As the overwhelming majority of all children in Central Asia live in rural regions, the 1988 data suggest that the earlier figures were inflated.

Although Central Asian officials constantly demand that raion officials provide more facilities, there is no evidence to suggest that this is a priority for either the local or republic officials. Rather, the opposite appears to be true; rural officials are content to allow older children to take care of younger ones, under the supervision of retired grandmothers.

However, in those areas where women are employed in industry, even in cottage industry, the social integration of women has proceeded more fully. Poliakov contrasts the situation in two villages in Leninabad oblast in Tajikistan; in Pangaz (Asht raion) 300 women are employed in cottage industry and another 130 in a local rug factory, whereas in Varuch (Isfarin raion) women are engaged solely in agriculture. In Pangaz, women appear in public without covering their faces, teen-age girls and boys go out together, and brides are married wearing European dress. In Varuch, women cover their faces and their heads; they do not talk to men in public or appear on the street unescorted; and girls are barred from extracurricular activities in schools. Poliakov attributes the difference in lifestyle directly to the presence of industrial employment in Pangaz, as lifestyles in the two raions were virtually identical before the factories were introduced in the latter community. However, most women living in rural Central Asia are not given the opportunity to be employed in industry.

Women also play only a minimal role in the government of Central Asian society. Every republic includes at least one prominent female office holder, who usually serves either in the area of cultural or youth affairs or in foreign relations. Now the new presidential councils boast a female member as well. Over the years a few of these Central Asian women have even turned into visible political figures, such as Rano Abdullaeva, who was the powerful but unpopular secretary for ideology in Uzbekistan in the mid-1980s.

However, such women are truly exceptional. When women do play a role it is generally under conditions that are sanctioned by religion, in single-sex and often quasi-religious organizations. Though women play no real role in the governing of Central Asian society, the local press has always written a great deal about the positive activities of women in neighborhood soviets and about all the good that is done by local women's committees. Most rural women's committees have existed almost exclusively on paper, having been formed to meet official Soviet guidelines but serving no other function. In reality, local authority is exercised by *mahalla* (neighborhood) committees in Uzbekistan and Tajikistan, and by clan councils in Kirgizia and Turkmenia, and these almost never include females among their members.

Islam and Women

For all the restrictions on the social life of Central Asian women, it would still be a mistake to label them second-class citizens. Central Asians generally accept that men and women have been allocated distinct social roles by their culture and faith, and women's daily lives are affected by Islam as much as those of men.

Most of the ways that a woman participates in the religious life of the community are indirect, though the role of child bearer is central to the community's survival. Almost all marriages are still celebrated with some form of religious ceremony, even if not fully in keeping with Islamic *Sharia* law. The responsibility to bear as many children as possible is understood as a religious obligation. The birth of each child is celebrated with customary rituals, as is a baby's naming. In the case of a boy, his circumcision several years later is again an occasion for the family to gather for a ritual Islamic observance.

Some more direct forms of participation are also open to women. Girls are able to receive limited religious education, under the direction of *bibiotuns*, female *mullahs*.[59] The level of religious learning of these women is substantially lower than male *mullahs*. Most only have the most rudimentary knowledge of Islamic doctrine and can generally only barely decipher the Arabic script. Nonetheless, they take on small groups of female students, and the most successful of their protegés become *bibiotuns* themselves.

The *bibiotuns* are active in rural areas. One of their prime tasks is to insure that women lead their lives in accordance with Islamic teachings and that young girls are properly prepared for marriage and the responsibilities of motherhood. They also assist *sheikhs* and *ishans* in superintending holy sites, and they attend to the religious needs of female pilgrims.

In recent years women living in cities have also begun to take a greater interest in Islam. Religious study groups have formed, and women as well as men are increasingly more interested in learning Arabic. The increased popularity of Islamic fundamentalist teachings has placed new pressures on women. In the past few years it has become more, not less, common for young urban Uzbek and Tajik girls to be modestly dressed. In large part this reflects many women's greater devotion to religion. But some choose to dress more modestly for more pragmatic reasons; women who are "inappropriately" dressed, in short-sleeved dresses with short skirts, may be subject to harassment, or worse yet even raped.[60]

Kirgiz party leader Absamat Masaliev has complained that the tasks of educating young women have become more complicated in recent years because of the increased religiosity of the population. In some parts of his republic, rural leaders are now demanding separate schools for boys and girls.[61]

The increased religious consciousness has also added to women's political activism, as Islamic women's activist groups have developed in

Kirgizia, Tajikistan, Uzbekistan, and Kazakhstan. Women have rallied around a variety of causes. One of the most popular has been the mothers' movement to oppose the draft in Uzbekistan, which succeeded in extracting from Uzbekistan's government the promise that local youths need no longer serve in construction brigades outside the limits of their republic. For the most part, the membership of these groups seems to be urban intellectuals, who see the religious-oriented format of their new organizations as affording them new rights of political participation.

There are also groups of Islamic women organized in Osh oblast, and the informal organization, *Birlik*, has a women's committee as well. The *Birlik* women are in contact with an Islamic women's group in Alma-Ata, which is pressing Kazakhstan's government to be more sympathetic to Kazakh national-religious goals. The agenda of the female activists in Kirgizia is similar. These women are pressing for government concessions that will make these republics Islamic national states.

For all the years of Soviet propagation of Central Asian "women's liberation," secular female activists are surprisingly quiet today. Moscow and the hypercentralized economy which Soviet rule imposed on Central Asia are viewed as the cause of the region's underdevelopment and of the hardships in the lives of most local women. The co-optation of the local elite by the "partocracy" is faulted but the traditional practices of the Central Asians are not. Secular ideologies are seen as tainted by their "foreignness," and even more so by virtue of their source–the Russians, who have long dominated the region. Islam, the direction that Central Asia was forced to abandon, has the advantage of seeming fresh, untried, and drawn from local roots.

The growing turmoil within Central Asia makes it very hard to predict what the future might hold. Soviet rule did not bring the promised liberation of women. If anything, the stresses on women were greater in the netherworld of partial economic and social development than they were when women lived in a fully traditional society. Over the next few years the political culture of Central Asia is sure to change, and is certain to become more rather than less Islamic. In the end this may make the lives of contemporary Central Asian women easier. It is hard to imagine that it can make their lives any harder.

Notes

1. *Vestnik statistiki*, no. 8, 1986, p. 77.
2. In Uzbekistan 2.8 vs. 3.1, in Kazakhstan 2.2 vs. 2.8, in Kirgizia 3.1 vs. 3.5, in Tajikistan 3.0 vs. 3.3, and in Turkmenia 2.7 vs. 2.9.
3. In Kirgizia women with only primary education had an average of 4.3 children, those with incomplete secondary education 3.5 children, and those

with higher education 2.0 children. In Kazakhstan 3.6, 2.9, and 1.6 respectively (*Vestnik statistiki*, no. 6, 1986, p. 76).

4. *Demografiia sem'i* (Tashkent, 1980), p. 10.

5. She found that women with higher education over thirty wanted to have 2.9 children, whereas workers wanted 3.6 children; both groups of women under thirty wanted 3.5 children. See V. V. Koroteeva, "Etnosotsial'nye aspekty rozhdaemosti u naseleniia mnogonatsional'nogo goroda," *Sovetskaia etnografiia*, no. 6, 1986, p. 17.

6. See S. P. Poliakov, *Islam and Traditional Life in Rural Central Asia*, edited by Martha Brill Olcott, translated by Anthony Olcott (M.E. Sharpe, forthcoming).

7. *Zhenshchiny v SSSR 1989*, (Moscow: Finansy i statistika, 1989), p. 33.

8. L. Khazan, "The World of New Arrivals," *Rabochaia gazeta*, Dec. 29, 1988, p.2, translated in *JPRS Report. Soviet Union Political Affairs*, JPRS-UPA-89-022, Apr. 6, 1989, pp. 54–56.

9. *Soiuz*, no. 30 (July, 1990), p. 7; as quoted by *JPRS Report. Soviet Union Political Affairs*, JPRS-UPA-90-056, Sept. 24, 1990, p. 90.

10. Annette Bohr, "Health Catastrophe in Karakalpakistan," Radio Liberty, *Report on the USSR*, July 11, 1989.

11. *Kommunist Tadzhikistana*, July 13, 1989.

12. *Turkmenskaia iskra*, Mar. 5, 1989.

13. K. Ormantaev, "Why Is Infant Mortality So High?" *Qazaq adebiyeti*, Apr. 7, 1989, pp. 10–11, as quoted in *JPRS Report. Soviet Union Political Affairs*, JPRS-UPA-89-037, June 1, 1989, p. 95.

14. *Komsomol'skaia pravda*, Oct. 14, 1988.

15. *Turkmenskaia iskra*, Mar. 5, 1989.

16. *Sovet Turkmenistany*, Jan. 21, 1989, as quoted in *JPRS Report. Soviet Union Political Affairs*, JPRS-UPA-89-035, May 23, 1989, p. 49.

17. *Izvestiia*, Jan. 2, 1989.

18. *Komsomol'skaia Pravda*, Oct. 20, 1990.

19. *Kommunist Tadzhikistana*, Jan. 26, 1990.

20. *Sovetskaia Kirgizia*, July 7, 1989.

21. In 1988 nearly 10 percent of all births in Kirgizia were premature, and 20 percent of all births resulted in low birthweight children. In the same time period, 16 percent of all newborn children in Osh oblast were reported to suffer from rickets or other dietary deficiencies (*Sovetskaia Kirgizia*, July 7, 1989 and June 8, 1989).

22. *Pravda Vostoka*, June 21, 1990.

23. S. Bakhramov, "Public Health in Uzbekistan," *Kommunist Uzbekistana*, no. 7, July 1988, pp. 27–32, as translated in *JPRS Report. Soviet Union Political Affairs*, JPRS-88-059, Dec. 21, 1988, pp. 84–86.

24. *Kommunist Tadzhikistana*, June 14, 1988 reports eforts by the Tajik SSR State Agro-industrial Committee to restrict manual labor of women in general and pregnant women in particular. Similar legislation has been introduced in the other Central Asian republics, but there is little evidence of law-enforcement efforts.

25. *Pravda Vostoka*, Jan. 3, 1989.

26. *Soiuz*, no. 30 (July, 1990), p. 7; as quoted by *JPRS Report. Soviet Union Political Affairs*, JPRS-UPA-90-056, Sept. 24, 1990, p. 90.
27. *Kommunist Tadzhikistana*, Feb. 3, 1989.
28. *Sovetskaia Kirgizia*, July 7, 1989.
29. *Soiuz*, no. 30, July, 1990. p. 7; as quoted by *JPRS Report. Soviet Union Political Affairs*, JPRS-UPA-90-056, Sept. 24, 1990, p. 90.
30. *Komsomol'skaia Pravda*, Oct. 14, 1988.
31. *Naselenie Srednei Azii* (Moscow: Finansy i statistika), 1985, p. 6.
32. Unless otherwise noted, materials in this section are drawn from S. P. Poliakov, *Islam and Traditional Life in Rural Central Asia*, edited by Martha Brill Olcott, translated by Anthony Olcott.
33. *Komsomolets Tadzhikistana*, Aug. 9, 1987.
34. Poliakov, chapter 10.
35. A. Soiunova, "O traditsionnom trude vospitanii v sovremennoi turkmenskoi sem'e," *Izvestiia AN Turkmensksoi SSR*, no. 2, 1983, pp. 10–16.
36. All of the women I met in Central Asia, from *kolkhoz* workers to Party elite wives, were busily collecting goods for their daughters' trousseaus. I also saw apartments in Dushanbe with the trousseau items on display.
37. Poliakov, chapter 14.
38. *Komsomol'skaia Pravda*, July 26, 1986, p. 3.
39. Poliakov, chapter 11.
40. For some examples see *Komsomolets Turkmenistana*, June 28, 1987, *Sobesednik*, no. 40, (Sept. 1988), p. 12, *Turkmenskaia iskra*, Oct. 14, 1988, and *Pravda Vostoka*, July 26, 1989.
41. *Agitator Uzbekistana*, no. 24, 1988, pp. 7–10.
42. Interview with Uzbek investigator Shukhrat Ashurov, August 7, 1990. Data for 1987 are from *Pravda Vostoka*, Jan. 31, 1988.
43. *Sovetskaia kul'tura*, Aug. 23, 1988.
44. *Turkmenskaia iskra*, April 26, 1989.
45. Poliakov, chapter 11.
46. *Kommunist Tadzhikistana*, no. 5, 1987, p. 19.
47. Poliakov, chapter 11.
48. It is only during the past few years that Central Asian officials have even admitted that prostitution exists. But even today they are unwilling to provide detailed data about the severity of the problem, let alone data broken down by nationality.
49. N. Kuliev, "A Torch in the Darkness," *Sel'skaia zhizn'*, Aug. 9, 1988, p. 3, as quoted in *JPRS Report. Soviet Union Political Affairs*, JPRS-UPA-053, Nov. 18, 1988, p. 62.
50. *Pravda Vostoka*, Feb. 15, 1989.
51. *Agitator Uzbekistana*, no. 24, 1988, pp. 7–10.
52. This is Bess Brown's conclusion in "New Theory on Suicides in Central Asia," *Radio Liberty Research*, Sept. 26, 1988, RL 431/88. See also Anne Bohr, "Self-immolation Among Central Asian Women," *Radio Liberty Research*, Mar. 20, 1988, RL 126/88.
53. *Pravda Vostoka*, Feb. 15, 1989.

54. Unless otherwise noted, materials in this section are drawn from S. P. Poliakov, *Islam and Traditional Life in Rural Central Asia*, edited by Martha Brill Olcott, translated by Anthony Olcott.

55. According to the 1979 census 15 rural Uzbek women per thousand complete their higher education as opposed to 51 men. In Tadzhikistan 6 women and 26 men per thousand, in Turkmenia 9 and 39, and in Kirgizia 26 women and 33 men, the only case where the difference in educational attainment is relatively small. All data are for nationals living in their titular republics. Data were provided by Soviet researchers in Moscow.

56. Review by P. I. Shmelin of "Sotsial'no-ekonomicheskiye problemy razvitiia Tadzhikskoi SSR," *Problemy nauchnogo ateizma. Referativnyi zhurnal*, no. 6, 1985, as quoted in *JPRS Report. Soviet Union Political Affairs*, JPRS-UPA-86-12, Mar. 12, 1986.

57. S. Iu. Isaeva, "Zaniatnost' zhenshchin v Tadzhikskoi SSR," *Sotsialisticheskoe issledovanie*, no. 1, 1990, p. 66.

58. Review by P. I. Shmelin and *Pravda*, Feb. 18, 1988.

59. The name of these female *mullah*s varies by community; they are called *bibiotun*s among the Uzbeks, *otyncha*s among the Tajiks, and *folchin*s among the Turkmen.

60. *Pravda Vostoka,* May 20, 1989. Eyewitnesses to the Feb. 1990 riots in Dushanbe spoke of how young girls in European dress were raped during the two weeks of civil unrest.

61. *Sovetskaia Kirgiziia,* May 20, 1989.

10

Central Asian Youth and Migration

William Fierman

Introduction

The most serious economic, political, and social problems of Central Asia are all shaped by the demographic processes described by Nancy Lubin in Chapter 2. Given other economic and geographic factors, excess labor is one of the greatest potential problems. Both Western and certain Soviet scholars have long recognized the serious challenges posed by the combination of underemployment and the various limitations on economic development in the Central Asian region of the USSR. Soviet and Western observers alike recognize unemployment as one of the factors contributing to the social tension which has served as a backdrop for violent outbreaks such as those in Fergana in the spring of 1989.

One of the suggested partial solutions to the unemployment problem has been out-migration from Central Asia to other regions of the USSR. Some Western scholars, although clearly the minority, have maintained that this is by far the most likely outcome of population pressures. Writing in the mid-1970s, Robert Lewis, Richard Rowland, and Ralph Clem claimed to be able to "forecast with some certainty that there [would] be considerable out-migration from 'non-European' areas" of the USSR unless conditions were to "change drastically." One of the bases for their conclusion was that "the universal experience" throughout the world has demonstrated that "when conditions analogous to those now [i.e., 1970s] developing in the USSR have occurred, they have ultimately been associated with much out-migration and ethnic mixing in multinational states."[1] Several years later Lewis and Rowland reasserted that although "there could be conditions specific to Central Asia that might impede migration, at least in the short run," as yet they saw "no particularistic factors in Central Asia that [were] sufficiently strong and resistant to change related to modernization to counter the strong demographic, economic, and social forces that [were] intensifying in

Central Asia and that elsewhere in the world generally have resulted in substantial out-migration."[2] Although the authors did not predict a specific time frame in which the migration would take place, they did feel that "pressure should be high in the 1980s and thereafter."[3]

Many other scholars, most notably Murray Feshbach, have argued that, taken as a whole, the balance of economic, social, cultural, religious, and linguistic factors has remained unfavorable for Central Asians to migrate from their native regions. In a paper presented in 1979, Feshbach predicted that there would "not be a mass movement out of Central Asia during the next decade."[4] In a slightly later explanation of his views Feshbach stated that out-migration of indigenous rural Central Asians (who comprise the bulk of the "excess population") "to their own cities—let alone to northern climes—[was] extremely unlikely" unless the Soviet regime was willing to resort to "administrative measures."[5]

The overwhelming evidence from the middle 1980s corroborates the prediction of scholars on both sides of the debate who saw the worsening economic (and specifically manpower) problems in Central Asia. Moreover, this situation was seriously compounded by the growing water shortage and ecological deterioration.

As a partial solution to these problems, the middle of the 1980s witnessed an intensification of the Soviet regime's efforts to urge Central Asians to migrate from their homeland. To judge from their published speeches, the Soviet leadership's promotion of migration was based not merely on a desire to redistribute the USSR's labor resources. One of its most important aims was also to contribute to the mixing of various nationalities and thus develop more bonds among the "Soviet people."

This chapter examines some of the organized attempts by the CPSU to encourage young Central Asians to move away from their native region in the middle of the 1980s and identifies possible reasons for their meager results.[6] Although we will briefly consider some "external objective factors" which have influenced the ability of the Soviet regime to encourage young Central Asians to move, we will focus primarily on young people's skills and attitudes. In particular, we will pay special attention to those attitudes and skills (or lack thereof) which have restrained mobility. We also will consider why it has been so difficult for the Party to teach skills and inculcate attitudes which make young Central Asians more willing to move and more employable elsewhere in the country.

One manifestation of the excess labor problem in Central Asia is the large number of people not employed in the public sector. According to one recent Soviet source, at the beginning of 1988 one quarter of the labor resources in Uzbekistan was not involved in public production (*obshchestvennoe proizvodstvo*).[7] The problem is most serious among youth, especially female youth. Half of the population not working in Uzbekistan in 1987 consisted of young people under age thirty.[8] In Tajikistan, over 136,000 men and women between the ages of sixteen and twenty-nine were neither working nor studying.[9] In 1987, in Tajikistan, women comprised 94 percent of the working-age population not involved in public production, while in Turkmenia (in 1986) their unemployment share was 98 percent.[10]

The excess labor is not evenly distributed in Central Asia. Labor resources in some areas, in particular the Fergana Valley, are said to be "spilling over."[11] In the Valley's Andizhan oblast it was reported that 18,143 Komsomol members were not working in 1986.[12] And there were allegedly some raions in the foothills and mountains of Uzbekistan where a majority of the population capable of working were not involved in public production.[13] The majority of excess labor has been concentrated in rural areas: in the late 1970s rural areas accounted for approximately three-fourths of those not working in Tajikistan.[14]

The employment situation worsened in the 1980s. During the Eleventh Five-Year Plan the manpower resources in Tajikistan increased by 16.9 percent, yet the number of individuals engaged in public production or enrolled in school increased by only 13.7 percent.[15] The picture was no better in Uzbekistan. In Fergana oblast alone during the late 1980s, 25,000 additional young men and women were becoming available to work in the oblast's farms and factories annually, yet there were only enough positions for 18,000.[16] Some of Gorbachev's economic reforms seem likely to aggravate the current situation. As farms and factories seek efficiency, a substantial number of workers may be released from their current jobs. The anxiety which such prospects evoke is apparent from articles with such titles as "Are We Threatened by Unemployment?"[17]

Despite "unemployment," there have been many unfilled jobs. In Uzbekistan these have tended to be in medium-sized towns and certain newly developed regions.[18] The vacant urban jobs have often been for skilled workers in factories. But there have also been other open positions. Uzbekistan, for example, has great expanses of desert and semi-desert to which the Party has attempted to attract pioneers.[19] Altogether, in Uzbekistan's Samarkand oblast (where 21,000 men and women of Komsomol age were neither working in public production nor enrolled in school), there were 16,000 vacant jobs in 1987.[20]

Although many economists have emphasized the need to encourage migration within the region and to reorient the Central Asian economy and vocational training in order to utilize more of the labor force within Central Asia, others have insisted that migration out of Central Asia is still an essential component in the solution to the region's labor surplus.

They have maintained that without such migration, Central Asians' standard of living will deteriorate further or else they will become recipients of ever larger amounts of "welfare" from the rest of the country. Based on the rates of growth for national income and fixed capital calculated for the Central Asian republics in the Twelfth Five-Year Plan, D. Ziuzin estimated that 7.1 million people would have to leave the region during the last fifteen years of the twentieth century just to maintain Central Asia's 1985 level of national income per able-bodied inhabitant. And even without a further deterioration, this level was 30 percent below the all-Union average.[21]

Like Western scholars' predictions of the growing labor surplus in Central Asia, those about the increasing labor shortage *outside* of Central Asia have also been correct. The latter seems likely to be further aggravated by plans for accelerated growth in Siberia and the Far East,[22] but the population necessary to carry out that development is currently not available there. As of the mid-1980s the population density in such regions as Tiumen and Amur oblasts, Krasnoiarsk and Khabarovsk krais, and the Buriat ASSR were only between 1.3 and 2.6 persons per square kilometer.[23] Some Soviet analysts blamed "limited manpower resources" for holding back agricultural production in some parts of the Soviet Far East.[24] In 1987, Soviet scholar Anvar Chamkin claimed that "relocation of one person from the southern to the eastern area of the country produce[d] a profit of 5,000 rubles." He estimated that "just a million immigrants" would yield "a profit of 5 billion rubles for the country."[25]

The above suggests that the economic benefits of migration of labor resources from Central Asia to the RSFSR and other regions in need of population are potentially very great. Nevertheless, as will be demonstrated below, very few indigenous Central Asians have been willing to make this move. In the remainder of this paper we will look at attempts by the CPSU in the mid-1980s to encourage greater migration of Central Asians to other areas of their own republics and the USSR. Although a number of measures have been intended to encourage migration within Central Asia from rural areas to towns, these have generally been diffuse programs which will not be our focus here. Rather, we will concentrate on specific programs intended to encourage people, especially young members of the Central Asian nationalities, to work or study either in distant parts of their own republic or elsewhere in the USSR. Although, strictly speaking, study by Central Asians in educational institutions in the Slavic republics is intended to train individuals who will return to work in their home republics (rather than "stay abroad"), it is useful to include these programs in the present context because they have encountered many of the same problems which face efforts to send labor outside of the region. Moreover, from

Moscow's perspective, one of the beneficial by-products of these educational programs was that a portion of the pupils sent "abroad" would remain there to work at least temporarily. In similar fashion, strictly speaking, some of the *temporary* employment of Central Asians in labor-short areas merits attention here. As will be demonstrated below, the Party, Komsomol, and state labor committees often attempted to offer incentives for those sent on temporary assignments "abroad" to remain longer. And, presumably, officials hoped that those who had a positive experience on one short-term project might consider signing up for another one on either a temporary or permanent basis.

Employment and Resettlement in New Locations: Opportunities and Incentives

Opportunities

The program with the largest number of participants in the mid-1980s was an almost exclusively temporary one. This involved the employment of higher education students in student brigades during the summer. Students worked, on average, approximately one and one-half months on these projects.[26] Although the total number of Soviet students participating in these detachments reached 806,000 in 1986, in 1987 the number was scheduled to be cut to 700,000.[27] Of the 700,000, more than 40 percent were to work on various construction projects, and the remainder in specialized brigades in agriculture, transport, medicine, education, and other areas.[28] Central Asian youth were well represented in these brigades; over the twenty years between 1966 and 1985, almost 130,000 Tajikistan students participated in them, with 12,000 in 1985 alone.[29] In 1987, 43,000 of Uzbekistan's student's took part. Not all students participating in these brigades were sent outside of their own republic; an undetermined but apparently fairly large proportion worked closer to home.[30]

A number of opportunities also existed for non-student laborers to work for a very short time (e.g., a season) in distant regions. One report tells of a group of 150 from Uzbekistan's densely populated Khorezm region who went to work for a season in Siberia's Chita oblast.[31] Volunteers for these jobs were frequently recruited through Central Asian newspapers. For example, one announcement published in Uzbekistan's *Pravda Vostoka* invited single men to work for a period up to six months in Arkhangelsk.[32] It is difficult to estimate the size of the work force involved in these programs since I have found no aggregate data, even for individual republics. However, if the modest amount of attention devoted to these programs in the Komsomol and republic daily press is any reflection, they were probably not very large.

The commitments for some of the other temporary work opportunities far away from home were somewhat longer. Announcements generally referred to "seasonal" assignments up to six months, with anything over a year being classified as "permanent" (*postoianno* or [Uzbek] *daimiy*).[33] Many of the newspaper announcements for these positions were from the republic State Committee on Labor (Goskomtrud). These programs, too, remained rather small. Uzbekistan sent out only 25,000 such workers through the entire Eleventh Five-Year Plan; the total for 1985 was only 5,700.[34] Fragmentary evidence suggests that most who agreed to these assignments were young: in Uzbekistan's densely populated Fergana oblast, the majority of the participants in 1987 were in their late twenties.[35]

Aside from those who went or were sent by the republic state committees on labor, many also went through the Komsomol to work on projects which had their high priority status indicated in the special designation as Komsomol "shock" projects. As in the case of the student detachments, Komsomol shock project detachments were dispatched both within the republic and beyond. The Uzbekistan Komsomol congress resolution in 1987 called for annually sending 3,000 youths to all-Union shock projects on Komsomol passes (*putevki*) and 2,000 to republic shock projects.[36] Although this was about the same number who on the average had been sent to republic projects during the previous five years, the number who were to go to all-Union projects represented a 50 percent increase over the earlier period.[37] Considering that its population is only one-fourth that of Uzbekistan, Tajikistan made a proportionally larger contribution to these shock projects, with a total of 13,000 volunteers sent from 1982 through 1986 (i.e., an annual average of 2,600) either to republic or all-Union shock projects. At least in the case of Uzbekistan the composition of the detachments sent out of the republic underrepresented the indigenous nationality. Between 1981 and 1985, 61.8 percent of the republic young people who went to a number of major all-Union shock projects were Uzbeks.[38] Although the proportion of Uzbeks in the republic's total population is not much larger (around 70 percent), this figure is much less than the percentage of Uzbeks in the cohort of youth. The Komsomol members who "volunteered" for these projects were obligated only for a set period. However, the benefits which they were to be given were often scaled in such a way so as to encourage them to remain longer. Thus, the bonus promised to those who volunteered for one project in the Far East reached 50 percent after the workers remained five years.[39]

While the Party clearly hoped that some of the participants in the Komsomol shock projects would remain in their new "homes," the individuals who went did not make any commitment to stay. This is very different from organized resettlement programs, in which volunteers were expected to commit to a permanent move. An article about a sovkhoz (state farm) in Uzbekistan's Kashkadarya oblast which welcomed new immigrants noted approvingly that half of the new immigrants were married. It took this as evidence that these people were "coming not just for a month or even a season." It concluded that these people "plan to put down roots in their new place."[40]

As illustrated by the above example, some of the resettlement programs merely involved the movement of people from labor-abundant to labor-poor regions of the same republic. This appears to have been especially true in Uzbekistan. During the Eleventh Five-Year Plan, about 20,000 families were resettled to the republic's virgin land farms.[41] Although there were plans to move 29,000 families over five years beginning in 1985 to the Karshi, Dzhizak, and Hungry Steppes,[42] it appears that at the beginning of the Twelfth Five-Year Plan the resettlement slowed. In 1985, over 4,300 families moved to virgin land raions of Uzbekistan,[43] but over the three years 1985–1987 the total was only about 10,000 families.[44] Although the resettlement of labor in this instance was voluntary, this was not always the case. Over 22,000 people in forty-five villages of Tajikistan's Komsomolabad raion were forced to move because the land which they lived on was to be used for a new water reservoir.[45]

At least in the case of Uzbekistan, organized resettlement of people outside of the republic was considerably less than that within the republic. In 1987, the *total* sent by the republic's State Committee on Labor either through organized labor recruitment or agricultural resettlement (presumably both inside and outside the republic) was only about 13,000.[46] It is true that the vast majority of out-migration was not connected with organized recruitment programs.[47] However, as indicated by the negligible increase in Central Asians living outside of their region (see below), it does not appear that "spontaneous" migration had a significantly greater effect than organized recruitment in redistributing the indigenous population to other republics.

Despite the relatively small number of individuals involved in these programs, these people were sent to a very broad range of locations. An announcement in Uzbekistan's *Pravda Vostoka* invited families with at least two able-bodied adults to volunteer to move to kolkhozes or sovkhozes in ten different areas of the RSFSR; some, such as Amur and Chita oblasts, were in the Far East and Siberia, but others, such as Pskov oblast, were in European parts of the country.[48]

In Uzbekistan, demographic forecasts for the end of the 1980s indicated that the government recognized that far less than 1 percent of the region's population might be encouraged to move out of the republic to the areas most in need of labor. In 1987, *Izvestiia* published an article by First Secretary of Tashkent oblast Alimov which said that "at the end of the [current] five-year plan the number of representatives of our republic employed in developing new economic regions will exceed 30,000."[49] It appears that Alimov did not include family members, but this was almost certainly not the case when former republic First Secretary Usmankhodzhaev predicted in 1987 that "140,000 of our envoys" would be sent to help develop the non-black earth zone, BAM, raions of Western Siberia, and Tiumen oblast.[50]

Incentives

In the mid-1980s, Komsomol and other Central Asian newspapers frequently printed articles about representatives of their respective republics who lived in distant locations. Although they admitted problems, the articles were generally upbeat and described a picture of an attractive challenge for young people and a successful adaptation. One, for example, recounted how an Uzbek who went to Siberia married a Russian whom he met there.[51] Although the Party and Komsomol called on young people to move to labor-short regions of the country on patriotic grounds, it is apparent that financial incentives were the most important attraction, especially in the case of people moving away from home only temporarily. This was admitted by a Fergana oblast official who said that the most attractive factor for those who went to other parts of the USSR was "high earnings."[52] Frequently volunteers for shock construction projects earned bonuses for working in particular zones of the USSR, plus an added percent of earnings (often 10 percent) for each of the first three to five years on the job.

Another major incentive was housing. Free housing was provided for the first two years to those who moved from Samarkand oblast to some sovkhozes in the Far East.[53] And Komsomol members who volunteered to work on a shock project in Khabarovsk were also promised individual apartments immediately upon arrival.[54] Although sometimes those who resettled first had to work before they received desirable housing, the waiting period was relatively short by Soviet standards. Turkmenia's Komsomol members going to labor on the construction of the Perm Hydroelectric Power Station were guaranteed apartments after three years of work.[55] Housing and land were also incentives in the case of intra-republic migration. According to a journalist for Uzbekistan's Komsomol newspaper, one of the major reasons that people were willing to leave Fergana for the Hungry Steppe was their desire to receive houses and large private plots of land.[56]

Aside from money and housing, the other incentives were probably of much lesser importance. They included, for example, extra vacation time, which those who went to work on some shock projects in Siberia were supposed to receive.[57] Other incentives were educational opportunity and desirable leisure and cultural facilities. Although it is difficult to judge how real opportunities matched up with promises, the press emphasized these aspects in announcements and positive vignettes of life in these places.[58] There is little evidence that coercion was ever used to convince people to move away from home for most of the "opportunities" described above; however, it was common in the case of students' summer work. Theoretically, of course, recruitment into student detachments was always voluntary, but increasingly at the end of the 1980s the press recognized that various sorts of pressure were being used to force "volunteers" to sign up.[59]

"Study Abroad"

Finally, for our discussion here, there were opportunities for Central Asians to study "abroad" in another part of the USSR, particularly in a vocational-technical *uchilishche* (abbreviated PTU) in one of the three Slavic republics. In most cases such PTU training lasted less than a year. Central Asians also studied in higher educational institutions of the RSFSR, Ukraine, and Belorussia, but the difficulties in motivating young people to accept these opportunities were very different from those of PTU education. In contrast to that obtained at a PTU, university and institute education (especially in central institutions) is very prestigious, and so young people are usually eager to apply. Although the number of students "abroad" at any one time was relatively large, the number of Central Asian students who actually received a higher education outside of the region was much smaller. This is because higher education generally takes a minimum of four (and in most cases five) years. Thus, for example, in 1987, there were 5,324 students from Uzbekistan in higher educational institutions of other republics, but the number to be sent in 1987 was only 1,400.[60] Significant numbers of Central Asians were also sent outside their republics to *tekhnikums*.[61] For example, in 1987, over 900 were to be admitted from Tajikistan through affirmative action-like programs ("outside of competition") by *tekhnikums* in other republics, primarily for training in specialties not taught in Tajikistan.[62]

The ostensible primary goal of sending Central Asians to PTUs in Slavic republics was to provide training in specialties which were not taught locally.[63] Many of these apparently involved factory machine operation or construction. But not all young Central Asians sent to other republics learned unusual or sophisticated skills. Many also studied such specialties as automobile repair, retail trade, and sewing.[64] Although, as we will see below, young Central Asians were not enthusiastic about going "abroad" to study in PTUs, officials tried to convince them to consider these opportunities. Second Secretary of the Tajikistan Communist Party Luchinskii tried to make the chance to "study abroad" look attractive by suggesting that instead of talking about these opportunities as the "international obligation of Tajikistan before the country," one should consider that the cities in other parts of the country were fulfilling *their* international obligation in providing places for Tajiks to study.[65]

Generally young Central Asians from the same oblast were sent to study together either in the same institution or in the same area. This was a result of pairing of Central Asian oblasts with what might be termed "sister" oblasts in Slavic republics. Thus, for example, a group of pupils from Uzbekistan's Navoi and Syrdarya oblasts went to Leningrad, a group from Bukhara oblast went to Minsk, and a group from Surkhandarya oblast went to Donetsk.[66]

Although the Party's primary goal in encouraging Central Asians to study in PTUs of Slavic republics was to train workers for Central Asia, demographers and other scholars recognized that one of the desirable consequences of this experience was encouragement of migrational mobility.[67] The number who remained in the Slavic republics immediately following graduation was in fact quite small. Of the 9,500 young people who went from Tajikistan to study in PTUs in the RSFSR and Ukraine between 1981 and 1985, 1,600 had remained as of the middle of 1986.[68] Likewise, very few of Turkmenia's pupils remained.[69]

It appears that the first organized groups of pupils from Central Asia went to PTUs in other republics in the early 1980s. The first ones from Tajikistan went in 1981,[70] and those from Turkmenia went the following year.[71] However, Kirgizia did not begin the practice until 1986, when for the first time 657 young people were sent to RSFSR and Ukrainian PTUs.[72] There was considerable variation among the Central Asian republics with regard to the proportion of PTU students who were sent "abroad" for study. No more than 2–3 percent of Uzbekistan's PTU students were trained in Slavic republics. In the late 1980s, the republic's own PTUs admitted an average of 180,000 to 190,000[73] and even as early as 1984 (before continued expansion of the PTU network) they trained 151,700 graduates.[74] But over the entire Twelfth Five-Year Plan the number of pupils sent to Slavic republic PTUs was supposed to be 25,000,[75] and in fact, to judge from the total of 3,100 sent in 1986, even this number may not have been met.[76] By contrast, in much less populous Tajikistan, the proportion of PTU graduates who "studied abroad" was much larger. It was planned to send 27,000 young people over the Twelfth Five-Year Plan to "study abroad," and in 1986 alone, approximately 6,000 went. Based on a total planned PTU contingent in the five-year plan for Tajikistan of 147,000, the 27,000 to be sent represented almost a fifth of those to be trained.[77] Even based on the figure of 9,500 who were trained in PTUs abroad during the previous five-year plan,[78] the proportion was much greater than in Uzbekistan. Turkmenia was more active in sending young people to PTUs "abroad" than Uzbekistan, but not as active as Tajikistan. In the Eleventh Five-Year Plan, 4,280 pupils from Turkmenia completed PTUs in the RSFSR,[79] and it was planned to send 8,000 to the Slavic republics in the course of the Twelfth Five-Year Plan.[80]

There is evidence that many PTU students sent to other republics were from poor families and had few other attractive opportunities. This is also suggested by the relatively low prestige of a PTU education. A report from a Kirgiz youth studying in a PTU of the RSFSR recounts that "To tell the truth, at the *uchilishche* we even enjoy privileges. We do not pay for food. And we are given free uniforms because many of the guys are from poor families with many children."[81]

Overview of Results

In the late 1980s, the Soviet Central Asian press devoted an enormous amount of attention to publicizing all of the programs described above. Besides frequent notices of opportunities to work or study in Slavic republics or to move away, there were also many articles which described the life of individuals or families who had made the move. Other materials described problems in the administration of the programs. But for all the publicity, the results were extremely meager.

In considering the effectiveness of efforts to encourage Central Asians to move outside of their traditional homelands, it should be noted that there are certain conditions under which members of Central Asian nationalities have exhibited high rates of migration. According to one Soviet scholar, Central Asians living outside of their home republics in fact have "higher indicators of migration intensity than Russians."[82] In their home republics, however, Central Asians are less mobile than the Slavs who live among them. Even in the mid-1980s, in Kirgizia, Tajikistan, and Turkmenia, the indigenous nationality accounted for less than one-third of those who moved, while in Uzbekistan, they accounted for slightly over one-third.[83]

Not surprisingly, a large proportion of those who move are young people. In an apparent reference to Uzbekistan, one scholar noted that the "migrational mobility" of those in the age group 20–24 was nine times higher than among the population at large, and even among the age group 15–19 years it was five times higher than that of the whole population.[84] In this same pattern, young people made up a very large proportion of the migrants from Central Asia to other parts of the USSR. In the case of Uzbekistan, over half of the heads of families who migrated to the RSFSR in 1985 were under thirty years old.[85]

But as a whole, migrational mobility in Central Asia in the mid-1980s was still much less than in other parts of the country. In 1983, 25 of every 1,000 urban dwellers in the entire USSR and 9 of every 1,000 rural dwellers "took part in migration." The analogous figures for Central Asia's most populous republic, Uzbekistan, were 14 and 7.[86] Moreover, whereas for the USSR as a whole only two-thirds of village inhabitants lived in their native villages, this was true for at least four-fifths of village inhabitants in Tajikistan, Kirgizia, and Turkmenia, and nine-tenths of those in Uzbekistan.[87]

Although there was substantial migration from Soviet Central Asia to other regions of the country in the 1980s, much of it was negated by migration into the region from other parts of the USSR. Indeed, until the middle of the 1970s the influx exceeded the out-migration. For the four Central Asian republics as a whole, the balance *into* the region from 1971–75 was 109,000.[88] At the beginning of the 1970s, the migration balance out of the republic was positive only for Kirgizia, and it passed the break-even point for Tajikistan, Uzbekistan, and Turkmenia only in 1975–76.[89] The average number of migrants who left Uzbekistan for other republics between 1976 and 1986 was about 23,000 to 24,000.[90] Although out-migration continues to surpass in-migration, it is of special importance here to note that this has been largely due to a greater number of urban residents of *non-indigenous* nationalities who have left.[91] Many of the members of the non-indigenous nationalities who leave are workers who have skills needed in Central Asia.[92]

Writing in the mid-1980s, one Soviet scholar noted that the development of migration in Central Asia in recent years had been above all "an intensification of the out-migration of the non-indigenous population from the cities."[93] Another stated "there are few individuals of the indigenous nationalities among those who are leaving Central Asia." Their observations are confirmed by statistics that no more than 10 percent of the families from Uzbekistan participating in the "organized agricultural resettlement" were Uzbek families.[94]

The low out-migration of Central Asians is also evident from recent population statistics. According to the 1989 census, there was a total of only 248,000 members of the four major Central Asian nationalities (Uzbeks, Kirgiz, Tajiks, and Turkmens) living in the entire RSFSR, the USSR's largest republic. This is only about 140,000 more than at the time of the 1970 census. Thus, even including births of Central Asians in that republic, between 1970 and 1989 the number in the RSFSR increased by an average of around only 7,000 per year.[95]

The extent of participation by indigenous Central Asians in the programs described here varied greatly from one program to the next. Although I have found no data to confirm this, it is likely that almost all of those who moved to set up homes in newly developed agricultural regions of Uzbekistan were members of the indigenous nationalities. Likewise, the Central Asians comprised the large majority in PTU training programs in the Slavic republics: almost 96 percent of those who went from Turkmenia to study in PTUs of the RSFSR during the last four years of the Eleventh Five-Year Plan were Turkmens.[96] On the other hand, most of the recruited labor force from Central Asia that went to work elsewhere was Slavic. As late as 1986, Uzbeks, who comprised approximately 70 percent of Uzbekistan's population, accounted for less than 10 percent of those who migrated to live on farms outside of the republic.[97] Likewise, a later report from Kirgizia recognized that few who went from that republic to work in distant parts of the USSR were Kirgiz.[98] And the programs for recruited labor in Tajikistan were also said to attract "few of the indigenous nationality."[99]

Dropouts

The Central Asians who volunteered to work away from home for extended periods or to move away often did not stay in their "new" place of residence or employment very long. Of the 3,000 young people who were sent to the Slavic republics in 1986 by the Uzbekistan State Labor Committee, only 300 remained as of the beginning of 1988.[100] And it is reported that most Tajiks from Tajikistan who left the republic through labor recruitment programs soon came back to Tajikistan.[101]

The Komsomol shock projects do not appear to have "kept" the Central Asians they attracted any better. Of the 500 young people from Uzbekistan who went to work on three projects in Tiumen oblast in 1986, only 58 remained at the end of 1987.[102] Available figures for specific oblasts reflect the same trend. Over one-third of those sent to various all-Union shock projects from the Tashkent oblast Komsomol quit within one year,[103] and of the 80 volunteers from the Andizhan oblast Komsomol who went to the Belovoshakhstroi project, half had left within fifteen days.[104] As a result of this phenomenon, Central Asians were underrepresented on shock projects outside their region: the proportion of Uzbeks, Tajiks, Kirgiz, and Turkmens working on the much-touted BAM (*Baikal-Amurskii magistral'*, a trans-Siberian railroad) was lower than these nationalities' proportion of the Soviet population by a factor of twelve.[105]

Those who moved away from home with the expressed intention of permanently resettling frequently did not return to their former place of residence even if they were dissatisfied with their new surroundings. Although less than half of the 1,014 families who resettled from Turkmenia to Amur oblast during the Eleventh Five-Year Plan remained at their "new home," many of those who left did not return to Turkmenia because they felt they would be laughed at and shamed by "the local elders and their relatives" there. One Soviet observer of this phenomenon remarked, "Thus we propagate nomads who will hardly be able to settle down, and thus live a full-blooded life and work full force."[106] Although, as will be argued below, nationality-related factors play a very important role in adaptability to new surroundings, some resettlement projects within the same republic did not "keep" their new inhabitants, either. For every 100 workers who were resettled in Uzbekistan's labor-short Kashkadarya oblast in 1980, 69 left in that same year.[107]

Even though young Central Asians who went to PTUs in the Slavic republics were supposed to be away for less than a year, a significant number returned even sooner. Four hundred (about 5 percent) of those who went from Tajikistan during the Eleventh Five-Year Plan returned home without finishing their courses; in 1986, the number was reduced to about 3 percent (192 our of 6,000).[108] To judge from the experience of one of the PTUs in Ivanovo oblast where pupils from Tashkent were sent, Uzbekistan's track record was worse: "almost half" of the fourteen pupils "ran away" from their school.[109] Although the rate at which they deserted is unclear, the same problem clearly affected Turkmen pupils.[110]

The difficulty which such programs had in recruiting volunteers indicates the lack of prestige enjoyed by these "PTUs abroad." Kirgizia, for example, was annually supposed to send 1,000 young people, mainly Kirgiz, to study in PTUs of Slavic republics. Yet in early 1987 there were only 510.[111] The city of Ashkhabad (Turkmenia's capital) annually fell about 100 short in its recruitment for these same institutions.[112] It was especially difficult to recruit women. In the case of Uzbekistan, Uzbek women comprised only 6 percent of the young people who went to study in PTUs of other republics in 1986.[113]

Although not necessarily a reflection of the training which they received "abroad," it should be noted that in fact many of the young people sent to the Slavic republics did not in the end take employment in the areas for which they received training. In part this may be due to administrative problems. In 1987, only 600 of the 2,000 who returned to Tajikistan after training in Slavic republic PTUs were given jobs through job placement agencies (*organy po trudu*). Most found work their specialty."¹¹⁴ In Turkmenia, many ... returned to their homes on collective ... they left for studies.¹¹⁵ Moreover, sometimes ... learned abroad were not even needed ... students were trained in the Slavic republics ... car mechanics, even though none of these ... supply in Tajikistan.¹¹⁶

The Problem: External Objective Factors

... divide the reasons for the failure of the above programs ... categories. One category concerns what might be termed ... "objective factors," i.e., the shortcomings in the organization, ... content and other factors of the program itself.¹¹⁷ The ... category concerns shortcomings in the students' beliefs, skills ... Although most of the focus of the remainder of this ... will be on the second category, it will be useful first to mention ... the most important external objective factors.

... of these circumstances was the difficult physical conditions in ... volunteers frequently found themselves. Many of the projects ... in Siberia and other places with harsh climates. Housing on many ... projects was crowded and primitive for newcomers, who sometimes had to live temporarily in trailers. Some housing facilities lacked hot water, gas, and even electricity. On many projects it was not possible to bring along family members. Other locations lacked leisure and educational facilities.

The effect of these conditions was compounded by the inflated promises which were made during recruitment for the above opportunities. Sometimes young people were promised housing, recreation, or educational opportunities which were entirely unrealistic. On one occasion volunteers for resettlement in new areas of Uzbekistan were falsely led to believe that they would receive individual houses and garden plots.¹¹⁸ Pupils reluctant to volunteer to study in the Slavic republic PTUs were misled to believe that they would learn desirable specialties—trades in which instruction was actually not even available at those PTUs.¹¹⁹

A major reason for dissatisfaction with work on shock projects was that many young people who had been lured by the prospect of high earnings soon discovered that they would not get rich as fast as they anticipated.¹²⁰ In order to combat unrealistic expectations, some articles warned prospective volunteers that although the wages were good, the really high earnings went only to those who worked very hard and remained for a prolonged period at one project.¹²¹

The conditions which young Central Asians encountered [...] a result of neglect or improper treatment by the organizati[ons] sent and received them. For example, once students were sent to study in PTUs, their home institutions and Komsomol org[ans] frequently felt they had fulfilled their responsibility and so forg[ot] the pupils' needs.[122] More often, the failure to provide good co[nditions] lay with the receiving projects or institutions. They were said [to dem]onstrate a "lack of necessary care."[123] Administrative confusi[on was] blamed when 60 of the 100 young people sent to a Komsomol [shock] project in Tiumen returned after only three months.[124] Some ve[ntures] were even stripped of their privileged status as shock projects be[cause] of failure to provide suitable living conditions for participants.[125] [Even] in the case of the very short-term summer student detachments, receiv[ing] organizations were not prepared to make good use of the availa[ble] hands,[126] and sometimes failed to provide necessary materials a[nd] equipment.[127] While in some cases these shortcomings were a result [of] inattention by overburdened organizations, in other cases the organi[-]zations' attempts to exploit programs inappropriately were at fault. Some PTUs which accepted young people from Tajikistan were said to do this as a way of "making up for their own shortcomings in filling their PTUs."[128]

Although no hint of this could be printed in the early 1980s, as glasnost broadened toward the end of the decade it became increasingly clear that newcomers from far away were often the object of discrimination. The potential for this was greatest in migration to distant parts of the USSR, but it also sometimes occurred to those who had moved within the same republic. For example, it was alleged that settlers from Fergana to labor-short regions of Uzbekistan were sometimes unable to get good jobs in their new locales because of "localism."[129]

These external, objective factors take on special importance in light of the attitudes, desires, expectations, and skills of the majority of today's indigenous Central Asian youth. As we will see, on the whole Central Asian young people lacked (and still lack) the skills and qualities which suitable candidates for a difficult move to another area of the country should possess.

Intractable Roots: Beliefs, Skills, and Attitudes

Much of the disagreement among Western scholars in the late Brezhnev era about the likelihood of migration from Central Asia to other parts of the USSR revolved around the importance of language, education, and factors related to ethnic consciousness and traditional beliefs. Such observers as Feshbach believed that these considerations posed a major impediment to Central Asians' migration outside of their region. Others, such as Lewis, Rowland and Clem, felt that economic factors were decisive. Although it is beyond the scope of this chapter to provide a detailed examination of the economic costs and benefits which Central Asians weigh as they contemplate migration, we will return to this question below. But before doing this we will reconsider the seriousness of the factors emphasized by Feshbach as they developed in the early and mid-1980s.

Attachment to Native Land, Ethnic Consciousness, and Traditional Beliefs

Without the kind of serious survey research which is only now being undertaken in Soviet Central Asia, it is still impossible to quantify in any meaningful way the importance of these factors in Central Asians' decisions of whether to migrate. However, it is clear from the Soviet Central Asian press and from modifications in policy that the Communist Party leadership acknowledged the importance of these ingredients and increasingly recognized that they did affect migration.

One of the most important reasons for Central Asians' (especially rural inhabitants') reluctance to migrate was (and is) their attachment to their native village or region and their very strong family ties. The editor of a Russian-language literary journal in Uzbekistan, for example, referred to the "blind love for one's native village and unwillingness to step beyond the confines of the family" which "acutely affect the economy."[130] Other authors were critical of young people who did not "want to see anything beyond their own village or raion."[131]

The significance of the same factors was recognized in the cases of Central Asians who returned "home" from life outside the republic or even in distant regions of the same republic. In this context the first secretary of the Tajikistan Komsomol cited the problem of Central Asians' "attachment to the home of their parents, where life with their parents provides them an imaginary stability and peace."[132] These feelings also caused people to return home from places where they had resettled within the same republic. Young people who left for other areas of Uzbekistan returned to their village of Sina in Surkhandarya oblast— even though there were no prospects of employment because, they said, "We grew up here."[133]

The Islamic environment is one of the strongest facets of "home" which Central Asians who leave the region are likely to miss.[134] At home Central Asians are part of a Muslim religious and social community. This is lacking in most other areas of the USSR. During the past decade Soviet scholars, journalists, and Party officials have all begun to recognize that Islam is an integral part of life in Central Asia. It is common knowledge that most of the Central Asian intelligentsia is very observant of such Islamic life cycle ceremonies as male circumcision (not widely practiced in the Soviet Union outside of Muslim areas), religious weddings and funerals. Some even participate in pilgrimages to holy sites. According to one survey, 42 percent of the students at Samarkand University (where the large majority of students are of indigenous nationalities) believe in God and 40 percent have positive attitudes towards religious ceremonies.[135] Many Central Asian youth who do not participate in religious ceremonies nevertheless display positive feelings towards Islam by wearing fashionable crescents and amulets with a religious significance.[136]

The maintenance of Islam has been supported by a number of social and demographic factors over which the Party has very limited control. Muslim families still tend to be large, age is venerated, and children are likely to spend much of their time with religious mothers and grandmothers. Even when religious practice was more actively discouraged young people frequently claimed not to be believers but said that they nevertheless observed religious rituals, such as weddings, so as "not to offend" their elders.[137] Soviet Central Asian young people, like their elders, confuse religion with nationality and see religious practices as "national" ones.[138] The confusion is evident from the responses to a survey conducted by the Uzbek-language Komsomol newspaper; some 50 participants filled the space provided for their *nationality* with the word "Muslim."[139]

Islam has also shown great vitality in Central Asia because it has adapted to the *sovetskaia deistvitel'nost'* ("Soviet reality"). *Mullahs* sometimes bless recruits before the young men leave for military service, parents often organize circumcision of male children when they enter school, and young couples frequently follow their ZAGS (official registry office) weddings with visits to mosques.

Recognizing the importance of the above factors, some Soviet scholars suggested that in order to encourage migration it was necessary to attenuate "those things which are connected with customs and traditions" in the Central Asian population's "need structure."[140] In the same spirit, *Izvestiia* published a call by the first secretary of the Tashkent oblast Komsomol committee to "defeat the inertia of [youth's] attachment to the 'land of their forefathers' and develop in them a desire 'to change places.'"[141]

But on the whole (as Rorlich's chapter in this volume demonstrates), policies of the Gorbachev era reflect a recognition that reinforcing old forms of anti-religious propaganda is not likely to be effective. In fact, in 1988 major Party policy pronouncements offered signs that the regime was ready to provide a more propitious setting for religious observance by Muslims living outside historically Muslim regions. The resolution on "cross-national relations" adopted at the Nineteenth Party Conference specifically called for efforts to provide more opportunities to "nationalities living outside the borders of their state-territorial formations" for realization of a variety of national-cultural needs. Among the areas listed was "satisfaction of religious requirements."[142]

Although it is likely that the resolution was written primarily with other populations in mind (in particular, those groups which *already* have large populations living outside their traditional homeland or, as noted in the resolution, those without state-territorial formations) it contained other provisions which might improve the availability of other products and services (e.g., educational institutions, mass media, and cultural institutions) and thus make the environment in other parts of the USSR less "alien" to the Central Asians.

This resolution reflected modest concrete measures in the same direction which had been taken in the immediately preceding few years. Thus, Central Asian music ensembles went to Siberia to entertain people there,[143] and native-language books were sent to PTU pupils studying "abroad"[144] as well as to those working on shock Komsomol projects.[145] And, at least according to the picture provided by one journalist, it had also become possible to hold a very traditional wedding ceremony in such a distant region as the Soviet Far East.[146]

Of course it is much easier to provide cultural facilities for Central Asians outside of their region if they live relatively close together. There are indications that as the Party recognized the problems associated with resettlement, officials began to take this into account. In 1988, plans for future arrivals from Turkmenia to the Far East called for the settlers to live on compact communes. Commenting on this, an official involved in this resettlement remarked, "After all, it's no secret how hard it is to adapt to a new place of residence, but that's if you're alone. But if you have your fellow-countrymen with you, your comrades . . . it will be much easier."[147] The author of another article in the all-Union Komsomol journal *Molodoi kommunist* emphasized the "kindred" (*rodstvenno-zemliacheskii*) principle in attracting new migrants and noted that specialists recommended resettlement in compact groups with opportunities to keep ties with their home republics.[148] This idea was also followed in the case of at least some of the pupils who "studied abroad" from the mid-1980s on. One of the principles followed in sending Tajiks to PTUs in Slavic republics was said to be "sending them only in groups."[149]

Despite all of this, however, it is doubtful that the ersatz traditional life away from home was or will be satisfactory, let alone attractive, to the Central Asians. Even with greater encouragement from Moscow, it is equally unclear how much of the cultural life of home the local Party or government organizations on the receiving end would support, encourage, or even permit. There are, after all, financial costs which local authorities in (for example) Western Siberia, might well be unwilling to bear for the promotion of Turkmen culture, let alone for the establishment of Turkmen-language schools. One of the crucial tests may be the attitude towards Islam. Despite the section of the Party conference resolution cited above, it may be especially difficult to convince local authorities, say in Siberia, to allow construction of a mosque, to accommodate Muslims who wish to fast during Ramadan, or to provide meat other than pork.

Educational Factors

In their 1976 work, Lewis, Rowland, and Clem pointed to improved Central Asian educational levels among the younger generation as a factor not only permitting, but indeed *encouraging* out-migration. Basing their assessment on the "dramatic rise" in educational attainment in both rural and urban areas of the region, they rejected the idea that rural Central Asians were a homogeneous group of uneducated, traditional Muslims. According to Lewis, Roland, and Clem, such a view was "very static," "not representative of reality," and "applicable only to the older cohorts."[150] Recent evidence, however, confirms Feshbach's warning about the questionable nature of Soviet statistics on rural educational attainment in Central Asia and indicates that education is indeed a factor which impedes migration.

Indeed, many Soviet scholars feel that educational (rather than cultural and religious) factors are of crucial importance. Anvar Chamkin, for one, has rejected as "unconvincing" the argument that the main reasons for the Central Asian indigenous population's low migrational mobility are "traditions" and "behavior characteristics."[151] Such scholars see technical skills as a more important brake on movement out of the region.

In illustrating that poor instruction in Central Asia hinders movement out of the region, Chamkin noted that labor education in Central Asian rural schools is based on "routine" techniques and technologies which do not prepare people to work in new fields.[152] Another Soviet scholar also claimed that Central Asian rural youth's lack of professional preparation to work in industrial sectors was a major reason for low migrational mobility,[153] while a third concerned with the problems of the Central Asian labor surplus simply said, "Let us be frank; [rural Central Asian youth] are prepared only for unskilled manual agricultural labor."[154] Even Chamkin, however, recognized the link between attitudes and inadequate skills. He claimed that Central Asians were "inwardly unprepared to take up an unfamiliar activity."[155]

The Soviet press confirms the importance of these skills: the announcements of opportunities outside the republic, described above, often stated that only those with the requisite skills should apply.[156] The press also carried many tales of problems due to "volunteers'" inadequate preparation. The contingent from Uzbekistan which moved to the Soviet Far East included many former waiters, bartenders, and taxi drivers, whose skills were not needed.[157] Of those sent to Komsomol construction projects from Kirgizia, almost half lacked appropriate specialties.[158] This lack of preparation was also said to lie behind a high turnover rate.[159] In general, those sent through organized labor recruitment from Uzbekistan to other republics included many who were "professionally unprepared."[160] Even in the case of Central Asians sent to PTUs of Slavic republics, poor educational background was a problem. For example, some Tajiks "sent abroad" had to spend two months of their year's studies on remedial work.[161]

Russian language fluency is an especially important skill for Central Asians' migration to or study abroad in other republics of the USSR. Attitudes undoubtedly also affect Central Asians' willingness to learn Russian. With the exception of military service, most rural youth encounter few occasions in which they cannot get by with their native language and very minimal Russian skills, and so they are likely to view learning Russian as an unnecessary burden.

It is not surprising, then, that some of the Central Asians who went to Slavic republics for PTU training were described as having only "minimal vocabulary" in Russian and requiring interpreters in order to communicate.[162] The language problem was especially serious for those who were supposed to learn more advanced technical specialties.[163] The Central Asian students' lack of Russian language skills was also said to impede social interaction with young people of other nationalities.[164]

In addition to the obvious effect that inadequate Russian language skills have on Central Asians' quality of life outside of their region, the full effect of weak language preparation on migration is incalculable because its impact is indirect and invisible. As individuals contemplating migration consider whether to move, they must certainly weigh the factor of the isolation which lack of Russian skills is likely to create.

Despite government efforts to improve Central Asia's educational system, the obstacles in the 1980s were enormous *and they remain so today.* Many of the more general Soviet educational problems of teacher shortages, poor facilities, and interruptions of the school year due to agricultural labor are worse in Central Asia than elsewhere in the country.

In the case of the teacher shortage, Uzbekistan alone had 7,500 unfilled positions in 1988.[165] The worst situation involved Russian language teachers: in 1987, the republic had 1,400 too few of them. Among other specialties, it also lacked 1,000 mathematics teachers, 500 chemistry teachers, and 340 biology teachers.[166] One of the ways of dealing with the shortage undoubtedly contributes to the profession's already low prestige. Teachers are often required to take on heavy loads and teach subjects outside of their specialties. (The latter situation applies to about one in eight teachers in Turkmenia.[167]) Aside from all else, Central Asian teachers are far more overburdened with non-teaching activities than their colleagues in other parts of the USSR.[168] Many are routinely "volunteered" to help harvest cotton, clean drainage ditches, and work on street patrols until late in the night.[169]

To make matters worse, new teachers often have a weak mastery of pedagogical techniques in even their "specialty" subjects. Turkmenia's Minister of Education described a "vicious circle" in which the secondary school produced unprepared graduates, who later returned from higher educational institutions and teaching colleges to the village as poor teachers.[170] Another problem has been teachers who quit their jobs or refuse to report for their assignments.[171] In Uzbekistan 23,000 teachers abandoned their positions in the course of a two-year period.[172]

Education in Central Asia is also plagued by a severely inadequate physical plant and by equipment shortages. Many schools are housed in structures originally built for other purposes or are in need of major repair[173]; they often operate in shifts,[174] and they are poorly heated in winter. Many lack cafeterias and most have no gymnasium.[175] In one of Turkmenia's oblasts approximately 60 percent of the schools in 1987 held classes in clay buildings, and nearly one-fourth of the total were in serious disrepair.[176] An indication of the relative state of Central Asia's schools is that in 1988 the equipment expenditures per pupil in Tajikistan's capital (Dushanbe) were only one-sixth of the Soviet average.[177]

Although in line with the new educational reform which was to be implemented in the late 1980s young people were supposed to learn such skills as metal-working and carpentry, at the time, 40 percent of Uzbekistan's schools lacked metalworking shops, and half had no woodworking shops.[178] The equipment for labor education which the schools do have is often outmoded and that which the pupils receive to work on is of poor quality.[179]

In most aspects Central Asian school facilities lag far behind even rural areas of the rest of the country. Whereas in the mid-1980s only 9 percent of rural secondary schools in the entire USSR lacked *kabinety* (instructional materials and equipment rooms) for biology, this was the case in 30 percent of the rural secondary schools in Tajikistan and 24 percent in Turkmenia.[180] And whereas in the Ukraine and Belorussia there were an average of thirty tractors for every agricultural PTU, in Uzbekistan there were only nine.[181] On the whole, one estimate indicates that Uzbekistan's rural PTUs have only a fifth or a sixth of the average technical facilities available to rural PTUs throughout the USSR.[182] Compounding the difficulties listed above is the fact that despite prohibitions of the practice, (at least late into the 1980s) pupils were still frequently removed from the classroom for prolonged periods in order to perform urgent agricultural work.[183]

Lack of a Social Conscience

The Western scholarly literature has paid little attention to the possibility of selfless patriotism as a factor motivating migration by young people out of Central Asia. Indeed, the prospects for such unselfish behavior by most Central Asians seemed remote in the mid-1980s and today they are virtually nil. However, it is worth briefly considering this aspect of the problem for two reasons. One is that until very recently the Soviet press pointed to such motivation as an important factor. Secondly, the gap between the selflessness which might motivate migration and the reality has widened to unprecedented proportions.

One example which described the idealistic motivation for migration to a distant location appeared in a March 1988 article in *Komsomolets Uzbekistana*. It reasoned "It isn't easy to tear oneself away from familiar places and to go to an unknown area to work in difficult and sometimes even severe climatic conditions." "But," the article continued, "there is such a word as 'must.' And someone—strong, brave, and skillful—must be a pioneer. He must be an example to the others."[184] The articles about pioneers who attempted to inspire others to follow positive examples told of individuals who felt a sense of obligation not only before their own republic or nationality, but before the entire Soviet people; such individuals were said to be willing to make sacrifices to provide "fraternal help." These models were often willing even to change careers: one Turkmen youth who was portrayed as unconcerned that he might not find a job which used his skills was reported to say, "If there is no work for an electrician on the kolkhoz where we move, I'll learn to be a farm equipment operator."[185]

For decades the Party used the external imperialist threat as one of its arguments to convince young people of the need to sacrifice. Even in 1986, Komsomol members were called upon to volunteer for a detachment because "While imperialism clangs its weapons, futilely hoping to frighten us, the Soviet people, including every Komsomol member, must be at the place where his conscience dictates, and where every one of us can be of maximum service to the Homeland."[186] But in the late 1980s the Party abandoned that effort. It is evident that today few Soviet youth view the "hostile" West as a threat. For many, the West represents a popular culture and life style which they seek to imitate.

Despite the occasional appearance of an ideal model, the Soviet press in the era of glasnost has published many articles which recognize that most Soviet youth do not at all resemble the models. For example, one story in Uzbekistan's daily *Pravda Vostoka* reported that over 12,000 Komsomol members in Dzhizak oblast alone "sat at home" rather than work or study, even when their help was needed for urgent agricultural tasks. Commenting on this, the reporter asked, "What kind of good things can one expect from a person who is just beginning adult life and is already looking for ways to avoid difficulties and social responsibility?"[187] Many young people were also said to "exhibit passivity in social-political life" and "be carried away by an obsession with material things (*veshchizm*) . . ."[188]

In the 1980s, the press frequently identified the lack of a social conscience and the preoccupation with money and consumer goods as reasons for young people's unwillingness to move. Sometimes it noted that this lack of social consciousness led to criminal behavior. A correspondent for *Komsomolets Uzbekistana* suggested that the reason why many young people refused to move to other areas of their republic (and instead remain in their home village without official employment) was that at home they could make large sums of money by growing opium poppies.[189]

A substantial number of those who did volunteer to migrate to new locations were said to go for the "wrong" reasons. Many Central Asians who joined detachments to work at Komsomol shock construction projects were described as violators of labor discipline, rolling stones, and in search of high wages and adventure; some even had police records.[190] Others who volunteered did "not want to work in an honest fashion"[191] or began to "demand both high salaries and apartments" immediately after resettlement.[192]

Not surprisingly, these same inappropriate attitudes were also blamed for the high dropout rate among migrants. Some of the Turkmens who "migrated" to the Far East were said to be "self-seekers, birds of passage, and rolling stones" who in fact intended to "migrate" only for a short time.[193]

Attitudes posed a special problem with regard to studying "abroad" in PTUs. As noted above, throughout the Soviet Union a PTU education has little or no prestige. But according to Soviet survey research, in the late Brezhnev era, the percentage of upper-grade pupils in Uzbekistan and Turkmenistan intending to enter PTUs was "significantly lower than in other areas of the country."[194] At least in part due to such attitudes, in the mid-1980s only 9.7 percent of the fifteen- to nineteen-year-olds in the USSR as a whole were studying in PTUs, while the analogous figure in Uzbekistan was only 5.6 percent.[195] The disinclination of Central Asians to enter PTUs applied particularly to technical skills which could be applied in industry. Despite the fact that Uzbeks comprised over two-thirds of Uzbekistan's population, they accounted for only 20 percent of those learning industrial trades in the republic's PTUs.[196]

Among those Central Asians who volunteered to study in Slavic republic PTUs, some went along "for the ride," and were soon sent back home by the institutions which received them.[197] Others quit their studies when they found out that they were being prepared for such unglamorous work as an "ordinary" painter, tailor, or turner.[198] And many of those who actually completed the PTU courses did so for selfish reasons. Some of them saw the PTU as the best way to enhance their chances for the much more selective higher educational institutions.[199]

Conclusion

In the conclusion to their 1976 book, Lewis, Rowland, and Clem stated that it was "obvious" that "when the economic crunch is on, people will migrate to other areas even if the movement is to an area with a different culture and less favorable climate." Therefore, in their opinion, although cultural and climatic advantages of a homeland may impede migration to another area, they "do not completely stop it."[200] As one looks at the current situation in Central Asia it is clear that the economy of the region is rapidly approaching or has already arrived at an economic crisis.

Why, then, have Central Asians been so reluctant to move to other areas of the USSR where they could find jobs and presumably enjoy a standard of living higher than in Central Asia? It must be assumed that on balance the vast majority of Central Asians still feel that the benefits of life in their region outweigh those available to them elsewhere. And while it is impossible to prove the degree of importance of the factors of culture, education, skill, and attitude described in this chapter, the growing evidence is that they are a far greater "drag" on migration than predicted by Lewis, Rowland, and Clem. Moreover, the broader interethnic tensions in recent years have probably made Central Asians feel that they would be even less welcome than before in most other regions of the country.

Most of the programs described in this chapter have received substantially less coverage and promotion in the Central Asian republic press since 1989. In the past couple of years the Komsomol papers cited above have rarely printed reports about their republic youths accepting temporary or permanent work assignments far away from home. True, the republic papers publish unadorned announcements of opportunities to move to the RSFSR. But they also carry articles which maintain that migration out of the region accomplishes nothing useful. Some of these arguments have linked Central Asians' working outside of their own region with an undesirable influx of outsiders (presumably Slavs) to Central Asian cities.[201] One Uzbek author who openly disapproved of these processes asked, "What will the future be like for the Uzbek families living in the endless expanses of Russia, an entirely alien environment?" Instead of calling on Uzbeks to consider their broader Soviet homeland (as was typical in the mid-1980s), this author stated, "There is nothing more precious or sacred for the Uzbek than his motherland. Even in the face of the most difficult tragedies our people has not abandoned the motherland, nor will it do so."[202] In less poetic fashion, two scholars have warned that "people are not equipment that can be moved around from place to place."[203] And in the words of a Turkmen writer, resettlement programs have been "contrived, ineffective, and, in the end, hardly needed by anyone."[204]

Some data suggest that "study abroad" may actually have grown at the level of higher education in recent years.[205] However, at the same time, the whole concept of sending organized groups of Central Asians to Slavic republics' PTUs seems to be under reconsideration. Some authors recognize that the problems more than outweigh any benefits, and they point to entire oblasts in the RSFSR which have refused to accept any more organized groups of PTU students from Central Asia.[206]

To return to the question of migration, it would, of course, be possible for the Soviet government to provide greater financial incentives to promote movement to labor-short regions of the country. Indeed, perhaps Gorbachev's policies intended to promote economic rationality will make it possible for the financial attraction of resettlement to rise. But this is most likely to draw the Slavic population from Central Asia before the indigenous nationalities. As indicated above, Russians and other Slavs already comprise a disproportionately large segment of the people from Central Asia who resettle to agricultural land in the Far East or volunteer for Komsomol shock construction projects. And the growing ethnic tensions in Central Asia are reinforcing the same trends for Slavs to leave the region. Unless the Soviet government were to differentiate financial or housing incentives for migration by nationality, which is highly unlikely, additional inducement to move out of Central Asia would accentuate the trend of a declining Slavic population in the region. To the extent that the indigenous population of the Central Asian republics becomes an even greater majority, this would complicate maintenance of Moscow's political control in the region.

The other set of circumstances under which life in labor-short regions of the country might become relatively attractive to large numbers of Central Asians is if the standard of living in Central Asia should decline. Alas, this deterioration is likely to materialize. In this case too, presumably, many of the Slavs would lead the migration out of Central Asia, but a large number of indigenous nationality Central Asians might leave as well. While this could help alleviate the excess labor problem in Central Asia and provide some workers for labor-short regions, this decline in the standard of living in Central Asia would bring on a host of serious new quandaries.

On the one hand, the Party would inevitably face increased ethnic tensions produced by the arrival of large numbers of Central Asians in Slavic regions and competition for scarce consumer goods, housing, and educational facilities. These are precisely the types of tensions which Lewis, Rowland, and Clem referred to in their 1976 work.[207] In turn, these could become factors reinforcing Central Asians' disinclination to migrate to other regions.

But there is another response to the "economic crunch" which is already in evidence. Rather than leave their native republics in order to enjoy higher standards of living elsewhere, Central Asians are beginning to demand that the Communist Party and Soviet government take measures to raise the standards of living in their native region. The most vocal proponents of such steps have been the creative intelligentsia, many of whom now see it as their mission to "awaken their people" to the crisis situation. Among other things, prominent Central Asian writers now publicly demand a higher state purchasing price for locally produced raw materials, control of the hard currency receipts for those materials, much greater investment in the educational and social service infrastructure, and stricter controls on pollution.[208]

At the time that Feshbach, and Lewis, Rowland, and Clem made their predictions about the likelihood of migration out of Central Asia, few could imagine the political reforms which would have made the public expression and dissemination of these sentiments possible in the USSR at present. However, today the Soviet Union seems to face a prolonged period in which ethnic ingredients aggravate the country's most serious economic and social problems. Perhaps in the distant future, in a "Soviet Union" with genuine political decentralization and a labor market responsive to rational economic criteria, Central Asians will willingly migrate to the Far East, Siberia, or the non-black earth region. However, in light of the degree to which the national problem in the USSR is still "unsolved," the factors described above seem sufficient to assure that by and large Central Asians will remain in their traditional homelands. Any wishes by the Party leadership for a mass migration of Central Asians to other parts of the USSR, and for their contribution thereby to a more socially stable, homogeneous, and prosperous society, seem farther than ever from fulfillment.

Notes

1. Robert A. Lewis, Richard H. Rowland, and Ralph S. Clem, *Nationality and Population Change in Russia and the USSR: An Evaluation of Census Data, 1897-1970* (New York: Praeger Publishers, 1976), pp. 380-81.

2. Robert A. Lewis and Richard H. Rowland, *Population Redistribution in the USSR: Its Impact on Society 1897-1977* (New York: Praeger Publishers, 1979), p. 424.

3. Ibid., p. 415.

4. Murray Feshbach, "Prospects for Migration from Central Asia and Kazakhstan in the Next Decade," in *Soviet Economy in a Time of Change* (U.S. Congress, Joint Economic Committee, 1979), p. 656.

5. Murray Feshbach, "Population and Labor Force," in *The Soviet Economy: Toward the Year 2000*, ed. Abram Bergson and Herbert S. Levine (London: Allen & Unwin, 1983), p. 103.

6. Although this chapter is concerned with *organized* migration, it should be noted that this kind of organization represents only a small proportion of migrants. According to one Soviet source written in 1975, in the "recent" period before publication, organized migration accounted for not more than 12 percent of total Soviet migration (A. V. Topilin, *Territorial'noe pereraspredelenie trudovykh resursov v SSSR* [Moscow: Ekonomika, 1975], pp. 13-14, cited in Lewis and Rowland, *Population Redistribution*, p. 19). Nevertheless, most of the factors discussed here as relevant to organized migration are also relevant to spontaneous migration.

7. Among others, this figure includes non-working mothers and those working on subsidiary plots (*podsobnoe khoziaistvo*) (*Pravda Vostoka*, Jan. 16, 1988).

8. *Komsomolets Uzbekistana*, Feb. 21, 1987.

9. *Komsomolets Tadzhikistana*, Feb. 22, 1987.

10. *Komsomolets Tadzhikistana*, Jan. 20, 1987, translated in JPRS UPA-87-002, June 8, 1987, p. 17; *Komsomolets Turkmenistana*, Sept. 4, 86. The figure for Tajikistan is for 1987, while the one for Turkmenia refers to 1986.

11. *Pravda Vostoka*, Dec. 22, 1987.

12. *Komsomolets Uzbekistana*, Apr. 30, 1986.

13. This comment was made by economist M. A. Zaidov in a roundtable published in *Kommunist Uzbekistana*, no. 7, 1986, p. 64.

14. *Komsomolets Tadzhikistana*, Jan. 21, 1987.

15. *Kommunist Tadzhikistana*, Jan. 20, 1987, translated in JPRS UPA 87-002, June 8, 1987, p. 16.

16. *Pravda Vostoka*, Dec. 22, 1987.

17. *Komsomolets Turkmenistana*, Dec. 24, 1987.

18. *Pravda Vostoka,* Dec. 22, 1987. One "solution" to the excess rural labor and shortage of urban labor is commuting. In 1988, approximately 200,000 rural residents of Uzbekistan commuted up to fifty kilometers to work in Tashkent and other industrial centers (*Pravda Vostoka,* Apr. 10, 1988).

19. This land comprises much of southwest Uzbekistan, the lower reaches of the Amudarya, and the Dzhizak Steppe (M. Zaidov, "Effektivnee ispol'zovat' trudovye resursy Uzbekistana," *Kommunist Uzbekistana,* no. 10, 1986, p. 17).

20. *Komsomolets Uzbekistana,* Aug. 8, 1987.

21. Dmitrii Ziuzin, "Varianty sotsial'no-ekonomicheskogo razvitiia sredneaziatskogo regiona," *Sotsiologicheskie issledovaniia,* no. 4, 1986, p. 21, cited in Anne Bohr "Current Trends in Central Asian Labor Redistribution," *Radio Liberty Research* 508/87, Dec. 22, 1987.

22. *Materialy XXVII s"ezda Kommunisticheskoi partii Sovetskogo Soiuza* (Moscow: Politizdat, 1986), p. 317.

23. L. V. Makarova, G. F. Morozova, and N. V. Tarasova, *Regional'nye osobennosti migratsionnykh protsessov v SSSR* (Moscow: Nauka, 1986), p. 73.

24. *Turkmenskaia iskra,* Mar. 12, 1987, translated in JPRS UPA 87-019, Aug. 10, 1987, p. 97.

25. "Razmyshleniia o glavnom" (roundtable), *Zvezda Vostoka,* no. 9, 1987, p. 13.

26. *Pravda Vostoka,* Aug. 20, 1987.

27. *Molodezh' Azerbaidzhana,* July 9, 1987.

28. Ibid.

29. *Komsomolets Tadzhikistana,* July 4, 1986.

30. *Pravda Vostoka,* Aug. 20, 1987.

31. *Yash leninchi,* Dec. 9, 1986.

32. *Pravda Vostoka,* May 16, 1987.

33. See, for example, *Sovet Ozbekistani,* Feb. 13, 1987.

34. T. Mirzaev and L. Raskin, "Organizovannoe pereraspredelenie trudovykh resursov," *Kommunist Uzbekistana,* no. 1, 1987, p. 14.

35. *Pravda Vostoka,* Dec. 20, 1987.

36. *Komsomolets Uzbekistana,* Feb. 25, 1987.

37. Between March 1982 and February 1987, 10,000 had been sent from the UzSSR to all-Union shock projects and 9,000 to republic shock projects (*Komsomolets Uzbekistana,* Feb. 21, 1987).

38. This figure was provided by economist M. A. Zaidov in a roundtable published in *Kommunist Uzbekistana,* no. 7, 1986, p. 66.

39. *Yash leninchi,* Apr. 3, 1987.

40. *Komsomolets Uzbekistana,* Apr. 28, 1987.

41. Zaidov, *Kommunist Uzbekistana,* no. 7, 1986, p. 65.

42. *Sovet Ozbekistani,* Jan 9, 1985.

43. Mirzaev and Raskin, "Organizovannoe pereraspredelenie," p. 14.

44. *Sovet Ozbekistani,* Nov. 17, 1987.

45. *Kommunist Tadzhikistana,* Sept. 26, 1987.

46. *Pravda Vostoka,* Jan. 16, 1988.

47. Of those who left Uzbekistan annually in the mid-1970s, only about 5 percent went through the lines of organized recruitment (Mirzaev and Raskin,"Organizovannoe pereraspredelenie," p. 18).
48. *Pravda Vostoka*, Jan. 20, 1988; see also *Sovet Ozbekistani*, Feb. 5, 1988.
49. *Pravda Vostoka*, Jan. 3, 1987, reprinted from *Izvestiia*, Jan. 2, 1987.
50. *Pravda Vostoka*, May 16, 1987.
51. *Yash leninchi*, Jan. 13, 1988. For an account of happy Turkmen families in Amur oblast, see *Turkmenskaia Iskra*, Mar. 12 1987, translated in JPRS UPA 87-019, Aug. 10, 1987, p. 97.
52. *Pravda Vostoka*, Dec. 22, 1987.
53. *Sovet Ozbekistani*, Mar. 28, 1987.
54. *Komsomolets Uzbekistana*, May 23, 1987.
55. *Komsomolets Turkmenistana*, Sept. 9, 1986.
56. *Komsomolets Uzbekistana*, Sept. 2, 1987.
57. *Yash leninchi*, June 13, 1987.
58. *Komsomolets Uzbekistana*, May 23, 1987.
59. *Komsomolets Uzbekistana*, May 30, 1987 and *Komsomolets Tadzhikistana*, May 11, 1988.
60. *Sovet Ozbekistani*, July 7, 1987. Presumably this figure refers only to civilian higher educational institutions. A large proportion were sent to pedagogical institutes: in 1986–87, 3,000 Uzbek students were studying in pedagogical institutes of other republics (S. M. Liashchuk, "Pomoshch' bratskaia, internatsional'naia," *Russkii iazyk i literatura v uzbekskoi shkole*, no. 5, 1986, p. 48).
61. *Tekhnikums* prepare specialists with a secondary specialized education.
62. *Komsomolets Tadzhikistana*, July 29, 1987. It is unclear where these *tekhnikums* were located; it is conceivable that many of them were elsewhere in Central Asia.
63. G. A. Shister, "Nauchno-tekhnicheskii progress i problemy popolneniia kadrov promyshlennykh rabochikh (na primere Uzbekistana)," in *NTR i natsional'nye protsessy*, (Moscow: Nauka, 1987), p. 71.
64. For a sampling of skills offered to young people from Kirgizia and Turkmenia respectively, see *Komsomolets Kirgizii*, May 13, 1987 and *Komsomolets Turkmenistana*, June 25, 1987.
65. *Komsomolets Tadzhikistana*, Jan. 21, 1987.
66. For a complete list of the pairing of Uzbekistan's oblasts see "Mustaqil hayat bosaghasida," *Sovet maktabi*, no. 7, 1987, p. 62.
67. I. R. Mulliadzhanov *Demograficheskoe razvitie Uzbekskoi SSR* (Tashkent: Uzbekistan, 1983), p. 217.
68. *Komsomolets Tadzhikistana*, June 22, 1986.
69. According to one report, 70 percent returned home. Of the remaining 30 percent, some (probably at least half) went into the army (*Komsomolets Turkmenistana*, May 8, 1986).
70. *Komsomolets Tadzhikistana*, Feb. 13, 1987.
71. *Komsomolets Turkmenistana*, June 25, 1987. No data have been found indicating when the first groups went from Kirgizia and Uzbekistan.
72. *Komsomolets Kirgizii*, Feb. 18, 1987.

73. *Yash leninchi*, May 20, 1987.
74. Shister, "Nauchno-tekhnicheskii progress," p. 70.
75. *Oqituvchilar gazetasi*, Dec. 17, 1986.
76. R. Ubaidullaeva, "Luchshe ispol'zovat trudovoi potentsial Uzbekistana" *Kommunist Uzbekistana*, no. 10, 1987, p. 28. At least according to the plan, a rather large contingent of 1,200 was to go to PTUs in Belorussia (*Komsomolets Uzbekistana*, June 11, 1987).
77. Figures taken from *Komsomolets Tadzhikistana*, Dec. 16, 1987; *Komsomolets Tadzhikistana*, Jan. 21, 1987; *Komsomolets Tadzhikistana*, Feb. 25, 1987.
78. *Komsomolets Tadzhikistana*, Dec. 16, 1987.
79. *Turkmenskaia iskra*, Aug. 30, 1986.
80. *Komsomolets Turkmenistana*, Feb. 14, 1987. This includes some going to the Ukraine, whose PTUs began taking groups from Turkmenia in 1986 (*Turkmenskaia iskra*, Aug. 30, 1986).
81. *Komsomolets Kirgizii*, May 13, 1987.
82. L. L. Rybakovskii, *Migratsiia naseleniia: prognozy, faktory, politika* (Moscow: Nauka, 1987), p. 174. Although it is not entirely clear, presumably Rybakovskii is comparing Central Asians and Russians who have already moved from their traditional homes.
83. Makarova, Morozova, and Tarasova, *Regional'nye osobennosti*, p. 89.
84. Mulliadzhanov, *Demograficheskoe razvitie*, p. 219. Although it is not entirely clear, it appears that Mulliadzhanov's figures refer to Uzbekistan only.
85. Mirzaev and Raskin, "Organizovannoe pereraspredelenie," p. 15.
86. A. Taksanov, "Razvitie promyshlennogo rabochego klassa na sele," *Kommunist Uzbekistana*, no. 7, 1987, p. 29.
87. Makarova, Morozova, and Tarasova, *Regional'nye osobennosti*, p. 21.
88. Ibid., p. 80.
89. L. L. Rybakovskii, *Migratsiia naseleniia*, p. 174.
90. L. Maksakova, *Migratsiia naseleniia Uzbekistana* (Tashkent: Uzbekistan, 1986), 57 cited in Bohr, "Current Trends."
91. Makarova, Morozova, and Tarasova, *Regional'nye osobennosti*, p. 83. Of course the tempo of this non-indigenous out-migration greatly accelerated at the very end of the decade.
92. Taksanov, "Razvitie rabochego klassa," p. 30.
93. Makarova, Morozova, and Tarasova, *Regional'nye osobennosti*, p. 83.
94. I. Bogdanov, "Uchit'sia pravde," *Zvezda Vostoka*, no. 5, 1988, p. 128.
95. According to the 1970 census, there were 61,588 Uzbeks in the RSFSR, plus 20,040 Turkmens, 14,108 Tajiks, and 9,107 Kirgiz. Except for Kazakhstan, the only other non-Central Asian republic with over 5,000 members of these nationalities was the Ukraine, where a total of about 16,000 were recorded (*Itogi Vsesoiouznoi perepisi naseleniia 1970 goda* [Moscow: Statistika, 1973], IV, pp. 321–24). It is possible that some additional natural increase is hidden in mixed marriages in which children were assigned Russian or another nationality.
96. *Sovet Turkmenistany*, Jan. 28, 1986, cited in JPRS UPS 86-018, Apr. 18, 1986, p. 49.
97. Mirzaev and Raskin, "Organizovannoe pereraspredelenie," p. 17. It appears that the proportion of Uzbeks increased after 1986. It is claimed that during

the first eleven months of 1987, the proportion of "the local nationality" among the 901 families who left Uzbekistan for farms of the RSFSR jumped from 17 percent to 42 percent (*Sovet Ozbekistani*, Nov. 17, 1987). Perhaps the seeming contradiction between the "under 10 percent" and "17 percent" figures is a result of a higher percentage of Slavic families who went to farms in other republics, such as Kazakhstan or the Ukraine. In any case, even 42 percent of 901 families who migrated is under 400 households.

98. *Komsomolets Kirgizii*, Feb. 27, 1987.

99. *Komsomolets Tadzhikistana*, Jan. 21, 1987.

100. *Pravda Vostoka*, Jan. 16, 1988.

101. *Komsomolets Tadzhikistana*, Jan. 21, 1987.

102. The three projects were Uraineftezhilstroi, Glavzapzhilstroi, and Tiumenstroi (*Yash leninchi*, Dec. 2, 1987).

103. *Komsomolets Uzbekistana*, Jan. 21, 1987.

104. *Yash leninchi*, Mar. 17, 1987.

105. Rybakovskii, *Migratsiia naseleniia*, p. 174.

106. Viktor Khatuntsev, "Za trideviat' zemel';" *Molodoi kommunist*, no. 6, 1988, p. 39.

107. Presumably most of those who went to these oblasts were Uzbeks from other parts of Uzbekistan (Maksakova, p. 155, cited by Anne Bohr, "Current Trends").

108. *Komsomolets Tadzhikistana*, May 24, 1987.

109. *Komsomolets Uzbekistana*, May 5, 1987.

110. *Komsomolets Turkmenistana*, Feb. 15, 1987.

111. *Komsomolets Kirgizii*, Feb. 27, 1987. It is unclear to what extent the shortfall was a result of underrecruitment and to what extent a result of dropouts.

112. *Komsomolets Turkmenistana*, Apr. 28, 1987.

113. *Pravda Vostoka*, Apr. 26, 1987.

114. *Komsomolets Tadzhikistana*, June 28, 1987. It appears that the situation of appropriate placement had gotten worse over several years. In 1983, 57 percent of those from Tajikistan who returned to their republic were not given specific work assignments, but were allowed to work wherever they wanted (*Komsomolets Tadzhikistana*, Mar. 11, 1987).

115. *Komsomolets Turkmenistana*, Feb. 15, 1987.

116. *Komsomolets Tadzhikistana*, Feb. 22, 1987.

117. Although it does not fit with the category thus defined, it should be mentioned that weather is also an "objective" factor which influences people's willingness to move and return home. For an example of this concerning work, see *Pravda Vostoka*, Dec. 22, 1987; for one concerning difficulty of students adapting to weather, see *Komsomolets Tadzhikistana*, Mar. 6, 1987.

118. *Komsomolets Uzbekistana*, Sept. 2, 1987.

119. *Oqituvchilar gazetasi*, June 3, 1987. One group of students was told they would learn to repair Zhiguli automobiles, but instead they were taught how to operate farm equipment (*Komsomolets Tadzhikistana*, Feb. 26, 1988).

120. *Yash leninchi*, Dec. 2, 1987.

121. *Komsomolets Uzbekistana,* Mar. 15, 1988; *Yash leninchi,* Dec. 2, 1987.
122. *Oqituvchilar gazetasi,* June 3, 1987.
123. *Komsomolets Tadzhikistana,* Dec. 16, 1987.
124. *Komsomolets Turkmenistana,* Feb. 14, 1987.
125. *Komsomolets Turkmenistana,* Feb. 21, 1987.
126. *Komsomolets Turkmenistana,* July 7, 1987.
127. *Komsomolets Tadzhikistana,* June 5, 1987.
128. (Roundtable) "Starye proschety, novye zadachi," *Molodoi kommunist,* no. 6, 1988, p. 22.
129. *Pravda Vostoka,* Dec. 22, 1987.
130. *Sovet Ozbekistani,* Nov. 23, 1986.
131. *Komsomolets Turkmenistana,* Mar. 19, 1988.
132. *Komsomolets Tadzhikistana,* Dec. 16, 1987.
133. *Komsomolets Uzbekistana,* July 15, 1987. Commenting on this phenomenon, the author wrote, "Yes, they grew up here, but who did they grow up to be? And who are they now? Passive people with a consumerist mentality who do nothing but sit back and watch."
134. Of course this does not apply to most migration within the republic or region.
135. *Pravda Vostoka,* Apr. 12, 1988.
136. For criticism of this practice see *Komsomolets Uzbekistana,* Sept. 1, 1983; *Sovet Ozbekistani,* Dec. 14, 1984.
137. *Yash leninchi,* Oct. 26, 1984.
138. *Islam v SSSR* (Moscow: Mysl, 1983), p. 73.
139. *Komsomol'skaia pravda,* Sept. 23, 1986, cited in Iu. A. Ponomarev "Nauchno-informatsionnuiu i kontrpropagandistskuiu rabotu—na uroven' sovremennykh trebovanii," *Obshchestvennye nauki v Uzbekistane,* no. 4 (Apr.) 1987, p. 16. The confusion, or perhaps fusion, of national and religious rituals, was brought home to the author personally during a tour of a kolkhoz museum near Namangan. The guide, a World War II veteran with medals covering his chest, was explaining how his farm had given refuge to citizens of other nationalities who had been evacuated there during the war. At the conclusion of the war, the guide proudly stated, some evacuees decided to stay and they became Uzbekified. As explanation, he added, "They even circumcise their sons!" A similar interpretation of the religious gesture of passing hands in front of the face after a meal was encountered in the Fergana Valley. When the author observed his hosts in doing this (including the mayor of one town), he asked if this was not a religious practice. The young mayor answered that this custom had "lost its original religious significance" and had become merely "national."
140. Rybakovskii, *Migratsiia naseleniia,* p. 173.
141. *Pravda Vostoka,* Jan. 3, 1987, reprinted from *Izvestiia,* Jan. 2, 1987.
142. *Pravda Vostoka,* July 6, 1988. It is very likely, however, that other nationalities living outside of their traditional homelands (e.g., Slavs in the non-Slavic republics) were foremost in the minds of those drawing up the resolution.
143. *Pravda Vostoka,* July 7, 1987.
144. *Yash leninchi,* July 1, 1987.

145. *Yash leninchi*, Sept. 22, 1987.
146. *Sovet Ozbekistani*, Feb. 13, 1988.
147. *Komsomolets Turkmenistana*, May 19, 1988.
148. Khatuntsev, "Za trideviat' zemel';" p. 40.
149. *Komsomolets Tadzhikistana*, Feb. 13, 1987.
150. Lewis, Rowland, and Clem, *Nationality and Population Change*, pp. 360–61.
151. Anvar Chamkin, "Uskorenie, iliuzii i real'nost," *Zvezda Vostoka*, no. 8, 1987, p. 138.
152. Chamkin, "Uskorenie," p. 138.
153. Rybakovskii, *Migratsiia naseleniia*, p. 174.
154. "Razmyshleniia o glavnom" (roundtable), *Zvezda Vostoka*, no. 9, p. 15.
155. Chamkin, "Uskorenie," p. 138.
156. *Komsomolets Turkmenistana*, May 19, 1988.
157. *Pravda Vostoka*, Dec. 20, 1986.
158. *Komsomolets Kirgizii*, Mar. 3, 1987.
159. Ibid.
160. Mirzaev and Raskin, "Organizovannoe pereraspredelenie," p. 14.
161. *Komsomolets Tadzhikistana*, Sept. 27, 1987.
162. *Komsomolets Uzbekistana*, Jan. 14, 1987; *Komsomolets Tadzhikistana*, Oct. 9, 1987.
163. *Pravda Vostoka*, Apr. 4, 1987.
164. *Oqituvchilar gazetasi*, May 15, 1987.
165. *Pravda Vostoka*, Apr. 12, 1988.
166. *Pravda Vostoka*, May 16, 1987.
167. *Komsomolets Turkmenistana*, May 26, 1987.
168. According to USSR Deputy Minister of Education Korobeinikov, teachers in Uzbekistan in the mid-1980s spent 50 percent more time on "public" (*obshchestvennaia*) work than teachers in the RSFSR (*Pravda Vostoka*, May 17, 1987).
169. *Oqituvchilar gazetasi*, May 16, 1987.
170. *Komsomolets Turkmenistana*, Feb. 15, 1987.
171. *Pravda Vostoka*, May 16, 1987; *Komsomolets Tadzhikistana*, June 7, 1987.
172. *Pravda Vostoka*, Apr. 12, 1988.
173. In Uzbekistan two-thirds of the schools are located in buildings constructed for other purposes or are in need of major repair (*Sovet maktabi*, no. 1, 1987, p. 6).
174. Almost 70 percent of Uzbekistan's schools operate in two shifts (*Sovet maktabi*, no. 1, 1987, p. 6).
175. In Uzbekistan 18 percent have no cafeterias; 63 percent lack gymnasiums (*Pravda Vostoka*, May 17, 1987).
176. *Pravda*, May 18, 1987.
177. The average in Dushanbe is 50 rubles, whereas for the USSR it is 300 rubles (*Komsomolets Tadzhikistana*, Mar. 30, 1988).
178. *Oqituvchilar gazetasi*, May 16, 1987.
179. *Komsomolets Turkmenistana*, May 26, 1988.

180. *Vestnik statistiki,* no. 5, 1986, p. 79.
181. *Oqituvchilar gazetasi,* Dec. 17, 1986.
182. *Komsomolets Uzbekistana,* Feb. 2, 1989.
183. See, for example, *Komsomolets Turkmenistana,* Feb. 15, 1987. Frequently agricultural work is disguised as "labor training" (*Pravda Vostoka,* Mar. 12, 1987).
184. *Komsomolets Uzbekistana,* Mar. 15, 1988.
185. *Komsomolets Turkmenistana,* Mar. 26, 1987.
186. *Komsomolets Tadzhikistana,* Aug. 24, 1986.
187. *Pravda Vostoka,* Nov. 15, 1986.
188. *Pravda Vostoka,* May 16, 1986.
189. *Komsomolets Uzbekistana,* July 15, 1987.
190. *Komsomolets Uzbekistana,* Feb. 21, 1987.
191. *Komsomolets Uzbekistana,* Mar. 15, 1988.
192. *Pravda Vostoka,* Mar. 25, 1987.
193. *Komsomolets Turkmenistana,* Mar. 16, 1987.
194. D. I. Ziuzin, "Puti sovershenstvovaniia sotsial'nogo sostava naseleniia Srednei Azii," in *Regional'nye osobennosti sotsial'nykh peremeshchenii v razvitom sotsialisticheskom obshchestve* (Moscow: 1983), p. 56.
195. Taksanov, "Razvitie rabochego klassa," p. 30.
196. Ibid.
197. *Oqituvchilar gazetasi,* June 3, 1987.
198. *Oqituvchilar gazetasi,* May 15, 1987.
199. *Komsomolets Tadzhikistana,* Mar. 11, 1987. Recruiters sometimes took advantage of the desire for *VUZ* entrance and misinformed students that they were going to study in a (higher educational) institute rather than an *uchilishche* (*Yash leninchi,* Jan. 14, 1987).
200. Lewis, Rowland, and Clem, *Nationality and Population Change,* p. 375.
201. *Yash leninchi,* Apr. 24, 1990 and *Ozbekistan adabiyati va san"ati,* Dec. 29, 1989.
202. *Ozbekistan adabiyati va san"ati,* Dec. 29, 1989.
203. K. Bedrintsev and A. Mirzaev, "Gde zhit' budushchim pokoleniiam uzbekistantsev?" *Kommunist Uzbekistana,* no. 12, 1988, p. 12.
204. *Sovetskaia kul'tura,* Dec. 1, 1988, p.6.
205. In early 1990, over 9,500 students from Uzbekistan were reported to be studying in higher eduational institutions of other Soviet republics (*Pravda Vostoka,* Feb. 1, 1990). Assuming the data are comparable, this is much higher than the figure of 5,324 cited above for 1987.
206. *Komsomolets Uzbekistana,* May 23, 1990.
207. Lewis, Rowland, and Clem, *Nationality and Population Change,* p. 348
208. See William Fierman, "*Glasnost'* in Practice: The Uzbek Experience," *Central Asian Survey,* 8, no. 2 (1989), p. 21.

Conclusion

William Fierman

Introduction

The preceding chapters, which deal with different political, economic, social, and cultural problems, all provide evidence of the Soviet regime's unsuccessful attempt to control Central Asia in such a way as to transform it in accordance with the aims of the Communist Party leadership. In illustrating the incomplete control exercised by the Party in the last decade, the above chapters demonstrate how much the Soviet Union has changed since the 1940s, 1950s, and even 1960s. In those years, most Western scholars still viewed the Soviet political system as a "totalitarian" one: they generally agreed that the Party's command of the means of armed combat, the means of communication, the terroristic police, and the economy, along with its manipulation of ideology, guaranteed "total" control of society.[1] Even in the late 1950s and 1960s, as analysts recognized that the USSR was beginning to emerge from its "totalitarian" origins, they recognized the utility of the "totalitarian" paradigm for understanding how Stalin managed to maintain control for almost three decades.

Although the few Western scholars studying the Central Asian political system in the Stalin and Khrushchev eras were more concerned with providing basic political and economic histories than with applying models, they, too, viewed the central Party apparatus as very powerful and able to impose its will on the region. In his important work *Russia in Central Asia* (published 1963), Michael Rywkin concluded with two scenarios which he felt could keep Central Asia from becoming a cause of serious conflict among China, Russia, and the Muslim world. One of the scenarios (which Rywkin apparently viewed as realistic) was for Russia to "accelerat[e] its process of colonization of the territory by Russian settlers and of continuous cultural absorption of the natives . . ."[2]

Conclusion

With the benefit of hindsight, we can appreciate that this assessment—like other assessments based on the "total" Party power—greatly overestimated the regime's ability to direct the transformation of Central Asia. Indeed, as several of the above chapters illustrate, Russia's ability for "continuous cultural absorption" was quite limited.[3] Nevertheless, if we consider the USSR of the time as just another example of a "totalitarian" system, it is easy to appreciate how scholars like Rywkin arrived at such "optimistic" conclusions. For all of its utility in explaining how dictatorships *maintain* power, the totalitarian model can obscure potential sources of change: if a regime truly has "total" power, there seemingly should be no political force able to challenge it.

In fact, however, there are forces which erode the "complete" power of totalitarian parties and leaders. Dictators age and subjects find ways to insulate themselves from terror as they pursue their personal goals. New generations are born whose fears, attitudes, knowledge, skills, and expectations differ from those of their parents. Moreover, as "totalitarian" regimes stifle innovation and risk-taking, the society's technological level is likely to lag. Such factors are easily ignored when focusing on how a dictatorship maintains "total" control.

On the other hand, if we approach the study of a political system from the standpoint of "political development," we are pointed in the direction of some of the processes which the totalitarian model overlooks, in particular those concerning change. Various theories of "political development" differ even on such fundamental questions as what constitutes "political development"; however, they are free of the static bias inherent in the totalitarian model and help to identify reasons for flux.

One of the central themes of this book is the failure of the Soviet political system to direct political and social change in Central Asia. Why was the Party "dictatorship" not able to achieve its goals? As we attempt to shed light on this question in the conclusion to this book, we will borrow and adapt some of the analysis of political development as interpreted by Leonard Binder and four co-authors (Myron Weiner, Joseph LaPalombara, Lucien Pye, and Sidney Verba) in a now classic work, *Crises and Sequences in Political Development*. According to these authors, modernization is likely to lead to new problems and aggravate old ones in five major areas of development.[4] These are penetration, participation, legitimacy, distribution, and identity. Although the title of the book by Binder et al. refers to "crises," not all of its authors focus exclusively "crises." In particular, Sidney Verba devotes much of his analysis to "problems" and "problem areas," and he reserves the term "crises" for a narrower purpose.[5] Because the discussion below will not merely be concerned with "crises," it will be useful here also to look at "problems" or "problem areas" more broadly. As we will see, some of the challenges which Moscow now faces indeed have become or are rapidly approaching "crisis" proportions. However, these crises may be understood as having arisen due to the Communist Party's failures in the "problem areas" of development.

Penetration

According to the definition of "penetration" provided by the authors of *Crises and Sequences in Political Development*, this phenomenon is a fundamental requirement of any government which seeks to exercise any real power. Joseph LaPalombara sees penetration as "conformance to public policy enunciated by central government authority." Thus, a high degree of penetration means that a government "can get what [it] wants from people over whom [it] seeks to exercise power."[6] Elsewhere, Verba states that the penetration problem refers to "how much effective control the central government has."[7] By definition, when a government no longer "penetrates," it no longer exercises effective control over a society.

Given the Communist Party's attempt to exercise very strict control over a broad range of activities, throughout most of its history it appeared to have been able to satisfy its almost endless appetite for "penetration." One of the key instruments was the control over appointments which both Carlisle and Critchlow discuss.

On the other hand, the evidence which both of these scholars present about appointments suggests that Moscow's ability to penetrate has declined and probably has been slipping for decades. Carlisle notes the degree of autonomy which allowed Rashidov and his supporters to fill positions with relatives and friends and thus escape some of Moscow's control. There were, of course, limits to autonomy and a price exacted from Rashidov and, presumably. other Central Asian first secretaries. In Uzbekistan's case, it was necessary to give the appearance that the republic was producing ever more cotton. In another area, Rashidov had to make convincing claims that huge numbers of his republic's natives were learning the Russian language. In fact, however, these "achievements" existed on paper only, and Rashidov was able to manage certain local matters with little interference from Moscow.

A primary reason for the decline in Moscow's control of Central Asia was the lessening of political terror. Under Stalin, terror was a chief instrument in effecting political compliance. In more recent decades, however, the use of terror has greatly declined. Moscow's reluctance to use violent means to achieve compliance with its policies is also evident in Fierman's description of the frustrated campaign to encourage migration by Central Asians out of their home region. Perhaps Stalin, too, would have sought ways to encourage voluntary movement, but faced with the lack of success which confronts Moscow today, he would have not hesitated to resettle Central Asians forcibly to labor-short regions of the country. Today, this solution seems highly unlikely. Without a doubt, Soviet leaders' inability or unwillingness to use terror played an important role in undermining the regime's penetration.

Identity

Unlike "penetration," which refers to the government's ability to enforce its will, "identity" is more closely related to the way in which the people in a given territory view themselves and their government. According to Sidney Verba, the identity problem concerns "the definition of the set of individuals whom it is believed appropriately fall within the decision-making scope of the government, i.e., the question of the appropriate members of the system." As Verba points out, a problem arises if "some members of the populace do not consider themselves as appropriately falling within the domain of the government or, conversely, feel that some other group not within that domain belongs within it."[8]

Soviet power in Central Asia can be viewed as one very long but unsuccessful attempt to solve the identity problem. It is true that, at least throughout the 1980s, virtually all Soviet Central Asians took a degree of "Soviet-ness" for granted. If nothing else, they viewed it as unavoidable. Moreover, the great majority of the population alive today in Central Asia has lived exclusively under Soviet power. Although there is no accurate measure of its impact, the system of political socialization (e.g., through study of the same history, participation in the same organizations, and—under circumstances of a perceived common enemy—service in the Soviet Army) probably did help to make Central Asians feel that they shared many things with the rest of what was called the "Soviet people."

As illustrated in the historical overview to this book, however, it must be kept in mind that the definition of the Soviet people—specifically the breadth of that definition—underwent tremendous change under Soviet rule. In the first period after the Bolshevik Revolution, until approximately 1933, the Party tried to carry out an "internationalist" policy as it distanced itself from the Russian "colonial" policies of the tsarist regime. But then beginning in the 1930s, "international" and "Soviet" became almost indistinguishable from "Russian." The greatest excesses of Russification occurred in the late 1930s and the first eight years following World War II.

But already under Khrushchev the leadership's definition of "Soviet" began to broaden in such a way that a "Soviet" identity became compatible with renewed pride in local or regional history and other roots of "separateness." The changes under Gorbachev might be viewed as a leap in magnitude, but also in the same direction of broadening the definition of "Soviet." Thus, today's Communist leaders in Moscow are willing to refrain from calling "anti-Soviet" or "reactionary" Central Asians' expressions of pride in an identity which is often blatantly juxtaposed to Russian culture and in clear distinction to it.

The Communist Party's task of inculcating a sense of identification with a "Soviet" community has been especially difficult in Central Asia because of the "alien-ness" of the "Soviet community" for Central Asians. Among other things, that community was based on a language and culture in which few Central Asians were comfortable; its leadership was largely Slavic, had a poor understanding of Central Asian society, and conducted policies which discouraged and ridiculed Islamic religious life.

Nevertheless, as Rorlich and Kreindler illustrate, the regime expended tremendous amounts of energy and resources attempting to make Central Asians feel that they belonged to a "Soviet" community. Given the special role of Russian as the "second mother tongue" for the Soviet people—a sort of linguistic glue—the statistics for Russian language competency from the 1989 census are very revealing. Only about one-fourth of all Uzbeks claimed to be fluent in Russian. The percentages for Tajiks and Turkmens were between 25 and 30 percent, whereas slightly over a third of all Kirgiz claimed Russian fluency.[9] These are very meager results.

Inasmuch as Central Asians' "rival identities" or "alternatives" to Soviet identity might provide a basis for a government under whose domain Central Asians might feel they should appropriately fall, it is necessary to reconsider these other sources of self-identification.

As several of the above contributions show, one of the most important "rival" identities has been Islam. Wixman and Rorlich demonstrate that Soviet Central Asians maintain a strong sense of Islamic identity. Rorlich also explains that glasnost and other policy changes have made it much easier for Central Asian Muslims to practice Islam and learn about it, thus reinforcing the sense of "Islamic" belonging.

It is significant that the Central Asian cultural intelligentsia took a leading role in calling for an end to Moscow's policy which treated Islam more harshly than Christianity. Back in the spring of 1987 (when Uzbekistan was just beginning to emerge from a period of very harsh anti-Islamic propaganda), the Uzbek poet Erkin Vahidov urged a less hostile attitude towards those who participated in religious funerals. He noted that unwarranted anti-religious vigilance had forced some people even to avoid attending their own parents' funerals.[10] By the beginning of 1988, another Uzbek writer, Nadir Narmatov, was calling for an end to the practice of ignoring the great works of Uzbek literature simply because classical writers praised religion or expressed religious views. Poking fun at the ideological straightjacket responsible for this situation, Narmatov asked, "Is it really possible to demand a knowledge of Marxism-Leninism from a twelfth-century person?"[11]

One of the most tangible ways in which the regime once attempted to destroy the Islamic identity was through the shift of Central Asian language writing systems from the Arabic to the Latin script at the end of the 1920s. Rorlich discusses important efforts to reacquaint Central Asians with this alphabet. It is still not clear whether most of the population (or even the literati) sees this merely as a way to enable Central Asians to be able to read writings from before 1930 or whether it is a step toward another shift of alphabet. Public expression of even the first more modest goal was impossible just a few years ago, and reference to the more radical one—reverting to Arabic letters—was entirely unimaginable. Yet in today's atmosphere this is a topic for open discussion.[12]

Analogous processes are occurring in other ways related to language. Many of the words of Arabic and Persian origin which were once "expelled" from the Central Asian languages are now reappearing. Even in such an "internationalized" (i.e., Russified) sphere as political vocabulary, in Uzbek, *jumhuriyat* is replacing *respublika* (republic), *katib* is replacing *sekretar'* (secretary), and *firqa* is replacing *partiia* (party). When this process began to acquire momentum a few years ago, one Kirgiz scholar justified it by saying that the Arabisms and Iranisms in the Kirgiz language were no more "reactionary" than the Greek and Latin elements in Russian which "in fact enriched [Russian's] vocabulary."[13]

Although the more open (and, presumably growing) identification with Islam is unmistakable, it must be kept in mind that "Islam" can mean many different things to different groups or individuals. Nevertheless, it seems that the "Islamic" identity which many of today's Central Asian intelligentsia feel reflects a view of Islam much like that of the *jadid* reformers in the early twentieth century. Central Asian scholars devote a great deal of attention to this group, among whom many of today's thinkers probably search for intellectual predecessors.

Closely related to the Islamic identity is another group identity—the "Turkic" one. This was also important to many *jadids*, as it is for many Central Asian intellectuals today. This rests above all on linguistic and historical links. Today many Turkic-language writers and scholars are seeking ways to reinforce bonds among their peoples; this includes, most importantly, the Central Asian Turkic languages, Tatar, Azerbaijani, and even Turkish, but excludes Tajik, which is not a Turkic language. One sign of this trend was a call published in the Uzbek cultural weekly to make the Azerbaijani press available to readers in Uzbekistan. The same article cited Azerbaijani scholars who maintain that "there is no language barrier" between Uzbek and Azerbaijani speakers.[14] Even if slightly exaggerated, this may seem almost a harmless expression of the obvious. But in the Soviet context such statements are very significant. As noted by the editor of the Soviet scholarly linguistic journal *Sovetskaia tiurkologiia* (Soviet Turcology), the epithet "pan-Turkism" was originally put forward in the USSR to prevent the "awakening of the genetic memory" of such Turkic peoples as the Gagauz, Azerbaijanis, Kazakhs, Kirgiz, and Yakuts. Sarcastically this scholar said that, even in recent decades, the label "pan-Turkism" performed this mission in "brilliant" fashion.[15]

It is worth noting, nevertheless, that even prior to Gorbachev, occasional manifestations of pan-Turkic sentiments found their way into print. One of the most striking cases was a historical novel by the Uzbek writer Mamadali Mahmudov published in 1981. Through the novel's heroes, Mahmudov suggested that if the Central Asian Turks had not been so divided in the nineteenth century, they would have successfully resisted the Russian imperial conquest.

Closely related to both the Islamic and Turkic identities is the "Turkestani" or "Central Asian" one. The reference group for this identity would be the indigenous population of the republics discussed in this book, plus possibly the Kazakhs and/or the populations of the broader geographical Turkestan (including territory in Afghanistan and China). Unlike the "pan-Turkic" category described above, "Central Asian" would include the Iranian-speaking Tajiks but not include the Tatars or Azerbaijanis.

Despite the many shared cultural traits and economic problems, until recently there has been less evidence of a Central Asian identity than an Islamic or Turkic one. This likely is in part attributable to the national delimitation and the consequence that through most of Soviet history the Central Asian republics have carried on relations with one another via Moscow. However, today, when Moscow is allowing the Central Asian (and all other republics) greater latitude to establish bilateral and multilateral *direct* ties, there are signs of substantial cooperation. Most importantly, in June 1990 the leaders of the Central Asian republics (as well as Kazakhstan) met and signed a number of agreements which provide for an unprecedented amount of cooperation and coordination among the individual units. At the same time, "informal" groups and fledgling political parties from the region have also begun to coordinate their actions.[16]

Conclusion

The Central Asian identity, as well as the Islamic and Turkic ones, must be seen against the background of mass interethnic disturbances in Central Asia in which members of one Muslim (and often Turkic-speaking) ethnic group have clashed with members of another Muslim Turkic-speaking group. For example, much of the fighting in Uzbekistan in the spring of 1989 was between Uzbeks and Meskhetian (Muslim) Turks (whom Stalin moved from their home in the Transcaucasus to Uzbekistan). Likewise, the adversaries in bloodshed in Kirgizia in 1990 were mainly Uzbeks and Kirgiz. Tajiks have clashed with Kirgiz on the border of Tajikistan and Kirgizia, and Tajiks have complained of discrimination against Tajiks by Uzbeks in Uzbekistan. Some Tajik intellectuals have even voiced objections about the present status of what they perceive as two centers of Tajik culture—Samarkand and Bukhara—under control by Uzbeks in Tashkent. Although greater economic cooperation could benefit all of the Central Asians, economic problems may also serve as a basis for conflicts. For example, proponents of Uzbekistan's case frequently point out that one of the reasons for the shrinking of the Aral Sea is Turkmenistan's diversion of some of the water.[17] Some Uzbeks also feel that some of the burden of supplying the USSR with cotton should be shouldered by neighboring Kirgizia and Kazakhstan.[18]

Many members of the Central Asian cultural intelligentsia maintain that in fact there are no disputes among "peoples"; they point out that fellow Muslims and fellow Turks have lived side by side for centuries in harmony. In their view, the disputes "between nationalities" or "between peoples" have been whipped up and manipulated by forces such as conservative political leaders in Moscow (who allegedly want to stir up trouble in order to make the Central Asians dependent on the center); they also see local organized crime leaders as inciting and fanning discontent.[19] Even if this is the case, there are still potential disputes which can weaken (or at least be exploited in order to weaken) any feelings of Muslim, Central Asian, or Turkic solidarity. Moreover, these disputes may ultimately force the Central Asians to turn to Moscow for help. In the summer of 1990, Uzbek Party First Secretary Karimov asked Moscow, through the all-Union Ministry of Defense, to take measures to help subdue the interethnic conflict in neighboring Kirgizia's Osh oblast.[20]

Before leaving the question of identities, brief mention should be made of the local identities, such as "Khorezmi" or "Bukharan." As suggested in Chapter 1, Moscow may have rejected the idea of a permanent Khorezm or Bukharan republic because these units might command genuine political loyalty. If this was a motivation, the Soviet leadership has probably achieved that goal. For although the people of Bukhara and Khorezm oblasts may indeed have a sense of "Bukharan" or

"Khorezmi" identity, the groups with which they identify probably do not correspond with the population of all of what was considered "Bukhara" or "Khorezm" before the national delimitation.

As Carlisle demonstrates, local identities have played an important role in Moscow's ability to "play off" competing political elites one against the other. But Moscow has probably consistently viewed these geographically small identities as complementing rather than undermining the "Soviet" one. On the other hand, if the thrust of Carlisle's hypothesis is correct—i.e., that (at least in the case of Uzbekistan) the republic identity is acquiring (or has acquired) a sense of loyalty which it never before possessed, it may now be serving (or beginning to serve) a purpose counter to what Moscow intended in the 1920s. Moreover, it may embody many of the elements of the "Islamic," "Turkic," and/or "Turkestani" identities.[21] Thus, instead of being a stepping-stone to a "Soviet" or "international" identity, it may stand in opposition to it.

The most remarkable evidence of the effect of this is the declaration of sovereignty by Uzbekistan (which was soon followed by analogous declarations in the other republics). According to Uzbekistan's declaration, all-Union laws will not enter force in Uzbekistan unless and until they are approved by the republic legislature. Even if it is not a stage on the way to a broader "Islamic," "Turkic," or "Turkestani" political unit and/or identity, this is certainly not what Stalin had in mind at the time that the Uzbek Republic was created.

Distribution

Unlike identity problems which are often most linked to symbols and perceptions, distribution problems are more closely tied to the material world. Joseph LaPalombara divides distribution problems into two "dimensions." In order to deal with the first dimension, governments try to find ways and means to produce more of the material things that are valued. In dealing with the second dimension, governments change the bases upon which the "valued" things are distributed among society's members.[22] Another way of looking at this is to say that a government tries both to increase the "size of the pie" of things produced and to bring about a more equitable distribution. LaPalombara states that when, for whatever reasons, the gap between demand for pieces and supply "reaches excessive limits, system-disintegrating forces are brought into play."[23] This may indeed be a major factor affecting Central Asia today.

Seen in these terms, the entire Soviet "pie" is falling desperately short of the demand for pieces throughout the country. At the base of this is the very inefficient organization of the Soviet economy. In the case of Central Asia, the local people feel that this inefficiency and its effects have been exacerbated by a colonial pattern which has kept the region dependent on Moscow.

Before considering this further, it is important to note that Central Asians' perspective is very different from the one that predominates among Russian economic planners at the center. The latter claim that, despite an alleged large share of investment in the region, Central Asia's economic performance (especially in recent years) has not been improving. During his visit to Tashkent in April 1988, Gorbachev pointedly noted that the allocation of funds for agriculture in Uzbekistan had grown by a factor of over four between 1970 and 1986. However, between 1980 and the time of Gorbachev's speech, the agricultural output had remained at the same level. In Gorbachev's view this meant that the potential created in Uzbekistan was "not yielding the necessary return."[24]

Rumer's chapter provides a number of examples which show how different Central Asians' perception of the problem is from Gorbachev's. The Central Asians see the widespread poverty of Central Asia and its social consequences (evident in Olcott's contribution) and bitterly ask such questions as why grain farmers—who live mostly *outside* of Central Asia—should receive an average of 60.5 kopecks for an hour's work while cotton farmers earn only 16 kopecks per hour.[25] And they want to know why over the past two decades the wages of almost everyone else in the country have been raised 50 percent or even 100 percent, while "only the wages paid to those who raise cotton have remained almost unchanged."[26]

Both in Moscow and in the Central Asian republics the leadership has called for moves toward a market economy and more republic control over the development of the local economy, including "self-financing" at the republic level. From the Central Asians' perspective, sovereignty over natural resources is one precondition for and a big step in the direction of improving their economy. They also see the ability to establish direct contacts with foreign governments and enterprises and to earn and spend their own hard currency in this same light. At the same time they also realize the need for a radical overhaul of the basis of the economy (e.g., replacing agriculture with more labor-intensive industry and services); and they know that this in turn will require massive construction of new facilities and a major change in the kind of training offered in local educational institutions.

In many ways the support for greater republic economic responsibility is shared by the Gorbachev all-Union leadership as well as the political leaders of the Central Asian republics. Each side supports it because it feels that the current arrangement is unfair to its own side. (The center does not want to "subsidize" Central Asia, and Central Asia does not want to be exploited like a colony supplying raw materials.) There is also a common interest in the greater efficiency which republic responsibility might produce. (This might be helpful in increasing the size of the "pie" referred to above.) But each side also wants to make sure—regardless of the size of the pie—that it receives a proportionally larger wedge. From the Central Asian leaders' perspective, this means that in any transition to a market economy, the Central Asian's poorer "starting position" (*startovoe polozhenie*) must be taken into account.[27]

Many Moscow scholars and political leaders appear to view overpopulation and a continuing high birth rate as factors which force the all-Union government to pour resources into Central Asia. As Lubin points out, some of the local economic planners share the perception that lowering the birth rate is part of a solution to Central Asia's economic problems. But, as she also indicates, some other members of the intelligentsia vehemently disagree. The intensity of the argument is indicated by Uzbek poet Muhammad Salih's insistence that "the question of whether a nation should grow or not should be decided by that nation's nature and not by some office."[28]

Regardless of the merits of each side's argument on the demography debate, environmental factors will play a key role in determining the kind of economic development possible in Central Asia. Rumer shows how one of these—water—will have major implications for how the "pie" is cut up. The Central Asians generally favor a "solution" which includes diversion of some of the Siberian river water southward. However, aside from the ecological damage to the Russian environment which this might cause, the water diversion schemes are very expensive. Given the terrible state of the Soviet economy, the Russians are even more reluctant to allocate billions of rubles to help a region of the country which they feel has been wasteful. The Central Asians seem more likely to achieve a degree of success in easing the water shortage—especially over the short term—by water conservation measures, including cultivation of crops which require less water. Thus they may also begin to make inroads on some of the terrible social and health problems facing the region; however, this prospect is far from being assured.

Inasmuch as the all-Union political leadership in Moscow desires some degree of tranquility in Central Asia (an assumption many members of the Central Asian intelligentsia seem seriously to doubt), the violent outbreaks in the region may convince Moscow that it has no choice but to help the Central Asians toward an economic solution. The Central Asian political, economic, and cultural elites stress that the "ethnic" problems of their region are really economic and social ones. In particular they point to the despair and crime which they see as logical products of unemployment. In the wake of the Fergana Valley violence, a whole series of measures was generated to relieve the social pressures; but most of these, just as water diversion, also will require financial resources. And even if the all-Union leadership is more sympathetic to these plans than to water diversion schemes, it may not be willing or able to provide the necessary funding.

Given the absence of market-determined prices, it is impossible to calculate accurately the "real" market values of Central Asia's exports to the rest of the USSR and the goods and services which the region has received in return. Thus, it seems unwise to offer a judgement about who have been the "winners" at which "losers'" expense. Perhaps, indeed, both Central Asia and Russia should be considered "losers" because the economic system has produced such a small "pie." Regardless of this, however, it is clear that the terrible state of the Soviet economy is accompanied by contradictory perceptions about "who owes." Therefore it appears that the gap between the demand for "pie pieces" and the supply is approaching (or perhaps already has reached?) "excessive limits." This could indeed add to "system-disintegrating" forces of the Soviet Union in Central Asia.

Participation

Whereas problems of distribution are most immediately economic ones, the problems of participation are most directly political. As Verba defines it, the participation problem is simply "the problem of who takes part (who has some influence over) governmental decisions."[29]

The entire Soviet Union has seen breathtaking changes in this area of political development under Gorbachev. In part this is a result of an emerging political culture fostered by the Gorbachev leadership's attempt to encourage more people to take part in various forms of decision-making. Even the origins of glasnost can be seen in this light. By urging people to articulate opinions which might not be popular among those in power and promoting multicandidate elections—not to mention by allowing public demonstrations, strikes, and the formation of "informal groups"—Gorbachev has promoted a much higher degree of participation among the Soviet population. On another level, Gorbachev's leadership has permitted much livelier and more spontaneous debates at all levels of Party and state bodies.

The early Gorbachev years witnessed popular support for these measures at the same time that Moscow attempted to reinstate a greater degree of control over the rest of the country. Although this may seem paradoxical, in fact it fits a familiar pattern. Myron Weiner notes that historically throughout the world "the growth of mass political participation has been primarily associated with the centralization of authority rather than with the growth of local institutions." In other countries, too, the central government has encouraged political participation "as a means of undermining local institutions."[30]

But these processes which Gorbachev himself set in motion have certainly gone far beyond what the leader must have imagined in the middle of the 1980s. In the second half of the decade, forces in the republics which the central Party apparatus could not control began more successfully to resist Moscow's direction, to put forth their own demands, and to insist on their own right to decide questions affecting their own lives. As Critchlow demonstrates, Moscow attempted to regain a greater degree of control over the selection of the major political participants in Uzbekistan, but this attempt failed. Indeed, as Carlisle suggests, Moscow's failed effort may serve as a catalyst which helps consolidate a more unified "Uzbek" identity; in turn, this may make it more difficult for any Moscow leadership to control participation in Central Asia. This, of course, has important implications for the Gorbachev regime's maintenance of "penetration." Thus, there is a direct relationship between problems of participation and penetration. When these problems are considered in combination with the problems of consolidating new identities, it suggests that any regime in Moscow which seeks to maintain control in Central Asia will have an extraordinarily difficult task in balancing "participation" and "penetration" concerns. As Verba notes, "New forms of participation, including mass elections, introduced in areas where problems of penetration remain severe, quickly threaten the stability, even the geographic integrity of a new nation."[31] Although Verba's observation refers to a "new" nation, it seems very applicable to the USSR. After all, the sense of "Soviet" nationhood does not presently appear to be very strong among Central Asians.

The language laws recently passed in Central Asia provide further evidence of how "participation"—even when it is promoted or at least tolerated by the leadership in Moscow—hampers the center's "penetration." Beginning in 1989, the Central Asian republics began to adopt laws raising the status of each republic's language (i.e., Uzbek, Tajik, Turkmen, and Kirgiz) vis-à-vis Russian. These changes can only be understood in the context of the fact that for over half of a century, i.e., ever since the era of *korenizatsiia*, Central Asians who sought access to certain prestigious types of education or jobs needed to pursue them through the *Russian* language. In Kirgizia, as in other republics, use of the local language had been equated with "nationalism."[32] Consequently, the result was that even when a single non-Kirgiz-speaking administrator attended a meeting where mostly Kirgiz were speaking, the meeting nevertheless had to be held in Russian; in rural areas this meant, for example, that collective farmers were forced to deliver their comments in broken Russian.[33] For the indigenous peoples, this was particularly infuriating when the administrators, who were born and raised in Kirgizia, still did not know the local language! Indeed, according to the First Secretary of the Uzbek Writers' Union Adil Yaqubov, there were actually "prohibitions against speaking in the native language at meetings."[34]

Until the recent surge of linguistic assertiveness, many Central Asians felt that a vicious circle leading to a decline in the status of the local languages had been created: because most Russians and other member of the non-indigenous nationalities did not know the local language, no one used it; and because of its limited use, no one bothered to learn to speak it well. This, in turn, further reduced the number of situations in which it was used. One manifestation of this was in the Tajik Komsomol, where many Tajik Komsomol leaders could not give a public speech in "their own" native language.[35] The worst situations probably existed in Kirgizia and in large "international" urban areas of the other republics, especially among a stratum of the more educated population. The erosion of the indigenous population's language was so serious in Kirgizia that, in 1988, 42 percent of the Kirgiz children in the capital (Frunze) were not even studying Kirgiz as a subject, let alone attending schools with Kirgiz as the language of instruction.[36]

Since 1989, however, the situation (at least on paper) has changed radically. In accordance with new laws, most public activities—paper work in government offices, public meetings, higher education, and many others—are scheduled to shift to much greater, if not exclusive, use of each republic's "official" language. If the laws are fully implemented, any emissaries whom Moscow may attempt to dispatch to Central Asia to impose the center's will at the republic or local levels will encounter a much more difficult task. Besides being uncomfortable due to resentment of Moscow's role, in increasing numbers of cases, these people will not even be able to read the relevant records.

Many Russians and other non-indigenous peoples living in Central Asia—especially among the large majority who do not know the local languages—perceive the recent language laws as having been devised by the "republic nationality" in order to discriminate against the non-native population. That is, they see these laws as poorly disguised efforts to limit participation by non-natives. This is very different from most natives' view, according to whom the laws are measures which had to be adopted in order to correct past injustices which limited participation by the local people.[37]

These language laws acquired a symbolic importance which also had major implications for participation. Language issues were the focus of public demonstrations and other activities by Central Asian "informal" groups in the late 1980s. Particularly in this early period of relaxed limits on political participation, the indigenous intelligentsia successfully utilized language questions to mobilize large numbers of people—especially students—who previously had been politically "inert."

Legitimacy

The last "problem area" discussed in *Crises and Sequences in Political Development* is legitimacy. Verba summarizes the legitimacy problem by saying that it refers to "the basis on which and the degree to which the decisions of government are accepted by the populace of a society because of normative beliefs on the part of the populace as to the 'rightness' of the ways in which decisions are made."[38]

Although through its extensive socialization network the Communist Party has always attempted to convince the Soviet population that the regime was legitimate, through most of the early decades the highest-ranking leadership most likely viewed legitimacy as something of secondary importance. This is because the Party's "penetration" depended heavily on terror. True, even at the height of Stalin's purges the dictator probably enjoyed legitimacy in the eyes of many Central Asians, particularly among the upwardly mobile and those who viewed Stalin as the embodiment of a revolution pledged to bring an end to social and national inequality; indeed, some subjects may have applauded Stalin for uncovering the "nests of spies" and "anti-Soviet conspirators." But certainly the purges were not launched in order to enhance legitimacy; during the late 1930s, as during most of Stalin's rule, the dictator relied much more upon terror in order to achieve "conformance to public policy."

The mixture of terror and legitimacy relied upon by the Soviet leadership began to undergo an important change in the 1950s, especially after Khrushchev's "secret" speech to the CPSU Twentieth Congress condemning Stalin's ruthlessness. As reliance upon terror declined in the ensuing years, the Party had a growing need for legitimacy in order to maintain "penetration." Unfortunately for the CPSU, however, this legitimacy continued to decline. Gorbachev attempted to reverse this: some of his innovative policies related to identity, distribution, and participation were part of an attempt to enhance the Communist Party's sagging legitimacy.

As part of this, with regard to identity, the contributions to this volume by Rorlich and Kreindler demonstrate that the Party greatly reduced its activities intended to create a homogeneous "Soviet" people. Instead of attempting to transform Central Asians into atheists with a Russian-like culture, today's Soviet leadership seems reconciled to the fact that Central Asians will remain Muslims with a culture very different from that of the USSR's Slavs. Naturally, the new policies which have emerged are not as offensive to the Central Asians as the old ones; and in this way, the Gorbachev leadership may indeed have enhanced its legitimacy.

Similarly, the need for legitimacy was likely a reason for Gorbachev's innovative policies relevant to participation. As Wixman's chapter notes, Central Asians have been very sensitive to their political domination by outsiders, i.e., Russians. It is quite plausible that the Party leadership viewed the broadening of limits on political participation as measures which could help support the Party's sagging legitimacy. Even more likely, Gorbachev may have realized that a refusal to permit greater political participation by Central Asians (especially while encouraging it elsewhere in the country) would have destroyed any remaining legitimacy for the regime in Central Asians' eyes.

Finally, the economic policies—i.e., the policies most relevant to the problem area of distribution—also have a close relation to legitimacy. As Rumer's chapter illustrates, Central Asians are still bitterly complaining about the small "piece of the economic pie" which they have been receiving. Certainly the regime's legitimacy among Central Asians relies in part on its ability to raise the living standard which, even in comparison with the rest of the USSR, is very low.

To date, Gorbachev has been able to achieve more legitimacy in Central Asia out of "identity" and "participation" policies than out of policies relevant to distribution. This is probably because in the short term the policies related to identity and participation can be implemented without great expense. This is true, for example, of the more relaxed policies toward Islam and toward expression of pride in history; to a lesser extent it is true in the case of broader limits on political participation and the new language laws. In contrast, such projects as the diversion of Siberian water to Central Asia or a great hike in the price of cotton would be very expensive.

Ultimately, however, many of these measures designed to *enhance* the regime's legitimacy (and, through it, penetration) could *undermine* Moscow's penetration of Central Asia and other areas of the country. This is certainly true in the case of distribution. If Moscow should give Central Asians a bigger piece of the same size "pie"—a prospect which, admittedly, seems very unlikely—this would clearly have a negative effect on the regime's legitimacy among the population of Russia. Likewise, the flexible policy concerning identity—by permitting greater expression of Islamic, Turkic, Central Asian regional, or nationality identities—complicates the task of convincing the people of Central Asia that it is appropriate for them to be ruled by a government in Moscow. And most clearly, permitting increased participation by local elites seriously confounds Moscow's attempts to "penetrate" the region.

Despite the unique nature of the situation in each part of the USSR, the economic, social, political, and cultural problems in Central Asia in many ways are parallel to those in other parts of the country. Naturally, the same can be said for the relations *among* problem areas. Thus, for example, the Soviet regime's increasing need to rely on legitimacy is true everywhere; and everywhere the decline in legitimacy is somehow linked to a deteriorating economic system and the failure of the educational system to produce a "new Soviet man." The "boom" in participation observable in Central Asia over the past few years and the re-linking of the modern national identity with old religious and historical traditions are also parallel to processes elsewhere in the country.

Inasmuch as a fundamental transformation was an integral part of what the Soviet government wanted from the people over whom it sought to exercise power, this suggests that the Communist Party's "penetration" was never quite so successful as the totalitarian model led most observers to believe. True, Central Asia did supply the Soviet Union with raw materials, and for decades Moscow was able to replace the leaders of the region in accordance with any Kremlin leader's whim. Moreover, Soviet power could and did prevent overt mass manifestations of Islamic or Turkic identities.

Over the long run, however, even the economic development of Central Asia did not proceed in accordance with Moscow's wishes. The tremendous padding of achieved economic indicators is evidence of this. Likewise, the Soviet system never successfully eliminated the shared ideas, practices, and other cultural phenomena which linked Central Asians to one another and even to other Muslims or Turks abroad. It achieved limited success—and apparently only temporarily at that—in inculcating Central Asians with a sense of "Soviet-ness." What is left of that seems to be rapidly unravelling. Indeed, the republics themselves, which were probably intended to facilitate assimilation into a Russian-colored "international" culture, seem to be serving a contrary purpose.

At the beginning of his tenure, Gorbachev was faced with a choice between two very different paths of action in Central Asia. One was to attempt to "rein it in," to regain effective political, economic, social, and cultural control of the region. It appears that Gorbachev initially attempted to follow this path, which had also been chosen by Andropov and Chernenko. But within three years after taking office, the new leader seems to have realized that this was an impossible task. (Not insignificantly, perhaps, this was about the same time that he announced the Soviet intention to withdraw Soviet troops from Afghanistan.) From about 1988 on, Gorbachev began to try to salvage the Soviet empire by agreeing to a political system with much less ambitious goals, one with a very limited degree of "penetration" achieved through much greater reliance on legitimacy. In part it is this policy which Central Asians can thank for their "gains" in policies related to identity and participation. However, given the Central Asians' anger, frustration, and distrust of any schemes which Moscow had to offer, by 1988 it was probably too late to hope for success via this path, either.

Moscow's failure, of course, will be celebrated—and perhaps already *is* being celebrated—by Central Asians who feel that they have finally freed themselves of the "Russian yoke." But as the Russian presence recedes, it is clear that Central Asians will have to face their own daunting problems. Nevertheless, for the first time since the Bolshevik Revolution, they will be doing so without the "help" of any "elder brother."

Notes

1. For a full treatment of the various aspects of a "totalitarian" regime, see Carl J. Friedrich and Zbigniew K. Brzezinski, *Totalitarian Dictatorship and Autocracy* (Cambridge: Harvard University Press, 1956).

2. The other scenario mentioned by Rywkin was to allow Central Asians to develop their own form of "national communism." At the time, however, Rywkin saw this as "still out of the question." See Michael Rywkin, *Russia in Asia* (New York: Collier Books, 1963), pp. 159–60.

3. Two decades later, when Rywkin finished an updated version of his 1963 book, the new title bore witness to the changes in perception of Soviet politics and specifically the degree of control of Central Asia. His new title was "Moscow's Muslim Challenge" (M. E. Sharpe, Inc. Armonk, NY, 1982).

4. Leonard Binder, "Crises of Political Development," in *Crises and Sequences in Political Development* (Princeton: Princeton University Press, 1971), pp. 3–72.

5. Sidney Verba, "Sequences and Development," in *Crises and Sequences in Political Development*, p. 299.

6. Joseph LaPalombara, "Penetration: A Crisis of Government Capacity," in *Crises and Sequences in Political Development*, p. 208.

7. Verba, "Sequences and Development," p. 299.

8. Ibid.

9. *Natsional'nyi sostav naseleniia* (Moscow: Finansy i statistika), draft version p. 3. With the exception of the Uzbeks, the figures for 1989 represented little change from 1979. The proportion of Uzbeks fluent in Russian *fell* from almost half to about a quarter! (*Naselenie SSSR. Spravochnik* [Moscow: Politizdat, 1983], p. 128.) Most of this drop is almost certainly attributable to the inflated figure reported in 1979.

10. *Ozbekistan adabiyati va san"ati*, Apr. 24, 1987.

11. *Ozbekistan adabiyati va san"ati*, Jan. 1, 1988.

12. Personal observations in Uzbekistan 1989 and 1990.

13. *Komsomolets Kirgizii*, Oct. 14, 1987.

14. *Ozbekistan adabiyati va san"ati*, June 17, 1988.

15. *Molodezh' Azerbaidzhana*, June 11, 1987.

16. *Pravda Vostoka*, June 24, 1990; Paul Goble, "Central Asians form Political Block," Radio Liberty, *Report on the USSR*, July 13, 1990, pp. 18–20.

17. *Ozbekistan adabiyati va san"ati*, Apr. 1, 1988.

18. Mamadali Mahmudov, "Bugun va erta," *Sharq yulduzi*, no. 4, 1987, p. 151.

19. I heard these views from a variety of members of the Central Asian intelligentsia in 1989 and 1990.

20. *Pravda Vostoka*, June 9, 1990.

21. One of the most startling manifestations of this is a proposal by the dramatist Abduqahhar Ibrahimov, which suggests that Uzbekistan, apparently in its *current* borders, be renamed "Turkestan" or "Turan" and that Samarkand be re-established as its capital. Ibrahimov dismisses the fact that this name could offend Tajiks, for, he says, "the absolute majority" of the population of the republics of Central Asia and Kazakhstan belongs to Turkic peoples (*Yash leninchi*, 26 July 1990).

22. Joseph LaPalombara, "Distribution: A Crisis of Resource Management" in *Crises and Sequences in Political Development*, p. 236.

23. LaPalombara, "Distribution," p. 255.

24. *Pravda Vostoka*, Apr. 10, 1988.

25. *Yash leninchi*, Feb. 25, 1988.

26. Otkir Hashimov, "Avladlarga nima deymiz?" *Sharq yulduzi*, no. 2 (Feb.), 1988, p. 155.

27. This is specifically mentioned in the declaration issued by the leaders of the Central Asian republics and Kazakhstan issued at their June 1990 meeting (*Pravda Vostoka*, June 24, 1990).

28. *Yash leninchi*, Feb. 25, 1988.

29. Verba, "Sequences and Development," p. 299.

30. Weiner, "Political Participation: Crisis of the Political Process," in *Crises and Sequences in Political Development*, p. 177.

31. Joseph LaPalombara, "Penetration," p. 215.

32. Chingiz Aitmatov, "Tsena prozreniia," *Ogonek*, no. 28 (July), 1987, p. 8.

33. *Komsomolets Kirgizii*, Oct. 7, 1987.

34. *Pravda Vostoka*, Apr. 12, 1988.

35. *Komsomolets Tadzhikistana*, Dec. 16, 1987.

36. *Komsomolets Kirgizii*, May 18, 1988.

37. The language situation, of course, is much more complex than can be presented here. Other important issues which would be raised in a fuller discussion include the ambiguous feelings of many Russified Central Asians and the attitudes of local minorities living in other Central Asian republics (e.g., Uzbeks in Tajikistan). For a fuller discussion, see William Fierman, *Language Planning and National Development: The Uzbek Experience* (Berlin: Mouton, forthcoming).

38. Verba, "Sequences and Development," p. 299.

Glossary

apparat: Party machine or apparatus
apparatchik: Party bureaucrat
bai: a wealthy individual or more broadly a local notable
basmachi: term applied to Central Asian anti-Soviet guerilla groups most active in the early years after the Bolshevik Revolution
buro: the Party's primary decision-making body at a given level
gorkom: the Party committee at the city level
ishan: leader of a Sufi brotherhood
jadid: late nineteenth and early twentieth century Islamic proponent of reform, in particular the "new method" school
kishlak: a Central Asian village
kolkhoz: (abbreviated form of *kolektivnoe khoziaistvo*) a collective farm
korenizatsiia: indigenization or nativization; the policy of encouraging the employment of national minority cadres
madrasah: Muslim school of higher learning
manap: traditional local leader among the Kirgiz
mufti: a senior Muslim religious official; the head of a Muslim ecclesiastical administration
mullah: a Muslim cleric
nomenklatura: roster of key political appointments or group of individuals who hold those appointments
obkom: the Party committee at the oblast level
oblast: a subdivision of a republic; a region
oblispolkom: government executive committee at the oblast level
PTU: (abbreviation for *professional'no-tekhnicheskoe uchilishche*) a vocational or trade school
raikom: the Party committee at the raion level
raion: an administrative district
sovkhoz: (abbreviated form of *sovetskoe khoziaistvo*) a state farm
Sufism: Islamic mysticism
VUZ: (abbreviation for *vysshee uchebnoe zavedenie*): higher educational institution

About the Editor and Contributors

Donald S. Carlisle is Professor of Political Science at Boston College and a Fellow at Harvard's Russian Research Center. He is author of numerous articles on Soviet domestic and foreign policy. In the fall of 1990 he was invited to lecture at Samarkand University. While in Uzbekistan he also visited Bukhara and the Fergana Valley. Dr. Carlisle has recently completed a book-length study titled "Uzbekistan Under Soviet Rule" which focuses on the period 1917–1941.

James Critchlow is a Fellow of Harvard University's Russian Research Center. Until his retirement in 1985, he was Planning and Research Officer at the US Board for International Broadcasting. He also served as head of Soviet and East European research for Radio Liberty in Munich. He has written and lectured extensively on Soviet affairs, especially the Islamic areas of the country. He has also written extensively on Soviet Central Asian affairs and is now completing a book on Central Asian elites.

William Fierman is Associate Professor in the Department of Uralic and Altaic Studies at Indiana University (Bloomington). He first went to Uzbekistan in 1976, when he spent a year conducting dissertation research. He has since then returned many times, including a 1989 visit to Tashkent at the invitation of the Uzbekistan Writers' Union. His publications include *Language Planning and National Development: The Uzbek Experience*, and numerous book chapters and journal articles on the politics of language and culture and on youth problems in Central Asia.

Isabelle Kreindler is Research Associate at Haifa University, Israel. She is the author of numerous journal and book chapters on language, education, and the nationality problem in tsarist Russia and the Soviet Union. She is editor of *The Changing Status of Russian in the Soviet Union* and of *Sociolinguistic Perspectives on Soviet National Languages: Their Past, Present, and Future*.

Nancy Lubin is Associate Professor in Soviet affairs at Carnegie Mellon University and a Fellow at the Woodrow Wilson Center for International Scholars. She spent one year at Tashkent State University (Uzbekistan) and travels frequently to Soviet Central Asia and other parts of the USSR. Her publications include *Labour and Nationality in Soviet Central Asia: An Uneasy Compromise*, and Congressional studies and testimony on Soviet affairs. She is a member of the Council on Foreign Relations and of the Board of the Institute for U.S.-Soviet Relations.

Martha Brill Olcott is Professor of Political Science at Colgate University. She is author of *The Kazakhs*, editor of *The Soviet Multinational State* and the forthcoming volume *Islam and Traditional Life in Rural Central Asia*, and has written numerous other articles on Soviet nationality problems. She has made numerous research trips to Central Asia and other parts of the USSR.

Teresa Rakowska-Harmstone is Professor of Political Science at Carleton University (Ottawa, Canada). Her books include *Prospectives for Change in Communist Societies, Communism in Eastern Europe,* and *Russia and Nationalism in Central Asia: The Case of Tadzhikistan.* She has directed and coauthored a four-volume study *Warsaw Pact: The Question of Cohesion* and has written many other articles and book chapters on problems of ethnic relations and nationalities policy.

Azade-Ayse Rorlich is Associate Professor of History at the University of Southern California at Los Angeles. She is the author of *The Volga Tatars* and a contributor to numerous other books and scholarly journals. Her research focuses mainly on the Turkic ethnic groups of the Russian Empire and the Soviet Union, particularly on their social, cultural, and intellectual history.

Boris Z. Rumer is Research Associate at the Russian Research Institute of Harvard University. He is author of numerous articles on the Soviet economy. His books include *Investment and Reindustrialization in the Soviet Economy* and *Soviet Steel Industry.*

Ronald Wixman is Professor of Geography at the University of Oregon. He has travelled extensively in the USSR, including Central Asia, and is author of numerous scholarly publications about ethnic relations and ethnicity in the Soviet Union. Among his major works are: *Language Aspects of Ethnic Patterns and Processes in the North Caucasus* and *The Peoples of the USSR: An Ethnographic Handbook.*

Index

Abdullaeva, Rano, 115, 249
Abdurakhmanov, Abdudzhabbar, 101, 103, 107, 110–111
Abdurakhmanov, Yusup, 23
Abortions, 237
Achebe, Chinua, 221
Adylov, A., 190
Affirmative action, 179, 182, 263
Afghanistan, 3, 13, 199, 200, 201, 203, 207, 306
Afrasiyab ruins, 11
Agriculture, 18, 20, 71, 83, 241, 247, 248, 299
Aitmatov, Chingiz, 227, 231(n41)
Akhunbabayev, Y., 23
Akkhurgansk raion, 82
Aksakalism, 143
Al-Afghani, 208
Alcoholism, 236
Alfalfa, 82
Algerian Ministry of Islamic Affairs, 200
Alimov, Arif, 104, 106, 107, 108, 116, 122(n8), 124(n17), 127(n42), 262
All-Union Turcological Congress (1926), 30
Allworth, Edward A., 221, 222
Alma-Ata, 2, 151, 251
Almalyk, 146
Alphabets, 1, 30, 31, 191, 227, 231(n42), 295
Amur oblast, 258, 268
Andizhan, 14, 33, 119, 147, 209, 257
Andropov, Yu. V., 80, 113, 118, 119, 306
Anishchev, V. P., 127(n37), 129(n51), 141

Anisimkin, I. G., 114
Annaberdi, Annamuhammed, 192
Antinomy, 20
Aquinas (Saint). *See* Thomas Aquinas
Arabs, 3
Aral Sea, 5, 56, 82, 89(n34), 150, 238–239, 297
Arkhangelsk, 259
Armenia, 1
Arrests, 135
Arts, 27
Arutiunian, Iu. V., 168, 169, 181, 184(n14)
Ashirov, Nugman, 196
Ashkhabad, 239, 268
Asriiants, S. A., 127(n37)
Assad, H. 127–128(n43)
Atabay village, 191
Ata-Mirzaev, O. B., 47–48, 51, 52, 54, 56, 237
Atheism, 26, 27, 28, 117, 129(n49), 186
  promotion of, 186, 203–207
  See also Propaganda/propagandists, atheistic
Avicenna, 11, 201
Azerbaijan, 1, 220, 229(n6)

Babakhanov, Shamsuddin (Mufti), 201, 208–209
Babur, 147
Baikal Amur Mainline (BAM) railroad, 49, 262, 267
Baku Muslim Conference (1986), 200–201, 205
Baltic republics, 2, 64, 66(table 3.4), 67(table), 71, 73(table)

BAM. *See* Baikal Amur Mainline railroad
Baranov, 205
Basmachi guerillas, 15, 18, 96, 153, 203
Bedrintsev, Nikolai, 84
Bekabad steel plant, 19
Beliaev, I., 194, 202, 214(n43)
Bells, 223, 226
Belorussia, 52, 60(n22), 71, 73(table), 144, 176, 263, 285(n76)
Belovoshakhstroi project, 267
Bennigsen, Alexandre, 133, 172
Bibiotuns, 250
Binder, Leonard, 291
Birlik organization, 118, 251
Birthrates, 31, 42, 44, 45(table), 46(table), 53(table), 54, 180, 236, 237, 300. *See also* Childbearing
Biruni, Abu al-Raihan, 11, 201
Blackmail, 149
Black marketeering, 179
Bolshevik Revolution, 13, 14–16, 99
Bolsheviks, 21, 22, 24, 26, 186, 235, 293. *See also* Bolshevik Revolution
Brezhnev, Leonid, 94, 223. *See also* Brezhnev era
Brezhnev era, 4, 19, 20, 25, 27, 28, 29–30, 32, 80, 132, 134, 138, 176, 186, 219, 235, 270, 278. *See also* Brezhnev, Leonid
Bribetaking, 135, 147, 148
Bride price. *See* Kalym
Bromlei, Iu. V., 221
Bukhara, 11, 12, 16, 27, 97–98, 103, 130(n56), 151, 240, 297.
  ethnic issues in, 160, 162, 167, 168, 170, 171–172, 175, 177, 184(n11)
  See also Bukharan Soviet People's Republic
Bukharan Soviet People's Republic, 16–17, 297–298. *See also* Bukhara
Bukharin, Nikolai, 110, 154(n8)
Burials, 172, 173, 174, 175, 214(n37). *See also* Funerals

Buriat ASSR, 258
Buturlin, A. V., 129(n51)

Cadres
  interrepublican exchange of, 134, 139, 144, 145, 146, 150, 151
  reserves, 144, 148
  resurfacing of ousted, 147
  See also Uzbekistan, cadre policy in
Capital, fixed, 64, 66(table 3.4), 74, 75(table), 88(nn 13, 21)
Capital investment, 64, 69–74, 70(table 3.7), 72–73(table)
Captain's Daughter (Pushkin), 222
Carrère-d'Encausse, Hélène, 172
Caucasus, 72(table)
Cemeteries, 194. *See also* Burials; Funerals
Center for the Study of Man, 206
Center/periphery relations, 207. *See also* Central Asia, and Soviet authority/control
Central Asia
  child-care/day-care facilities in, 248
  and colonialism, 79, 86, 169, 170, 178, 182, 183, 290, 293, 299
  Communist Parties, 25, 26, 206
  economy. *See* Economy, Central Asian
  identities in, 4, 96, 117, 120, 121(n5), 187, 293–298, 302, 304, 305, 306
  infant mortality, 56, 57(table), 58, 150, 238–239, 240, 241
  national delimitation, 16–18, 21, 22, 98, 297–298
  nationality composition, 37, 40–41(tables), 42, 280–281
  native language status, 231(n42)
  native village inhabitants, 266
  population, 2, 3, 5, 36, 37, 38–39(tables), 50(table), 51, 54, 55–56, 63, 66(table 3.4), 88(n13), 180, 187, 238, 258, 300. *See also* Population; *under* Uzbekistan

Index

pre-Soviet history and revolution, 11–16
republic relations within, 296
rural higher education, 254(n55). See also Education, VUZy/specialized secondary
Russian conquest of, 12–13
Russian fluency in, 294, 307(n9). See also Languages, Russian
Russians in, 2, 11, 42, 140, 146, 185(n28). See also Uzbekistan, Russians in
sex ratio, 52
and "sister" Slavic republic oblasts, 264
and Slavic republics, 258
and Soviet authority/control, 4–5, 21, 25, 33, 85–86, 93, 109, 290, 291, 292, 293, 307. See also Central Asia, national delimitation; Uzbekistan, cadre policy in; Uzbekistan, Moscow relations
State Committees on Labor, 260, 261
underemployment of women, 247–248
vital statistics, 45(table), 53(table). See also Birthrates; Deathrates; Population, natural growth
See also individual republics
Cereals, 77
Chamkin, Anvar S., 206, 258, 274
Chauvinism, 128(n49), 185(n28)
Chaykhanas, 160, 164–165, 171
Chechmek (term), 176, 185(n27)
Chemical fibers, 74, 76
Chemicals, 19, 56, 63, 82, 150, 241
Cherkezova, M. V., 224
Chernenko, K. U., 119, 306
Childbearing, 237–241, 250, 252(n21). See also Birthrates
Childrearing, 242
Children, 46, 55, 78, 81, 83, 190–191, 193, 225, 226, 227, 228, 240, 241, 248. See also under Ethnic attitudes/relations

Chimkent, 12, 198
China. See People's Republic of China
Chirchik Hydroelectric Complex, 114
Cholera, 14
Christianity, 172, 187, 199, 202, 205, 211, 294. See also Russian Orthodox Church
Churbanov, Yu. M. (son-in-law of Brezhnev), 95, 179
Circumcision, 172, 173, 174, 192, 193, 214(n37), 250, 272, 287(n139)
Clem, Ralph, 255, 271, 274, 279, 281
Climate, 62, 89(n34), 241, 269, 286(n117)
Coal, 19
Collectivization, 18, 48
Colonialism. See under Central Asia
Commission for Turkestan Affairs, 26
Communist Party of the Soviet Union (CPSU), 5, 29, 108, 109, 290, 304
Central Committee, 25, 105, 123(n12), 147
membership, 138, 189
and migration, 258, 259, 277–278
Nineteenth Congress, 123(n12)
Nineteenth Party Conference, 189, 273
Politburo, 25, 105
Presidium, 105, 108
and religion, 186, 272–273
Seventeenth Congress, 23
Twenty-Seventh Congress (1986), 131, 138
See also Central Asia, and Soviet authority/control
Competence vs. reliability criteria, 22, 23, 24
Computers, 220, 229(n7)
Construction, 19, 71
Consumer goods, 68, 243, 278, 281
Consumption, 69, 70(table 3.6), 87
Contraception, 58, 237
Corruption, 25–26, 81, 94, 113, 114–116, 135, 140, 144, 148, 149,

152, 179, 182, 189, 190. *See also*
Cotton affair; Crime
Cotton affair, 4–5, 80–81, 95, 117
Cotton production, 13, 18, 19, 20–21,
69, 71, 83, 247, 299
crisis in, 76–79
exports, 74, 76
infrastructure serving, 63
and pollution, 238, 241
prices, 86–87, 99, 305
quality/quantity issues, 76, 77, 86
superspecialization in, 80
"Tragic Experiment" of, 79–83
water requirements, 78, 79
See also Cotton affair; *under*
Uzbekistan
CPSU. *See* Communist Party of the
Soviet Union
Crime, 137, 145, 278, 297, 300. *See
also* Corruption; Law
enforcement personnel
Crises, 291–292
*Crises and Sequences in Political
Development* (Binder et al.), 291
Cultural issues, 11–12, 26–30, 97,
132–133, 175, 294. *See also*
Ethnic attitudes/relations;
Languages, acculturation/
communication functions;
Religion
Currency, 74, 86, 29
Cycles, action/reaction and attack/
retreat, 93–94, 95

Dairy products, 87
*Day Lasts More than a Hundred Years,
The* (Aitmatov), 227
Dead Souls (Gogol), 222, 226
Deathrates, 42, 45(table), 53(table)
Death sentences, 135
Defoliants, 82, 241
Demidov, S. M., 203
Democratization, 146, 149
Demographic issues, 33, 54–59, 119.
See also Central Asia, population;
Population

Demonstrations/riots, 33, 55, 111,
117, 118, 119, 129(n50), 146, 151,
179, 208, 211, 255, 301, 303. *See
also* Ethnic attitudes/relations,
tensions/violence
De-Stalinization. *See under* Stalinism/
Stalinists
Didorenko, Eduard Alekseevich, 152
Diet, 240, 252(n21)
Discrimination, 178–181, 270, 303
Diseases, 240, 252(n21)
Distribution problems, 298–301, 305
Divorce, 244–245
Dollars, 86
Dowries, 243
Draftees, 55
Drugs, 236. *See also* Opium poppies
Dushanbe, 33, 201, 239, 276
Dzhizak oblast, 113, 126(n32), 190,
278

Earthquakes, 71, 110
Economy, Central Asian, 13, 14, 18–
21, 25, 32, 33, 58–59, 64, 87,
236, 255, 256, 306
agrarian-colonial model of, 79, 86.
See also Central Asia, and
colonialiam
and atheism, 186
and central planning, 85, 299
crisis in, 279
economic growth, 65(table)
investments, 71, 72(table)
and national economy, 63–69,
64(table), 66(table 3.3), 66(table
3.4), 68, 305
and population, 55–56, 64,
66(table 3.4)
second economy, 247, 248
sovereignty over natural resources,
299
See also individual republics
Education, 13, 30–33, 99, 281, 306
and atheism, 186, 203. *See also*
Propaganda/propagandists,
atheistic

Index

and cadre placement/advancement, 140, 145
equipment shortages, 276–277
and family size, 237–238, 251–252(nn 2, 3, 5)
females, 32, 235, 237–238, 247, 250, 254(n55)
health/hygiene, 239
higher education. *See* Education, VUZy/specialized secondary
and Islam, 191, 193
kindergartens/nursery schools, 220
language instruction, 29–30, 31, 219–221, 228(nn 2, 3), 229(n5). *See also* Ethnolinguistics; Literature, Russian
and migration, 263–265, 274–277
non-enrollees, 257
pedagogical institutes, 284(n60)
primary schools, 31, 247
religious, 197, 207, 250. *See also* Islam, schools
teachers, 31, 32, 220, 229(n7), 275–276, 288(n168)
tekhnikums, 263
vocational-technical *uchilishche* (PTU), 263–265, 267, 268–269, 273, 275, 277, 278–279, 285(nn 76, 80), 289(n199)
VUZy/specialized secondary, 31–32, 35(n46), 247, 254(n55), 263, 289(n199)
Elders, 143, 173, 174
Electricity, 20
Elites, 25, 94, 95, 99, 132–133. *See also under* Uzbekistan
Embezzlement, 135, 147, 189
Employment. *See* Labor issues
Environmental issues, 5, 20, 119, 134, 150, 240, 256
cotton production, 82
and infant mortality, 238–239
pollution, 238–239, 240, 281
and population density, 56
See also Water
Esenin, S. A., 225, 228
Estonians, 169–170

Ethnic attitudes/relations, 159–183, 185(n28)
and children, 162, 166–167
and competition among groups, 169, 178–181, 182, 281
head coverings, 171, 173, 174, 185(nn 22, 26)
housing, 163–164, 178–179, 182, 184(n10)
husband-wife relations, 162, 166, 184(n14)
and languages, 163, 177–178, 181
and migration, 270, 271, 279, 280
rural vs. urban groups, 170
school/workplace colleagues, 161–162, 164
as situational, 160–161, 177, 183(n4)
and social interaction, 161–169
studies concerning, 183–184(n9)
tensions/violence, 279, 280, 281, 297, 300. *See also* Demonstrations/riots
Ethnolinguistics, 224–228, 230(n30)
articles, 227–228
experts in, 225
Eugene Onegin (Pushkin), 225

Faculty of Oriental Languages (Dushanbe), 191
Fainsod, M., 99
Family life, 271. *See also under* Women
Family size, 46–47, 47(table), 52, 54, 58, 59, 163, 166
expectations of married women, 237
See also under Education
Far East. *See under* Union of Soviet Socialist Republics
Farms, state/collective, 136. *See also* Kolkhoz
Fathers and Sons (Turgenev), 226
Fazylov, E. I., 190
Fergana/Fergana Valley, 2, 14, 15, 33, 55, 84, 96, 117, 118, 119,

129(n50), 130(n56), 148, 209, 242, 255, 257, 260, 300. *See also* Tashkent/Fergana cadres
Fertility rates, 46, 47, 49
Fertilizer, 56, 86
Feshbach, Murray, 256, 270–271, 274, 281
Fishing industry, 89(n34)
Five-Year Plans
  First, 18, 22, 27, 31, 99, 100
  Eleventh, 71, 257, 260, 261, 265, 267, 268
  Twelfth, 258, 261, 262, 264, 265
Fruits, 83, 89(n56)
Frunze, 239
Fundamentalism. *See under* Islam
Funerals, 188, 194, 272, 295. *See also* Burials

Galiev, Sultan, 16
Gas production, 19–20, 21, 63, 71
Gdlian, Tel'man, 135, 150
Generational analysis, 95
Georgia, 220
Germans, 168, 175, 177, 178
Gil'manov, Khazret, 198
Glasnost, 6, 86, 144, 146, 150, 187, 204, 211, 270, 278, 294, 301
Gogol, N. V., 222
Gök Tepe, Battle of, 12
Gold, 20, 87(n7)
Golodnaia Steppe, 79
Gorbachev, Mikhail, 71, 95, 117, 133, 280, 294, 304, 306
  and political development, 301, 305
  and reforms, 187, 257
  and Uzbekistan, 80, 119, 131, 134, 146, 151, 299
Grain, 18, 19, 299
Grapes, 89(n56)
Great Fergana Canal, 110
Guliamov, Rasul, 116, 124(nn 17, 18), 127(n42)

Hairy Ishans order, 191
Harasymiw, Bohdan, 132

Hashimov, Otkir, 83
Health issues, 56, 82, 212, 238–241, 252(nn 21, 24)
Holidays, 193
Hospitals, 239
Housing, 262, 269, 281. *See also under* Ethnic attitudes/relations
Hungry Steppe, 262
Hurshid, 196
Hydroelectric power, 19, 20, 63

Iavan Electrochemical Plant, 20
Ibn Sina, 11, 201
Ibn Sina Medal and Prize, 201
Ibragimov, Abdukakhar, 129(n56)
Ibragimov, M. I., 118
Ibrahimov, Abduqahhar, 308(n21)
Identity issues. *See* Central Asia, identities in
Ikramov, Akmal, 23, 94, 107, 110, 154(n8)
Ikramov, A. S., 127(n37)
Ikramov, Kamil, 128(n47), 154(n8)
Industrialization, 48, 87
Industry, 18–19, 20, 63, 71, 84, 247, 249
Infant mortality. *See under* Central Asia; Union of Soviet Socialist Republics
Infertility, 244–245
Institute for Teaching Russian to Non-Russians, 227
Intelligentsia, 21–22, 23, 120, 272, 281, 294, 295, 297, 300, 303. *See also under* Uzbekistan
Intermarriage, 165–168
Iran, 203, 207
Iron, 21
Irrigation, 18, 56, 62–63, 79, 82, 99
Iskanderov, I., 85
Islam, 3–4, 13, 26–27, 28, 30, 117, 133, 147, 186–212, 235–236, 294
  believers, 190–191
  clergy, 204, 208–209
  and foreign policy, 200–201
  fundamentalism, 207, 209, 250

international conferences, 200–201
and internationalization, 195, 199
Islamic state, 208
and migration, 271–273, 274
modernization, 195–201, 206
and native officials, 189–190
observances, 192–195, 198, 206, 272. *See also* Religion, rituals/customs
official and parallel, 187–189. *See also* Sufism
schools, 13, 171–172, 175, 191, 202
sermons. *See* Khutbas
and socialism, 195, 196
as threat, 198–200
tolerance toward, 209–212
unity, 195–196
unregistered communities, 188, 212(n6)
and women, 249–251
See also Muslims
Islamskaia Pravda, 207–208
Iusupov, Usman, 101, 103, 105, 107, 108, 110, 111, 123(nn 12, 13), 125(n24)
Ivanov, Nikolai, 135, 150
Izvestiia, 110, 262, 272

Jadid movement, 13–14, 22, 23, 101, 133, 196, 295
Japan, 87
Jews, 167–168, 170, 174, 176, 177, 199
Jihad, 198–199
Juvenile delinquency, 236

Kadyrov, G., 208
Kaganovich, Lazar, 123(n 13)
Kaiumov, Favaris, 82
Kalym, 242, 243
Kamalov, Sabir, 101, 104, 106, 107, 109, 116, 122(n8), 128(n44), 192
Kamenetskii, Boris, 125–126(n25)
Karakalpak Autonomous Soviet Socialist Republic, 58, 98, 148, 238, 240

Karakhanid state, 189
Karakirgiz Autonomous Oblast, 17
Karimov, Islam, 117–118, 119, 129(nn 52, 56), 190
Karklins, Rasma, 159, 168, 183(n4)
Kashkadarya oblast, 98, 136, 240, 245, 246, 261, 268
Kasym, Abdurassulkhan, 192
Kazakhstan, 2, 3, 19, 27, 59(n1), 71, 145, 151, 179, 187, 189, 198, 209, 237, 251, 296
Kazakh steppe, 12
KGB, 129(n50)
Khaidarov, G. Kh., 114, 126–127(n33), 127(37)
Khalmukhamedov, M. Kh., 189, 206
Kharchev, K. M., 209–210
Khiva, 12, 16. *See also* Khorezm
Khodzhaev, Asadilla A., 109, 112, 113, 126(n31)
Khodzhaev, A. R., 113, 114
Khodzhaev, Faizulla, 23, 94, 107, 110, 111, 125(n23)
Khomeini (Ayatollah), 208
Khorezm, 11, 12. *See also* Khiva; Khorezm oblast; Khorezm Soviet People's Republic
Khorezm oblast, 79, 98, 240
Khorezm Soviet People's Republic, 17, 297–298
Khrushchev, Nikita, 19, 27, 32, 105
de-Stalinization campaign, 28, 103, 109, 304
removal, 110, 125(n22)
sovnarkhozy experiment, 19, 69–70
See also Khrushchev era
Khrushchev era, 25, 235, 290. *See also* Khrushchev, Nikita
Khudaiberdyev, Narmakhonmadi D., 109, 112, 113, 114, 125(n21)
Khudaibergenova, Rimadjan M., 152
Khutbas, 187, 196–197
Kirgizia, 3, 17, 222, 251
Council of People's Commissars, 23
economy, 64

education/employment in other republics, 264, 265, 267, 268, 275
ethnic violence in, 297
hydroelectric power, 20
Islam in, 188–189, 213(n23)
language use in, 302, 303
Pedagogical Research Institute, 224
population, 37. *See also* Central Asia, population
Public Education Department, 83
urban dwellers, 169
VUZy/specialized secondary education, 32, 35(n46)
Women's Pedagogical Institute, 225, 227
See also Central Asia
Kirgiz Soviet Socialist Republic (Kirgiz SSR), 17. *See also* Kirgizia
Kirgiz SSR. *See* Kirgiz Soviet Socialist Republic
Kirgizstan madaniyati, 192
Kirichenko, A. I., 124(n19)
Kocharli, K., 196
Kokand, 12, 15–16, 130(n56)
Kolbin, Gennadii, 2, 145, 179
Kolkhoz, 99, 169
Komsomol, 259
  shock projects, 260–261, 262, 267, 269–270, 273, 275, 278, 280, 283(n37)
  See also under Uzbekistan
Komsomolets Uzbekistana, 277
Komsomol'skaia Pravda, 81
Koran, 30, 188, 191, 194, 197, 206, 209
Koreans, 19
Korenizatsiia, 22–23, 24, 29, 145, 302
Koroteeva, V. V., 238
Kostomarov, V. G., 224
Kretov, V. G., 129(n51)
Krokodil, 226
Kuala Lumpur, Malaysia, 184(n10)
Kunaev, Dinmukhammed A., 2, 145–146, 151, 179
Kurandykov, I., 192

Kurbanov, Rakhmankul, 109, 111–112, 124(n20)
Kurbanov, R. O., 196
Kurgan Tiube, 208
Kyzylkum Desert, 20

Labor issues
  child labor, 83
  and commuting, 283(n18)
  cotton production, 77–78, 83, 84, 241, 276
  Komsomol shock projects, 260–261
  labor excesses/shortages, 20, 255, 256, 258, 281, 283(n18)
  labor productivity, 64, 66, 67(table), 68, 69
  specialized brigades, 259
  student/non-student opportunities, 259–260
  temporary/seasonal employment, 259–260
  See also Migrations; Underemployment; Unemployment; Women, employment
Labour and Nationality in Soviet Central Asia (Lubin), 128(n45)
Land, 55–56, 262
Languages, 26, 27, 29–30, 163, 180, 181, 308(n37)
  acculturation/communication functions, 221–226
  connotations, 222, 225–226
  decrees, 219–220
  Kirgiz, 295, 302, 303
  language laws, 302–304
  literary, 18
  and migration, 275
  Russian, 29–30, 177–178, 181, 219–224, 228(nn 2, 3), 229(n5), 275, 292, 294, 307(n9). *See also* Ethnolinguistics; Language, language laws
  Tajik, 4, 17
  translations, 191
  Turkic, 4, 295–296

Uzbek, 4, 177, 295
  See also Alphabets
LaPalombara, Joseph, 291, 292, 298
Latvians, 176
Law enforcement personnel, 136–137, 145, 152
Legitimacy problem, 304, 305, 307
Lenin, V. I., 5, 209–210
Leningrad, 179
Lermontov, M. Iu., 222
Lewis, Robert, 255–256, 271, 279, 281
Ligachev, Egor, 118, 119, 132, 134–135, 139, 144, 145, 146, 151
Literacy, 31, 35(n39)
Literature, Russian, 222–223, 224, 225–226
Literaturnaia gazeta, 80–81, 194
Lithuanian Popular Front, 1
Living standards, 59, 150, 170, 258, 281
Localism, 141–142, 270
Lomonosov, M. V., 222
Lubin, Nancy, 128(n45)
Luchinskii, P. K., 264

Machine building, 19, 63
Madrasah. See Islam, schools
Mahmudov, Mamadali, 296
Makatov, I. A., 204–205
Makhkamov, K., 188, 191, 194
Makhmudov, N., 109
Malaianov, A., 103
Man and Religion (radio journal), 206
Market economy, 299, 300
Marr, Nikolai, 30
Marriage, 4, 173, 175, 188, 192, 193, 214(n37), 241, 242–246, 272, 273. See also Divorce; Intermarriage
Masaliev, Absamat, 250
Massacres, 15
Massell, Gregory, 24
Matchanov, Nazar, 109, 112, 126(n27)
Maududi, al- (Pakistani leader), 208

Mausoleum of the Samanids, 11
Mazipov, R. G., 223
Media, 210. See also Press
Meilakh, B. S., 224
Mercury, 20
Meskhetian Turks, 297
Metals/metal industries, 19, 87(n7)
Middle class, 120
Migrations, 48–49, 50(table), 58, 77, 180, 182, 255–282
  age groups, 265–266
  dropouts, 267–269, 278
  and education. See under Education
  incentives, 262–263
  of indigenous/non-indigenous nationalities, 265, 266, 280, 281
  labor resources to RSFSR, 258, 261
  organized/spontaneous, 282(n6)
  program failures, 269–279
  and resettlements, 259–265, 268, 273
  and skills, 274–275
  and social conscience, 277–279
Mikhailovskaia, N. G., 221
Mir-i Arab Madrasah, 27, 35(n38)
Mirza-Akhmedov, M., 106, 107
Modernization, 100, 291
Moldavia, 1
Moldokasymov, 192
Molodoi kommunist, 273
Mongol invasions, 12
Monuments, 175
Morality, 194, 197, 236
Moscow, 179, 180
Moscow Show Trial (1938), 107
Mosques, 26, 27, 175, 187, 188, 190, 191, 192, 208, 210, 211
  numbers of, 212(n4)
Muhammad (Prophet), 197, 210
Muhammad Yusuf, Muhammad Sadiq, 196–197, 209, 211
Mukhamedzhanov, Mirza ali, 82
Mukhametzhanov, Sh., 198
Mukhitdinov, N. A., 103, 104, 105–107, 108, 109, 116, 122–123(nn 8, 9), 123(n12), 124(nn 16, 19), 127–128(nn 42, 43)

Mullahs, 191, 192
Murtazaev, Kayum, 109
Musakhanov, M. M., 109, 113, 114
Music, 29, 273
Muslimov, S., 188
Muslim Religious Boards, 187–188
  Fourth Congress (Kurultay), 206, 209, 210, 211–212
Muslims, 2, 3, 14, 15, 17, 24, 25, 95, 99, 152, 168, 169, 170, 187, 297, 304. *See also* Islam
Muslim Spiritual Directorate of Central Asia and Kazakhstan, 198, 200

Nachal'niki, 99, 100–101
Namangan, 209, 211
Narmatov, Nadir, 295
Nasriddinova, Iadgar, 106, 108, 109, 111–112, 123–124(n14)
National delimitation. *See under* Central Asia
National income, 68, 69, 70(table 3.6), 258
Nationalism, 95, 119–120, 128(n49), 131, 133, 206, 302
Nationalities, 1, 37, 39–41(tables), 138, 139, 141, 145, 176, 183(n5), 256, 273. *See also* Ethnic attitudes/relations
Nativization, 107, 180. *See also* Korenizatsiia
Nauka i religiia, 210
Naumkin, V. V., 196
Navoi oblast, 147, 150, 240
Nepotism, 141, 148, 179, 182
Newspapers. *See* Press
Niiazov, Amin, 102–103, 104, 105, 108, 123(n12), 189
Nishanov, Rafik, 115–116, 117, 124–125(n20), 127(n39), 194
Nomadic herdsmen, 18
Nomenklatura, 132, 134, 137, 141, 142
Non-black earth zone, 49, 262
Novosti Press Agency, 201
Nurek Hydroelectric Station, 20

Nurutdinov, Sirodzh, 101, 102, 104, 106, 107, 109, 110, 123(n14), 124(n170
Nysanbayuly, Ratbek, 209

Obituaries, 122(n7), 125(n24)
Ocherki istorii Kommunisticheskoi partii Uzbekistana, 125(n22)
Oil production, 19, 20, 63, 71, 74
Opium poppies, 278
Orenburg-Tashkent railroad, 13
Orlov, 128(n47)
Orlyonok Pioneer Camp, 81
Osetrov, T. N., 114, 127(n34), 128(n47)
Osh oblast/city, 33, 83, 117, 119, 129(n50), 188, 191, 240, 251
Ostrovsky, 226

Pakhtakor Incident (1969), 111–112
Pan-Turkism, 296
Parks, 160, 165, 171
Participation problem, 301–304, 305, 306
Patriotism, 28, 96, 277
Peaches, 83
Peasants, 99
Penetration problem, 291, 292–293, 302, 304, 305, 306
People's Republic of China, 3, 74, 76
Perestroika, 55, 131, 132, 146, 149, 189, 190, 197, 210, 211
Perm Hydroelectric Power Station, 262
Persia, 4
Pesticides, 56, 80, 82
Petroleum. *See* Oil production
Pigs. *See* Pork
Pilgrimages, 203, 210, 245, 250
Pipes, Richard, 15
Poliakov, S. P., 238, 242, 244, 245, 248, 249
Police, 25
Political development, 291–307
Pollution. *See under* Environmental issues

Index

Polygamy, 242
Population, 59(n1)
  age groups, 52, 54–55
  Muslim (Central Asian), 187
  natural growth, 42, 44, 45(table), 46–48, 50(table), 53(table)
  rural/urban, 51–52, 53(table), 56
  See also under Central Asia
Pork, 163, 170, 172, 173, 174, 184(n10)
Pospelova, E., 84
Pravda Vostoka, 110, 122(n7), 128–129(n49), 259, 261, 278
Press, 49, 81, 85, 129(n50), 148, 149, 185(n28), 205, 207–208, 210, 236–237, 242, 244, 249, 262, 263, 265, 275, 277, 278, 280, 296
Prices, 86, 281. *See also under* Cotton production
Professions, 143
Prokofiev, 221
Propaganda/propagandists, 28, 58, 79, 176, 202
  atheistic, 186, 188, 189, 197, 203, 204–205, 206, 212
Prostitution, 236, 245, 253(n48)
Prozorov, M., 199–200
Prusakova, N. G., 196
PTU. *See* Education, vocational-technical *uchilishche*
Pulatov, Timur, 81, 150
Purges, 23–24, 101, 145, 304. *See also under* Uzbekistan
Puritanism, 211
Pushkin, A. S., 222, 225, 228
Pye, Lucien, 291

Qadiriy, Abdulla, 28
Qazaq adebiyeti, 191, 203

Racism, 181. *See also* Ethnic attitudes/relations; Discrimination
Railroads, 49, 84
Rakhimov, Rashid, 68

Rakowska-Harmstone, Teresa, 25
Ramadan, 193
Rapes, 250, 254(n60)
Rashidov, Sharaf, 25–26, 80, 94, 95, 98, 103, 104, 105, 106–107, 108–109, 111, 112, 113, 115–116, 118, 119, 123(n12), 124(n18), 126(n31), 128(n49), 133, 135, 179, 292
  cadre legacy, 137–143
Refugees, 19
Religion, 128(n49), 146–147, 186, 206
  and ethnicity/nationality, 207, 272, 287(n139)
  law of 1990 concerning, 207
  political lines of, 204–205
  rituals/customs, 172–175, 193–194, 204, 287(n139). *See also* Islam, observances
  See also Atheism; Christianity; Islam; Russian Orthodox Church
Religious Board of the Muslims of Central Asia. *See* Muslim Religious Boards
Resettlements. *See under* Migrations
Riga, 239
Riots. *See* Demonstrations/riots
Rituals. *See* Religion, rituals/customs
Rowland, Richard, 255–256, 271, 279, 281
RSFSR. *See* Russian Soviet Federated Socialist Republic
Rubles, 86
Russia, tsarist, 12–13, 14, 86, 140, 172, 293. *See also* Literature, Russian
Russia in Central Asia (Rywkin), 290
Russian Language Resource Centers, 220
Russian Orthodox Church, 205, 210, 223
Russian Soviet Federated Socialist Republic (RSFSR), 16, 144, 258, 261, 263, 264, 280, 305
  birthrates, 44, 45(table)
  Central Asian nationalities in, 48, 266–267, 285(n95), 285–286(n97)

Central Industrial Region, 180
economy, 71, 73(table)
family size, 47(table)
infant mortality, 57(table), 238
population, 37, 38(table), 50(table), 52
Uzbek cadre training in, 145
vital statistics, 45(table), 53(table)
Russification, 1, 27–28, 100, 165, 293
Rywkin, Michael, 290, 307(nn 2, 3)

Sagadeev, A., 199
Saidbaev, Talib, 214(n37)
Saidov, A., 208
Sajudis. *See* Lithuanian Popular Front
Salih, Muhammad, 58, 59, 86, 89(n51), 149–150, 239, 300
Salikh, Mukhammad. *See* Salih, Muhammad
Salimov, A. U., 113–114, 115, 127(n40)
Samarkand, 17, 97–98, 103, 109, 121(n4), 129–130(n56), 140, 148, 245, 257, 297, 308(n21)
ethnic issues in, 160, 162, 167, 168, 170, 175, 177, 184(n11)
Samarkand University, 211, 272
Satin, B. F., 129(n51), 146
Satybaldyev, A., 191
School Reform of 1984, 220
Science/scientists, 141, 198
Self-immolations, 244. *See also* Suicides
Sel'skaia zhizn', 245
Sewerage, 239
Sex education, 58
Shamat Ishan, mosque of, 190
Shanskii, N. M., 223–224
Sheiman, L. A., 224, 227
Siberia, 63, 258, 259, 261, 262, 273
Simon, Gerhard, 133
Slastenko, E., 84
Slavs, 2, 37, 42, 44, 46, 48, 52, 94, 96, 129(n51), 138, 139, 151, 152, 170, 265, 280, 281, 294
and ethnic issues, 163, 166, 168, 169, 170, 174, 176, 177, 219

Slavic republics, 264, 265, 267, 268, 269, 273, 275, 279, 280
urban dwellers, 169, 170
Smolensk Under Soviet Rule (Fainsod), 99
Socialism, 194, 195
Social sphere, investment in, 71, 74, 88(n13)
Soils, 82
Soiuz, 238
Sokolov, Vladimir, 152
Solokhiddinov, Z., 69
South Korea, 87
South Tajikistan Territorial Production Complex, 20
Sovetskaia Kirgizia, 221
Sovet Turkmenistany, 198
Soviet of Soldiers', Workers', amd Peasants' Deputies, 15
Soviet Union. *See* Union of Soviet Socialist Republics
Sovnarkhoz experiment. *See under* Khrushchev, Nikita
Spiritual Directorate of the Muslims of Central Asia and Kazakhstan, The, 188
Stalin, Joseph, 28, 103, 145, 292–293, 298, 304. *See also* Stalin era; Stalinism/Stalinsts
Stalin era, 95, 290. *See also* Stalin, Joseph; Stalinism/Stalinists
Stalinism/Stalinists, 95
Class of '38, 100–103, 106
de-Stalinization, 28, 101, 103, 107–108, 109–111, 124(n16)
Great Retreat, 99
two-tiered approach, 100
See also Stalin, Joseph; Stalin era; Uzbekistan, Stalinism in
Standard of living. *See* Living standards
Starvation, 55
Steel, 19
Stepanenko, Iuliia L., 125(n24)
Stolovaias, 165
Stores, state run, 170
Storm (Ostrovsky), 226

Sufism, 14, 175, 188, 191, 192, 201–203, 205, 208, 211
Suicides, 236, 244, 245–246
Surkhandarya oblast, 98, 147
Suskin, V. I., 127(n37)
Sviderskii, B. E., 190

Tairov, K., 127(n37)
Tajik Aluminum Plant, 20
Tajikistan, 3, 4, 17, 18, 20, 58
  collective farm workers, 169
  Commission for Establishing New Rites and Customs, 195
  divorce in, 244
  education/employment in other republics, 259, 260, 263, 264–265, 267, 268, 269, 273, 275, 286(n114)
  Islam in, 188, 189–190, 202, 207–208
  population, 37. *See also* Central Asia, population
Tajiks in Uzbekistan, 162, 167, 168, 177, 182–183, 185(n28)
  rural schools, 276
  unemployment, 257
  urban dwellers, 169
  VUZy/specialized secondary education, 35(n46)
  women's employment in, 247, 248
  See also Central Asia
Tajik Soviet Socialist Republic, 17. *See also* Tajikistan
Talhatan Baba Mosque, 192, 197
Tamerlane, 12, 147
Tariffs, 84
Tashkent (city/oblast), 12, 14–15, 71, 84, 96–97, 98, 111, 121(n4), 130(n56), 136, 140, 145, 151, 238
  ethnic issues in, 160, 162, 168, 170, 175, 177, 178, 179, 184(nn 11, 14)
  infant mortality, 239
  Shaykh Zaynutdin Mosque, 187
  Tilla Shaykh Mosque, 208
  See also Tashkent/Fergana cadres

Tashkent Conference (1980), 200, 201
Tashkent/Fergana cadres, 103, 109, 112, 114, 116
TASSR. *See* Turkestan Autonomous Soviet Socialist Republic
Tatars, 2, 14, 16, 19, 178, 193, 206
Tatarstan, 206
Taxation, turnover, 68, 69
Tchaikovsky, P. I., 221–222
Teahouses. *See Chaykhanas*
Technology, 78, 87, 198, 291
Terror, 292–293, 304
Textile industries, 63, 83–87
Third World, 200
Thomas Aquinas, 199
Tiumen oblast, 258, 262, 267, 270
Tobacco, 241, 247
Totalitarianism, 290, 291, 306
Tourists, 171, 172
Toynbee, Arnold, 93
Transcaspia, 12–13
Trans-Caspian railroad, 13
Transcaucasus republics, 2, 64, 66(table 3.4), 67(table), 71, 180
Transportation, 71
Turan Lowland, 62
Turgenev, I. S., 226
Turkestan, 3, 13, 14, 15, 16, 296
  General-Governorship, 12, 15
Turkestan Autonomous Soviet Socialist Republic (TASSR), 16, 31
Turkic national epics, 28
Turkmenia. *See* Turkmenistan
Turkmenistan, 3, 12–13, 18, 193, 214(n37), 246
  childbirth mortality of women, 239
  collective farm workers, 169
  Communist Party, 25
  cotton production, 20–21, 83
  Council for Scientific Atheism and Progressive Tradition, 195
  education/employment in other republics, 265, 268, 269, 273, 278–279, 285(n80)
  gas production, 19–20, 63

population, 37. *See also* Central Asia, population
rural schools, 276
self-immolations, female, 244
teachers in, 276
unemployment, 257
urban dwellers, 169
VUZy/specialized secondary education, 35(n46)
See also Central Asia
Tursunov, A., 205–206

Ubaidullaeva, R., 59
Ukraine/Ukrainians, 71, 138, 144, 175, 177, 263, 264, 276, 285(nn 80, 95)
Ulema, 13
Ulmasov, Akhmed, 80
Ulughbek, 12
Underemployment, 246, 247, 248, 255
Unemployment, 55, 148, 246, 255, 256–257, 300
Union of Soviet Socialist Republics (USSR), 74
  Chief Prosecutor, 136
  collective farm workers, 169
  Communist Party. *See* Communist Party of the Soviet Union
  Constitution of 1977, 186, 197
  cotton production/exports, 21, 76
  Council for Religious Affairs, 187, 209
  economy, 54, 65(table), 66(table 3.4), 86, 88(n13), 134, 298, 301
  ethnic Russian population, 36
  Far East, 258, 261, 262, 273, 275, 280
  foreign policy, 200–201
  infant mortality, 57(table), 238, 239
  law on religion (1990), 207
  medical care, 238
  migrations of urban/rural dwellers, 266
  Ministry of Health, 241
  non-Slavic population, 2
  People's Deputies, 209
  population, 38–39(tables), 50(table), 66(table 3.4)
  rural schools, 276
  southern tier, 54–55
  vital statistics, 45(table), 53(table)
United States, 74, 173–174, 177, 179, 180
Uranium, 20
Urbanization, 49, 51, 169
Usmankhodzhaev, Buzrukkhodzha, 126(n30)
Usmankhodzhaev, Inamzhon B., 108, 112–113, 114, 115, 116, 126(n30), 128(n49), 135, 136, 149–150, 154(n17), 262
USSR. *See* Union of Soviet Socialist Republics
Uzbekistan, 3, 4, 17, 19, 249
  age of officials in, 143
  agriculture, 299
  birthrates, 44, 46
  cadre policy in, 118, 131–153, 302
  cadre reform in, 137, 144–147, 151, 153. *See also* Cadres, interrepublican exchange of; Uzbekistan, purges
  collectivization in, 18
  Communist Party, 23, 25, 101, 108, 110, 114, 118, 122(n8), 128(n49), 136, 143, 147, 148, 151, 154(n17), 189, 195, 210. *See also* Uzbekistan, purges
  cotton production, 20, 21, 62, 69, 74, 76–77, 80, 83, 86, 137, 150, 292, 297. *See also* Cotton affair
  Council of People's Commissars, 23
  draft opposition, 251
  economy, 64, 71, 88(n21), 148
  education/employment in other republics, 259, 260, 261–262, 263, 264, 267, 268, 275, 278–279, 283(n37), 284(nn 47, 60), 285–286(n97), 289(n205)
  elites, 111, 118–119, 147–150, 153, 155(n48). *See also* Uzbekistan, cadre policy in

Index

ethnic issues. *See* Ethnic attitudes/ relations
"European" officials in, 139–140
family size, 52, 54, 58, 237–238
First Congress of the Uzbek Intelligentsia, 107
first-secretary positions in, 138–139
independence declaration, 131, 298
industry, 19
infant mortality, 238, 239
intelligentsia, 107, 128(n49), 150
irrigated land, 55–56
Islamic rituals in, 214(n37)
and Komsomol, 101, 189, 260, 283(n37)
living standards, 150
meat consumption in, 87
Memorial Day, 194
migrations from, 266. *See also* Uzbekistan, education/ employment in other republics
Moscow relations, 94, 116, 118, 119, 121(n5), 131, 153. *See also* Uzbekistan, cadre policy in; Uzbekistan, cadre reform in; Uzbekistan, purges
nationality composition, 40(table 2.3), 42, 43(table). *See also* Ethnic attiudes/relations
nomenklatura, 80
population, 2, 5, 17, 37, 44, 48, 54, 55–56, 60(n22), 88(n21). *See also* Central Asia, population
purges, 26, 94, 95, 113, 114–116, 118, 119, 135–137, 147–150
raion organizations, 152
regions, 96–98, 97(fig.)
Republic Council of Veterans of War and Labor, The, 127(n42)
Russian fluency in, 307(n9)
Russians in, 138, 162, 171, 175–176, 177, 178, 180, 181, 182, 183
self-immolations, female, 244
Stalinism in, 99–104
subnational networks, 141–142
Supreme Soviet, 131, 138, 139, 142, 143, 154(n23), 194
teachers in, 31, 275–276, 288(n168)
Uichinsk raion, 202
unemployment, 55, 256–257
urban dwellers, 169, 178, 181, 266
violence in, 297
VUZy/specialized secondary education, 32, 35(n46)
VUZy student exchanges with other republics, 145
water contamination, 240
work force, 84
See also Central Asia
Uzbek Soviet Encyclopedia, 121(n3)
Uzbek Soviet Socialist Republic (Uzbek SSR), 17. *See also* Uzbekistan
Uzbek SSR. *See* Uzbek Soviet Socialist Republic

Vagabov, N. M., 19
Vahidov, Erkin, 294–295
Vasiev, A., 212
Veils, 24, 27, 249
Verba, Sidney, 291, 292, 293, 301, 302, 304
Vereshchagin, E. M., 224
Vilnius, 239
von Kaufman, K. P., 13
Voslensky, Michael S., 133
VUZy. *See* Education, VUZy/ specialized secondary

Wages, 299
Wahabis, 211
Water, 55, 56, 78, 79, 238, 239, 240–241, 256, 297, 300, 305. *See also* Irrigation
Weddings. *See* Marriage
Weiner, Myron, 291, 301
Wimbush, S. Enders, 172
Women, 24, 27, 52, 54, 84, 99, 100, 143, 144, 152, 172, 198, 211–212, 235–251, 268
activist groups, 250–251
childbirth mortality, 239, 240
dress issues, 249, 250, 254(n60)

employment, 241, 246–249, 252(n24)
and family life, 241–246. *See also* Marriage
and Islam, 249–251
social integration and industrial employment, 249
travel restrictions, 246–247
See also Education, females; Ethnic attitudes/relations, husband-wife relations; Suicides
Workers, 143

World War II, 19, 24, 27, 31, 48, 176–177
Writers, 28, 29, 79, 80, 145

Yakuts, 1
Yaqubov, Adil, 83, 86, 303
Youth, 257, 265–266. *See also* Education; Migrations
Yuldashev, Dzh., 212

Ziuzin, D., 258
Zvezda Vostoka, 210